LANCASTER
PHOTO ALBUM

LANCASTER

PHOTO ALBUM

compiled and edited by
NEVILLE FRANKLIN

PSL Patrick Stephens, Cambridge

First published 1981

British Library Cataloguing in Publication Data

Lancaster photo album.
   1. Lancaster (Bombers) — Pictorial works
   I Franklin, Neville
   623.74'63   UG1243.B6

   ISBN 0 85059 477 4

Text set in 9 on 10 pt Univers by Manuset Limited,
Baldock, Herts. Printed in Great Britain on 100 gsm
Huntsman Velvet coated cartridge, and bound, by
The Garden City Press, Letchworth, Herts, for the
publishers, Patrick Stephens Limited, Bar Hill,
Cambridge, CB3 8EL, England.

INTRODUCTION

When I had completed writing my section of *Classic Aircraft No 6, Lancaster,* so many photographs were left over, and others have been collected since, that I was able to persuade Patrick Stephens to allow the compilation of this *Photo Album* covering this historic aircraft, its variants, test-beds, civil adaptations and overseas usage.

The Lancaster originates from the end of 1936 when a specification was issued for a twin-engined bomber to carry a maximum of 8,000 lb of bombs, or 3,000 lb for 2,000 miles at 275 mph and 15,000 ft. Although three manufacturers tendered, only Avro completed an aircraft to the basic specification, the Vulture-powered Manchester which made its maiden flight from Ringway on July 25 1939. Although dogged throughout its life by problems, having, as it did, an insufficiently developed X-type 24-cylinder engine, the Manchester entered service on November 1 1940, and, although only about 200 were completed, it served with 13 squadrons in Bomber Command.

With the virtual scrapping of the Vulture by Rolls-Royce, an airframe was selected from the Manchester production line around the middle of 1940 and modified to take four Merlins in the already-developed Beaufighter II power plant. BT308, the first prototype, made its first flight on January 9 1941, and proved an immediate success. The last Manchesters were converted on the production lines and Bomber Command received the first Lancasters by Christmas, joining 44 Squadron at Waddington. Four Lancasters laid mines in the Heligoland Bight on March 3 1942, and the first bombs were dropped on Essen a week later, a sign of what was to come! A total of 7,377 Lancasters was built, the highest production of 293 being achieved in the month of August 1944. 5 Group, Bomber Command, became an all-Lancaster group, whilst 6 (RCAF) Group flew both English and Canadian-built aircraft, and others were used by 8 Pathfinder Group. A total of 68 squadrons was completely equipped with Lancasters.

By the time the last raid of the war was made, on Kiel early in May 1945, Lancasters had taken off on 156,000 sorties, dropped over 600,000 tons of bombs, and 3,349 aircraft had failed to return from operations. With the end of hostilities, the Lanc took on two more roles, dropping 6,684 tons of food to starving Dutch people, often from house-top level, and flying home 74,178 ex-prisoners of war.

Whilst the development of the Lancaster went almost hand-in-hand with that of radar, very little change was made in its basic configuration. The only major power-plant change was the fitting of Bristol Hercules radial engines to 300 Mk 2 Lancasters built by Armstrong Whitworth Aircraft at Baginton, but this did not give the expected performance improvement found with the Halifax B III. Later Marks of Merlin were fitted, and tail-turrets were of varying types, but the main modifications were necessitated by Barnes Wallis' bigger and more-beautiful bombs. Bomb-doors were bulged to accommodate 8,000 lb 'Cookies' and 12,000 lb 'Tallboys', whilst they were cut away to carry the Dambusters' cylindrical bouncing mine and 22,000 lb 'Grand Slam'.

The Airborne Lifeboat was developed for dropping from the Lancaster, and Coastal Command received a maritime reconnaissance version of the aircraft after the war, this being the last operational version, only retiring on October 15 1956. L'Aeronavale received 54 MR Lancasters under NATO defence plans, five more were also supplied for French ASR squadrons, 15 were sold to the Argentine and nine more went to Egypt. Canadian-built Lancs soldiered on until April 1 1964, some in much-modified form.

Probably the most publicised use of the Lancaster in the post-war era was as an engine test-bed, a duty for which its very strong airframe was peculiarly suited, sprouting jet and turbo-prop engines in nose, tail and bomb-bay, as well as the usual positions!

Several Lancasters were converted for civil use and a quantity were built as Lancastrians for the Royal Air Force and various international airlines, but the major civil version was the York, with a new fuselage specially adapted for both passenger and freight carrying. Being unpressurised, it could not compete with specially-designed American Skymasters and Constellations, and quickly disappeared.

At least two Yorks have been preserved for posterity, whilst many Lancasters still exist. Four are in Britain, one being lovingly flown by the Royal Air Force's Battle of Britain Memorial Flight at Coningsby, and now coded AJ-G (Guy Gibson's 617 Squadron dambuster), and another, at Strathallan, should eventually fly again. Others exist in Australia and New Zealand, whilst at least one Canadian survivor is being rebuilt for flying.

Without a doubt, the Lancaster was a war-winning aircraft, and I am proud to be able to compile this photographic record, assisted by my good friends: Chris Ashworth, Bill Baker, David Bennett, Roy Benwell, Dave Birch, Roy Bonser, Paul E. Branke, Don Burton, Roy Cross, Philippe Denis, Dave Elvidge, Sid Finn, Peter Green, Barry Halpenny, Bob Hambidge, Keith Hayward, Harry Holmes, George Hopp, Robert Löfberg, Peter Lord, Ian MacDonald, Greg Marshall, Brian Robinson, Patrick Tilley, Alan Todd, John Walls, Brandon White and anyone else I have forgotten! Thanks also go to Rolls-Royce and Anglian Aeropics for photos supplied.

Neville Franklin
Newark, June 1980

THE PHOTOGRAPHS

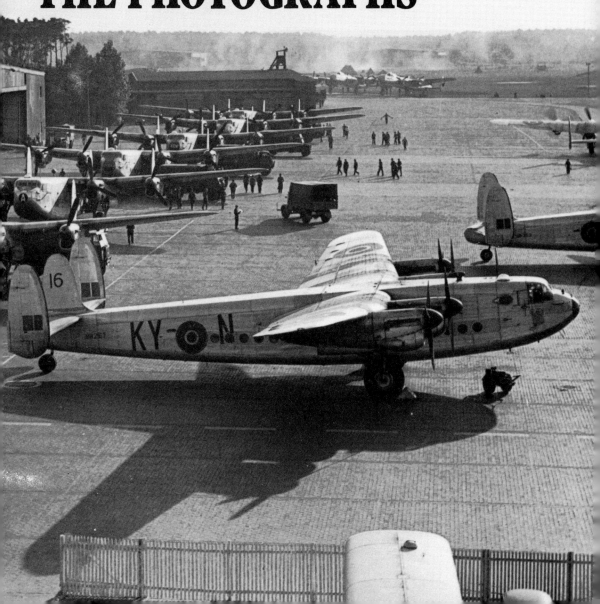

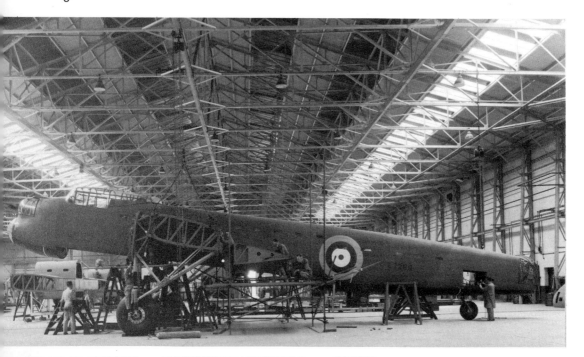

Above Manchester L7280 in Woodford erection hall shows undercarriage detail.

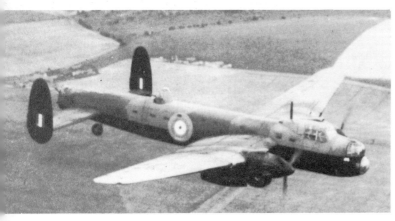

Above left and left Two shots of Manchester IA, L7320, flying near Boscombe Down in 1941. The starboard undercarriage door has not closed. Note pre-war roundels with small red centre.

Above 207 Squadron Manchester I, EM:A-L7378, on an unidentified snow-clad airfield.

Right Manchester IA planform shows 33-foot span tailplane.

Above left Manchester power—the complicated Rolls-Royce Vulture 24-cylinder 'X' engine.

Left Rear view of triple-finned Lancaster prototype BT308 in January 1941.

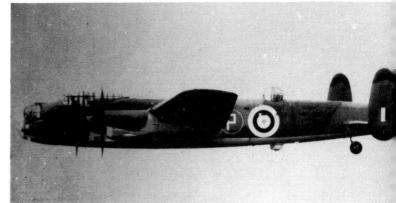

Above Manchester IA, EM:S-L7515, of 207 Squadron, airborne in November 1941.

Above right Second prototype DG595 in flight—note yellow undersides of experimental aircraft.

Right Lancaster B.1, R5700, being over-flown at Press presentation, mid-1942.

Overleaf Unidentified Lancaster B.1 being prepared for its 11th sortie in mid-summer sun. Incendiary containers make an unusual resting place! The unusual nose motif still needs explaining.

KM:Y, W and S of 44 Squadron fly in 'Vic' formation.

R5849 used as a test aircraft by Rolls-Royce at Hucknall. The mid-upper turret does not have a fairing fitted.

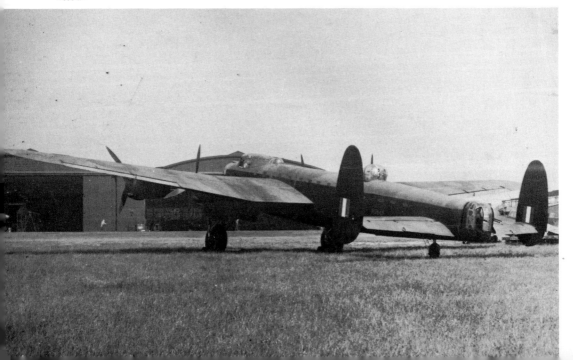

PG:H-LM446, of 619 Squadron, flies over cloud early in 1944.

JO:X from 43 Squadron poses for the cameraman.

Above 576 Squadron's UL:I-LM227 taxies out on its first raid from Elsham Wolds on July 4 1944. Ground staff signal their best wishes.

Left 'U' Uncle, of 12 Squadron, Wickenby, displays its anti-gas disc, twin ·50-in Rose tail turret and H2S blister.

Right R5727, a B.1 pattern aircraft in Canada, 1943. Fortress II behind.

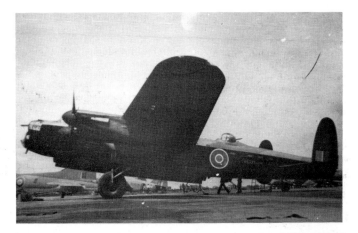

Right Reduced to spares after a raid on Berlin on November 28 1943 was frost-covered PH:O-JB354 of 12 Squadron.

Below 'G' George strains against its brakes at the start of its take-off run. A wartime censor has blanked out the H2S radome, serial and nose aerials!

Left A fresh-looking Lancaster unusually parked on the grass by Rolls-Royce at Hucknall.

Left This B.III has its rudders hard over to counteract engine torque. N^2 — 'Nan Squared', already carries ten rows of bombs on its nose, but is unidentified.

Below 467 Squadron Lancasters taxiing out in the snow at Waddington in the winter murk of 1944/5, clearly showing shape of mid-upper turret.

Right Much used B.1, OL:F-R5857 of 83 Squadron, in 1942. Despite its short life, June 1 to November 7, it also shows painted-out codes of 207 Squadron (EM). Note trestling marks under nose and wing.

Right Mepal-based AA:U of 75 Squadron displays its daylight tail markings — two horizontal white bars.

Below Another 'U' Uncle gets victory signals as it taxies out. It is believed to be a 100 Squadron Lancaster at Waltham.

With undercarriage just beginning to retract, 'M' Mike lifts off from Waddington's main runway.

43 Squadron Lancaster landing back at Graveley after a sortie in 1945.

ABC-equipped Lancaster, SR:B, of 101 Squadron, dropping incendiaries.

Side view of 170 Squadron's TC:C-LM732, with Rose tail turret and H2S.

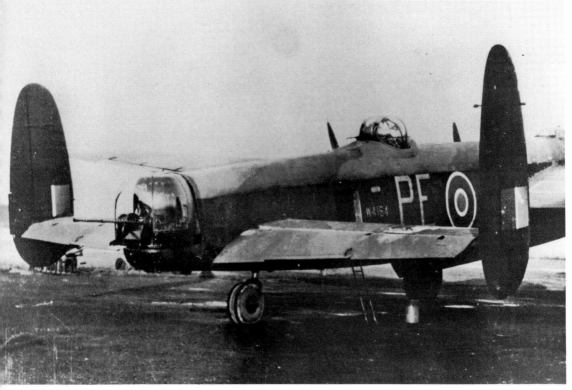

Above Good detail of 1662 HCU Lancaster B.1, W4154, showing Rose tail turret with its twin ·50-in calibre Colt-Brownings, at Blyton.

Left How to bale out from the Rose turret—just raise the guns and leave head first!

Below left A Lancaster B.1 of 1661 HCU, W4113, coded GP:J, from Winthorpe. It was later transferred to No 5 Group Lancaster Finishing School at Syerston, and became 4969M.

Above right Good view of a 1668 HCU Lancaster B.III, coded J9:H, which overshot Bottesford.

Right RAF Lancasters were usually named, but, when Canadian and Australian squadrons adopted American-type nose-art, albeit censored, the RAF followed suit. 12 Squadron Lancaster B.III, WS:R-EE136, was 'Spirit of Russia' at Bardney in 1943. It eventually completed 109 operations.

Above Alex Henshaw tested Lancasters at Castle Bromwich. Here he is airborne in their first, HK535, which later joined 463 Squadron.

Left This 463 Squadron Lancaster B.III, PO:D-LL847, had two Walt Disney characters on its nose.

Left QB:P-NG347 of 424 (Tiger) Squadron, Skipton-on-Swale, 1945, settled for 'Piccadilly Princess'.

Above 'MacNamara's Band', a B.III of 101 Squadron, had made 16 raids.

Right 'X' X-Ray of an unidentified Australian squadron, would you believe?

Below 'Jock's Revenge', PO:M-LM233, of 467 Squadron, was at Waddington in 1944, with 32 raids—and a tipsy Kangaroo!

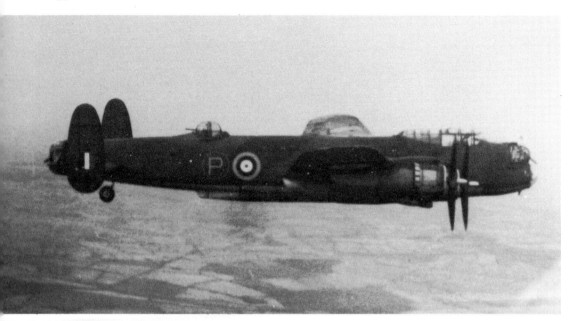

Above Only 300 Hercules-powered Lancaster B.IIs were built, by Armstrong Whitworth at Baginton. This was the prototype, DT810, the only one built by Avro, with bulged bomb-doors and yellow undersides.

Left Unusual plan view of radial-engined Lancaster prototype DT810, with roundels under its yellow painted wings.

Above right Only six squadrons, three of them Canadian, used the B.II. This is OW:N-LL621, 426 Squadron, taking off from Linton-on-Ouse in 1944.

Right EQ:D-DS729, of 408 Squadron, ground-looped with flak damage at Linton-on-Ouse, January 7 1944.

Pages 28 and 29 'O' Oboe, with standard bomb-doors and single gun in its ventral turret, had completed 32 raids when it was photographed. Engine cowlings appear to have individual names.

Left YZ:O-PD129 of 617 Squadron, at Woodhall Spa, with 'Grand Slam' ready for loading. A crew member gives scale — 46-in diameter.

Below left Dambuster ED909 (AJ:P), YF:B, was allocated 6242M, and scrapped at Scampton in 1947.

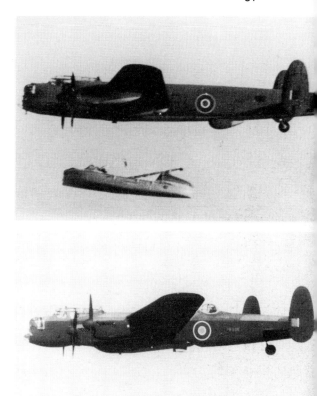

Right The first Mk II Airborne Lifeboat being dropped from Lancaster ASR.III, EL:A-RF310, of 279 Squadron, Thornaby-on-Tees, on December 10 1945.

Right PB995, a B.1 (Special), flying at the Aircraft and Armament Experimental Establishment in 1945, carries a 22,000-lb 'Grand Slam' — and still has turrets fitted.

Below Another Dambuster, ED906, once AJ:J, became YF:A of Scampton's Station Flight in 1945.

Left 'Elizabeth', OF:A-R5548, burnt at Woodhall Spa at the end of 1942, when its photo-flashes caught fire. This Lancaster had been named by Queen Elizabeth when she visited the Lancaster Aircraft Group's Yeadon shadow factory on March 20 1942, with King George VI.

Left JB675, a rare B.VI, with two-stage Merlins in circular cowlings installed by Rolls-Royce at Hucknall, served with 635 Squadron at Wyton (F2:U) and 7 Squadron (MG:O) at Oakington, flying at least 18 sorties in the latter half of 1944.

Below In one of the last raids of World War 2, on Berchtesgaden on April 25 1945, 12 Squadron's WS:V, piloted by Flight Lieutenant Watkins drops its 'Tallboy'.

Right Many unfortunate crashes occurred during training flights—B.X, KB879, of 428 (Ghost) Squadron, Middleton St George, dived in from 16,000 feet, near Hixon, Staffs, on April 30 1945.

Below The Möhne Dam in 1965, now used as a museum. The breached, and repaired, centre-section can just be detected.

Postwar, the Lancaster soldiered on with ASR duties. This ASR.3, SW368, was with 210 Squadron at St Eval in Cornwall . . .

. . . and this one, RF313-'Y', served with 38 Squadron at Luqa in Malta in 1953.

This GR.3, RF289, was coded BS:G of 120 Squadron, Kinloss.

NX739, a B.7/FE, with rear turret removed, was used by the Ministry of Supply as a photographic mount, and was operated from Blackbushe.

Above This GR.3, L:U-SW283, from 210 Squadron, waits attention by Avro at Langar in 1952. It was scrapped in 1957 after service with the School of Maritime Reconnaissance as H:Q.

Left End of the line for PA414, seen travelling north through Grantham in October 1948. It bears 7 Squadron codes, MG:G, from Upwood. Strange that it was dismantled so carefully!

Above right This Mk 7/FE, NX773, seen at Istres, France, on June 8 1951, is 'Capella' of the CNCS, coded FGG:C. Light grey top and glossy black undersides.

Right 4S:AU-PA444, was with the BCDU at Tangmere in 1949, in black and white finish.

Left A Lincoln-type radome was fitted to Lancaster PB820. Note Junkers Ju 188 and Heinkel He 162 in the background.

Left ME540 was flown on trials fitted with the Boulton-Paul Gust Alleviator.

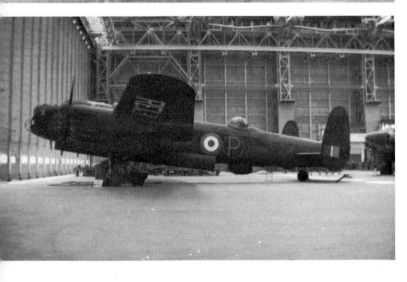

Left After service with 44, 75 and 207 Squadrons, B.III RE131 was used by Bristol at Filton for testing Brabazon controls.

Right CXU:?-RE219, of the Empire Flying Training School, demonstrates that a Lancaster could fly on its port inner engine only, in this poor but unique photograph.

Right 617 Squadron's B.7/FE, KC:E-NX791, stored at Aston Down MU before being refurbished for use by the Flying College in 1949.

Right Originally a pathfinder, OF:C-RE115/G, of 97 Squadron, this Lancaster was converted to ASR.3 for 179 and 210 Squadrons and is here seen at Langar in 1954 in GR.3 configuration before joining 210 Squadron. Scrapped in May 1957, when H:P of the School of Maritime reconnaissance.

Left TW661 of the Telecommunications Flying Unit shows off its black and white finish.

Below left This B.I/FE, TW655, with ferry time only, was brought up to RAF Maritime Reconnaissance standard and became WU:17.

Bottom left This unidentified dark blue Lancaster, with French Navy markings, was being prepared for test flying at Avro's Langar workshop on June 2 1952.

Below G-AJWM, still in bomber colours, was the only Lancaster B.1/Special (PP741) to have double curvature bomb-doors to enclose a 22,000-lb 'Grand Slam'. It is seen here at White Waltham in 1947 marked ALITALIA ROMA and was used for training Italian Lancastrian crews.

Above right G-11-14 was PA375, one of 15 Lancasters overhauled for the Argentine Air Force in 1948, becoming B-031. B-006 was a Lincoln, ex-RE353, which also went to Argentina.

Right 54 Lancasters were refurbished by Avro in 1952 for l'Aeronavale under NATO defence plans. NX668, an Austin-built B.7, photographed at Langar on June 2 1952, became WU (Western Union) —24.

Left WU:01 during flight trials before delivery, clearly showing the French markings, blue, white and red roundels, with orange outer ring, and anchor superimposed. It was a B.7/FE, built by Austin Motors as NX613.

Below WU:14, ex-NX623, numbered '5', in flight showing clear radome and scanner bowl.

Right WU:27, ex-TW651, repainted acrylic white, served in New Caledonia and is here photographed in Fiji. It was 9S:2 of the 95th Flotille, Tontoute.

Below Another Austin-built B.7, RT673, again photographed at Langar on June 2 1952, became FCL.04 of the French Navy in 1954 and was based in North Africa.

Bottom Lancaster PB922 was modified by Flight Refuelling and used for trials with a Meteor in 1949 as G-33-2.

Left G-AGJI, ex-DV379, was a civil Lancaster with turrets faired over and used by BOAC in camouflage. Red, white and blue stripes underline the civil registration.

Left It is not generally known that 'Aries', PD328, developed for the Empire Air Navigation School's long-range flights, was actually a Lancaster fitted with Lancastrian-type nose and tail fairings. Here, with codes FCFA, it is seen at Negombo, Ceylon, in 1946.

Below left One of the last public appearances of the Lancaster was in July 1953, when four were lined up for Royal Review. GR.3s, RE164 and RE181 frame the Royal Daimler at RAF Odiham.

Opposite page Filling nose fuel tank and last minute servicing at Blackbushe in 1946 before yet another world flight. The listing indicates visits to many countries, and Record Flights.

Above Lancastrian starboard outer wing at Langar. Underside only marked MW17!

Left Nice side view of Lancastrian VM728 in flight shows sleek lines. The Lancastrian's top speed was 315 mph.

Above right We wish we knew where this superb shot of a Lancastrian was taken. Its radome identifies it as a long-range aircraft. An Anson and Lancaster are behind.

Right Lancastrian 'Star Watch', G-AGUL, takes off from Heathrow on a training flight in 1947.

Pages 48 and 49 Lancastrians in production, with Tudors behind.

Above Immaculate G-AKMW, British South American Airways' 'Star Bright', poses for its portrait.

Left Speed Pack, designed, manufactured and installed by Airtech Ltd on BSAAC Lancastrian, to carry bulky cargoes.

Below First BOAC Lancastrian, G-AGLF, ex-VB673, in the snows of 1945. Civil markings still underlined by red, white and blue stripes, despite natural metal finish.

Above Freighter Lancaster G-AGUJ, 'Star Pilot' of British South American Airways Corporation.

Right Silver City Lancastrian, G-AHBV, 'City of Canberra', one of three used by this airline.

Below BSAAC Lancastrian 3, G-AGWK, 'Star Trail', crashed in Bermuda on September 5 1947.

Above Hucknall shot of Victory Aircraft-built Lancastrian, CF-CNA, ex-FM187, which joined Flight Refuelling as G-AKDJ at the end of 1947.

Left First prototype York, LV626, Experimental Aircraft No 178, being erected — fuselage jig in foreground.

Above right First civil York, G-AGJA, ex-MW103, being towed out on January 14 1944.

Right Jeep being loaded in a York freighter — four could be carried.

Pages 54 and 55 Camouflaged York, MW169, was the first combined passenger/freight version.

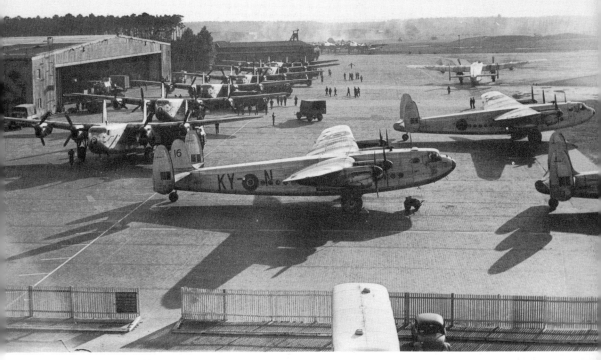

Above left MW140's nose showing the Governor General of Australia's crest. The York was named 'Endeavour' and allotted RAAF type A74 but no serial.

Left This York, MW?32, was displayed at an early post-war Waddington Battle of Britain display—did it become G-ANTK now preserved at Lasham?

Above Heyday of the York was the Berlin Air Lift in 1948 and 1949. Ten Yorks and two Lancastrians can be counted in this Official photo. The nearest York is KY:N-MW287, of 242 Squadron, '16' on its fin.

Above right MW260 is being loaded at Gatow. The rear door was at truck-bed height and very convenient.

Right The Air Lift saw many casualties. This York, YY:S-MW145, of 241 OCU, didn't quite make Wunstorf!

York MW139, at Khartoum Airfield in 1951, was used for general transport duties and ferried the Sudan Defence Force to Port Said during rioting. It is believed to have been the last York in RAF service.

G-AHEX, 'Star Venture', shows off its Lancaster wing as it climbs away from Heathrow.

BSAA's 'Star Speed' G-AHEZ at Langley.

York G-AMUU joined Hunting-Clan in 1956 and is ex-MW183. It was scrapped at Heathrow in 1959.

Left PA.1, ex-MW234, was one of three Yorks operated by Aeronavale in 1960. PA.3 lies behind.

Below left G-AGNN, ex-TS798, and marked as MW100, is now displayed in the Cosford Aerospace Museum. It was once in the Skyfame Collection at Staverton.

Right Lancasters have been featured in many films, and several B.7s were converted in 1954 and repainted at Scampton for use in *The Dambusters*. Here RT686 loses its underwing serial. It already has 617 Squadron's code 'AJ'.

Right Dan-Air used the last Yorks and have preserved G-ANTK, ex-MW232, at Lasham.

Below Once 'Star Quest', G-AHEY was one of many Yorks operated by Skyways of London, and used the trooping serial WW806. It later became JY-ABZ.

Lancaster B.6, JB675, at Hucknall, with hybrid Merlins installed for a 500-hour endurance flying programme. The inboard engines were Tudor power-plants (102s) and DC-4M Merlin 150s were fitted outboard.

Previous page Gibson's 'AJ:G', and 'AJ:P' flying over Lincolnshire during filming. The dummy mine carried was spherical, with flat sides, as the actual weapon, now known to be a cylinder 50-in in diameter and 60-in long, was still secret!

SW342 had a Mamba fitted in its nose by Armstrong-Siddeley's Flight Test Department at Bitteswell in 1949.

Hive of activity at Bruntingthorpe as Lancaster 6, ND784, with AS.X turbojet installed in its bomb-bay, is prepared for a test flight.

ND784 was later fitted with an Armstrong-Siddeley Mamba in its nose by Air Service Training at Hamble, and this photo illustrates relative size as well as detail of the circular Merlin power-plants.

Above This Lancaster later had a Viper turbojet mounted in its tail, becoming the only six-engined Lanc.

Left Underside detail of water spray rig on the Mamba engine, with cropped propeller, for icing trials.

Above right This Lancastrian, VH742, had Nene RN.1 turbojets fitted outboard.

Right Avon-powered Lancastrian, VL970, with spray gear fitted, in front of Hucknall's slag heap.

Above Lancaster NG465 was flown with a Rolls-Royce Dart turbo-prop in its nose. Note Barracuda under port wing, slag-heap and propeller-less Lanc behind.

Left NG465's career came to an abrupt end on January 22 1954 when it made a forced landing on Hollinwell golf course just north of Hucknall, the last Lancaster to be used for test flying.

Below left VM733 was converted to have Sapphires outboard by Air Service Training Ltd at Hamble during 1949.

Above right The old and the new. Merlin and Avon RA.2 fitted to Lancastrian VM732 and first flown on August 15 1948. Despite its similar size, the Avon delivered many times the power of the Merlin.

Right Python power—Lancaster TW911, the last B.I/FE built by Armstrong Whitworth Aircraft and delivered in March 1946, had these powerful turbo-props fitted outboard and first flew on January 3 1949.

Side view of TW911 flying on February 25 1949 solely on its Python turbo contra-prop engines each of 3,500 hp. This engine was only used in Westland's Wyvern strike fighter.

Previous page Superb shot of Lancastrian VM733 flying on the power of its two Armstrong-Siddeley Sapphire turbo-jets, circa 1950.

STAL Dovern Lancaster Tp.80 flew 125 hours with this huge belly-mounted nacelle.

Excellent shot of Lancaster TW911 flying on March 8 1950 after its Python cowlings had been cut back by 4ft 9in to improve airflow to the compressor.

Overseas, Avro Canada flew this Orenda-powered Lancaster 10-0, FM209.

Left Converted by Air Service Training at Hamble, RA805 had its Dovern engine fitted in Sweden. A Swedish Ju-86 lies behind. The Bomber Command grey/gloss black finish was originally retained. Note twin retractable tail-wheels and stainless steel undersheath on fuselage.

Right Long-nosed Lancaster 10-MR, KB976, runs up its engines.

Right Lancaster II, LL735, with Metropolitan-Vickers Beryl fitted in its tail.

Left KB700 was the first of 430 Victory Aircraft-built Lancaster B.10s and first flew at Malton, Ontario, on August 6 1943. It served with 405 Squadron as 'The Ruhr Express', LQ:Q, at Gransden Lodge before joining 419 Squadron and being lost on its 49th op.

Right Serialled 80001, and marked Fc, but now natural metal, Tp.80 flew with RM28 (reheat Ghost) No 5327 installed. This was fitted in mid-1953 to test the Svenska-Flygmotor designed after-burner for the J-29F 'Tunnan'.

Left This RCAF Lancaster, FM213, was at Prestwick on June 19 1957.

Below left A Ryan Firebee under a Lancaster's wing-tip.

Below One of two 10-DCs, Firebee Drone carriers, KB848, at Cold Lake experimental base.

Right KB976 (see top of page 75) was further converted to 10-AR configuration, ending its life with 408 Squadron at Rockcliffe, coded MN:976.

Below right KB889 became a Mk 10 SR (Search & Rescue) with Maritime Air Command. It was later converted to a Mk 10 MP (ex-MR + Maritime Reconnaissance) and ended its service life at Greenwood, Nova Scotia.

Greenwood's Gate Guardian Mk 10/MP, KB839.

Canadian Warplane Heritage are working on Mk 10/MR FM213 at Hamilton to get it airworthy again.

Nose of Mk 10P, FM199, MN:199, of 408 Squadron, a photographic unit based at Rockcliffe for aerial mapping in the Arctic. Note ILS aerial on cockpit.

Mk 10/AR, KB882, shows off its special equipment, aerials and camera ports at Greenwood.

Left This Lancaster probably has the most original interior — KB944 of the Canadian National Aeronautical Collection at Rockcliffe and coded NA:P.

Below left Port cockpit.

Right Nose of KB944 — 'Winnie' — displays 72 bombs.

Below Starboard cockpit.

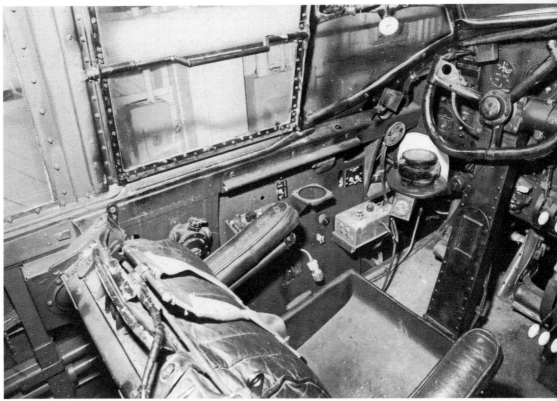

Flight Engineer's position.

Right Navigator's position.

Rear fuselage looking forward.

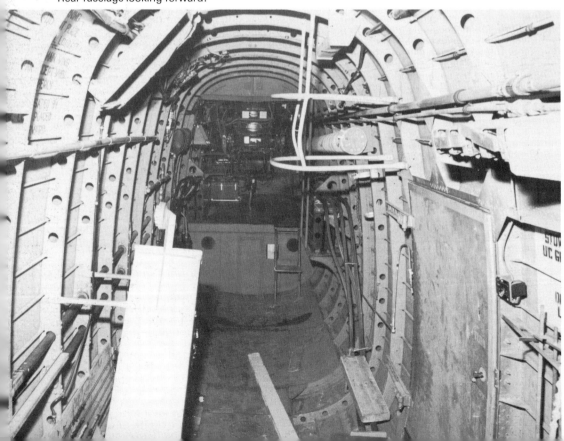

Left 'VN:N', FM136, on its pylon at Calgary International Airport.

Left KB882 at Edmundston, New Brunswick.

Right KB889 at Oshawa Airport is being overhauled, hopefully to fly again.

Left FM212 at Windsor, Ontario.

Right This shot-up hulk at Shilo, Manitoba, is supplying spares for other Lancasters.

Two Lancasters flew to Australia in World War 2, AR:G-W4783 of 460 Squadron, which made 90 raids and was presented to the Australian War Museum, and A66-1, ex-ED930, supplied in May, 1943.

FM104 in Toronto Exhibition grounds. Much neglected and parts missing.

One Canadian Lancaster is in the United Kingdom. G-BCOH, ex-KB976, taxies out for a test flight on May 14 1975, prior to issue of its CA for ferry flight across the Atlantic to Strathallan.

It is now being slowly refurbished by the Strathallan Collection to fly again.

In New Zealand, MoTaT displays an ex-Aeronavale Lancaster VII. It was WU-10 and has been restored as ND752/PB457, although it was NX665.

At Perth, the Air Force Association's Historical Group cares for NX622, another ex-Aeronavale Lancaster, formerly WU-16.

The Imperial War Museum proudly displays the nose of Lancaster B.III DV372, ex-467 Squadron and 1651 Conversion Unit.

'G' — George, allocated A66-2, which it apparently never carried, is now displayed in Canberra.

Above Once at Scampton's gate, where it was originally displayed without trees in front of it (!), and coded PO:S, the well-known 'Sugar'. . .

Above left and left In 1970, whilst coded OL:Q, it was dismantled, and moved to the Royal Air Force Museum at Hendon, where it is now displayed with a 'Cookie'.

Right . . . just as it had been earlier, joined by two Barnes Wallis's bombs, 'Tallboy' and 'Grand Slam', at Scampton.

Below and bottom HAPS were presented with an ex-Aeronavale Lancaster, WU-15, once NX611, and this was flown from Caledonia to Australia where it was prepared for its 12,000-mile journey home. Leaving Sydney on Anzac Day, April 25 1965, it arrived at Biggin Hill on May 13 for the annual Air Fair, after an adventurous journey.

Left NX611 was eventually repainted as HA:P (218 Squadron) and flew into a reunion at Scampton on May 19 1967.

Below left After that, its history becomes sordid, and it arrived at Blackpool, via Lavenham and Hullavington, where it began to deteriorate badly in the sea air. Eventually it was put up for auction but bought privately by Lord Lilford who offered it, on loan, for display at Scampton's gate, where it now sits, marked as YF:C of their Station Flight.

Bottom left It is reasonably complete internally as can be seen from this cockpit view.

Top right Starboard inner Merlin exposed during painting shows good detail.

Above right This photo shows that a 'Dams' mine is now also on display at Scampton.

Right The Mk VII Lancaster has a twin ·50-in Frazer-Nash FB.82 rear turret.

Left That only leaves PA474. This Lancaster, after use by 82 Squadron as a PR.1, was based at Cranfield as a test aircraft, carrying various wings, etc, on its specially strengthened back, for icing and other research. Here it taxies out with a Folland Midge wing, fitted with Handley Page's laminar flow section.

Left It was also used for aerodynamic research on other airfoil sections until replaced by a Lincoln.

Below It was reclaimed by the Royal Air Force and eventually arrived at Waddington, via Wroughton and Henlow. Here it was taken in hand by 44 Squadron and restored as KM:B, Squadron Leader J.D. Nettleton's aircraft in which he gained the VC during a daylight raid on Augsburg on April 17 1942.

Right Originally only fitted with a tail turret, it soon had a nose turret fitted and appeared at many air displays.

Right and below Next modification, after moving to Coningsby where it was incorporated in the Battle of Britain Memorial Flight, was the fitting of new jacks to enable its bomb-doors to be operated.

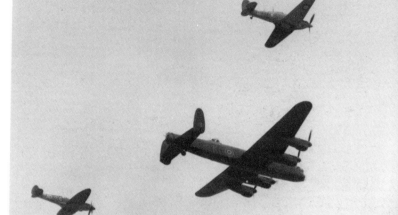

Left Adopted by Lincoln, this City of Lincoln crest appeared on its nose.

Left A mid-upper turret, found in Argentina, was fitted at Coningsby.

Below 1980 saw a change in squadron markings and now PA474 is coded AJ:G, Guy Gibson's dambuster Lancaster of 617 Squadron.

CW0404685

Behind the Headlines

Behind the Headlines

An Autobiography

Michael Lindsay Charlesworth

Greenbank Press

Published by
Greenbank Press
Greenbank
East Horrington
Wells
Somerset BA5 3DR

Reprinted January 1995

British Library Cataloguing in Publication Data
A catalogue record for this book is available from the British Library.

ISBN 0 9523699 1 5

Typeset by Create Publishing Services Limited

Printed by Bookcraft (Bath) Limited, Midsomer Norton, Avon

Contents

For All Friends Round the Wrekin – especially one.

More The Dean of St Paul's offers you a post; with a house, a servant and fifty pounds a year.

Rich What? What post?

More At the new school.

Rich (*bitterly disappointed*) A teacher!

. . . . .

More Why not be a teacher? You'd be a fine teacher. Perhaps a great one.

Rich And if I was, who would know it?

More You, your pupils, your friends, God. Not a bad public really.

From *A Man for all Seasons* by Robert Bolt

Preface

That this book is an exercise in self-indulgence, I at once admit. On the face of it my life has been in the main conventional, without the slightest impact on the affairs of the world, interesting – if at all – only to family and friends. But it happens that much of it has been spent – on and off – at Shrewsbury School with which I have not been wholly out of touch for more than sixty years. I have no wish to trespass on the ground covered by Colin Leach in his excellent book *A School at Shrewsbury*, but this memoir may perhaps be seen as complementary to the story he tells of twentieth century Shrewsbury and it is my hope that some Salopians may find interest in these recollections of people, attitudes and events as seen from a position close to the action.

If there is any sort of theme to the Shrewsbury parts of the book it is to describe the death of the Public School and the rise of a very different educational establishment albeit inside the same structure, a development which has not, I think, been adequately described – or even realised – elsewhere.

Many may think the lives of those whom Cowper called 'public hacknies in the schooling trade' to be 'cabin'd, cribb'd, confin'd'. To those who need a wider field it may be so. But there cannot be many occupations in which there is so broad a range of interest for the energetic, not only in the central work of the form room where discussion can be so wide ranging but in opportunities for music, drama, art, expeditions, a variety of games and a multitude of human relationships. This field of activity has suited me and I have enjoyed the continuous activities of the boarding school for which there are never enough hours in the day and where the distinction between work and play is finely drawn.

My account is, of course, entirely subjective. Readers may well disagree with my comments, my judgements and indeed my accuracy, though I would claim to have a better memory than many who write about their schooldays, when exaggeration and selection often present a much-distorted picture, sometimes tinted by a later-acquired philosophy. Only occasionally have I kept a diary but I do not readily throw away pieces of paper and I have drawn on a mass of letters and documents of all kinds, some significant, some trivial, ranging from letters written from my prep school to weighty headmagisterial documents. I have consulted little with others, though for the years when I was in Pakistan I have drawn on the memories of those then present at Shrewsbury, particularly on those of Peter Hughes and Laurence Le Quesne for whose assistance I am grateful.

Without the help of Richard Hudson, to whom by a strange quirk I was at different times form master, housemaster and headmaster, this book could never have appeared. His skills as editor and publisher have made all things possible and my gratitude is boundless. My thanks also go to Dee Dakers for cheerfully and efficiently transforming my ill-typed manuscript into respectable copy.

Michael Charlesworth

May Day 1994
Shrewsbury

CHAPTER I

Early Years

I remember, I remember
The house where I was born,
The little window where the sun
Came creeping through at morn.
                              Thomas Hood

One winter day in November 1918, Ellen Terry, then in her seventies, was selling flags for a war-time charity outside Harrods. My mother was shopping at Harrods on that day and hastened to buy a flag from her great heroine whom she had so many times seen at the Lyceum with Henry Irving. Pinning the flag on my mother's coat, she said "I wish you get what you most wish for". Then, looking my mother in the eye, she asked "And what do you most wish for?". "For a baby boy", said Mother. I was born some two months later and have always regarded Ellen Terry as a quasi-godmother.

My parents came from very different backgrounds. My father, George Lindsay Charlesworth (the Lindsay came from a supposed and sketchy descent from an early 18th century Earl of Crawford and Balcarres), was a Yorkshireman and his father was a miner, killed in a pit accident when Father was nine. He, his brother and two sisters, were brought up by their mother in harsh conditions at Thornhill, near Dewsbury. She was a woman of character and determination. With the help of the Vicar of Thornhill, Archdeacon Brooke, my father – a bright boy – won a free place at Bradford Grammar School. Archdeacon Brooke was the family guru, an Anglo-Catholic of the Oxford Movement, directing his energies, as did so many others of that persuasion, to bringing hope and encouragement to the less well off in those days before any sort of social security provision. He moved amongst the mining families with a sure touch, leading their worship and from the position of comparative influence which the clergy then had, alleviating their lot and lightening their lives. Certainly the Charlesworth family owed all to him. My father's brother, Tom, became in time the village schoolmaster at Thornhill, respected by several generations of boys and possessing an encyclopaedic knowledge of the neighbourhood; the sisters, Amelia and Lettie (Laetitia), taught in the primary school, though Amelia was 'delicate' and soon retired to be an invalid, paradoxically outliving all the others.

Amongst Father's contemporaries at Bradford Grammar School were John Coates, later one of the best known tenors of his time, and Frederick Delius. Studying the classics, such good progress was made that he won an open exhibition to Magdalen College, Oxford, a considerable achievement for a miner's son, and was in residence from 1884 to 1888. I have looked up the list of freshmen for 1884. Thirty-three came from the well-known public schools, including the 7th Duke of Newcastle, and six from grammar schools. Fifteen described themselves as sons of gentlemen, six as sons of clergy. The President of the college was Sir Frank Warren, whose opening remark to the freshmen was, "Gentlemen, we live in a palace...". And a palace indeed it must have seemed to the boy from Thornhill. He never spoke much of his time at Magdalen but was intensely proud to have been at the college, reading Mods and Greats, attending college chapel where he enjoyed the music, bicycling into the countryside, his machine being looked after in the original garage in Longwall where Lord Nuffield began his career, and living as full a life as his restricted finances allowed, albeit in a community whose social *mores* must have been far removed from the simple Yorkshire life at home.

Intending to teach, he did not find it easy to get a job but after quite a long interval was engaged by the headmaster of Suffield Park Preparatory School at Cromer, a place which was always high in his affections. Sometimes we used to go to Cromer or to Sheringham for our summer holidays where, walking on the golf course, he would lament the disappearance of various holes as the sea eroded the cliffs. From Cromer he went to Derby School and then at the turn of the century to Northampton Grammar School, where he became Second Master at a time when the school was rapidly expanding. One of the young men who joined the staff at Northampton was S.S. Sopwith, who became a good friend; later he moved to Shrewsbury where he was my housemaster.

Father was now an established professional man in his mid-thirties. Always keen on games, he was a member of the County Cricket Club on whose committee he was to serve for many years. He was a member of the Northampton Club in the centre of town, a typical gentlemen's club of the period with billiard tables, a card room, dining room and bar. The game which he played most was bridge; a very competent and knowledgeable player, he used in later life to go to the club virtually every day from five until seven. Bridge suited him for he was a most accurate and painstaking person, strong on fact, less strong on imagination, a man of habit and routine, keenly interested in history and contemporary politics – he read

The Times thoroughly every day – with an essentially conservative stance. He had a good bass voice, played the piano a little and enjoyed music. He told me that once, getting into the train at Dewsbury to go to Leeds, he was asked if he could sing bass; replying affirmatively, the other occupants incorporated him into their group and they went through the main Messiah choruses before they reached Leeds. He followed the Anglo-Catholicism of Archdeacon Brooke and became familiar with the church music of Stanford, Samuel Wesley, Stainer and the other Victorians. He was also attracted to Wagner's music, stemming from concerts conducted by the great Hans Richter at Oxford.

Although always a Yorkshireman at heart, he had in middle life accustomed himself to living in the Midlands and established a secure niche in Northampton, a bachelor schoolmaster like so many others, and seemingly likely to remain so as he entered his forties. Then in the Easter holidays of 1908 he went abroad with a friend and colleague, a tour which was to include Paris, Rome, Naples, and Venice. Going down to dinner in the lift in a Paris hotel were two ladies, travelling on the same tour. The four were asked if they would mind sharing a table and so Father met Mother – Constance Emma Turle. He was forty-three, she thirty-one. As sometimes happens in mature age, when my father fell in love (for the first time?), he fell completely. My mother's discreet diary survives. "Mr. Charlesworth" soon becomes "L" (Lindsay). "L told me about his people", "I told L about my people", "L and I saw Miss Bell home and then...", "Evening gondola, L and I". He proposed after twelve days, was accepted after twelve weeks and married after twelve months.

Who was Constance Emma Turle? Her father, Richard Turle, was a provision and wine merchant, first at Taunton where he carried on business at the Tudor House, Fore Street, an old timbered mansion where it was said that Judge Jeffreys stayed when conducting the Bloody Assize, and then at Beckenham in Kent. His forebears were either in trade or farmers, a remarkable family to which he was related by marriage being the Cookes of Ashburnham, Sussex. In 1798 William and Elizabeth Cooke presided over a family of eighteen children – *all* in that year alive and well.

Richard Turle (1843–1912) married Emma Noakes (1839–1926) and they had two daughters, Marion ('May') and my mother ('Con'), born respectively in 1875 and 1877. The Noakes family lived in Battle, Sussex, at a house which still stands called 'The Lake' – tradition said that it was a lake of blood after the Battle of Hastings. The Noakes were a family of typical Victorian entrepreneurs, rising from the lower middle class to relative affluence by the exercise of solid Victorian virtues, a Forsyte family at one remove down the social scale. The family business was in leather and the Battle tanyard was well known in the trade. My grandmother, Emma, was one of the thirteen children of William Noakes whose solid tomb is in a prominent position in the Battle churchyard. Of the seven sisters only two married, one without issue, and of the six sons only one, my mother's Uncle Fred. The sons worked in the tannery or in related trades, the unmarried daughters lived all their lives at The Lake, the last, my great-Aunt 'Min' (Matilda) surviving there until 1935, when she was ninety-two. I can just remember my grandmother, Emma Turle, who lived as all good grandmothers should, at Tunbridge Wells. The garden of her house abutted the railway line and I used to wave to the engine drivers. Dressed always in black, she was a scaled-down version of Queen Victoria. I remember her telling me of the 1848 Chartist disorders in London and how her uncles were enlisted as special constables (along with the soon-to-be-Emperor Napoleon III) to cope with the expected riots in Hyde Park. I didn't understand what 1848 was all about, but I remembered the special constable bit which much enhanced the family in my seven-year-old imagination. When my grandmother died, I was told that I could choose one thing from her house. Surprisingly I chose a gilt clock, a copy of an eighteenth century French clock, which I have enjoyed ever since. At the time I think I must have thought it was made of solid gold.

My mother, born in 1877, lived the first years of her life in a small Beckenham house which had no bathroom and where a man called daily to deal with the sanitation. However, as her father's provision business flourished, the family moved to a more commodious villa, Vere Lodge, Cedars Road, Beckenham, where she lived until she married. Life was severely restricted by the class structure of the day. May and Con were not to play with the children next door as the father was only an assistant in a drapery shop, whereas Mr Turle owned his own business. The principal residents of Beckenham were City men who did not mix with the local tradesmen. My mother therefore could not join the tennis club or the drama society. The Turles were really suspended between those above them by whom they did not wish to be patronised and those below who were not their social equals. The house was a substantial one and they had the usual two maids to look after the family. Even so there was no bathroom; a hip bath hung in Mr Turle's dressing room and was brought out on Saturday nights for the family baths. Mother never saw a fitted bath with taps before she went to boarding school; she was so flustered by it that she left her towel in the bedroom and was in an agony of indecision as to whether to shout for help or put on her nightdress while still wet. Fortunately a kindly schoolmistress came to her rescue.

Education for girls – or indeed boys – was not highly thought of in the Turle and Noakes families. My mother went to no less than six academies for young ladies. One was Vanburgh Castle at Blackheath (it still stands) where, for fifty guineas a term (boarding), Mrs and the Misses Hart gave instruction "in every branch of English literature, use of the globes, French,

Piano Forte, Pencil Drawing, Dancing and the Exercises". Mother's education was completed by residence for a time at Potsdam in the house of a good Frau who took foreign girls to teach them German and ran a sort of finishing school. Mother and her sister May used to go to the Potsdam city church, which was also attended by the Kaiser when in residence. They were pleased when he was there as he had let it be known that sermons must not exceed a stated – short – time.

This lady-like education for the drawing-room and wifehood did not satisfy my mother, who had an enquiring mind and needed intellectual stimulation which she did not find in the family, where reading did not encompass more than *The Daily Telegraph* and three-volume novels, so popular at that time. She made a determined effort to seek the education denied her. Reading lists for 1907 and 1908 included titles like *Spiritual Adventures, Essentials in Architecture,* and *Realities and Ideals.* She tackled Gilbert Murray's translations of the Greek classics and was drawn to the philosophy and poetry of Browning and Matthew Arnold, though reading without guidance or encouragement. Her sister May did not have similar tastes.

One of Mother's major interests was the stage; and here she encountered much frustration. Her secret ambition was to act professionally, which was of course socially unthinkable. She took elocution lessons, she gave recitals for charitable causes; but there was little or no opportunity to act in proper plays. May used to tell me how good Mother was, for in addition to the sentiment – and the sentimental – beloved of Victorians, she could also manage humour, so much more difficult. Even as late as the 1930s *Little Orphan Annie* was still given an occasional outing giving a glimpse of what might have been. She went frequently to London to the theatre in the heyday of the great Edwardians: Forbes Robertson, Mrs Patrick Campbell, Granville Barker, Frank Benson, Irvine himself and – beyond all others – Ellen Terry. She recalled that, when a child, she saw Ellen Terry sweep her train over the footlights; thinking they were candles, Mother only just restrained herself from calling out. Once at Rye, where Ellen Terry lived, my mother met her at a sale of work, carried her basket and was given a pink pin cushion. She tried to summon enough courage to say that she wanted to be an actress but failed.

For twelve years after she 'came out' she lived at home with her sister and parents, a circumscribed and somewhat frustrated life. The family circle was large: her mother had twelve brothers and sisters, her father seven. So there was much visiting, especially visits to The Lake at Battle. But from all the thirteen Noakes uncles and aunts, there were only two cousins. Uncle Fred became an important figure; widowed early in life he several times took his daughter, Dorothy, and his nieces May and Con, to places abroad, operating through Mr Thomas Cook. They saw the sights in

France and Italy, once going as far as Egypt, and on another occasion visited Madeira where in Reid's Hotel they met Dr Jameson, famous for his Raid. Mother was always a keen traveller, interested both in the buildings of antiquity (she was a disciple of John Ruskin) and in the life of the people. Uncle Fred, who ran the tanyard, died in 1912; he was comparatively well off and his fortune gradually filtered down the family. (A much meaner uncle was Richard who, when home for Christmas, tipped the maid two shillings and sixpence, and then asked for sixpence change).

By 1908 Mother was thirty-one, May thirty-three, both unmarried and apparently destined to be amongst those numerous daughters who never left the family home. Travelling with her friend Florrie Aitchison, she found her destiny in that lift in a Paris hotel. After a suitable interval, while both families accustomed themselves to the marriage, the plain-spoken Yorkshire Charlesworths from a mining village with hearts of gold and the more sophisticated Turles in their Beckenham suburb, the marriage took place at Christ Church, Lancaster Gate, on 14th April 1909, a time of political turmoil when Lloyd George introduced his famous Budget.

'Masetti', Church Avenue, Northampton, was a semi-detached house in a quiet suburb, opposite the parish church of St Matthew, an imposing essay in Victorian Gothic, then twenty years old, built by the local brewer, Pickering Phipps, who was also the landlord of 'Masetti'; a feeble attempt was made to call the area 'Phippsville'. As the church was built on beer money, the spire was known as 'Phipps's Fire Escape'. The church was Anglo-Catholic and the vicar, Canon Hussey, a long-standing friend and neighbour. 'Masetti' had six bedrooms on two storeys; it was a commodious house with cellar and boxroom and a good garden. A sparsely furnished bedroom on the top floor – with no heating – contained minimum furniture for cook and housemaid, and space also for a nursemaid, when necessary. Gas provided heat and light, though candles were mainly used in the bedrooms; there were coal fires in the drawing room and kitchen, otherwise gas fires throughout. There was a bathroom and two lavatories, though all the bedrooms had chamber pots, emptied daily by the maids, whose lavatory was outside the house. The full-time gardener, Denton, was in my parents' service for more than twenty-five years.

Mother was good at running the domestic establishment. She could not cook but she knew how to direct and it must have given her much satisfaction to be free at last from living with her parents and sister. Dinner parties were frequent, she had her 'At Home' days, and there were constant bridge evenings.

When he married, my father was Second Master at the Grammar School. He had hopes of being appointed headmaster when the vacancy came but in this he was disappointed as he was in his applications for other posts. In 1910 he decided to leave the Grammar School and set up his own preparatory school. Marriage had much improved his financial position as my mother brought part of the Noakes money with her. A pleasantly symmetrical record of their estimated income and expenditure survives, undated but presumably from early married life:

Con's Income	£475	Rent, rates, taxes	£70
Lindsay's ditto	£225	Food	£70
	£700	Dress	£70
		Insurance & save	£70
		Give away	£70
		Clubs & pocket	£70
		Wages, laundry	£70
		Light, heat, doctor, books	£70
		Holidays	£70
		Save	£70
			£700

The new school was set up in two semi-detached houses only a few hundred yards away from 'Masetti'. It was called Waynflete House School, taking the name from Magdalen's founder, William Waynflete. The initials WHS were interwoven in a gold monogram imposed on bright red caps. Here from January 1911 a school was gradually developed, building up to forty boys including twelve boarders; in 1917 a Montessori class was added so that the school numbered about sixty. The Montessori development was fostered by my mother who was fired by Madame Montessori's ideas, held meetings to discuss them and once organised a visit by the lady herself. The boys were straightforward middle class sons, many being sons of my father's friends at the Club and included the Vicar's sons, Walter and Christopher Hussey, the former ultimately succeeding his father at St Matthew's and then becoming Dean of Chichester, in both places acquiring a considerable reputation for bringing the Church and the Arts together. Another pupil was Francis Crick who won a Nobel Prize for his work on DNA. The school was staffed by the seemingly inexhaustible supply of maiden lady teachers, so numerous then, so rare today.

A jotting in one of my mother's notebooks reads, "When I was married at thirty-two, I did not know the facts of life. I asked my Mother to tell me but all she said was, 'You will know soon enough'". Children became of paramount importance in my mother's life, not only her own but children in general. My brother Richard was born in 1910, my sister Olive in 1912. On the nursery and general theories of education, my mother concentrated her very considerable energies. Soon she became involved in the Maternity and Infant Welfare movement which was a major occupation for the rest of her life. She became leader of the Abington Avenue Infant Welfare Centre where mothers from the surrounding mean streets, where the shoe operatives lived, brought their babies every Thursday to hear talks on baby upbringing, buy baby foods, see the district nurse and also, as my mother was quick to encourage, to be members of a club with social activities. She was an 'advanced' thinker for her time and often in demand as a speaker on such subjects as 'Breast Feeding' (of which she was a strong advocate), 'Fresh Air', 'Constipation', 'Habits', and subjects of basic health and hygiene in the home. She conducted a war on 'dummies' (now called 'comforters') even to the extent of, when walking down the street and seeing a baby sucking a dummy, saying loudly in mock amazement, "Look, a baby with a dummy!" Her enthusiasms soon led her on to various local and later London-based committees.

Thus Richard, a good looking little boy with impressive curls, and Olive, quieter but thoughtful, were the objects of all Mother's progressive educational thinking. On 4th April 1915 another son, Alan, was born. At Christmas he developed some internal trouble and, partly through incompetent nursing, died on 4th January 1916. The wound was very deep.

In the first ten years of married life, the matching of two very different temperaments must have been difficult. In his mid-forties, my father was well-established, cautious, conservative, and found pleasure in watching cricket and football, in bridge and in a quiet domestic routine. My mother was intuitive, energetic and enterprising, keen for new experiences, intellectually curious and glad to be rid of the claustrophobic frustrations of her spinster life. Whereas Father, not a particularly religious man, nevertheless stayed with the Anglo-Catholicism of his background which was practised over the road at St Matthew's, Mother was moving fast into the rationalist-humanist camp. She expressed her own philosophy thus, "What the world needs is a body of ethics and morals (without superstitions or supernationalisms) to belong to, to be one with. It is the greatest need of the human heart", and she quoted with approval George Eliot, "...that Faith that life on earth is being shaped to glorious ends; that rushing and expanding stream of thought, of feeling, fed by all the past". Her comment on Christianity was severe: "A God who begets a son and sacrifices him in order to appease his own wrath against his own creatures appears to me to be incomprehensible". One *cri de coeur* survives. It is headed Good Friday 1915. "Every time I go to church I vehemently desire that my children shall not be brought up in the Church of England. Have I been weak or wise in not stating my views more definitely? Ought I to have endeavoured not to have them baptised? It is impossible to teach them to be Christians and not Christians. If only I had someone to talk things over with".

So married life developed at 'Masetti', outwardly placidly, my father content with his work in creating a well-liked school, my mother constantly seeking new initiatives whether of thought or action; between them there was perhaps not much communication below the superficial level. In May 1918 Mother knew she was again pregnant. In this last year of the war life was hard, shortages real and in the autumn the 'flu epidemic swept away more than the war itself had done. Mother was ill, though not with 'flu: her doctor, as was the fashion, recommended bed rest and she hardly came downstairs for three months. Was it a difficult pregnancy? Did the devastating depression of later years afflict her at this time? Whatever the causes, they did not prevent a healthy baby being born on 31st January 1919, the day after her forty-second birthday, in that curious time between the Armistice and the Peace, the year of the creation of the League of Nations, of the crossing of the Atlantic by air, of the first woman Member of Parliament, of the first performance of Elgar's cello concerto.

With a brother nine years older and a sister seven years older, I grew up in many ways like an only child. As the youngest and much-desired child, born when my mother was almost past child-bearing age, with a father who was in his Fifties in my early years, I was spoiled, shy, selfish and solitary. Although I did not know it at the time, my mother suffered constantly from a heavy depression which sometimes lasted for months at a time. She concealed this, but it must have affected our family life. On the other hand, when well, she was full of energy and initiative – a typical manic depressive. As was often the case in those days, I spent much time with nursemaids and with the maids in the kitchen. A succession of girls were employed, several staying for years. They may have been poorly paid and hard worked but some became very much part of the family, for my mother was very sensitive and understanding in dealing with the servants. Amongst those who looked after me, wheeling me out in my push chair in the afternoons, was Joan Hickson, much later a successful actress who achieved wide fame on television as Miss Marple in Agatha Christie's stories. I wrote to her in 1989 to see if she remembered me. "Of course I remember you and your family. You were an extremely good looking little boy with dark curly hair, going to dancing class and sitting *under* the table to have your tea"; which reminds me of how I disliked those dancing classes, where I met *girls*, all of whom I much despised for not being boys.

At the age of three-and-a-half I joined the Montessori School at Waynflete, though I have little recollection of those early school days. More clearly I remember the imaginative games I played in the garden, great deeds of derring-do with myself as hero, cowboys and Indians, my first Raleigh bicycle to which I was passionately attached, my mongrel terrier Cracker, and elaborate battles with the great army of lead soldiers which Richard and I built up. I avoided the company of other boys until a friendship developed with near neighbours, Ted and Alan Hicks and Richard Cartwright; we formed an inoffensive gang, bicycled furiously round a dirt track we had set up in the garden, swapped theories about the facts of life on which we were notably ill-informed and spent some time in our box-room, a long, dark room which we at one time turned into an airship and from whose skylight windows I carried out extremely dangerous climbs on the roof amongst the chimneys; today, looking at those same roofs and chimneys, I can hardly credit my courage in one naturally uncourageous.

When I was three, Richard went off to the Dragon School at Oxford, a school unorthodox enough to satisfy my mother and successful and academic enough to satisfy my father. He was at first very unhappy but grew to love it, somewhat handicapped at first by being sent with nightgowns and 'combinations', my mother not having caught up with the new fashion of pyjamas, pants and vest. Thence he won an exhibition to Winchester, not a school my mother wholly approved of – the boys "need more air, less work, more variety of work and a proper High Tea". Richard grew into a proper Wykehamist and, encouraged by his housemaster Harry Altham, bowled himself – nearly – into the cricket XI; but in the end was twelfth man. Olive went off to Benenden in 1926, a new school much approved of by Mother. In that year my father retired and thereafter lived a contented life of bridge, cricket, football, driving the car, and reading *The Times*.

One activity which absorbed much of my rather solitary life was the construction of a hut of considerable proportions in the garden, measuring about forty by fifteen feet. I mixed concrete by the ton, dug down so that the floor was two feet below the ground, built a wooden roof covered with roofing felt, fitted drainage, painted and re-painted the inside, cultivated a garden with pond, installed an internal heating system for warmth and hot water, had some primitive cooking arrangement and connected myself to the house by a field telephone, a war-time relic. I cannot well say how many hundreds of hours I devoted to this work. I was constantly pulling bits down and re-planning so that the work never ended. No help was required, except from adults who knew about cement and sand and had technical knowledge of electricity when I came to light it. I suppose this was the centre of my leisure life for four or five years. My mother noted in her diary, "Michael plays too much by himself"; and, when a boy (of her choice) was asked to tea it was "not a great success". So I went my way, devoted to my own activities, shy of others, apprehensive of new situations, full of imaginative and self-centred thoughts. In the boxroom, where I sometimes played alone, I was quite convinced that there also lived there a little black man, whom I can still see, going across one end of the room; fearful and fascinated, I was quite old before I was persuaded that he was a figment of my imagination.

In two interests I was sedulously encouraged by my mother – reading and the theatre. She used to read to me every tea time. I did not always care for her choice of books, 'improving' literature on the whole, but I remember certain of them, notably *The King of the Golden River* by Ruskin. *The Children's Newspaper* was similarly tainted, its editor, Arthur Mee, stating that his aim was "to make goodness news"; it seldom does. I soon learned to read and devoured adventure stories. Mother was fascinated by the epic of Captain Scott and, similarly inspired, I turned the nursery into a replica of Scott's Antarctic hut. Dr Dolittle books were read again and again; when Arthur Ransome's *Swallows and Amazons* books appeared they carried me away completely to the Lake District and the Broads.

I saw my first real play at the age of six, J.M. Barrie's *A Kiss for Cinderella*. I quite failed to grasp what was going to happen and that the curtain in front of us would go up and I concentrated my attention on the boxes where I thought the action would take place. Most vividly I remember *Show Boat* with Paul Robeson, astounded that anyone could have a bass as deep as that; the tunes stayed with me for months. In the late twenties the Stratford Shakespeare season was continued in a cinema, the theatre having been burned down in 1926. I was taken to *Henry V* at the age of eight and saw my first *Hamlet* a year later; I had difficulty in keeping still and earned a rebuke from the lady behind me. So much did it catch my imagination that at the age of nine I talked my three friends, Ted, Alan and Richard, into doing our own production in the nursery. Needless to say, I was Hamlet and the rest of the cast had to cover all the other parts, though Ophelia only appeared as a cushion with a long flowing dress. I was particularly pleased with the Ghost who was draped in a long rug and had a flashlight under it to illuminate his face, a red light when addressing the soldiers, a green light when talking to Hamlet. The King was murdered by having secatine squeezed in his ear. Particularly enjoyed were the fights and death scenes. In the interval, wishing to see the audience, I cut a hole in the "curtain" which was actually one of our best bedspreads, attracting a rebuke from the audience who paid 4d. for a stalls seat, 1/- for a box and 2d. for the gallery, where the maids sat. My promise, "There will be quite a lot of Shakespeare's own words in the play, Mother" was fulfilled. A later production was of *The Prisoner of Zenda* in which I was able to strike dramatic and romantic attitudes as Rudolf Rassendyll; the rest of the cast seem to have reacted meekly to my autocratic direction, much as must have happened in Donald Wolfit's company. Perhaps I felt with David Garrick that "any fool can play Hamlet; but comedy is a very serious business".

I am grateful to my mother for so firmly launching me into the theatre and into literature. But one of the great excitements of my childhood was undoubtedly the motor car. My father bought his first car, a large and ponderous Humber, in 1924. He had tuition from various employees of Mr Lane of the Autocar Garage who sold us the car. Much skill was required to navigate this heavy machine and particularly to change gear. Journeys were adventures. Poor road surfaces, few signposts, no speed limits, only occasional garages, hazards in the shape of pedestrians, cyclists, horses, cattle and dogs. One could never be quite sure of actually reaching a destination without a break-down. Once we set out for Winchester to see Richard. The engine gave trouble three times and in Hampshire we had a really serious accident, colliding with a motor cycle and side-car and breaking the cyclist's leg. We arrived at 11.30 p.m. There were as many as fifty or sixty different makes of car on the road, all with different contours and recognisable by the shape of their bonnets. Richard and I used to have recognition competitions as we drove along at 30 or 40 m.p.h.; 50 was fast, 60 unthinkable. Into our view came Standards, Morrises, Austins, Deemsters, Armstrong-Siddelys, Beans, Sunbeams, Morgans, and the aristocratic Alfa-Romeos, Daimlers, Hispano-Suizas and of course the occasional Rolls Royce.

In the car we went on our holidays, conventional visits to watering-places, staying in small hotels: Sidmouth, Walton-on-the-Naze, Cromer, Thorpeness, Harrogate, Woolacombe, Thurlestone – all came within our family orbit. Once only we ventured abroad, to St Briac in Brittany, my mother's love of foreign travel overcoming my father's distaste for 'abroad'. We stayed in a small hotel kept by White Russians and I – untypically – found a friend in Nicky Toudendoff, the son of the establishment, said to be a Prince, though all White Russians were thought to be of noble blood. In 1928 we went on the Broads for the first time, though without my father who now retired for his summer holiday to Harrogate where he took the waters and played bridge, while my mother and the children struck out more adventurously. I loved the Broads and went several times, Richard and his Oxford friends being willing to take me as a cabin boy. Sailing was a major interest for some years, encouraged by seeing the famous 'J' Class yachts racing off the south coast.

Certain events stand out in these first dozen years of my life. Only dimly do I remember being taken to the Wembley Empire Exhibition in 1924, but the sight of a model of the Prince of Wales carved in Canadian butter stayed with me. The excitement of the aeroplane was brought home when we were one day motoring down to Benenden to see Olive. In a field stood a little De Havilland Moth two-seater aeroplane; we stopped and, finding that flights were being offered at ten shillings per person, my mother typically seized my hand and bought two tickets. I was very frightened, especially as the cockpit was open and it seemed most likely that we would fall out. But I enjoyed the flight in retrospect and it certainly was something to speak of at school. Could it have been part of Sir Alan Cobham's circus which I was to see at a later Air Show? Not many miles from home was the airship headquarters at Cardington; here my father took me to see a sight which was unique – the visiting Graf Zeppelin, the R101 and the R100 (in its shed) congregated for the first and last time, a time of confidence in lighter-than-air travel before disaster struck.

The event which most stands out however, was the opening of the new theatre at Stratford. My mother had been a subscriber to the building fund and managed to get two tickets for the first performance on 23rd April, Shakespeare's birthday, in 1932. So, amidst the theatrical personages and politicians (Baldwin and Bernard Shaw were there), we saw *Henry IV Part I*, after the official opening by the Prince of Wales in his shy way. I thought it marvellous but the critics didn't: "an uneasy performance" wrote Ivor Brown; "dull and spiritless" said W.A. Darlington. In truth the cast were very tired, having had to rehearse five plays in three weeks. Randle Ayrton, the doyen of Stratford (*The Times* compared him to Woodfull), was the King with the young Giles Isham as Prince Hal and Roy Byford, whom I was to see many times, as Falstaff. The bored Prince of Wales left after Act I, a singular discourtesy. The theatre building, designed by Miss Scott, who was only twenty-nine when commissioned, came under much criticism. "Soviet barracks", "Jam factory", "Teutonic", were some of the epithets. Inside I thought it was splendid, with its comfortable dunlopillo seats, rolling stage, lack of footlights and details such as a clock with no numbers, and ash trays let into the wall labelled ASHES which smacked of the crematorium. But the actors found it difficult and there have been many modifications since 1932. For me it was a great day; meanwhile Newcastle were beating Arsenal in the Cup Final, receiving the cup from the King while his son scuttled out of the theatre at Stratford. Not content with the first performance at Stratford, my mother also managed tickets for the first night at the new Sadler's Wells theatre, the triumphant achievement of the indomitable Lilian Baylis. We saw *Twelfth Night* with a cast which included both Richardson and Gielgud, but all I really remember is that the curtain several times fell actually on the heads of the players, presumably because, with the front of the house open, currents of air altered the curtain drop by a yard or so.

It was in 1928 that the dread decision was taken to send me away to school. Much as I disliked it both in prospect and in practice, I have no doubt that it was the right decision. My Aunt May, always forthright, told me much later just how intolerable I was at that stage. As I have said, I lived quite a solitary life, enjoyed my own company, was essentially selfish and skilled at wheedling what I wanted out of my parents, who were 'old', Father being over sixty, Mother over fifty, at a time when these ages implied 'old age' more than today when we all live so much longer. Mother was suffering from her periodic depressions, Father getting rather ponderous, neither being in very close touch with their moody youngest child. Father now had a new toy – a radiogram, a most impressive instrument and important in my life as a constantly expanding library of records was built up, the old HMV and Columbia 78s. From these I became familar with Beethoven, Brahms, Tchaikowsky, Bach and Handel, providing me with a musical base from which I have developed a real love for music, although never a performer.

Richard went from Winchester to Hertford College, Oxford, with a classical exhibition; Olive went to Girton College, Cambridge, after Benenden, thus having the education which my mother had missed. Richard loved Oxford, where he met Freda, his future wife, and it bulked large in his memory for the rest of his life. Olive was less happy at Girton, where she read economics, but nevertheless emerged with a decent degree. Even at this stage she was showing something of Mother's depression, which dogged her hereafter. I cannot say I was very close to either brother or sister but we got on well together. I have always been reluctant to reveal my real feelings and certainly did not do so in the family circle. But Northampton and our house and its environs exercised a strong fascination, dull as is the town and neighbourhood. The local shops, the back alleys where I bicycled, the nearby park, the trams, the County Ground only a few hundred yards away, the old Racecourse, and beyond all my hut and the garden – these were the scenes of childhood which retained and evoked my strong affection, from which I was now to be temporarily sundered.

CHAPTER II

Abinger

I a stranger and afraid
In a world I never made.
Housman

My parents searched far to find a suitable prep school for me and it was my mother's influence which was strongest in deciding on Abinger Hill. The moving spirit in founding this progressive and unusual school was a Miss Belle Rennie, who provided most of the money. She had been fired with enthusiasm for the Dalton Plan of education which she had seen working in the United States where it originated. The basic idea was that there should be no forms in the accepted sense but that each pupil should go at his own pace. Each curriculum subject had a room where was the relevant member of staff. The pupil was supplied with a series of assignments in the different subjects which were divided into units. Every morning the pupil planned his day's work – how much time to spend on each subject – and progressed round the subject rooms, following his assignment and taking his work up to the master for advice and correction. The units were then marked up on his chart. In this way the pupil devoted more time to subjects which he found difficult, less time to those which he found easy and so moved at a pace in accordance with his abilities. Planning his own progess day by day was expected to make him more self reliant. Such was the theory.

Miss Rennie gathered about herself a Council headed by a noted educationalist, Dr C.W. Kimmins, and including a bishop, various members of the aristocracy and Dr Percy Nunn, well known in education circles of the day. She purchased a country house with 130 acres, situated in the Surrey woodlands between the villages of Abinger and Holmbury St Mary, places which seem to me in retrospect remarkably like Miss Marple's St Mary Mead. Looking for an enterprising headmaster, she lighted on G.J.K. Harrison, then teaching at Horris Hill, twenty-five years old and recently married, a man who – as it turned out – was to set the whole course of my life and at whose memorial service fifty years later I was to give the

Address. The staff were, for some years, all under the age of thirty, the chief assistants being Henry Brereton and Pat Delap, both later to move north, Henry to Gordonstoun where ultimately he became Warden, and Pat to be headmaster of the Gordonstoun prep school nearby. Both were enthused by the ideas of Kurt Hahn, founder of Gordonstoun and father of the philosophy of Atlantic College and the Outward Bound movement.

The enterprise was launched in 1927 when four boys were surrounded and outnumbered by a staff of boundless enthusiasm and limited experience; two of the boys were Persian. ("I hear Jim Harrison has a school where half the boys are black"). The next formative years were exciting as numbers rose while at the same time the Harrisons, Breretons and Delaps were increasing their own families and babies always seemed to be arriving. The school was officially opened by the Duchess of Atholl, nicknamed the 'Red Duchess' by the Press because she was always taking up 'progressive' causes (like Abinger Hill), though in fact *The Times* obituary described her as an 'earnest, dowdy committee woman'. Still she was a fitting symbol to usher in this new brand of education. *The Morning Post* headlines were: 'A New Phase of Education. Public Preparatory School. Not Run for Profit'; which meant that the school was a Trust unlike the normal proprietary schools of the day.

'Staffing on a scale which permits individual teaching and the encouragement of independent methods of work' was an educational approach which appealed to my mother, though my father must have had doubts about a wholly untried school in the formative stages, run by an idealist but inexperienced staff. So in January 1929 to Abinger I went, the twenty-seventh boy to join. At the same time arrived Llewellyn and David Lawrence Jones, both to be good friends. Their father had interviewed Jim Harrison in the holidays at the Adelphi Hotel in Liverpool; after some desultory conversation he asked if Jim's father was coming, not realising that he was in fact talking to the headmaster himself.

Going away from home for the first time was hell; the January weather was cold and wet; the strangeness of everything overwhelmed me. "I am very very miserbale" I wrote. My birthday occurred after a fortnight and I was worried about receiving parcels, worried about the cake and crackers my mother kindly sent, worried that I should be teased or my presents commented upon. The matron – Miss Snook (no less) – tried unsuccessfully to be motherly. Jim Harrison was altogether cast on too large a scale for me at that stage. I wrote unhappily, demanding things from home, not so much "please send" as "I must have", which perhaps indicates what a spoiled child I had been. Only very slowly in that first year did I begin to find my feet, thoroughly lacking in self confidence. I attached myself to a sympathetic older boy called Tim Craxton, acting (for some obscure reason) as his little dog, curling up in some lockers as a makeshift kennel and acquiring the nickname 'Toby' by which I was thereafter known. All this, I now see, was in a desperate effort to be accepted, to fit in – even as a dog. I was constantly writing to my parents and they visited me every three weeks, staying at the little Abinger Hatch hotel, a scene of delight on Saturdays and of unhappiness as those Sundays drew to their inevitable conclusion – back to school for evening prayers, 'The day Thou gavest, Lord, is ended', ever afterwards for me a tune of profound melancholy.

But of course things improved. I did not then realise that we were to some extent educational guinea pigs or that we did strange things. Our very dress marked us as 'progressives' – corduroy shorts and shirts with enormous V-necks, thus ensuring a big intake of air unimpeded by tight collars or ties; out of school we often wore dungarees and wellington boots though on Sundays we had more conventional tweed suits (costing £2.12.6d.) and Eton collars. The school colours were brown and orange, pleasant autumn colours which fitted the footballers into the natural ambience of the woods which surrounded the pitch. Before breakfast we all stood on the terrace, facing Holmbury Hill, and blew our noses on the order being given, first one nostril, then the other, then both at once. After breakfast we ticked off our names on a list signifying that our bowels had moved; frightened as to what would happen if I didn't sign, I appended my tick daily, regardless of what my bowels were or were not doing. Our diet was laid down by Dr Corry Mann whose experiments had shown him that boys were much fitter and grew faster if they drank an extra pint of milk a day which we duly drank. I was not then a tea drinker and when the other boys had tea at meals I had milk, in addition to the Corry Mann pint. My milk intake being enormous I quickly grew fat and when my parents first came down to Abinger, I was bursting out of my suit. Another man who had a hand in our diet and general life was Dr Murray Levick, who had been with Scott in the Antarctic, and later was one of those who ran the Public Schools Exploring Society – thought by some to be a charlatan. He exhorted us to be tough and manly – not to have soft carpets in the bedroom but to feel the hard linoleum with one's feet as one got out of bed and "to go to the window and throw your chest out"; a difficult physical feat, we thought. His son, perhaps not strangely, was a weak and puny child who did not stay long at Abinger.

We also had some rather esoteric drill or dancing connected with Margaret Morris, then a fashionable name in this sphere, who herself once came down to inspect us. I wrote home, "She felt me when breathing and said I was 'tight'. I thought she meant I was drunk at first but it turns out she was only referring to my chest!" Another extract from a letter seems mysterious. "In the afternoon we were all photographed with nothing on, first in our ordinary position and then in our best position to show the difference". What does this tell one? Nothing seems to have been spared in enabling us to burst with health; even the windows were fitted with Vita glass which enabled the sun's rays to penetrate more easily. In summer we all sun-bathed on the terrace for half an hour after lunch, with shirts off, while the headmaster's baby daughter crawled naked amongst us, giving us an elementary biology lesson. When it was really hot, we slept in a makeshift outdoor dormitory in the woods.

The woods! The handsome half-timbered house built in 1893 by William Flockhart, with later additions by Lutyens, was surrounded by woodland which winding paths and rides crossed and re-crossed. Today the smell of pine trees in hot weather brings back to me those woods in which we roamed entirely freely – frightening to me at first, as boys formed gangs and rival gangs, hunting each other through the thickets. In Nicholas Mosley's memory, new boys were buried up to the neck in pits which they themselves had to dig. Nicholas was burdened by the nickname 'Baby Blackshirt', his father being Sir Oswald Mosley, then leader of the British Fascists. Tree houses were at one time the rage; wide games and organised hide and seek were played over what seemed a vast area. Jim Harrison developed cross country running on the Shrewsbury model of a Hunt, covering distances through the woods which to a slow hound like me assumed marathon proportions. The woods also provided an area of constructive activity in that we all spent one afternoon a week on estate duty of some sort. I belonged to the Honourable Company of Foresters, cutting and clearing, sweeping and burning and once making a list of all the trees on the estate by type and attempting an estimate of their ages. Next door to Abinger was a large house and estate called Parkhurst, out of bounds to us, where Rousseau once had been a guest. I went there with Tim Craxton (his faithful dog) and we dodged the gardeners amongst the trees and shrubs. I have seldom been so frightened but Tim navigated with confidence.

Amongst all this unusual activity took place the more mundane prep school activities – cricket and football and some hockey; and a peculiar type of wall game in the Riding School, converted into a sort of gymnasium. I was keen on games and increasingly enjoyed them, though my ability was never more than ordinary. I was thought to be a promising bat but only at the end of my Abinger time did I begin to fulfil that promise. Naturally with few boys to choose from, it was not difficult to get into the 1st XIs but my batting average one year was two. Wicket keeping I took up late and this was to be my stock in trade. We were coached at one time by a vast man called Mr Halliley, given to telling the boys stories of his cricketing feats. Did he really play for Somerset? We certainly all thought so. He decided to make me into a professional type of wicket keeper, perhaps with Duck-worth in mind, the current England keeper. So I was given enormous gloves whose surface was treated with eucalyptus oil, raw steak on each hand, over-large pads, and an abdominal protector, though I hadn't much to protect. All this was meant to make me more confident but I found it most cumbersome; not that this mattered as wicket keepers in those days were expected to be entirely static in contrast to today when, in the Godfrey Evans and Knott tradition, small pads, light gloves and extreme mobility are the professional characteristics. Just as I found my niche in wicket keeping, so I drifted into goal keeping at which, at prep school level, I was competent; indeed on leaving, the school magazine described me as a 'sound and brilliant goalkeeper, by far the best we have ever had'. Early matches at Abinger were hard work – we had few boys and were playing against established schools like Boxgrove and Edgeborough. In our first cricket match against Boxgrove we were all out for 24, facing a bowler of terrifying speed whose name was Passy; Christopher Robin Milne was amongst their batsmen as they slaughtered us. Every year we played the estate staff who had solid and comfortable country names – Harber, Bridger, Covey, Foreman. The latter was in fact one of a group of young men taken on as domestics from the Durham area during the great slump of 1931–32. James Foreman became a commanding figure at Abinger on the domestic scene and stayed at the house for the rest of his life, revisited by Abinger boys for the next forty years.

I made my first dramatic appearance in a little play called *The Brothers* (Joseph and his Brethren), in which I was Joseph's steward – I also played Bluck in an adaptation of *The King of the Golden River* – both small parts for me who had after all played Hamlet at the age of nine. But I much enjoyed this tiny whiff of the stage. There were other typical prep school activities – a well equipped train room, to which my brother Richard's excellent collection of Basset-Lowke rolling stock was given, a lively debating society at which we solemnly discussed whether one preferred Summer to Winter or whether the Channel Tunnel was desirable (at an estimated cost of £31 million), a mock election at the time of a general election at which I was the 'Reformers' candidate (I lost), an exceptionally good art room where leatherwork, basketry, pottery and lino-cuts were produced; and, like so many other boys of that age, I started the piano. The Primary exam I passed but, alas, the Elementary was too much for me. I don't know why I didn't flourish as I was quite musical; perhaps I didn't have the patience to practise, though most days a boy called Howard and I went over to the Old Barn (the music school) to do our half hour at the scales and exercises, gloomily walking back and saying how much we preferred history. (Michael Howard later became Regius Professor of Modern History at Oxford.) My teacher, Miss Deveson, somewhat despairing, taught me simple improvisation as I did not seem to get on well with the written notes. This I took to with enthusiasm, gave up formal lessons and was soon able to play simple tunes (in certain keys only) to my own enjoyment, if not to the enjoyment of proper musicians. I am grateful to Miss Deveson for this small skill, useful later in a variety of army messes.

Some effort was made to introduce us to classical music. Sir Robert Mayer was then organising special concerts for children in London, conducted by Malcolm Sargent. I was immensely impressed by seeing and hearing a full symphony orchestra. Malcolm Sargent was an excellent guide to the young, explaining the instruments, choosing exciting pieces and attracting us all by his personality, not to say his dapper appearance with the ever-present carnation in his button hole. Also in the audience was the Duchess of York, now the Queen Mother, bringing Princess Elizabeth.

Robert Mayer sent his son Adrian to Abinger, one of several figures in the world of art and music who were attracted to this progressive school. Once Harold Craxton, Tim's father, Professor at the Royal College and a well-known accompanist, came to play for us. To my astonishment he was preceded by a lorry with CHAPPELL written on the side which disgorged a grand piano; why could he not use one of our ordinary school uprights? His performance of Beethoven's Moonlight Sonata made a profound impression on me and I eagerly wrote home suggesting that a gramophone record be bought.

Over all this activity presided the larger-than-life figure of James Harrison. An enthusiast for the Dalton Plan and also for the generally liberal approach to education, he nonethless kept his feet on the ground, modifying Dalton so that there were a number of class periods and balancing the emphasis on individual development ("We go flat out for the ego here") with a disciplinary structure which put some curbs on our freedom to run wild. John Gale, later a distinguished journalist with *The Observer*, relates in his autobiography that, having committed some misdemeanor, he was beaten with a long-handled clothes brush on which were imprinted the initials of the headmaster, G.J.K.H. Inspecting himself afterwards in the dormitory mirror, he found G.J.K.H. firmly implanted on his nether regions; and symbolically those initials were stamped on all of us. Jim had a remarkable ability in communicating with prep school boys and was able to strike a balance between the boys' world which he took seriously and the adult world to which he belonged. He used our slang, read the *Modern Boy*, presided over wrestling matches in the bedrooms, ran the debates, entered with enthusiasm into the train room activity, and led our cross country runs. He never lost his sense of wonder and this capacity to stay young was wonderfully attractive to boys. Yet he was at home with all types of parent – the aristocratic, the artistic, the academic, the professional – a ready conversationalist and a splendid raconteur. Abinger owed everything to his enthusiastic leadership, which to us had a charismatic quality and a touch of unusual panache. His wife Jo was exceedingly beautiful. On Sunday nights I remember her reading to us, *The Thirty-Nine Steps*,

The Prisoner of Zenda and *Robbery Under Arms*. But a prep school was too limited a sphere for anyone with her zest for life. After having produced two children, she achieved her life's ambition of going on the stage and, after training at the Guildhall, joined a repertory company. After the war she became 'out of town' editor of *Vogue*. Thus, though the family kept together, she was little seen at Abinger.

Jim Harrison's two main lieutenants were Henry Brereton and Pat Delap. Henry taught history and English, subjects which I increasingly enjoyed under his tutelage. He also ran the football and cricket. Pat taught French, had a slight stutter and had been a Half Blue at Cambridge in the Low Hurdles. Seeing him effortlessly gliding over hurdles (which we had made in the carpentry shop) caught my imagination so completely that I determined to be a hurdler. I read coaching manuals, did my exercises nightly, knew who held the records (Forest Towns (USA) held the world record of 13.7 seconds) and modelled myself on D.O. Finlay, Britain's leading performer. The result of all this effort was only moderate; the plain fact was that throughout my hurdling career, which lasted for the next twenty years, although I could twist my body into the right shape and do the splits, I was never a fast enough sprinter.

Other members of the staff came and went but it was on Harrison, Brereton and Delap that the school was founded. In fact Abinger was such a pleasant place that numerous adults seemed to drift in and out of our lives. In the holidays the grown ups had splendid house parties, using all the excellent facilities of the estate. Charlie Smirke the jockey came and married the school secretary, Miss Charlton. We were also visited by the earnest educationalists to see how the Dalton plan was faring. At the end of my time, Jim asked me to show round a visitor called Mr Coade, who was eager to know all about Dalton. I did my best for him and on that foundation he built a brilliant career as the headmaster of Bryanston.

What, then, of the Dalton Plan? Frankly it did not entirely suit me. I required very direct supervision and help; and direction. Being bad at maths and not liking the maths master, I put in as little time as possible in the maths room. As no one knew where any boy was at any given time, it was easy to slip off to the lavatory for a whole period and read the *Modern Boy*, though I was not bold enough to do what Nicholas Mosley did, marking up his own units on his chart. Well-organised boys who had their own motive power did well. For others the structure was too loose. My own progress was also handicapped by a grumbling stomach ache which went on for some months. "Can't something be done about my stomach *please*, it's awful!" I wrote with my usual exaggeration, but in fact this time my troubles were not superficial. Soon after the beginning of term in September 1930 I was whisked up to London in an ambulance and had my appendix out. This was a painful and long drawn out process in those days.

I was in hospital for at least two weeks, a time which coincided with the R101 disaster when that great airship crashed in France only a few hours after leaving England on what was meant to be an epoch-making flight to Karachi. I read every account and comment, becoming an expert on the whole subject. But I missed weeks of school work and on top of this, when I did return, there was an outbreak of measles and we were all sent home, resulting in my missing nearly half a year's work in all. No wonder that as I approached Common Entrance there was some anxiety, not least in my own mind. "Worried about work", was a constant theme in my letters. How vulnerable were schools in those days to the common diseases: it seems that frequently we were in quarantine for something or other and nurses were often imported. In my last term scarlet fever killed Robin Arnold Forster. My close friend Llewellyn Lawrence Jones died in his first year at Harrow. To us these illnesses were not without their positive side – extra holidays, special food and the usual fuss which surrounds the sick bed. We did not much worry about missing lessons. The school motto was 'Labor Donum Dei' – Work is the Gift of God – but we thought nothing of it and were totally disbelieving of Sir Rennell Rodd (a retired ambassador) who told us at Speech Day to "give your whole self to the job you are doing because only the very best can help your country. Does not work give you greater pleasure than anything else in life?" Nods of approval from the adults and a resounding (silent) negative from the boys.

Dalton and I did not get on well, but that did not prevent me from writing enthusiastically if hypocritically of my experiences. Many years later I came across a book entitled *The Triumph of the Dalton Plan* with a section by boys sententiously entitled 'The Judgement of Youth on the Dalton Plan' where in reply to the queston, "If you like working on the Dalton Plan, say why", I found that M.L.C. Aged 10½ had written:

> Because (as I said to the larst question) boys who do not work do not keep the form back, and if you are very backward in any subjects you do not just do it as the time comes along for you to do so, but you can specialise in it, and if you get bored with it you can do some other work and come back refreshed and with new vigeur on to it till you get it right.

Alas, I cannot remember carrying out my precept or returning to the maths room refreshed and with new "vigeur".

As might be expected, Abinger attracted a wide variety of 'progressive' parents. Julian Huxley sent his sons as did the musicians Harold Craxton and Robert Mayer; Oswald Mosley and David Margesson, the Government Chief Whip, represented the political extremes; Montagu Norman, Governor of the Bank of England, sent his stepson Peregrine Worsthorne; aristocratic families were well represented – Billy Buckhurst, later Earl de la Warr, Julian Mond, later Lord Melchett, Martin Pollock, later Lord Buckmaster and Lord Bruce Dundas were all contemporaries. A little later came Edward Boyle, nicknamed at school 'the Prime Minister', later to be Minister of Education and Vice Chancellor of the University of Leeds. John Gale tells a rather revolting anecdote: at milk time, Eddy Boyle could pull out a fold of fat in his stomach, pour the milk in and bend over and drink it. Industry and commerce were also present, notably in Tony and John Mills, whose father we all thought was a real tycoon, then chairman of Mills & Rockley, the advertising firm. Then there were the cranks – Murray Levick, already mentioned, Lady Heath who insisted that her son Geoffrey follow an extraordinary diet proposed by a Dr Damoglu and, most extreme, a Mrs Clark whose son Jimmy had a difficult start in life as an illustration to the Glaxo advertisement 'Glaxo Builds Bonny Babies', which featured Jimmy as a fat, naked baby lying on a cushion. Mrs Clark was a devoted Nazi and after a few terms took Jimmy away to Germany to follow Der Führer, both becoming members of the Goebbels propaganda machine in which Jimmy became chief assistant to Lord Haw Haw, frequently broadcasting from Berlin in 1939–40. He later became disillusioned with the Nazis and left the party, thus escaping being shot after the war.

Several contemporaries of mine have made their living by the pen. In addition to Peregrine Worsthorne, recently editor of the *Sunday Telegraph*, and Nicholas Mosley, now a leading novelist, Johnny Gale was a journalist with *The Observer* until his premature death, and John Halcro Ferguson specialised on South America. He married a black girl at a time when this was unusual; showing her photograph to a contemporary at an Abinger reunion weekend, the friend innocently but unwisely asked if the photograph was a negative. Then there was Michael Howard, Professor of History, first at Oxford and then Yale. I do not know what became of Alexander Royds, who had a fine turn of phrase. When we were both about nine years old, sitting at lunch, the master asked him if he would like more pudding to which he solemnly replied, "No, thank you Sir, my bowels are bound with fetters of brass".

In my last year I was made Head of the School. I am still surprised. Did I really have enough confidence at this stage to show any sort of leadership? I was by now to the fore in the sporting scene and still remember an innings of 42, a lot of runs for me, against a school called Hillside who were all out for 41. I threw myself about dramatically in goal but failed to win the hurdles (again) through being out-sprinted. The last summer term was dominated by the Common Entrance and by the school Pageant. In the former I did poorly, partly through my own fault in putting genitive singular instead of genitive plural and making other elementary mistakes. But Shrewsbury accepted me.

Henry Brereton wrote and produced the Pageant – scenes from history –

the Stone Age, Egypt, Rome, and so on. In the Middle Ages scene, I rode on horseback at a steady trot to make an impressive appearance with my page Billy Buckhurst, clad in cardboard armour and dyed dishcloth chain mail. Then I handed the Arrow of Progress – the symbol of continuity in the Pageant – to David Lawrence Jones, the modern boy, who shot it out of sight into the future. It was all very fitting for my own farewell to Abinger. To the school I owed much, particularly the friendship with Jim Harrison which continued throughout his life, and the companionship of several boys with whom I remained in touch for many years.

As it turned out, it was Jim's advice that settled the course of my whole career. It was intended that I should follow my brother Richard to Winchester and Harry Altham, Richard's housemaster, had offered me a place – subject to entrance examination – at the age of twelve. My father balked at this and as it seemed to be difficult to fit me in a year later, thoughts began to turn elsewhere, especially as my mother was never very happy with Winchester and my own academic standard was not such that Winchester might accept. Jim suggested his old school, Shrewsbury, which my parents looked at and liked; and, by coincidence, my father's old colleague at Northampton Grammar School, S.S. Sopwith was – at short notice – to become a housemaster in September 1932. So to Shrewsbury I went, a step into the unknown for me who had taken a long time to settle into my little world of Abinger Hill and to whom the prospect of a school of five hundred boys was daunting. Still I was confident enough to cross London by myself and organise my train home on that last journey from Abinger.

Abinger was five years old when I left; there were only to be another eight years. In that extraordinary summer of 1940, when the world as we had known it seemed to crumble, the whole school together with some sisters packed up and went to Canada for the duration. Jimmy Clark on the Berlin Radio reported that Abinger Hill was crossing the Atlantic in the 'Duchess of Richmond', and that a torpedo was in store for her, but the school arrived in Ottawa safely. After the war Jim Harrison found it impossible to re-start at Abinger owing to financial problems, so began again at Ashfold School in Sussex which he tried to turn into Abinger Redivivus. Ashfold is now situated near Thame and flourishes. But it is a far cry to those days in the Surrey woods, noseblowing facing Holmbury Hill as the sun rose, the open air dormitory, planning one's day and all the enthusiasms of the pioneering age. Small wonder that John Gale wrote that Stowe was "a lifeless sham in comparison with my prep school".

CHAPTER III

New Boy

The English Public Schools are the best in the world: and very bad.

Talleyrand

At the beginning of the Michaelmas Term on 27th September 1932, three people started new phases of their lives at Shrewsbury School. In decreasing order of importance but increasing order of nervousness, they were H.H. Hardy, Headmaster, S.S. Sopwith, housemaster, and myself – a 'new scum'. That I would myself one day assume the positions of housemaster and headmaster was not a thought that occurred to me as we drove up to the front door of Oldham's Hall in the family Rover. The formality of the traditional new boys' tea party, the stilted conversation, the tense atmosphere, the awkwardness of the Eton collar and the lack of appetite – these will be common memories to generations of Salopians. Three or four monitors assisted; giant men of great maturity, they seemed to me. Here I met John Malins, Head of House, James Hill and Donovan Allen, all destined to be long-term friends, unlikely as it seemed at the time as I gazed at them with awe. I recollect but little of the occasion, but I do remember staring at a boy who seemed neither a new boy nor monitor; he was not wearing an Eton collar but was in fact a new boy too, John Ferguson, far advanced in puberty unlike the rest of us, and from that moment, one might guess, destined to be Head of House which indeed in four years' time he was.

Presiding over the party and (as he admitted to me at a later stage) as nervous as we were, was my housemaster, S.S. Sopwith. He had been a colleague of my father's at Northampton Grammar School, which was one of the reasons for my coming to Shrewsbury, and had now been on the Shrewsbury staff for seventeen years, having been chosen by Alington to succeed Ronald Knox. An urbane and witty man, he was a brilliant teacher of English, especially at the VIth form and scholarship level; he coached a boat on the river though no sort of sportsman himself, and was a man of wide friendships and interests, retaining a remarkable freshness of mind throughout a long career in which he was a civilising influence on the boy community. When he retired many years later, the then Headmaster wrote of him that "he stands for something which no one else quite supplies". His wife, Effie, was well named, for effervescent she certainly was; red-headed, lively, talkative, she carried on non-stop chatter at our tea party. She was also, as later became apparent, quite a snob, and the presence of so many boys with double barrelled names in Oldham's was – quite wrongly – attributed to her.

At last the Rover disappeared down the drive and I was left marooned in a strange sea whose uncharted waters looked very threatening. Shy and with little self-confidence, I had revealed a series of worries to my parents. "How will I find the lavatory?" was one, to which my Mother sensibly replied that this worry would be short-lived as, after all, the lavatory did not move and once located, stayed put. I had even asked my brother if homesickness meant that one was physically sick. Today every endeavour is made to see that new boys are incorporated into continuous activity immediately after arrival, but in my case there seemed to be endless empty hours before the other boys returned. I surveyed my fellow victims – Ferguson, Bevan, Day, Fowler, Lee, Grundy and Vint; we used surnames almost throughout our school careers. With Lee I walked round and round the Site indulging in sketchy and forced conversation. My play-box was quickly unpacked in Study V; my bed in Bedroom 1 had been identified; so had the lavatory.

In the evening the flood of large and seemingly self-confident boys swept into the House, moving possessions and books, arranging studies, taking stock of their new study companions and largely ignoring the new boys, their conversation sprinkled with words unknown to me. James Hill was my study monitor. How fortunate that was. James became a very close life-long friend and even at that stage was kind in introducing me to study life, together with the other inhabitants: Cemlyn-Jones (fat), Dawson (thin) and Forbes (shy). One of my first tasks was to clean the ancient pictures which had been passed down from boy to boy. With vigour I washed them in the swill room, not realising that water would penetrate the picture itself with deleterious effect. Panic. Would I be beaten for wrecking the pictures? But James, a happy-go-lucky character, was reasonably kind.

John Malins was my bedroom monitor. Humorous, wise, quizzical, with a thoroughly civilised outlook and idiosyncratic turn of phrase, he seemed to me to be wholly adult. His very presence quickly killed any nastiness and his own values were communicated without didactic elaboration. The second in command of the bedroom was Cuthbert Brooke-Smith, quiet, solid, a distinguished oarsman and a boy of integrity. Twenty-six years later I was to marry his widow and inherit his children. With these two in charge, new boys could feel a certain confidence. But getting up in the morning was a real trial: the ringing bells, the cold swill (standing for a few moments under a jet of cold water which gushed from a roseless pipe), the Eton collar and the studs, and fast dressing so that one reached First Lesson on time at 7.45 am. I soon learned the trick of putting on all my clothes at the same time – vest, shirt, pullover – without having to do up buttons. After First Lesson was Chapel, at a most unsuitable time of day, when breakfast called louder than God. Meals were in house halls, supervised by Matron and served by domestics. One advantage of having a lesson before break-fast was that there were only three periods in the morning before a spell of free time, called 'after 12', when for an hour one might play fives, practise the piano, go for a run or do nothing. Lunch was thus late at 1.45 pm, followed by an hour for games, two periods of school lessons (except on half holidays of which there were three), tea and Top Schools, the Salopian name for prep, done in Hall under a monitor's supervision for one-and-a-half hours. House prayers were followed by bed with lights out – for all – at 10.15 pm. A long day for a prep school boy.

Having done poorly in the Common Entrance, I was placed in a lowly form called Lower IV2A under P.W. Pilcher ('Pa P.'), a senior member of the staff whose disposition was benevolent. He spoke sometimes of our getting "the rough side of my tongue" but his tongue was in fact wholly incapable of producing a rough edge. I am grateful to Pa P. for introducing me to the book we read in his English lessons, *The Riddle of the Sands* by Erskine Childers; I still have the book we then used and have re-read it with relish.

The first school occasion of the term was 'Reading Over'. The whole school assembled in the Alington Hall and the name of every boy, in form order, was read from the top of the school to the bottom. At my first Reading Over I was somewhat astonished when, as the masters entered one by one from the side of the stage, they were accorded vociferous applause which varied greatly in intensity depending on the popularity of the recipient. This practice also evidently surprised Hardy, for it did not occur again and the staff were thus robbed of a useful barometer of popularity. Reading Over – the same happened at the end of term – continued until the 1950s, for no obvious reason as the information about the composition of forms was available on form lists.

Another ceremony to which we were soon introduced was Hall Elec-tions. All assembled in the house hall and a number of posts were filled by democratic voting, without benefit of ballot. All douls (fags) were eligible and the most unpopular (or shyest) was elected to the office of Hall Crier which meant standing on a bench and giving out announcements as monitors thought fit, such as the award of house colours or information concerning the presence of the barber on the premises. (Mr Griffiths cut hair, rather badly, in the changing room in dim light). Announcements

were preceded by the ancient warning, "Oyez, Oyez, Oyez", and con-
cluded with another ancient formula which must have dated from the early
nineteenth century, "God Save the King and down with the Radicals".
Other offices were those of Hall Postman, Hall Scavengers, etc. As a doul
one did not look forward to the ceremony but in Oldham's it was carried
out with due decorum, unlike times distantly past when the Headmaster
gave a half holiday on it being confirmed that the elections had taken place
without actual rioting.

Another not-looked-forward-to event was the Tucks run. Dating it was
said from the time when Shrewsbury Races were held at nearby Harlescott,
the whole school without exception was compelled to run five miles under
the direction of the officers of the Royal Shrewsbury School Hunt, resplen-
dent in distinctive dress with the Huntsman carrying his horn, and whips
wielded by the Senior and Junior Whips. All assembled and coupled up by
the Alington Hall, cheering with enthusiasm those masters – and there
were many – who took part. On this first occasion the Headmaster himself
came to run; such was his reputation already that he was greeted with the
Nazi salute – Herr Hitler Hardy. I was hopeless at cross country running
and much feared the Tucks; the Junior Whip at the rear was said to wield
his whip in a practical manner on stragglers. Exhausted, I just kept out of
range. Later I enjoyed the Tucks as a social occasion, though I was never in
the first twenty to whom, by tradition, Freddy Prior awarded 'hot suppers'
at the Shop.

The house matron was Miss Booker. Appointed many years earlier,
Sopwith had inherited her. Firmly set in her ways, she looked like a witch,
wore a wig and was never known to show any sign of good temper. The
more gullible new boys were told that she was actually a man in disguise.
Sopwith stood her for a year by which time he noticed that his whisky bills
were higher than his own – quite generous – consumption could warrant.
Private investigation revealed that the teapot on Miss Booker's mantelpiece did not contain tea. Thus the Booker left, unmourned; John Malins
engineered a whip-round for her to which grudging contribution was
made by those who had suffered under her tongue. I forget the total sum
but it might have been £2 or £3 which John duly presented, to be met by
spitting ingratitude in a phrase which was preserved in house lore, "When
I saw the paltry sum, I gave it all to charity".

Gradually, as my first year unfolded, I gained a little confidence though
always content to be a silent member of any group I was in. Life revolved
round the bedroom and the study – here were the two central social
groups. The inhabitants were changed every term, so there was constant
uncertainty as to who one would be with and how one would get on with a
new social mix. As so often is the case, those whom one feared turned out to
be quite reasonable on closer acquaintance and, living as we did, acquaint-

ance was indeed close. Tempers and temperaments had to be accommodated, friendships were formed and broken, injustices supposed or real had to be endured, fraught situations defused, individual eccentricities admired or ridiculed. People revealed themselves bit by bit, particularly in the bedroom at night in the uninhibited period of darkness before sleep. Was I happy or unhappy? It is difficult to say; moods came and went. Always anxious about not knowing my work, I toiled quite hard and came near the top of the form in the many orders that were compiled. I was at the foot of a long, long ladder on which there were many weary rungs to ascend before reaching the upland plateau of the School Certificate forms and the stratosphere of the VIth. A number of boys never even reached the School Certificate, and as a thirteen-year-old I sat alongside a boy entering his fourth year in the school. Much of the work was construe – Latin and French – varied with 'slips', foolscap paper torn vertically, on which were recorded one-word answers to oral questions. Sitting in cramped double desks, boys corrected each other's work with varying regard to accuracy and honesty. There was little that was imaginative in the teaching. One period a week, 'Drawing,' was our introduction to 'Art'. This was taken by J.M. Woodroffe, in appearance a fierce Old Testament prophet, who swept round the desks, giving advice and admonishment in about equal proportions. To be put on 'Extra Lesson', which took place on Saturday afternoons, one had to accumulate three 'penal marks'. Woodroffe had a system of 'floating' three penal marks whereby the first miscreant was given three penal marks which were then transferred to the next miscreant and so passed round the form. The last ten minutes were generally deadly quiet as we strove to avoid being left with the three penal marks at the end of the period. If given, the penal marks were recorded in the Punishment Book, which was brought round all the form rooms by the school porter, Ernie Hartshorne. Small in stature, with a slight stutter, often running to keep up with himself, Hartshorne was a pivotal figure. He carried the Punishment Book and the notices book round the school tirelessly. Hardy was a great man for notices, couched in his tortuous but grammatical English, and in the book were notices in red for the master and in blue ink to be read out; naturally every endeavour was made to get new masters to read out the red ink ones. Hartshorne's day was one of perpetual motion; persuaded to carry a pedometer one day, he clocked up eleven-and-a-half miles. In the boxing ring he was a lightweight killer.

Games bulked large. Oldham's had a record of defeat at all levels for the previous five years or so; in fact the only cups won had been those for shooting and for singing, both of which activities flourished from year to year. Between 1926 and 1932 only one cup for games was won – the not very significant Under 16 fives cup. As new boys we played everything and a 'change' a day was the requirement – football and fives principally, with

running and swimming worked in. If we were not playing we were
watching, as spectating was compulsory not only for 1st XI matches at
which the whole school was present, but for house matches as well. I
enjoyed fives, once I got the hang of it, and I played goal for various league
teams. That traditional sport, cross-country running, organised at Shrewsbury as the Royal Shrewsbury School Hunt, probably the oldest cross-
country running club with continuous records in the world, was however
not for me. I laboured round the local short course or 'Benjy' with pain.
Much more fun was yard football, an Oldham's speciality. Basil Oldham
had built the yard beside the house and three-a-side football was played
with energy and enjoyment by a large number of boys, with an inter-study
tournament every term – not that there was much skill in Study V. The
school's facilities for games were more than fully taxed; football grounds
were often out of use because of the weather, fives courts were hotly
competed for and allocated by the school captain of fives; rowing was
limited by the number of boats – and coaches. There was no gymnasium.

As I have written elsewhere, the Public School of that date contained
within it elements of the Rule of St Benedict, of the Court of Louis XIV, and
of HM Prisons. St Benedict puts much stress on obedience – "the first step is
obedience without delay", a precept which any praepostor or monitor
would echo. Of tradition – "a monk does nothing but what the common
rule or example of his seniors encourages him to do". Of chastisement – "if
he does not mend his ways, he is to be rebuked publicly ... but if he be
thoroughly bad, let him undergo corporal punishment". Seniority is to be
exactly observed, "The monks are to keep their order as determined by the
date of their entering monastic life". Monitors supervising Top Schools
were doing just what St Benedict enjoined: "It is very important that one or
two seniors are appointed to go round when the brethren are supposed to
be reading, to keep an eye on them in case somebody may become restless,
and spend the time in idleness and gossip instead of being intent on his
book ...".

The exacting pattern of worship laid down by the saint was not repro-
duced at Shrewsbury School but was reflected in the frequency of prayer.
The Shrewsbury word for to pray or prayer is 'to dick' or 'dicks'. I am not
aware of the etymology of the word though it may be connected with the
Latin *dico*. It is a word which is still in use, though its original meaning has
now been obscured. We used to dick frequently. Private prayers on rising
were encouraged (though little practised), Chapel took place every day
with the same monotonous liturgy – psalm, lesson, hymn, prayer. Even the
opening sentences by the priest were standardised. The first time I was in
the chapel I was in the back of the gallery; when the sermon started I
remember it was a minute or two before I could actually locate the pulpit
and preacher, so far away did I seem to be in that seemingly vast and

strange building. Evening prayers took place in each House, taken by the housemaster – set prayers for each day of the week; in Oldham's we occasionally had a hymn, played at first by Sopwith himself, who took off his glasses to read the music – the only time he was ever known to take them off and so a notable occasion. Then prayers at the bedside, generally after dark, were said or pretended by almost all. On Sundays there was a voluntary service of Holy Communion at 8.00 a.m., generally attended by fifty or sixty boys; a school service at 11.00 a.m., with sermon; and Evensong, also compulsory. Although Hardy soon made a change, the weekly Divinity period was set at 2.15 p.m., thus filling the afternoon. How much were the Hours of St Benedict in mind and how much the desire to fill every space, so that morning, afternoon and evening were all effectively blocked off from other possibly less desirable activity?

A small pink booklet was given to every new boy on arrival entitled 'Rules and Privileges'. The Rules, which emanated from the Headmaster, took up two pages; the Privileges, built up over the years with the weight of tradition behind them, took up the remaining twelve pages. Here, *mutatis mutandis*, is the Versailles of Louis XIV and Saint-Simon. Carefully detailed is the long list of what you may wear, what exercise you may take, where you may go, where you may sit and so on. The boy hierarchy was socially rigid and apparently unchanging. At the head stood the praepostor, known elsewhere as a school prefect. There were some fifteen in all, lords of all they surveyed. The Pink Book records that a 'Postor' may:

  i   Carry a walking stick
 ii   Wear a praepostor's tie
iii   Stand outside chapel while the bell is ringing
 iv   'Doul' scums from other houses
  v   Walk through the Praepostor's Walk
 vi   Accompany school runs on a bicycle
vii   Watch fives from the concrete

In addition he wore a soft collar, a coloured handkerchief in his top pocket, and a butterfly collar on Sundays.

Below the praepostor came the house monitor; and then the other castes, divided like racehorses into 4-year-olds, 3-year-olds, 2-year-olds, and 1-year-olds. The lower two classes were 'douls' or fags (*doulos* = slave in Greek). Each class wore an appropriate collar: Eton collars for the juniors, rounded collars for 2-year-olds, collars with short points for 3-year-olds, with longer points for 4-year-olds. All collars were of course starched. Thus at a glance one could tell on which rung of the ladder a boy was. Blue suits were worn on weekdays, tails and top hats on Sundays (or Eton suits – 'bum freezers' – for the lower classes). Off the Site a straw hat with house colour ribbon was worn. The differentiation between years was carefully delineated; in Oldham's, for instance, one might not sit on a radiator nor have a cushion on one's chair in the study until one was a 2-year-old. Douls were also known as 'scum', not a pleasant word though it tripped readily off the tongue. Basil Oldham had an explanation, namely that junior boys in times past had to answer 'adsum' to a call-over and this got corrupted to 'scum'. An unlikely tale.

Douling or fagging has featured large in many a school story and the ill treatment of fags is legendary. Interestingly the nineteenth century origin of fagging lay in the need to establish some sort of order in a chaotic boy-world; the fag's monitor was his protector as well as his director, and the idea of defining what boys could command other boys to do was meant as a shield against abuse. By the time I was at Shrewsbury douls were very much at the beck and call of monitors; a loud and prolonged shout of "Doul..." meant that every doul must run to the monitor, the last getting the job – going to the Shop to get some food, running an errand to another House, cleaning football boots, etc. Another way of summoning douls was to strike the heating pipes with a swagger stick; as the pipes ran through the House all could hear and came running. In addition there were private douls who were really valets. So the monitor was powerful: he could enforce his authority by corporal punishment, with a swagger stick (as used in the OTC) or with the slipper. Those who write their memoirs generally have horror stories. Brian Inglis (also in Oldham's) and Kyffin Williams, both near contemporaries of mine, have written of their unpleasant experiences as have others. How corrupt was the system? Of course it depended entirely on two things – the inherited tradition of the particular House and the outlook and attitudes of the monitors of the time. Brian Inglis experienced a reign of terror in the two years before I arrived in Oldham's, largely traceable to one sadistic boy. Oldham, his housemaster, must have been aware of what went on but kept to his principle of letting the boys run the House under the mistaken impression that his trust in them would not be abused. Yet when I arrived, with monitors such as they then were under John Malins's leadership, I recollect little abuse or suffering. I myself was beaten, I would say unjustly, by a present Anglican clergyman, due largely, I believe, to a misunderstanding, and I did not enjoy those six strokes in Headroom (the monitors' common room). No one today would dream of re-inventing the fagging system, but like all systems it depended entirely on those who administered it; I was lucky. It did have the effect of making one very careful what one did. Those who speak of being 'damaged' psychologically may indeed have been so, but the great majority accepted the system with reasonable composure as a peculiar but not obtrusive part of school life, unless – as was indeed sometimes the case – the power was abused by a bully. I still find it strange that abuse was allowed to take place with little or no safeguard. In my experience, however, the relation between doul and monitor was generally harmonious, and in later days culminated at the end of term in the monitor taking his doul down town to tea.

Knowledge of the Pink Book of privileges was expected after three weeks when a dreaded Colour Exam took place in the bedroom, where other fields of Salopian knowledge were also covered, such as the names – and appearances – of masters (Brushers), house colours, notable personalities and the names by which topographical features of the Site were known; for instance the trees in front of the School Buildings were Castor and Pollux, the lights on the Moser Building were Adnitt & Naunton (the school stationers), those beside the school clock were Romulus and Remus, and outside Oldham's were at one end the Gallows (a double light), at the other the Oasis, a small group of trees.

The third institution on which the Public School seemed to have been modelled was an HM prison. Though the atmosphere had considerably changed from the early nineteenth century, when 'Boy Republics' threatened to take over from the Headmaster and staff – Dr Butler (Headmaster 1798–1836) had on one occasion been forced to ask the Mayor for police protection – the thought that boys would be up to no good, unless strictly supervised and ridden on a short rein, was still present in the ethos. There were strict rules about Bounds and much detail as to who could go beyond them and when. Leave to go into the town was possible through the housemaster but only for a specific and limited purpose; off the Site the straw hat or the Sunday top hat was always worn, even for a short walk into the neighbouring fields. Recognition was thus always immediate. Call Overs were very frequent. There would certainly be five, perhaps more, on a normal working day. On half holidays the whole school had a Call Over, by forms, on the Drum, a space in front of the School Buildings, when every boy had to answer his name, called out by a praepostor dressed in tails and supervised by a Brusher in gown and mortar board. The older Houses had bars over the study windows to make the prison picture more complete. In the winter evenings before Top Schools (prep), there would be study lock-ups, when one was confined to one's study for a period of quiet and did not leave it save for an essential purpose. Exit and re-entry to the House was by the housemaster's door, names being entered in a book. It must often have been the case that a boy did not leave the Site more than half a dozen times a term, if that.

Until Hardy's time there were few expeditions and the rhythm of life was broken only by visits from one's parents. My father being retired, he and my mother came two or three times a term but even this was looked on with a little suspicion as taking my mind off school life. Few boys were visited more than once a term; there were no nights away, no half term. Contact with local inhabitants was minimal. Girls, of course, did not exist.

I recollect the enormous scandal when a boy in Ridgemount was said to have had an assignment on the School Bank with one of the ladies who served in the Shop. (I doubt if he did but it made a good story). Miss Minnehay (?) and Miss Thorpe were the only females whom we saw, apart from Miss Booker, if she could be thus categorised.

There were, of course, domestic servants in the Houses but they were virtually invisible save while serving meals in Hall. A massive iron gate shut off the bedrooms in day time; the domestic staff living quarters were totally unknown territory at the back of the House. Effie Sopwith supervised the domestics who included a house man, called by the boys, as were all male servants, a John; however, he was carefully trained, as were the maids, to refer to Sopwith as 'The Master'. Elsewhere in the school, Johns proliferated in the days when there were few machines. There was the Baths John, the Chapel John who pumped the organ by hand, the 'green baize John' (from his apron), and the various groundsmen Johns, headed by Len and Albert, who lived in the Johns' hole below the Baths, and who were at least accorded the dignity of names, unlike the unfortunate John who delivered Adnitt & Naunton's books who was designated 'Creeping Paralysis'. The longest lasting John must have been 'Corps Boots'; unemployed in Durham in the slump years, he walked south looking for work and found it at Shrewsbury, continuing until the 1960s.

Boys were not expected to do domestic work. Shoes were cleaned for them and beds made. The bedroom itself is worth recalling. Each boy had an iron bed and underneath it what Oldham had called an 'under bed wardrobe' but which had always been known as a 'coffin' in which suits and trousers were kept. There was a wash hand stand to every bed, with basin, jug and glass, and a rail for the towel; below it a chamber pot; in the space between the beds an 'alley mat' on the linoleum floor. Chamber pots sustained casualties from time to time; an exciting game was to bowl them up the floor from opposite ends, seeing how near they could pass each other without actually hitting; sometimes they didn't pass and there followed a shamefaced admission of breakage to Miss Booker. Every evening the bedroom doul would carry round large hot water cans and fill each boy's basin. Another unpopular duty was to open all the windows when all were in bed, for the Oldham emphasis on fresh air did not die with him. Hence the freezing winter temperature when getting up at 7.15 a.m. – ice sometimes formed on the basin – and the unattractiveness of the cold swill.

One of the least popular of the duties performed by douls was cleaning one's monitor's corps kit. The Officers Training Corps continued as a major institution in school life until the 1960s. In theory voluntary, only a few miserable pacifists failed to join. In one's first year one was a recruit, attending 'rookey parades' and learning to drill. Then one was incorporated in the house platoon, training on a half holiday every week. The Corps was enjoyed by few, unpopular with most, and seemed to take an enormous amount of effort and time – cleaning uniform, getting into it, being inspected, cleaning rifles, marching and counter-marching, cold in winter, sweating in summer. We wore the old long puttees of the First World War which required to be put on with skill, otherwise one had the nightmare of one's puttees coming down on parade and trailing along the ground like the tail of a comet. We could not hope to rise to the sartorial perfection of our commander, the dazzlingly immaculate Major J.M. West, late Rifle Brigade, whom we followed with that unthinking confidence found in the rear ranks of the Gaderene swine.

CHAPTER IV

Lower School

Editique caro colle
Matri quam amamus
Arte, libro, remo, folle
Gloriam petamus.
            C. A. Alington

Into all these activities I was quickly absorbed during my first two years – my time as a doul. I did not find it difficult to live in a tightly organised community, not being individualistic or imaginative enough to feel the constraints as some others did. At that age, I did not examine or criticise the values by which we lived. I made friends. I warily avoided so far as possible those I did not like. Boys at any age can be unpleasant to their fellows, and verbal bullying can be more devastating than physical. But in general I lived in a House where reasonably civilised standards prevailed. Outward conformity there indeed was, but I do not subscribe to the view that individuality was thus crushed. Looking back, there were a lot of lively and intelligent people who led their lives, within the system, in their own way. Nor did I find the hierarchical system an oppressive one; in the growing years and certainly to someone very unsure of himself, it was in some ways a comfort to know where you stood and where the boundaries lay. For instance I do not think that anyone in the west with any liberal tendencies would support the caste system in India and particularly its excesses, but without it that vast population, unstructured, would dissolve into chaos. So, despite its absurdities, the hierarchy supported at least some of us, who were not subject to its distortions and excesses.

I was for some time the private doul of James Hill who held the position of Choregus, that is head of the chapel choir. I did a lot of work for James, who was fairly chaotic, and enjoyed it, putting out music and programmes, and reminding James of choir practices and engagements. The Director of Music – did we call him by that exalted name? – was W.H. Moore, universally known as 'Black Death'[1], a name which in no wise suited a man of convivial disposition and cheerful outlook. He was now in his last year. Also in the choir were Freddy Prior ("profundo basso is my name"), housemaster of Moser's, looking exactly like Bruce Bairnsfather's Old Bill, with his straggling walrus moustache, now completing the last of forty-two years on the staff, as was Rashleigh Duncan, who sang tenor, now aged seventy and also in his last and forty-second year. These were venerable figures. Freddy Prior was a humorist: after Duncan had hit a particularly high note, Freddy turned to his neighbour saying "Just see if Mr Duncan has laid an egg". Duncan taught modern languages and was always known as 'The Dwinks', I believe because he used to say "We shall be having a few friends in to dwinks after Chapel". New boys' voices were tested by Black Death, each having to sing solo a verse of the National Anthem. I was classified *beta* but nonetheless was put in the trebles. Our standard was not very high but higher, so Black Death said, than his earlier choirs; he had to get a small piano to put between the choir stalls so that he could actually make the boys sing by looking at them; at the organ he had had his back to the choir. After a term I was made an alto: I had no idea what this meant but endeavoured to follow the alto line in the music when it was pointed out to me, as did my fellow decani alto, Geoffrey Lane, who enlivened choir practices by his *sotto voce* sharp wit. (When he became Lord Chief Justice he reminded me that he was the first LCJ since Judge Jeffreys; "funny how Salopians run to type".) The Concert Choir was voluntary and rehearsed throughout the term for the annual School Concert in December. This was very formal and one of the high points of the school year. As an alto I was dressed up in a dickey (the word must have disappeared), that is a stiff artificial shirt front, with a green rosette in my buttonhole (green = alto); we sang a miscellaneous selection of songs, the only one I remember being *Rolling Down to Rio*. The choir was about seventy strong, accompanied by the school orchestra of about fifteen boys and fifteen masters and ladies. The final item was as always a song composed by Freddy Prior, listing the achievements of the year; Freddy was a neat versifier and the song had a tremendous reception. To hear these mythical figures like Prior and Duncan unbending was to us a remarkable experience, for they were not credited with human feelings and it seemed impossible that they should sing such lines as

> Oh what a full delight through my bosom thrills
> And a wilder glow in my heart instils,
> Bliss unfelt before, hope without alloy
> Speak with raptured tone or my heart the joy.

1   Said to have originated in a weak schoolboy jest. In Latin, the black death was Mors Nigra (Mors = Moore's).

The last thing we connected with such figures were words like 'rapture', 'bliss', 'wilder glow', let alone 'bosom'.

A necessary part of Salopian education was to learn the language. Most public schools had a vocabulary of slang, with perhaps Winchester and Charterhouse having more than most. Shrewsbury had forty or fifty words which a new scum had quickly to pick up. The derivation of some is obvious – for example 'sap' = to work – but others have no known origin. Two of the most descriptive seem to me to be to 'wazz', which means to be nervous about a forthcoming event – wazzing for house matches, wazzing for an examination; and 'scale' = to be sarcastic or critical. Much used was the word lift (= cheek); 'lift off' was a frequent expression, a reprimand to one who essayed to be above his station. The hierarchical lines were narrowly drawn and lift was tightly interpreted. In addition there was the vocabulary of the Royal Shrewsbury School Hunt, the Gentleman of the Runs, the Whips, the Huntsman, the all-ups, the killing hound and so on. A word liable to misinterpretation was 'erection'. This arose from a curious three-sided structure of football posts into which shooting practice could take place simultaneously from three angles; the structure was known as the 'erection' from which the term was transferred to any football practice anywhere. A master from another school, bringing his team to play at Shrewsbury, was startled by the polite Captain of Football who met the visitors with the question, "Would you like an erection before lunch or afterwards?" It was remarkable how quickly one learnt and found oneself saying, "I'm going to ram off leagues as I'm stiff for sap and wazzing about being shipped". There was also a general consensus of correct and incorrect behaviour – what was 'done' and 'not done'; a withering reproof for a remark or action which lay outside the code was that it was 'not much done'. It doesn't sound much but it stung.

Entertainment did not figure very much in one's life. In the House the monitors had a radio and a gramophone (hand wound) in Headroom. There was a flourishing Oldham's Hall Cinematograph Society which showed a weekly 16mm film of doubtful technical quality, but we sat with great content through the flickering pictures – usually thrillers like *The Cabinet of Dr Cagliari*. I recollect one on the white slave traffic featuring the electric line "Me Tondeleo" simpered by an engagingly forward nubile native girl which caused a communal heart flutter. School entertainment was limited to occasional lectures; 'Our Relations with Native Races', 'The Colonial Services', 'Life and Humour in the South Seas', and 'The Territorial Army' were some of the subjects and there was a visit from that complete charlatan 'Grey Owl' who was universally accepted as a North American Indian but who hailed from the back streets of an English town and had perfected an act about 'my people', which both took him to and took in most of the schools in England. There was an occasional visit from a wandering acting company, one with the banal name of Miss Owen's Players. They did *Macbeth* for which we had been prepared by Sopwith who, amongst other points, singled out the importance of the porter scene as coming after the murder, the dramatic contrast etc. Miss Owen saw fit to omit the scene entirely. We thought it odd that certain players always carried hats until we realised that they were reading their parts therefrom.

School societies flourished, generally with boys reading papers which was a salutary thing for both writer and audience; debates were lively if on fairly dull subjects. In the absence of any other entertainment, we were glad to go to anything which was different. On Speech Day in Hardy's time, as he later wryly admitted, we had a succession of stupendously dull speakers – the Director of Education of the London County Council was the dullest, though Field Marshal Lord Milne and the Earl of Liverpool ran him close. In the House we made our own entertainment, for Sopwith decreed that there should be some sort of dramatic performance at the end of the Christmas term. So from small beginnings was born 'House Turns', crude study 'turns' eventually evolving into quite humorous and enjoyable playlets, mostly home written and needless to say incorporating current events and imitations, often with a standard of wit and satire which even now I think was remarkably high. There were very occasional musical events and the Shrewsbury Orchestral Society's concerts, conducted by a well-known local personality in Freddy Morris, were attended by many.

Outings were rare. Most of our lives were spent on the Site and largely in the House. How did we fare, these new boys who sat awkwardly at the new boys' tea party in 1932, the 'new scum', the very bottom of the social pyramid, and whither did we go in life? John Lee was probably my closest friend. A scholar from the Dragon School, his father was a don at Magdalen, later to be my tutor; John soon showed his ability at games which was a passport to acceptance; more important he had sterling qualities and integrity, a happy disposition and, as was later seen in the war, unusual powers of leadership. But for the war, he would have joined that legion of Blues ruling Blacks in the Sudan; instead he joined the King's Shropshire Light Infantry, was one of the last away from Dunkirk in 1940, became Adjutant of his battalion and was killed at Anzio. He was recommended for a high decoration but given no posthumous award at all. His enthusiasm and freshness made him a delightful companion, and those who fought with him know that he ranked with the bravest of the brave.

My other close friend was Peter Fowler, also a competent games player, who became keen on flying, was in the RAF in the war and passed his life in aviation, at one time a test pilot for Hawker Siddeley. Adding culture to our year were Roger Bevan and Patrick Day, both musicians of ability. Roger made his mark while still at school as a singer, conductor and composer, as well as being a scholar. His Old Salopian father was the Archdeacon of

Ludlow and had inherited the bogus Quatford Castle, near Bridgnorth. We saw quite a lot of the Archdeacon and indeed there was quite a lot to see as he was

> Most typical in size and girth
> Of the church militant on earth[1]

Per contra, Roger was of slight physique as a boy; indeed he seemed unlikely to be able to fight his way out of a paper bag but his virility later in life saw the rest of us off as, having become a Roman Catholic and married a Roman Catholic, they happily produced fourteen children, later to form The Bevan Family Choir and to tour Europe.

Patrick Day was of a measured and thoughtful disposition; he did not get a scholarship to Shrewsbury but his academic life thereafter was fruitful; a First in PPE was followed by various posts as a philosopher, partly in America, finally as Reader at the University at Keele. Of lighter weight, when at school, were Lewis Grundy, who later made a successful business career in Australia, and Ronald Vint, a north country solicitor. Lastly there was John Ferguson, 'Fergie', shy in manner but immensely solid in performance, with a very transparent honesty which led him to call a spade a spade. A scholar to the school, the Shrewsbury science staff were emphatically unenthusiastic about his future in medicine, but he had the last laugh as Surgical Tutor and Sub-Dean of the Middlesex Hospital, living at No. 1 Harley Street.

We were a mixed bunch but not lacking in ability, and our mutual relations, despite differences of both temperament and interests, were on the whole harmonious considering how closely we lived together. I steadily climbed the Lower School ladder, gaining five promotions in six terms. Shrewsbury's main claim to fame had been and still was the tradition of classical teaching started by Samuel Butler in the early nineteenth century, and maintained by his successor headmasters, B.H. Kennedy and H.W. Moss. It would be difficult to surpass the classical teaching in my own time of J.M. Street, H.N. Dawson, R.W. Moore (later Headmaster of Harrow), D.S. Colman (one time Fellow of The Queen's College, Oxford), R.St.J. Pitts-Tucker (later Headmaster of Pocklington), and R.P. Wilson (later Bishop of Chichester).

But in the lower reaches of the school things were very different. I ascended from Pilcher to Dick Sale. A superlative sportsman, he had adopted a wholly idyosyncratic style in the form room, expecting to be rotted (= teased) and apparently enjoying it. His remarks were mostly preceded by a hum and we hummed back; we swung the pictures, wrote 'For Sale' on the outside of the windows, filled the reversed lightshade with

1 Harry Graham.

chalk and received his admonitions ("My good owl...") with equanimity. Some work got done, but not much. My next move was to Hans Pendle-bury, massive in figure, devoted to Masonry on which he spent most of his time, and an expert lepidopterist, but as a form master undistinguished; there was a rather cruel joke about "not doing a hans turn". From him to Russell Hope-Simpson who really did teach and who would brook no disorder. Like the others, however, his teaching had followed a narrow treadmill for many years. Very much later there was a moment when he was heard to say that he really must revise his history notes. It transpired that this did not mean bringing them up to date in the light of new knowledge, but copying out the same notes he had been using since the early 1920s as his notebook was falling to pieces. My last form master was A.E. Kitchin – 'The Bull' – and he too was intolerant of disorder. With a magnificent physique, a mass of fair hair and penetrating blue eyes, he was a rowing coach of national repute. To this day the society of those who coach in the major rowing schools is called the Kitchin Society. You never quite knew what to expect from the Bull. In his younger days he would surprise his form by taking off, that is climbing round the four walls of the room on furniture and window-sills without his feet touching the ground, to be received with respectful applause. We treated him circumspectly. One day a boy in Moser's was reading the inevitable construe with a 'cab' sheet in his book, one of Mr Kelly's popular keys to Caesar. Alas, Kelly had somehow slipped up; the boy read Kelly's words "and to fight from a near position", but there were no corresponding words in the Latin text. The Bull stopped the construe dramatically and asked to see the book; in fear and trembling the book was taken up and Kelly revealed. I have never forgotten the Bull's reaction which was to look out of the window up the river without comment for what seemed an age; we held our collective breath, the tension unbearable. But there was no explosion; the boy left the room; at the end of term he left the school.

The Lower School was indeed a rough and tumble place and the aca-demic education provided was very sterile, mostly the endless preparation of Latin and French construe, a barren exercise for a large number who would never get beyond the School Certificate and some who would never even reach it. Latin might be a vehicle for the introduction of the culture of the ancient world but for many it was sheer drudgery leading nowhere. French was similarly taught, with little emphasis on oral work. One term with James West teaching French was spent exploring, with a map, the sights and streets of Paris where presumably James had been in the war. The French language hardly entered in.

Science was taught to us by the Revd W.S. Ingrams, known as "The Tush". Rumour had it that Moss, the Headmaster, rather unwillingly feeling bound to appoint a science master, went to Oxford and found the man with the worst degree of the year, namely Ingrams with his Fourth in Botany. The Tush had been a member of the staff since 1883 and, having 'retired' in 1921, was still doing some administrative work and a little teaching in 1933, fifty years after his appointment, at the age of seventy-eight. He was the father of two exceptionally able sons: Harold, who was said to be the most influential man in the Middle East since T.E. Lawrence; and Leonard, a most successful merchant banker, father of four sons one of whom is Richard Ingrams, a founder of *Private Eye*. The Tush was a dear old man when I knew him and started all his remarks with "Dear Boy", "Dear Man", "Dear Lady", as appropriate. His lessons were a riot. The standard joke, handed down, was still going; when the Tush blew into a test tube of liquid which then turned white, thus illustrating some chemical process, we asked "Will anyone's breath do that, Sir?". It was a great moment when we sang Psalm 73 in Chapel and with loud emphasis roared out the line, "... 'Tush' say they, 'how should God perceive it...' ".

Another who taught me was A.H. Pearson, a mathematician. Here was another eccentric. He was in fact Major Pearson, MC, who had been in the Machine Gun Corps in the war, which may have been the reason why he spoke in such sharp and staccato sentences. He taught in his own peculiar way; in geometry every theorem had a story. He was a Cambridge athlete of many parts as is illustrated by the doubtless apocryphal story of his being set upon by a thug in London's docklands. 'Pearcrack' (as he was known) confidently shaped up to him for a bout of fisticuffs, saying "Boxing Blue", whereat his assailant ran for it. Pearcrack ran steadily beside him commenting "Running Blue". Desperate to escape, the man dived in the Thames only to find Pearcrack swimming easily alongside him with the inevitable comment, "Swimming Blue". Pearcrack used to take parties of boys out on Sunday afternoons, often to climb the Breidden. Each boy carried a stone to the top to add to the Pearson cairn which grew to nearly six feet in height and whose remains must still be there.

In my first days in Oldham's I was somewhat mystified by many, generally hilarious, references to "the Gush". Who or what was he? I was told that he was J.B. Oldham, founder and for twenty-one years house-master of the House, who had had a nervous breakdown and retired that very year. The full story of Oldham's life I only pieced together bit by bit many years later; it was such an extraordinary tale that I wrote a book about him. But he needs some introduction here as playing an important part in the life of the school and in my own story. An Old Salopian, he had joined the staff after Oxford on a purely temporary basis in 1906. It was always said that the headmaster, Moss, forgot to tell him not to come back and he stayed for the rest of his life. Not entirely true, but he was not really appointed to the staff until C.A. Alington became headmaster in 1908. To his surprise he was invited to be a housemaster in 1910 – provided that he built his House. Nothing daunted he borrowed the whole cost, £17,749.16s.7d., from Lloyds Bank, designed and built the House and was in occupation, at the age of thirty, for the Michaelmas Term of 1912 with thirty-two boys.

For twenty-one years Basil Oldham ran his House on his own special lines. He was a bachelor and made a virtue of being so, thus being able to devote himself entirely to his boys. He embodied the full Victorian/Edwardian public school philosophy – manliness, *mens sana in corpore sano*, strong religious principles, loyalty, sense of duty, leadership, team spirit and patriotism. But Basil sought more than this, for he aimed to build up close personal relationships with 'his' boys – and he really wanted them to be 'his'. He devoted all his energies to them and much of his money, for he lost heavily from being a housemaster where others grew comparatively rich. He was absurdly generous, entertained freely and took foreign holidays, always accompanied by boys. In 1931 he took all his monitors to ski in Switzerland entirely at his own expense. Women did not feature in his life, apart from a loved mother who had died when he was sixteen; this may have had an important bearing on his development.

Since its origin in 1897, the word 'homosexual' has travelled a long way and Basil was happy so to describe himself in the sense the word then carried, that is one who preferred the company of men to that of women. Shrewsbury was for years dominated by bachelors – Chance, Pickering, Moser, Ingram, Prior, Mitford. But his wholehearted desire for the friendship of 'his' boys could lead to an emotional intensity and depth in relationship which many boys found difficult to handle. The "free and informal talks" which Basil had with individual boys in his study after lights out were the opposite of what Basil intended. His constant probing led many to subterfuge, to suspicion, and sometimes to outright dislike. Talks on what Kurt Hahn has called "the poisonous patterns of puberty" often resulted in acute embarrassment.

One of Basil's main principles was that of trust: he commissioned his monitors with due solemnity and then let them get on with it, largely unsupervised. Consequently, there were continual explosions when things went wrong, when trust was abused and Basil found himself let down – and such crises were highly personalised and emotional. Though there were some boys who became Basil's friends for life, there were many who found their quirky housemaster difficult to deal with, relationships being often made more difficult by Basil's habit of mangling his words so that it was impossible to understand what he was saying.

Thus Oldham's, despite the high ideals, had seldom been a very 'successful' House. Basil himself moved from boundless optimism to deep gloom. In 1929 he had written "I am simply broken-hearted as the whole of my system has crumbled to its foundations..." and "I have practically not a friend to rely on". And yet soon afterwards, "The atmosphere

here among my boys is like a breath of fresh air''. Then in 1932 his whole world did indeed collapse. Basil had been staying in a hotel in London with, as was his wont, a boy in the House as his guest, who shared his bedroom. Something transpired which worried the boy to the extent that he told his mother (his father was dead) who in turn was deeply upset and told his uncle, a KC and Salopian himself, who took a most serious view leading to an interview with the Headmaster. Misunderstanding and exaggeration may well have happened in this chain but the result was that Basil had a breakdown, was sent abroad to recuperate and medical opinion decreed that he should not undertake the burden of housemastering again.

Quite broken in spirit, he went to live at Little Grange, Kennedy Road, adjacent to the school, where – remarkably – he recovered his full health and lived vigorously for nearly thirty years. He had some status in the school as Librarian, an office he had held since 1911 and was to hold for fifty years. Here lay his main occupation. He became a world authority on the bindings of books, on which he toiled with immense patience, producing three major works and being appointed in 1960 Sandars Reader in Bibliography at Cambridge University. His occupation was in bindings, but his interest still lay with boys. Thus it was that new boys in Oldham's received at some stage an invitation to tea at Little Grange; ''tea with the Gush'' became an institution. Thither I and others wended our way to meet this legendary man whose speech we found it difficult to understand, to be shown the 'museum', a room in which were collected his many treasures, to see Ruskin's writing desk, the collection of walking sticks, the elephant tusk gong. I was a frequent visitor to Little Grange and, as others had done before me, found myself showing interest where I had none, admitting to feelings which I did not have and generally keeping up with a talkative and emotional man. He had always looked on the relationship of housemaster and boy as one akin to a sort of marriage, and now he invented the position of 'step-housemaster' for his relationship with us. Being gullible and unwary I fell for it all, though Sopwith's reaction to all this was to lead to future strife.

So in my first two years I had become, I suppose, a typical Salopian, not without the anxieties of developing adolescent life, but at any rate established in the community with a small record of success; in the summer of 1934 a form prize, an English literature prize, captain of the house under-16 cricket team; and, in an unlikely role, I had been incorporated into the house jazz band – the Hot Chocolates. With the quite considerable musical talent that we had, we were a passable imitation of Henry Hall and Harry Roy, with our signature tune *Goldiggers of 1933* ('We're in the money...'). I played the drums in a rather military fashion for I had joined the OTC band as a drummer. In those days it was a drum and bugle band, but in my joining it I had started an activity which was ultimately to be my sole claim to fame at Shrewsbury School.

But it is time to raise the sights from my small beginnings in Oldham's Hall to the broad panorama of Shrewsbury School and its Headmaster in the 1930s.

CHAPTER V

The Salopian Scene

There were giants in those days...
Gen. 6.4

The year 1932, though I was hardly conscious of it at the time, was an *annus mirabilis* at Shrewsbury School, for it marked the completion of the first fifty years on Kingsland and the resignation of the headmaster, Canon H.A.P. Sawyer, after fifteen successful years. Bob Sawyer has sometimes had a less than adequate press. Succeeding the Revd C.A. Alington, who had himself done more in eight years than most headmasters in twice that time, following too the Alington charisma which dazzled staff and pupils alike, Bob Sawyer had a difficult task. Totally uncharismatic, looking like a cheerful and rotund country grocer, without academic distinction, his first years found him grappling with problems caused by the war, not yet over, and in finding his niche in a community which at first was not sympathetic. After a turbulent Reading Over, Tommy Twidell, Head of the School, threatened that there would be no extra half holidays, which lay largely in his gift, if unruly behaviour continued.

Gradually Bob's genial integrity, devotion to the school and essential goodness won him a place in the hearts and affections of almost all. His forgetfulness, perhaps to some extent cultivated, is much remembered but behind it lay a certain shrewdness and wisdom in assessing both people and situations. Bob stories used to abound. As typical as any is that of Bob in Oxford in later life, bicycling to a library to borrow a book, coming out and seeming lost in thought as he prepared to remount his bicycle. Seeing a policeman standing by, he enquired from which direction he had come; the policeman indicated and Bob, mounting and riding off in the other direction, was heard to murmur "Ah, then I've had my lunch". Part of his strength lay in his selection of staff, however unusual the method. When A.E. 'Tom' Taylor was being considered, he came to play football (he was an amateur international player) and stayed in School House with the

Headmaster. No mention of the appointment was made until Tom Taylor, about to depart, tentatively raised the matter himself. "Of course – splendid! You must come". Months passed and Tom heard nothing further. At last he wrote, to receive a telegram appointing him to teach divinity and maths. (Tom was a physicist). That was the only communication he ever received.

When Bob said in his usual simplistic way, "Oh, I don't do anything, I leave it to the housemasters", he was over-stating the point but there was some truth in what he said. He was surrounded by men who spent their lives at the school, who owned their houses and kept a large proportion of the fee, which was paid by the parent to them, passing on a smaller proportion to the school. Chief amongst them was A.F. Chance, a distinguished scholar who was on the staff for fifty years; austere and frightening to a small boy, he was a man of the highest standards both in the form room and out of it. He had taken a major part in adapting the rough fields (the Common) of Kingsland after the Move and their transformation into the fine playing fields of today; it is right that a field and pavilion should be named after him. He ran his very successful House – seldom more than thirty strong – with total devotion. In his teaching he insisted on the most rigorous standards and he was a keen supporter of football and cricket. He had no time for rowing. A colleague remembers him crossing the Kingsland Bridge with measured tread, looking to neither right nor left, when his own house crew were actually rowing in Senior Challenge Oars beneath, and on an occasion when he enquired where Kitchin was and was told that he had gone to Oxford for the Trial Eights, expressed astonishment and said he was thinking of going to Cambridge for the Tripos. It was Sopwith who, at a masters' meeting in Bob Sawyer's time, thought of the quotation from *Paradise Lost*:

> Chaos umpire sits,
> And by decision more embroils the fray,
> By which he reigns; next him, high arbiter,
> Chance governs all

These lines, oft quoted, do not however do justice to Bob. He maintained a real control of the school, made many decisions (such as standing out against and abolishing a cruel ritual in School House, whereby new boys were subjected to running the gauntlet and made to sing to the accompaniment of noisy comment), and made it clear that the object of masters' meetings was "to raise questions and give the Headmaster material for action and pass resolutions merely on matters of convenience. Questions of principle must inevitably be decided by the Headmaster" (a recorded minute in 1929). It is impossible that Shrewsbury should have flourished as

much as it did in Sawyer's years without leadership, however camouflaged, from the top. During his time numbers rose from 394 to 517.

Although he had retired comparatively early in the Sawyer regime, a
powerful influence since the Move was E.B. Moser, another distinguished
classic, another Old Salopian – and another bachelor who gave his whole
life to the school. He had a kind heart but an acidulated tongue; not many
escaped it. Two stories well encapsulate his 'humour'. Duncan asked
Moser whether when he retired he should continue to live in Shrewsbury
or move elsewhere; Moser thought for a moment and said, "I don't know,
but whichever you do you'll regret it". On an occasion in town he saw W.H.
Moore across the street looking in a shop window; going over to him he
remarked, "So it is you, Moore; as I was coming along I said to myself,
'That's what Moore will look like in ten years time'". Such stories accumu-
lated and Moser – as others – became a legend in his own lifetime. Pickering
was another such: he served for fifty-one years, for many of which he was a
housemaster as well as School Librarian; again he was an Old Salopian and
a bachelor. A keen cricketer, he had been most successful as a schoolboy
but in the freshmen's match at Cambridge he was no-balled for throwing
and never bowled again. W.D. Haydon, housemaster of Rigg's for thirty-
two years, compensated for the numerous bachelors by marrying twice
and having ten children, "with power to add to that number", as Moser
said. A keen oarsman, he was also domestic bursar and dealt with property
matters on the Site. By 1932, his physical powers were declining and in the
form room he tended to nod off. A School House boy, John Hanmer, once
took the obvious opportunity provided and went to sleep himself; he was
much incensed when Billy Haydon, having woken up first, put him on
Extra Lesson for sleeping in form.

These and others were the men by whom Sawyer was surrounded;
narrow minded they might have been, but they knew exactly how to keep
the school running even if the lines on which it ran were those laid down by
Moss in the nineteenth century. Hidden from the boys by a curtain of awe,
the staff relaxed in private. Even Chance had a store of droll stories which –
it is said – contained three ingredients – a classical element, a Cambridge
element, and a bawdy element. He had a good cellar and Neville Cardus,
for a time assistant cricket professional, said in later years that he never
tasted a really good claret without thinking of Chance.

To celebrate the fiftieth anniversary of the migration from the town,
celebrations were held to which came the Prince of Wales, later Edward
VIII. Landing in his light aircraft on the site of the Battle of Shrewsbury, he
was addressed in Latin by R.E. Hill, the Head of School, and granted an
extension to the holidays as requested. He laid the foundation stone of the
re-sited School Wall, which had been brought up from the town, reviewed
the guard of honour, and returned to the town by ferry with an escort of

School VIIIs. The school were kind enough to buy Fred the Ferryman a suit for the occasion. To general surprise, the Prince wore a straw 'boater'. Not lacking in enterprise, Frank Newton, who had a shop in Castle Street, ordered a consignment of straw hats from Luton by telephone and the next day was selling them at 7/6d. each.

To crown a memorable summer term, the 1st VIII won the Ladies Plate at Henley, then a competition most difficult for a school to win, being open to both Oxford and Cambridge colleges as well as schools. When the news reached Kingsland a major riot took place: rockets were fired, masters (if unwise enough to appear) were chaired round the Site, bicycles ridden in all directions, a car commandeered, trousers flew from flagpoles and an attempt was made to roll the captured German guns (regrettably melted down in the Second World War) into the river. In a state of high excitement, the mob swept down to the river with the intention of throwing Mr Dunn, the unpopular toll keeper of the Kingsland Bridge, into the river. He defended himself with a broomstick, but in whirling it round his head accidentally hit his wife who was standing behind him, causing him to shout dramatically, "You have killed my wife!". Rowley Hill intervened to prevent further mayhem; Dunn's hat was brought back and put on 'Apollo', a lamp by the Alington Hall. James Hill wrote to his parents, "Freddie Prior was livid with all the brushers for going away into safety and not helping to keep order. I think it was just as well they did though. They would not have had nearly such control as the postors, and probably added to the chaos". An interesting comment on the disciplinary scene at the time. The boys were reproved in strong terms by the Headmaster. It was said that in chapel the next day penitence was shown: "we have done unto Dunn those things which we ought not have done unto Dunn". A markedly humourless correspondence, which went on into Hardy's time, was conducted between the Kingsland Bridge Company and the school. Reparation was paid for Mrs Dunn's injury, in fact she went to the sea for a week to recover and a domestic had to be employed to look after Dunn in her absence; an estimate had to be made as to how many boys had failed to pay their penny toll when rioting; and Dunn's hat had to be replaced. But Bob Sawyer had a light touch (though a firm hand on occasion) in disciplinary matters. The School House woke up one morning to find that the tree on Doctor's Grass had bloomed overnight. To every branch were attached apples, pears, apricots, bananas, peaches and plums, in a dazzling display of exotica. The Headmaster smiled with the rest, probably knowing that the author was Bunny Winfield (who rowed in the winning VIII at Henley), well known as an original humorist. It was his rockets which exploded high above Churchill's one evening, to the intense annoyance of the Revd J.O. Whitfield, his housemaster.

Thus Bob Sawyer's last term, when the sun appeared to shine every day, seemed in retrospect to those who were there, a golden age. In that and the previous year the list of scholarships to Oxford and Cambridge was long and distinguished. At Oxford there were three Salopian Fellows of All Souls, Basil Blagden, Geoffrey Hudson and John Austin. Four Salopians rowed in the Boat Race; there were three football Blues and one cricket Blue. That year the Old Salopians, led by Lionel Blaxland, again won the Arthur Dunn Cup. But the end of term was clouded; a boy in the School House, J.C.L. Mellersh, in leaning out of a window to look at the school clock before First Lesson, slipped and fell to his death. He was a poet of outstanding promise; his friend Paul Dehn commemorated him in some moving lines published in the end of year *Salopian*.

So ended the Sawyer era. He handed over a school in good condition and with high morale, and went out with a flourish of trumpets. Addressing the school for the last time in chapel he found himself unable to continue, overcome with emotion.

H.H. Hardy had been headmaster of Cheltenham College for twelve years; before that he had taught at Rugby, where he commanded the OTC and he had had three years' war experience with the Rifle Brigade. With his short, clipped moustache, upright carriage and spare figure, he looked a soldier, accustomed to command. The governors had had a response of some quality when advertising the post. Names familiar in the school world – or to be so – abounded: J.T. Christie, later head of Rugby; R.V.H. Roseveare, later head of Cheltenham; J.D. Hills who went to Bradfield; J.G. Barrington-Ward, a Tutor at Christ Church; the then headmasters of Sedbergh, St Bees, Trent, Merchant Taylors, Leeds Grammar School, and St Lawrence, Ramsgate; and the Revd J.W. Hunkin, OBE, MC, DD. The field looked formidable. Also standing was Stephen Lee, a don at Magdalen. (Curiously Hardy was one of his referees!) From this strong field, Hardy appeared to stand out, in fact he was the only name put forward by the sub-committee of governors to the main meeting, and he was the only one interviewed, so high was his standing and reputation. Had the staff in Hardy's early years known of the strength of the field, they would have wondered about the competence of their governors ... actually, they did anyway.

The Michaelmas term, then as now, started for the new boys with an address by the Headmaster. Housemasters ushered their charges into Top Schools (the long room at the top of the School Buildings) and thither Sopwith led us from Oldham's. There then took place a momentous incident of which, I fear, I have no recollection whatever. The Revd J.O. Whitfield, short in speech and temper, brought his new boys from Churchill's late. Hardy had already begun. Without hesitation the Headmaster, in front of boys and housemasters, addressed Joe with a withering reproof. Never did Joe forget that moment; during the whole of his headmastership

Hardy was never invited to Churchill's. It was the opening shot of battles to come.

In fact Hardy had already been embroiled in controversy with his governors. Hitherto the Headmaster had always lived in the School House and was its housemaster. Hardy proposed not to do so, reckoning that headmastering was enough of an occupation apart from looking after eighty-seven boys, even though a house tutor did much of the work. In Michaelmas 1931 a new boarding house had been opened in the recently purchased Kingsland House and H.G. Broadbent installed as housemaster. The establishment of Kingsland House had been a matter of controversy, for the housemasters had felt that it was injudicious to open a new house in the prevailing conditions of the economic depression; however, although Sopwith, Street and Moxon all refused the offer of the housemastership, H.G. Broadbent was established with twenty-four boys. Hardy now proposed that he and his family should live there as in a private dwelling, and the boys dispersed to other houses as opportunity offered. This indeed set the cat among the pigeons. Sawyer was for keeping the Headmaster in touch with the boys through being a housemaster; he had had lunch daily in Hall, went round the bedrooms and took his evening cocoa with the School House boys. His suggestion was that Hardy should stay as housemaster but have his responsibilities alleviated by having a housekeeper, secretary, and a house tutor with greater scope and powers – all financed by the school. In a letter to Lord Bridgeman, the Chairman of the Governors, Sawyer was frank about the financial profits, having saved £1,000 a year over the last ten years, after all expenses, public and private, had been met. "One feels some delicacy in making big profits out of boys", he wrote. To salve his conscience Bob had personally paid the allowance of his house tutor, his secretary's salary and all expenses of Speech Day. And he and Mrs Sawyer had entertained freely. (There is a well-known story of Mrs Sawyer being heard on the telephone to the butcher, "Please send two pounds of best steak and 25 pounds of boys' meat".)

After much argument, Hardy won his case. He moved into Kingsland House, being *pro tem* housemaster to the boys there but with J.B.C. Grundy as house tutor. He was on a salary of £3,000 p.a. plus £500 entertainment allowance, £100 petty cash and £300 for a secretary. But the governors – perhaps a rather spiteful thrust – made him pay rent and rates on Kingsland House. For more than a year Kingsland House went on, though now a Waiting House. In October 1933 Hardy wrote to the governors, "I am bound to admit that financially the position is distinctly adverse to us and to point out that no previous headmaster, though in a position to make large profits from the School House, has been charged for rent and rates on his House. In other respects than finance, the position is one which I can only continue under protest...".

The preliminary bout was followed by a long slugging match between Hardy and the housemasters over the question of the fees. The 'old system', which Hardy sought to change, was that the housemaster owned his House, was responsible for its care and maintenance, enlisted the boys and kept a proportion of the fee – which was paid to him personally by the parent. Since 1921 the annual fee had been £180, of which the housemaster kept £105 and passed £75 to the school. Was housemastering a profitable occupation? The answer must be an emphatic 'Yes'. Few bothered to keep more than the roughest of accounts, but the housemasters themselves worked out that the average figure of profit per annum per House was £1,319 – this after all expenses of maintaining the structure and the boys, the housemaster and his family, and of general entertainment had been met. And this over a long period; of the housemasters in 1932, one had an expectation of twenty years housemastering, three of nineteen years. On the other hand it must be said that there was no pension scheme save an inadequate insurance policy to which the older housemasters did not belong; and housemasters did not progress to the upper reaches of the salary scale, being pegged at £600 p.a.

Hardy's proposal was that housemasters should receive full salary and an allowance – £500 was suggested – plus free living, the Houses becoming the property of the school. The housemasters strenuously opposed this and a majority at a staff meeting supported them; it was felt that the identity of a housemaster with his House was important and that his efforts might fall off without a financial carrot. Junior members of the staff themselves hoped to succeed to Houses and the comparative wealth which they brought, compared to their present meagre salaries. The most that housemasters would do was to offer to give up £6 per boy per annum to the school in return for a deal on pensions. In the end a compromise took place: housemasters gave up £5 per boy per annum to the school with a gentleman's agreement that this should not be changed "except in exceptional circumstances" – not defined. But Hardy's suggestion that the fees be paid to the Bursar, not to themselves, was thrown out.

Hardy was eventually successful in this long battle but there was already much blood on the field of combat. He had won the first round by showing that housemasters at Shrewsbury received a greater percentage of the fee than at any similar school in England. He was now able to improve the staff salary scale which, from 1935, ran from £350 to £800 and to get the governors to lay down that Houses should be held for fifteen years with retirement for all at sixty. The present housemasters remained, bloody but unbowed, on the 'old system' of profit-making; only gradually was Hardy able to bring the House finances under central control. It should be said, to complete the picture, that both housemasters and the school contributed to the central fund from which assistance with the fees was given to a high proportion of parents who might comprise some twenty per cent of the whole. It was, one must remember, a time of slump and financial uncertainty. The governors were hard pressed; their balance sheet showed an overall loss of £504 on the income and expenditure account for 1932–33; and this was at a time when they had had to purchase Rigg's from Billy Haydon and – unexpectedly – Oldham's from Basil Oldham as a consequence of his breakdown. There must have been considerable irritation with Hardy when they considered the money wasted on equipping Kingsland House as a boarding establishment.

This conflict was, of course, entirely hidden from the boys in the school. A considerable gulf was fixed between us and the staff; a solid green baize door between us and our housemaster. The more senior staff we regarded as Olympians, living in a rarefied atmosphere; one might experience people like Chance and Moser but one did not know them in a human sense. Many were referred to with the definite article before their names – the Banks, the Barnes, the Bling – as though they were institutions; others had nicknames – the Bull, 'Cuddie' Mitford, the Hobo (Hope-Simpson), the Joe (Whitfield). When Hardy took on the housemasters, he was confronted by a formidable team and it is worth looking at these men who, to a considerable degree, ran the school and all of us in it.

Foremost was 'Cuddie' Mitford who had been on the staff for twenty-four years, seven of them as housemaster. In his autobiography *Across the Straits*, Kyffin Williams, perhaps the most distinguished artist the school has produced, writes of his misery at school, attributing much of it to Mitford. A tall man, with a small head and the remains of wavy fair hair, he towered above most boys, having (it was said) a bicycle of immense height specially constructed for him with two cross bars. More frightening than his physical appearance was his tongue, which was sardonic at best and sarcastic at worst. He believed firmly in the current philosophy that the boys should run the House, and he left the monitors to get on with it, to the infinite terror of legions of small boys. He was keen on games, though bad at them himself; rumour said he had been a gymnast in past days. Tombling once said that golf was too good a game to play as Mitford played it. Mitford was a mathematician and had his figures well under control when taking on Hardy in the arguments about fees; there was not much love lost between these two determined men. When at a housemasters' meeting Hardy took an unpopular decision and reminded those present that a headmaster was paid to be a cad, Mitford's whispered comment to his neighbour was that he earned every penny of it. A bachelor, he seemed devoid of human feelings though there was a certain sardonic humour which boys seldom saw. In the great 'flu epidemic of 1918 when three boys and two masters died and the school was again in chapel for a funeral, Mitford commented to his neighbour that he was glad St Paul was not at

Shrewsbury as apparently he died daily. Improbably there was a musical side to Mitford and he played the bassoon in the school orchestra; as Paul Dehn said, on regarding the length of the bassoon and the length of Mitford, one could not really tell whether Cuddie was playing the bassoon or the bassoon playing Cuddie. Formidable to the boys, he was equally formidable to his colleagues, none of whom ever called him by any but his surname. When Sopwith arrived on the staff, he lived with Mitford and three others on 'the Staircase' (one end of the school buildings); a colleague wished him well and said it would probably take him a term to settle down, but on hearing that he was living with Mitford amended this to two terms. He was related to the famous Mitford girls, daughters of Lord Redesdale, one of whom, Unity, was a notorious fascist in the pre-war days. She once visited Hitler and there was some speculation in the cheaper press that he might marry her. When she returned still single, Mitford was heard to say, "Well, I'm glad we haven't got Cousin Adolf in the family".

The Revd J.O. Whitfield was housemaster of Churchill's. We were puzzled as to why he ever became a clergyman, though it was rumoured that it was necessary in order that he could marry Megan, one of the daughters of Billy Haydon whose children's marriages spread tentacles across the Site. We who knew him little were conscious mainly of his short temper, the peculiar emphasis he laid on unlikely words, the tense atmosphere his presence created in the form room and the speed with which he conducted chapel services. He took unholy pleasure in starting the eight o'clock Communion service on Sunday mornings as the clock struck, knowing that Hardy, always two minutes late, would at that moment be half way across the Common. Having gradually built up a stock of sermons, he used them indefinitely. Most famous was his Trinity Sunday sermon in which he tied himself into a hopeless theological knot in explaining the Trinity, and having got into a single yet double and slightly bifurcated yet trinitarian position from which there was no escape, he would glare at the congregation and say, "It is all very difficult and neither you nor I will ever properly understand it – And now to God the Father . . ." For years Tony Trench and I would say to each other on Trinity Sunday, "Somewhere, in some pulpit, in some town or village, Joe will be preaching it again". Micky Jones, in his first days at the school as a timid new boy, had acquired a snap file of which he was proud. In Joe's form he made a slight noise with it, at which Joe seized it from him and flung it straight out of the window on to the wet grass where it rapidly deteriorated. His best known punishment in form was to order a boy to copy out the Bible backwards, alternate letters in red and black. This punishment was always rescinded at the end of the lesson but, according to Jimmy Street, if carried out in full would take a hundred years, working twenty-four hours a day without intermission for food or sleep. In fact Joe did have a softer side; there was a genuine concern for boys in his house, there were acts of unobtrusive kindness and generosity, and he was willing to sing "Poor old Joe" at house Bump Suppers, to the delight of all. At the time of the Calcutta Sweepstake – organised in Ireland and illegal in England – which brought vast money prizes to the winners, there was some publicity as to the fate of those who won, so many of whom being in the end ruined by their riches. Joe preached on the theme, asking with great emphasis, "Could you afford to *win* the Calcutta Sweep?" whereat every master's head in the back row of the stalls nodded vigorously. Joe's morality was ahead of his underpaid colleagues.

J.H. Tombling was the housemaster of Moore's. He had an unusual background having been born in humble circumstances in Bermondsey. Through the good offices of the Oxford Mission he had been sent to the City of London School and thence to University College, Reading. Always known as 'the Bling', he was much imitated because of an abrupt intake of breath before beginning a sentence. He was another who concealed a sharp wit behind an unsmiling facade. A close friend of Jimmy Street, they shared various interests – reading, food and wine, games, anecdotes, the countryside of Shropshire and North Wales – and spent much time together, both as bachelors but also later in their married states. In 1931 Bobby Armitstead, who had a fast left-hand slinging action, shattered Repton, taking 9 for 22. Someone suggested to Bling that he could be compared to the England bowler – Larwood's companion – Voce. "Rather *sotto voce*", said Bling. On another occasion he and Jimmy Street, looking out of the Common Room window, saw boys departing early from their lesson in the Art School where timekeeping was not of the essence. Bling's pithy comment was "*Ars Brevis*".

Jimmy Street became a housemaster at the same time as Hardy arrived, but he had already been on the staff for sixteen years. He was a splendid and inspiring teacher of the classics, a man of wide general culture, a ready wit, and with all the arts of the raconteur. He was a part of the school until 1960 and had an immense knowledge of Salopians and an excellent memory, enjoying Salopian reunions and dinners up and down the country. Shrewsbury and Street were inseparable in the memories of many, though Richard Cobb in *A Sense of Place* describes his intense dislike for his housemaster, and it was perhaps in that capacity that he lacked patience and sensitivity in understanding those with whom he did not have a natural affinity. Clearly there was a head-on collision between Street and Cobb whose memoirs are a remarkable amalgam of fact and the wildest flights of fiction.

To complete the list of housemasters, I have already mentioned the physically dominating figure of A.E. Kitchin; and Dicky Sale, who had very little grip on his House but was a delightful man, whose contribution to the school's games was immense. Apart from Sopwith, my own housemaster, that leaves only H.G. Broadbent and J.R. Hope-Simpson. The former (the 'Broadbean'), after a less than happy year in the School House, went to Moser's. With his shiny bald head, he somewhat resembled Lenin. Gruff and brief of speech, he was a capable physicist and had a passion for bridges. He had run the school's engineering society with efficiency and initiative, but in Hardy's time it came to a dead stop for reasons unknown. The Broadbean was a cultured man and ran such concerts as there then were; to Shrewsbury he brought Schnabel, Solomon, the Dolmetsch family, and on one occasion the Hallé Orchestra then under Adrian Boult. At one famous dinner party he had served fish flown from the Rhine the day before, with appropriate wines of the Rhine to the accompaniment of Wagner's music, played on his gramophone, which had a long horn as seen on the old HMV labels. But again, the boys saw little of this side of a person who appeared to them more a machine than a man. In Moser's as in all houses, the boys ran their side of the House, for better or for worse, the housemaster as referee only intervening in extreme circumstances; the whistle was seldom blown even when the most blatant fouls were committed. Hope-Simpson, variously known as 'the Hobo' or 'the Bo' and to his colleagues as 'Juggins', spent his whole working life at Shrewsbury, much of it in the School House where he had been Sawyer's house tutor. From 1933 to 1948 he was housemaster, spending in total seventy terms in the House, more than any of his colleagues of Hardy's time. No one better personified the Roman virtues; very straight in speaking, very clear on principles, he ran his large House by force of his own personality. He did not keep records, he had no bureaucratic instincts, but he had a wide knowledge of boys. Praise was only grudgingly given but when given was sincere. He was much respected and much liked; he had a strong disciplinary structure but everyone knew where they were within it and he was abundantly fair minded. His three major interests lay in photography, in gardening, and on the river where he probably spent more hours coaching than any other master. His photographs were often exhibited (though he disliked any sort of publicity) and he was a gardener of outstanding expertise and skill.

These then were the formidable team of housemasters whom Hardy faced. Still around on Kingsland, like a group of not wholly exploded volcanoes, lived Chance, Moser and Pickering; Haydon was still employed, and Ingrams in his fiftieth year of service to the school, still making lists, compiling the Brown Book (the school list), keeping the Punishment Book and acting as Sacristan in Chapel; while Oldham, licking his wounds in his tent in Little Grange, was still Librarian with his involved bundle of prejudices and traditions.

CHAPTER VI

H.H.H

Hardy, Hardy, Hardy
Lord God Almighty,
Every day in morning dicks
Our song shall rise to thee.

For the past twenty-five years, the office of headmaster had been filled first by Alington, who had flashed like a meteor across the Salopian sky illuminating all that he encountered, and Bob Sawyer with his genial air of general good will, radiating to all his deep love of the school. Now there was to be a harsher and altogether more authoritarian note sounded. Whether Hardy had any particular brief from the governors is not known but the general line of his policy soon became clear: the school was to be more centralised and there was to be a greater control by the Headmaster himself of all that took place. Bureaucracy, unknown to Sawyer who carried everything in his head, was to spread its tentacles across the Site. The part-time Bailiff and Bursar was then a solicitor in the town, the domestic bursarial matters being dealt with by Billy Haydon on the Site; on his retiring from Rigg's he was to bursar more fully, but illness and death removed him in Hardy's first year. In typical military phraseology, Hardy described his position as that of commanding a battalion with no Adjutant and no Quartermaster. Given the administrative bent of his mind, he was indeed severely stretched in his first years until the appointment of the first full-time Bailiff and Bursar, S.A. Tippetts (St Paul's and Merton), a barrister, latterly Governor of the Red Sea Province and holder of the Order of the Nile, who was uncomfortably ensconced in an Alington Hall room adjacent to the piano practice rooms and the boys jumping about in their gym lessons a few feet away.

The staff now found themselves receiving a barrage of instructions. Hardy was strong on the administrative detail on such subjects as marks, orders, correcting examinations, lists and timetables. Notices which others had been accustomed to publishing on their own subjects now had to be countersigned with the magic initials H.H.H. A boy going away for an interview or other similar business had to have his exeat signed by the Headmaster, and his train timings would be personally checked in a copy of Bradshaw kept by the headmagisterial desk. I recollect that when Patrick Gower, a contemporary of mine, had been in London, his exeat designated that he should return on the 4.10 p.m. train. Knowing that if he caught the 6.10 p.m. ('the Zulu' – because it had been running on the same timings since the Zulu War), he could get a good dinner on the train, he took the risk thinking that no one would notice. Seating himself luxuriously in the restaurant car, he found himself opposite a man obscured by a double spread of newspaper; when the paper was folded, Hardy was revealed. Patrick said that they had a reasonably genial journey, Hardy going to sleep after dinner as was his custom, but he was punished on his return.

Toby Barnaby, a member of the staff from 1928 to 1943, had a considerable gift for parody. Here is his adaptation of Cowper's well-known hymn (tune: Winchester New):

> H. moves in a delirious arc
>> Whilst weathering the storm.
> He plans his projects in the dark
>> And writes them on a form.
>
> Deep in unfathomable reams
>> Of complicated cock,
> He dishes up his darkest schemes
>> And issues them *ad hoc*
>
> Ye fearful staff, with terror quake,
>> Name, set, initials, age,
> And all the bloomers that you make
>> Are cross-checked by the sage.
>
> Ye timid few, fresh courage take,
>> The forms you have not read,
> Are big with bullshit. In the break
>> Hear ye our lucid Head.
>
> There in a rigmarole verbose
>> And fierce *pro hac vice's*
> He will propound the cons and pros
>> In flaccid journalese.
>
> Crass underlings are prone to err
>> And 'strue his words in vain,
> For there is no interpreter
>> Nor will he make it plain.

The boys soon felt the force of Hardy's administrative reorganisation. The school porter, Hartshorne, made repeated journeys round the class-rooms with the Notice Book. The headmaster's style was pithy, grammatically correct and sometimes peppered with tags of Latin.

"The rumour that Whit Monday will be a holiday has no basis in fact".

(On Armistice Day) "The Two Minutes Silence being observed, all will at once return to work, like the rest of the nation".

"Inside form rooms it is clearly at the Master's discretion to let boys loosen uniform collars, or remove ordinary jackets or OTC tunics, for greater comfort. But all Masters are asked to see that boys do not come out in public in any sort of disarray. It was distressingly noticeable this morning".

"All Masters are very definitely reminded that they should insist on boys getting out of their form rooms during the ten minute break, unless actual rain prevents it. Mere cold need not stop anyone from taking a brisk turn out of doors. Loitering in form rooms may lead, and has led, to avoidable troubles".

"The Upper School will attend the lecture on 'The Colour Problem in the British Empire and Mandated Territories'. I hope the absence of Masters, thus relieved of a period, need not, on this occasion and similar occasions, be so marked as on some recent occasions". (Hardy clearly enjoyed back-handers to his staff).

And sometimes his rather heavy humour came through:

"I have to be in London tonight, leaving at 3 p.m., and I shall not return until Tuesday evening at 9.30 p.m., having succumbed to the temptation of spending Tuesday afternoon, on what may be called University business, in a London suburb". (Which meant that he would be going to the Boat Race).

Some Hardy phraseology remained encrusted in school notices. In 1960 boys were still directed to their seats in chapel "in accordance with previously circulated lists". In admonishing the school for coughing in Chapel, he called for "corporate self-restraint". At a discussion as to whether boys should have to wear black ties on Sundays, he declared himself in favour of "Sabbatical nigritude".

If the staff were finding Hardy a difficult headmaster to deal with, the boys, while respecting his general grip and energetic presence, found his facade both harsh and threatening. It was very soon that H.H. Hardy became Herr Hitler Hardy and he was referred to as 'Hitler' for most of his time at Shrewsbury. He soon put a stop to what had become a popular feature on Sunday afternoons, a film show in the Alington Hall. Hardy reported to his governors, "I frankly dislike these displays and feel no disposition to sanction them in the future". Discipline was stiffened. A Head of School lost his position – though later restored – in Hardy's first term, over a bottle of beer consumed at the Mission in Liverpool. An episode with a car saw two members of Ridgemount disappear forever. It is interesting to note that in a recent publication on Cheltenham College (*Then and Now*), Hardy's years there are summarised, "This was not, apparently, a very happy period". He was concerned with personal smartness and had all the Great War officer's devotion to short hair. A limerick appeared in a scurrilous school magazine:

> There once was a fellow of Shrawardine
> Whose hair with grease was o'erlarwardine
>   Said Hardy, H. Harrison,
>   With a witty comparison
> You're less like a man than a marwardine.
>
> (Shrawardine is pronounced 'Shraden').

At the end of his first year, the Headmaster on Speech Day seemed to be conscious of his wide unpopularity; he finished his speech with a story from the bar of a Wild West tavern which ended, "Don't shoot the pianist, he is doing his best". As parents were also liable to receive a few rounds from Hardy's six-shooter, this plea would have a point. At a much later stage the mother of John Lea (he was in Ridgemount), having written to Hardy on points concerning her son's future, was disconcerted to have her letter returned with the spelling mistakes corrected in red ink. Nor were parents the only people in the firing line; prep school headmasters – very important people – received short and sharp notes on the supposed shortcomings of their charges. Tony Barnaby's descriptive lines do not mince matters:

> When Satan old shot up from Hell
>   A swift ascent he made,
> Involved with sulphur, flame and smell,
>   Half rocket, half grenade.
>
> But when on earth he next was seen
>   He chose another shape
> An Hardy monster, Gadarene,
>   Part lupine and part ape.

He drills this ancient school; he drills
　　Whom Ashton bade triumph
In nought but God's good works; and fills
　　The whole damn place with Bumph.

But all this is to paint only the worst of H.H.H. (He was irritated that a wine merchant in the town had the same initials – H.H. Hughes.) Hardy's reforming zeal spread widely. From the boys' point of view perhaps the best thing he did in his early days was to rearrange the divinity lesson which had been on Sunday afternoon at 2.15 p.m. and lasted an hour. Now it was placed on Sunday morning before Chapel. On weekdays Chapel had been after First Lesson – as unproductive a time as could be thought of with all longing for breakfast. Now it was placed after breakfast, before morning school. Also there was now a five minute break between lessons and a ten minute break in the morning at 11.30 a.m. Hardy was a great man for the countryside and he made every effort to encourage boys to enjoy and appreciate the splendid county in which the school was lucky enough to be placed. Thus bicycles, hitherto for the few privileged, were now for all. On Ascension Day there was a whole holiday after Chapel for boys to get out and about, often in groups led by enterprising masters; and then, a little later, Country Expedition days were instituted when every boy had to leave the Site.

Hardy also made some attempt to improve the primitive facilities in the houses. The sanitation and washing provision in Moser's were, according to Hardy, "altogether behind modern school standards and have to be concealed from visiting parents with great care". In Whitfield's House there were in the changing rooms "some basins and a trough in which one can paddle and upstairs two baths for 46 boys". An inspection of the fire escape in that house showed that on the top floor the windows were too narrow for an average boy to get through and the swinging rope ladders "could only be used by a practised gymnast with an exceptionally steady head".

One of the areas in which Hardy operated with circumspection and meticulous care was in appointing staff, often interviewing them in a favourite place – the landing half way up the stairs in the Athenaeum. He recognised at once that, as the first lay headmaster since the seventeenth century, he needed a chaplain but, then as now, chaplains were hard to find. He started with the Revd E.C. Crosse, DSO, MC. A strange man he seemed to us, still living with the War and the palpable untruth, fashionable at the time, that "there were no atheists in the trenches". On asking confirmation candidates in his room to sit down he said "Squattez vous", the remains of army French presumably, which caused smirks. How he got the name "Wee Wee" I know not but it was universally used and we would sing, "When I survey the Reverend Crosse" in Chapel, just as we sang "Hardy, Hardy, Hardy/Lord God Almighty...". However, Wee Wee did not last long, leaving in Hardy's first year to become Headmaster of Ardingly.

More successful was the appointment of J.B. Johnson as director of music, on the retirement of 'Black Death' (W.H. Moore). Johnny, a man of wide interests and much enthusiasm, really put life into the school's music which hitherto had been an area not much regarded. Hardy instituted the Congregational Practice on Fridays and Johnny, slowly but successfully, made the school sing with remarkable enthusiasm, especially after the introduction of a new psalter. He loved the psalms and knew many by heart; he had his idiosyncrasies in stressing certain words and phrases. "Hailstones and coals of fire", several times repeated, lifted the roof as did those valleys which were thick with corn and laughed and sang. The concert choir's concerts at Christmas were changed; the Old Salopian song was dropped as were the humorous items; an effort was made with both choir and orchestra to play and sing more ambitious works. The house singing competition, which in Hardy's phrase had been "a deplorable farce", took on new life and became one of the events of the year. Johnny had a musician's temperament and his reactions were often incalculable. He hated Congregational Practices and many years before his retirement he had them all numbered off in a notebook, crossing one off every week with evident relief. He kept elaborate commonplace books; he took notes on sermons in Chapel – provided they were proper sermons starting with a text. If, as occasionally happened, a preacher was a conversational story teller, those near the organ could hear a notebook snap shut with condemnatory finality. For services in exceptionally cold weather, Johnny would arrive with a hot baked potato to keep his hands warm.

In 1935 the school was inspected by His Majesty's Inspectors, and a thorough visit it was with much to praise and much to criticise adversely. They reported that the classics were taught (in the upper forms) by "an admirable combination of masters (three with double firsts) and some of the teaching is brilliant"; but there was a note of doubt while recognising the very high standard of scholarship; "in the interpretation of the classics, is enough encouragement given to independent reading and thought or are the boys' minds too much over-looked and over-taught?" A relevant question. But when it came to the Lower School the inspectors let rip: "In most subjects syllabuses may be said not to exist"; "The position assigned to geography is several places below the salt"; "The accommodation for teaching science is quite inadequate". It was noted that in Upper IVA – four forms up from the bottom – there were three boys over seventeen, and that if one started in the Third Form (the very bottom) and missed one promotion, one would never reach School Certificate. Modern languages were not well reported on. Some parts of the inspectors' report were blacked out in the version shown to the staff and no one was ever able to find out what was thus concealed.

All this gave Hardy some ammunition in striving for a new science building and in trying to improve the form rooms; but there was little he could do about the staff in the lower regions of the school. A rather feeble attempt was made to appoint what are now called Heads of Faculties but they had little power or influence: everyone went on teaching what they had always taught and the timetable was still arranged so that Kitchin, Tombling and Street could play golf on Tuesday afternoons and so that Hans Pendlebury, the 'monumental Mason', always had Mondays off and the regular bridge evenings were not broken up by meetings or overmuch correcting of work. Hardy also made an attack on the considerable amount of cheating, cribbing, or in Salopian parlance, 'cabbing', which went on in the lower regions of the school. This was encouraged by the narrow double desks which prevailed in most of the form rooms and which Hardy gradually had replaced with single desks or tables. He was not pleased when a publication included a 'Sixth Form Hymn' whose opening stanza was:

> Though lowly here our lot may be
> High work have we to do;
> We had to sap to climb the tree
> Now cabbing sees us through.

For almost all his time, Hardy was worried about the numbers in the school and generally took a pessimistic view. In his early days, the Depression lay heavy on the country. Speaking in Birmingham in 1933 he described the public schools as being "up against it". "That all the Houses at Shrewsbury were full was a matter for the greatest satisfaction, but how long the British public could go on filling even Shrewsbury anyone must, in his less enthusiastic moments, doubt". Yet in 1936 the total was 535, the highest in the school's history. Despite this, two years later Hardy was radiating general gloom at the decline in numbers of the school age group owing to the War, a decline "to be reckoned not in thousands but in hundreds of thousands. It is perfectly clear that from now onward and for at least twenty years, either some of the public schools must cease to exist or all but a very few indeed must count on a marked decrease in numbers. My own belief is that both these misfortunes will occur simultaneously". How wrong one can be.

As a one time soldier himself, Hardy took a close interest in the Officers Training Corps. Whereas on the annual Inspection Bob Sawyer had appeared in top hat and morning coat, Hardy wore his old uniform, which looked increasingly ancient year by year. As has already been indicated, his whole stance was military, an attitude which did not lie in the Salopian tradition; nor did his keenness on physical training, hitherto a neglected backwater despite the efforts of RSM Joyce, one of Bob Sawyer's last appointments, a brilliant gymnast himself who had risen to the top of the Army's PT structure. It was only under Hardy that Joyce, much loved and much imitated, began to play a real part in the school with the building of the Gymnasium in 1937. Hardy insisted that all forms had a PT period in the timetable and both boxing and fencing had their keen adherents. At a later time he went further and instituted PT in small squads in the morning break, under house arrangements, which was universally unpopular. This, in 1938, led to a failed *coup d'état* when a manifesto was circulated – "A Spectre is haunting Shrewsbury..." – and a demonstration planned to take place in the break in the form of a refusal to do PT. This was nipped in the bud by Ronald Prentice, the Head of School, but there were consequences for the conspirators, one of whom, Douglas Scott, a boy of literary promise, had to leave the school, while a group of 'left wing' masters came under suspicion and Humphrey Moore (called 'Pisa' Moore as he carried his head on one side) was not confirmed in his appointment and left. It was on his typewriter that the manifesto had been written. Hardy discounted the incident: "a few boys made a misguided attempt to get up an agitation". He also wrote, "Unless I am extraordinarily deceived the School is enjoying PT". Extraordinarily deceived he was.

There was a considerable contrast between Hardy as an individual and Hardy as a headmaster. He could be quite outstandingly rude to his staff. George Simmons never forgave or forgot his treatment and recounted to me, when on his deathbed more than fifty years later, the derogatory terminology which Hardy had used about him. Yet he was a most generous and good tempered host and a perfect guest. All the time, behind the scenes, was Mrs Hardy, of whom no one at any time said a bad word. Sympathetic and forthcoming, she was a friend indeed and friend in need to the ladies of the staff. As David Bevan said, "It only needed one of the children to have a chicken pox spot for Mrs Hardy to be on the doorstep with a grape". When Hardy, as often he did, walked the hills on a Sunday afternoon with a colleague, clad in his Norfolk jacket, they returned to a sumptuous tea in Kingsland House and Mrs Hardy was presented with the wild flowers which had been gathered. Many unobtrusive acts of kindness and consideration emanated from this happy home. To quote again from the Notices Book, "After the (alfresco) play there will be physical restoratives at Kingsland House, where we much hope that as many as care to come will join us and restore their circulation".

Behind the lupine exterior, there lurked softer feelings than often appeared in public, though it is difficult to envisage Hardy, as was recorded in his Cheltenham days, reading Romeo in the Shakespearian

Society (it was also remarked that he three times took the part of Richard III). What he felt in his heart about his first years at Shrewsbury is not recorded but he did let slip this sentence to his governors in 1933, "Anyone coming here from outside, could not fail to remark, gratefully, on the general amenableness of boys in the school".

In 1937 there appeared in a "*Wollopian*", an occasional scurrilous magazine, two verses from the pen of Toby Barnaby which perhaps sum up what the school thought of its headmaster:

> O H.H.H., though here a ribald laugh
> Scurrility may raise against your School,
> Indulge our folly, sifting from the chaff
> Some grains of sense as *hardi* as your rule.
>
> For your large-hearted wisdom did present
> New liberties, new music, much beside,
> Granting to scholars sometimes mewed and pent
> The freedom of the Shropshire countryside.

CHAPTER VII

Public School Life

Oh History Side the Golden
With toasted teacakes blest...

It is time to turn from this Salopian *tour d'horizon* and the dominant
characters on the Salopian scene to life lived on a lower level. I had
survived my two years as a doul successfully and though I had not risen to
bark with the rest of the pack, I could at least wag my tail. Being a
two-year-old brought enhanced status: I had crossed a considerable divide
and was now wearing my two-year-old collar and able to sit on a cushion,
at the same time being suitably patronising to those below me with whom I
nevertheless used to get on very well – Frank Allen, later to be a Clerk in the
House of Commons after a serious wound in Burma; Claude Boys-Stones
from Northumberland, who went into his family stockbroking firm; James
Arkle, an able medic; Dennis Page, later a bishop; Nicol Cooke, who died
unduly young and who was somewhat dogged by a professional Old
Salopian uncle, Vicar of a Shropshire parish, who seemed always to be
dropping in and whom we called "Cooke's – yer'uncle". And there were
others whom one remembers for particular reasons – George Bidder of
very considerable girth who was said to have eaten twelve eggs at a session
in the Shop and Brian Suckling, not a happy name to bear in a school,
physically very tall on arrival; it was his lot to sit in Chapel in full view of
everyone else in the south gallery. When we reached the psalm which
contained the line "out of the mouths of babes and sucklings" all eyes
would be turned on him.

"He has done well to clear the Lower School in two years", wrote Hardy
on my report, so here I was in a School Certificate form taken by Johnny
Key. He was a man who knew exactly what the School Certificate required
and he was going to see that we knew, by rigid drilling and strict discipline;
we had the fruits of his long experience and were grateful. I passed in all the
necessary subjects with a reasonable showing of credits. When Hardy
thought that injustice had been done in the divinity marking and "chal-
lenged" (his word) the Oxford and Cambridge Board to re-mark, they

reluctantly did so and another credit came my way. I admired John Key but he did not admire me. "I hope he has profited by his year but with his aloofness and taciturnity he makes so little impact – positive or negative – that it is difficult to say. He is a difficult boy to estimate". There must have been more of a facade than I thought protecting my private life.

I had long enjoyed history, partly perhaps because of interesting teaching at Abinger, and partly because of my father's own interest and the fact that we went to see places in the holidays which caught my imagination. So, in Michaelmas 1935, I joined the History Side. For many years this small group had been taught by Basil Oldham and for long had adopted the motto, "Otium Cum Dignitate". Of the twenty-one history periods in the week under Oldham eleven were private reading periods; this had been adversely criticised by the 1930 inspectors. To replace Oldham, Hardy had appointed Murray Senior, lately an undergraduate at Christ Church, whom we credited with a First Class in his final Schools but who in fact got a Second.

Here was a man who had a lasting effect on his pupils and on the school. With an impressive profile, from which his nickname 'The Duke' is said to have come (though a counter theory pins it to the time when he read Duke Senior in *As You Like It*), he had a fine bass voice and an impressive personality. He based his teaching on the Oxford tutorial system and we used to read our essays to him in pairs in his home on Canonbury; in the form room his teaching was wide ranging, encouraging us to think and read outside the confines of the syllabus, constantly straying into what was then called Current Affairs, broadly liberal and even radical in his own stance, always with sympathy for the minority and the outsider. As Richard Wainwright recalls, a visiting inspector was quite nonplussed on being invited to participate in a hard-fought discussion on the ethics of nudism. He was a reader of the Gollancz Left Book Club publications, not necessarily because he had any socialist leaning, but so that all sides of a case might be properly presented, and we read them too. His only expression of his personal belief lay in commending the works of Henry George, the apostle of social credit, and we were meant to take an interest in what Major Douglas was doing in Alberta. His teaching was geared to university scholarship and he fought and won a battle with Hardy in getting the History Side exempted from the Higher Certificate, which everyone else took, sometimes two or three times.

Although our form room was decidedly inhospitable, a tiny room with a north-west facing window, inadequate heating and with no space for maps, plans, posters or any of the clutter now found in history rooms, there was a real atmosphere of hard work, debate and good humour. And the results were spectacular. There were never more than ten boys in all, sometimes fewer, yet amongst my companions on the History Side over three years, there were ten open awards at Oxford or Cambridge. I was not one of them and indeed I was at first quite overwhelmed at the cut and thrust of minds much sharper and better stocked than mine. At the head of the form were Richard Wainwright and David Gieve, close friends in Severn Hill, the one small with a curds-and-whey complexion, the other saturnine and hirsute. ("Two shaves a day, you know, and two blades a shave".) Richard became a long-serving Liberal MP. David Gieve, after running his famous family firm in Bond Street, retired early to the remoteness of a West Scotland village, choosing a life of different values. Then there was Ian Hogg, a quiet spoken Scot; Alexander Cumming-Bruce, destined for an unconventional career in the Civil Service; Maurice Craig, Irish journalist and author, who at school used to wear a green carnation on Oscar Wilde's birthday. In the year before me were Richard Cobb, later Professor of Modern History at Oxford, and Brian Inglis, journalist, author and TV presenter. Following me was Dennis Dobson, a publisher of genius and a man of legendary eccentricity.

Although our form room was so bare, we did have access to the VIth Form Library, a delightful panelled room with comfortable chairs, bookcases and in winter – a coal fire! Luxury indeed, and here we, at times, luxuriated. A much later parody catches well the atmosphere:

> O History Side the golden,
>   With toasted teacakes blest,
> Beneath thy contemplation
>   Sink we with sleep opprest;
> We know nought! O we know nought!
>   For work we do not care;
> To lie in peaceful slumber,
>   This is our only prayer.

Our concentration was, of course, on our own subject; and I fear that we tended to treat other subjects with disdain. Science we never touched. (As Lord James once said, "You have to go to a very good school indeed not to learn any science at all".) Mathematics was given up once the School Certificate pass was obtained. But we had the statutory divinity and kept up our Latin and French – that is to say, some kept them up but for me and others languages retreated fast. We would not take them seriously, much to our discredit. Harry Dawson had the misfortune to teach us Latin. A very good scholar himself, he spent most of his time with the Classical VIth, where (I believe) behaviour was sometimes not good but not as bad as on the History Side. Harry, a most kind-hearted man with a quiet wit, had never found the secret of controlling a class of lively boys. He was much imitated and his expressions preserved. One was, "I don't mind a little light hearted badinage but I will not stand for a concerted effort". We thought of all kinds of things to make his life difficult though an ingenious plan devised by James Wales was never carried out. This was to wire the electric heater, which Senior had wrung from an unenthusiastic bursar, to the master's seat, thus creating an electric chair. Once, however, when mayhem had again broken out, Wales did actually read the Riot Act, a copy of which he had thoughtfully obtained from HM Stationery Office.

French was in the hands of George Simmons and he encouraged us through unseens and plays with his own combination of light-hearted comment and unexpected repartee. But then one term a comparative newcomer, Frank McEachran, appeared to teach us – what? I think it must have been divinity but as all came to know as time went on, it was immaterial what Mac (later known as 'Kek') taught as it always turned out to be a study and recitation of 'Spells' – his name for wide-ranging quotations from literature, which became his hallmark, known to generations of Salopians spread over forty years; and if one was in range, one heard the oft-repeated rendering of the Horst Wessel song by the modern linguists, though the sound never seemed to reach Hardy.

In Oldham's a different House was emerging from that run by the founder. For one thing – and what an important one in the climate of the day – we began to be successful in games, with one great star, Guy Thornycroft, goalkeeper in the 1st XI, captain of fives, a punishing batsman of immense power, a left-handed slow bowler and withal one of the nicest people of whom many years later, Willie Jones – an unlikely National Service officer – would write, "Guy Thornycroft, ideal gentleman, whose charm would always draw the best from us".

Guy stood for much that was good in Oldham's, quite apart from the games field, and there were others such as Brian Inglis, who describes his misery in his first years under Oldham in his autobiography, but who added much to our lives in his latter years with his critical Irish intelligence, his wit and general ability, in contrast with, for instance, Patrick Studdert-Kennedy, who suffered under the handicap of having a brilliant father, "Woodbine Willie", famous chaplain of the War and a maverick clergyman after it. Pat bowled fast, ran fast, was not in a particularly high form and surveyed the world in a rugged four-square way which led him to be nicknamed 'Trog' (Troglodyte), which in the fashion of the day was reversed to 'Gort'. So with others of some ability participating, Oldham's won the 1st House Football cup, then all three House Fives cups (John Lee and I were the Under 16 pair), and finally at the end of the summer term of 1935, the 1st House Cricket bat – much sought after and never seen in Oldham's before. The final match lives in memory, a stern tussle with Ridgemount, then the most successful sporting house under Kitch, and we naturally owed much to Guy and to the Gort's fast bowling. But with 150 or so to get and standing at 70 for 3, Ridgemount edged nearer and nearer until some 25 only were needed with two wickets to fall. Here was my moment of glory behind the stumps. The Gort had been put on in a last attempt to win the match and, standing back, I just hung on to a catch at full stretch with the sort of dramatic dive that wicket keepers specialise in. The last man hit a four and then I caught him: we were home by sixteen runs. Hardy was writing my report that evening: "I write on the day of his famous catch". That term I played in the school 2nd XI, unusual for a boy under sixteen, but to be a wicket keeper seemed an advantage. Having been given my 2nd XI colours, I proudly wore my 2nd XI blazer – alternate blue and white stripes – with wholly conscious pride. I don't think there has ever been a garment which I was more pleased to own. Yet my great hopes in the games world were to be disappointed and I was never to win that elusive School First status, achieved by most of my friends. My contemporary Peter Blagg was both a wicket keeper and a goalkeeper of far greater skill than I, having time to get a cricket Blue at Oxford before the war took him to his death in the Burmese jungle. So 2nd XI status was to be my lot and my Joseph's coat was more than worn by the end of my third season in the 2nd XI – though our results, unbeaten for two years, were a slight consolation and I did at least score a century against Malvern 2nd XI. Nor did my keenness and enjoyment of fives take me near the school team. At least I thought I could win the hurdles in the School Sports, training hard (by the standards of the day) doing my exercises nightly in the bedroom, as I had done since Abinger days. I could twist myself into unlikely shapes, but I was just not fast enough as a sprinter; one year my friend John Pooley, with his very long legs, defeated me; and in the next year I touched the easily dislodged hurdle tops of three hurdles and was thus disqualified, the same absurd rule which had prevented my distinguished predecessor, R.M.N. Tisdall, from a world record in the Olympics of 1932, though he did at least win a gold medal. Much as I enjoyed keeping goal, I had to face the fact that others were better. Tom Taylor then ran the Football, an outstanding international player himself, and a skilled coach prone to realistic and sometimes sardonic criticism. At the beginning of one season I recollect his comment on my performance, "Charlesworth is more spectacular this season but I do not know if he is any better".

Status was, of course, absurdly important. How I would have liked to walk across the grass (a privilege), to wear a soft collar, to go to Chapel on the day of a 1st XI match in white flannels! The nearest I got to the charmed circle was to be taken to Uppingham, a two-day match, to score for the 1st XI. I was sitting with Geoffrey Lane in the bus going there. As we went through Leicester, he made the authoritative remark, "The best looking women in England live in Leicester". I was amazed by this show of sophistication and experience. No wonder he became Lord Chief Justice. Before the match, batting in the nets, Peter Blagg received a nasty blow in the abdominal region and was taken away to rest; I hardly dared to hope that this might be my big chance ... but Peter recovered.

To us in those days, the Officers Training Corps was a necessary evil to be borne with such endurance as one could summon up. Occasionally there was a boy of extreme keenness such as Ian Fraser in Tombling's, who licked his house platoon into shape with the same efficiency he was later to show as a Conservative Opposition Whip in the Commons, after a war in which he was badly wounded and taken prisoner. But normally we just got on with it, grumbling the while and hardly living up to the example of our glittering commander, Major James West, who when booted, spurred, beribboned and moustached, looked the very model of the modern Major-General which surely he would have been had he not, perhaps mistakenly, devoted himself to schoolmastering. Wonderfully pompous, James ran the Corps immaculately, earning our grudging admiration. The War was not far behind us in those days and those who had been in the trenches seemed to have a special aura about them which impressed us who were to be the participants of the next conflict, dimly to be discerned on our horizons. Thus we weekly adorned ourselves in all the panoply of battle in our First War uniforms, with long puttees, blancoed belts and peaked caps, drilling a complicated bayonet drill which included the injunction "On the command 'Fix', yer don't fix". The Sergeant Majors who instructed us in all this were the objects of affectionate mimicry: RSM Evans, badly wounded and lacking an eye, had won the Military Cross, a rare award for a Warrant Officer. He was a real disciplinarian but one experienced in the art of boy management. At the opposite desk in the Orderly Room sat C.S.M. Blud, MM, pounding away at the ancient Orderly Room typewriter, instructor of the recruits in their first stages, coach of the Bisley VIII, and a magnificent shot himself. Some incident buried in regimental history had led to a quarrel. Evans and Blud did not speak to each other except in emergency; communication took place through notes placed in each other's in-trays. Blud was theoretically, perhaps actually, related to a famous ancestor, Sir Binden Blud, C-in-C in the Punjab in the nineteenth century. (When building a new town in his day it was said that they did not know whether to call it Bludibad or Bludipore.) C.S.M. Blud's dog was called Binden and every day he and Binden walked to work past the Oldham's studies, with Blud giving the orders, "Come along Binden, one-two, one-two".

But there was a third Sergeant Major, who played a large part in my life. Sgt. Major Addison (originally Badcock but that proved difficult in the Shrewsbury OTC) ran the Band. What prompted me to become a drummer I do not know; probably the idea that in the Band one got out of things, and Patrick Day, Roger Bevan and I volunteered. So we made the evening hideous in the Armoury on practice nights, with the bugles and the big drum. But here as elsewhere, Hardy had ideas. He wanted there to be a brass band and persuaded the governors to put down £260 for a full set of instruments. On a memorable evening in 1935, twenty-three volunteers were introduced to those shining machines and, selecting one at random and deciding which end to blow and which end the noise came out, we attempted in unison the scale of C. I do not know what induced me to choose the E flat bombardon (or bass, or tuba) but that was what I landed myself with. Gradually, coached and encouraged by Sgt. Major Addison, we became a band, and played on Inspection that year after only a few months practice. To keep the enthusiasm going, which was not at all easy, half a dozen bandsmen formed a band committee of which I found myself chairman. We seemed to have very little encouragement from the authorities and the Band was entirely run by ourselves, an occupation which took much of my time. Soon we were able to march the Contingent to the railway station on Field Days. Looking back, it all seems an extraordinarily elaborate procedure. We paraded on the Site – by platoons and then by companies, then as a battalion; led by the striking figure of Major West we gave our eyes right at the War Memorial, broke step crossing the Kingsland Bridge and then marched up Pride Hill, four hundred or so strong, we in the Band straining every nerve but enjoying the fine resonance in the narrow streets where all traffic was suspended; so to entrain, travel to say Cressage, fight a battle in the fields, the tactics of which were obscure to most, discharge our blanks, charge the enemy in a final assault and be stopped by the bugle sounding 'Cease Fire', generally the signal for the discharge of volleys of unexpended blanks. So to tea and buns, the return train and, disguised as exhausted warriors daubed with camouflage cream, the march up to Kingsland, to pull through with four-by-two and on to house tea.

The annual Inspection meant standing, generally in the hot sun, for what seemed hours, waiting for some General to walk round with Major West and Major Hardy. In other days, bolder boys had played a trick or two on the somewhat wooden-headed inspecting officers. One platoon, anticipating the oft asked question, "Where do you come from?" decided that all would answer "Wigan". The first three (this was the Headroom platoon), keeping straight faces, answered "Wigan, Sir", but the strain was too much for the fourth boy; although his lips were conjuring up "Wigan", he actually said "Chester, Sir". On another occasion – in times past – the Doctor's platoon, ordered to number, smartly shouted in sequence "One-Two-Three-Four-Five-Six-Seven-Eight-Nine-Ten-Jack-Queen-King-Ace". But we, under the eye of H.H.H., attempted no such tricks. In the Band, we stood in rear until it was time to head the march past when we let fly with 'Colonel Bogey' or 'Blaze Away'. The bass was a singularly dull instrument to play, most marches allotting us no more than two notes in a bar, a perpetual pom-pom. But when there was a bass solo to enjoy we made the most of it, aided by the trombones, always the most volatile and undisciplined part of the Band, especially when John Sharp was first trombone, an actor then and ever since, later to be seen as Mr Biggins in the TV programme 'All Creatures Great and Small'. One had to admit, reluctantly, that there was a certain satisfaction in carrying out the ceremonial inspection drill with competence – every boy rock-like with arms at the 'present' – the (comparatively) straight ranks in the march past in line – the click of 400 bayonets being fixed in unison; at the end we had put on an impressive show, though how much it had to do with fighting a war was to us obscure.

However, the climax to the whole OTC year was the annual August Camp when contingents several hundred strong from seventy or eighty schools would go under canvas at Tidworth or Tweseldown or Thirsk. Again, the military content seemed small but the social impact was great. For the first time we were with hundreds of our contemporaries, in the lines, in the NAAFI, at evening concerts, playing improvised games; and in the tents, where we lay uncomfortably on our palliasses. Some schools were instantly disliked; with others, we had happy relations – I particularly remember Bradfield and Malvern in this respect. But not Repton. As we went to bed we would sometimes shout in chorus, across half a mile of intervening tents, "Good Night Bradfield" or whoever it might be. Another school of whom we thought little was Skinners. So our nightly ritual, well acquainted with the Litany as we then were, was to shout across the camp, "Good-night, Miserable Skinners", with the correct intonation. Discipline was strict in one way yet the inhibitions of life on the Site were in other ways abandoned. Cookhouse fatigue with regular soldiers was a new experience, so was communal urinating in the open buckets provided in the lines; those so inclined smoked like chimneys in the latrines – in themselves an experience in primitive living. We in the Band found ourselves popular as contingents vied for our services to march their troops across those many miles of dusty Salisbury Plain. The climax to Camp, so far as I was concerned, was the band competition. This was judged both on marching and playing. In our first year we found ourselves against, amongst others, a bagpipe band from Scotland and a drum and fife band from Ireland, beautifully turned out and, having no music to play from, marching in good order. We struggled to clean all our uniform ourselves – we had white belts and accoutrements – while other bands had everything done for them by regulars; we had no drum major and so invented one for the occasion, arming him with a 'mace' which had done duty as Prospero's wand in a recent staff play. To our great joy we were placed second. The next year we set out to win and by this time our playing and marching were really quite good. With bated breath we awaited the results: but again, "Shrewsbury, second". I was bitterly disappointed; for few things in life was I to work harder. As I turned away, David Bevan laid a heavy hand of sympathy on my shoulder, "Well done, Charlesworth, you did splendidly". It was too much; hot tears fell.

When appointed to the teaching staff of Shrewsbury, many anticipated they would remain there for their working lives. Hardy commented wryly to his governors in 1935 that only one master would retire (at the age of sixty) in the next ten years and, in theory, there would be no change of housemaster until 1945, which well illustrates how static the staffing position was. Most hoped for Houses with the status and financial security that would bring. But in addition to the housemaster barons whom Hardy sought to control, there was a rising tide of young and energetic masters, appointed in Bob Sawyer's last years or by Hardy himself. With them the senior boys had some social contact and some *rapport*, though within a formal structure. During the First War when Ronald Knox had taught for a short time at Shrewsbury, he had found teaching enormously attractive and the company of those who lived in a bachelor colony, The New House, wonderfully stimulating. He wrote in *A Spiritual Aeneid*, "I can honestly say that I never came in contact in all my life with a group of minds so original". Much of that New House tradition lived on. The doyen was K.B. Banks ('Banquo'), a man of striking appearance, very tall, very straight, with flaming red hair. He had been a naval officer and there was talk of an incident on the Clyde with a destroyer, which had led to his change of occupation. He brought a tang of the sea and the quarter deck, his voice loud enough to overcome a North Sea squall.

Alec Peterson, with original teaching methods, a man well read and original in thought, was another lively person to have on any staff and was to go on to headmasterships and then to be Director of Education at Oxford. Mike Powell had been at Cheltenham under Hardy and was to take over the rowing from Kitchin, a handsome and energetic young member of the Shrewsbury scene which he was to adorn for thirty-three years. David Bevan was to devote his life to Shrewsbury, a painstaking teacher, much imitated and much liked. And then there was, more remarkable than any, Hugh Brooke, who had come as a 'creeper' – the word then used for a man attached for a term as part of his training for the Diploma of Education. Hugh failed that particular exam, having danced at the Mayfair for the whole of the previous night but nonetheless Hardy appointed him to the permanent staff. He used to say that the first question on his history of education paper was "What influence did Roman Catholicism have on girls' schools in Mid-Wales in the 18th century?"; an unlikely story which shows how far from answering any of the questions Hugh had been. He was a cricket Blue and shortly took over the cricket from Dick Sale. He often wore the Harlequin cricket cap which well reflected his colourful personality; debonair, with his silky moustache, even exotic, his was a flamboyant contribution to the Salopian scene. His conversation was studded with Latin tags, obscure verse, terrible puns and abbreviations. It was some time before we learnt that an experience described as F.W.D. really meant Fate Worse than Death; a colleague given to pungent and verbose criticisms on the other hand was described as F.W.H. – face working horribly; while adverse conditions were "utter gloom". When umpiring he puzzled the scorers by shouting "Quattuor abs". John Kitchin – at a later period – recalls his leaving the cricket field early muttering "V.C.P." (Very Controlled Panic) and, being questioned further, "TM²" (Too Much Married).

From this lively bachelor group emerged the Suckers' League. Like the rest of the staff, the New House disliked Hardy, or at any rate affected to do so. Points in the League were scored by sucking up to Hardy. For instance:

Saying how well the School was running in His hearing	3 points
Accompanying Him to the Mission	4 points
Reminiscing with Him about Cheltenham (Mike Powell)	3 points
Playing Him at squash and letting Him win (Hugh Brooke)	5 points
Speaking to Him after Chapel	2 points

David Bevan scored eight points for asking if he might be away on a Good Friday night so that he could take his old Mother to the Messiah. It is not known who finished at the top of the League but when Peter Hawkesworth joined the New House, he threatened to win outright, by showing the book to Hardy.

Hugh Brooke used to recount that in his earliest days in the New House, he encountered Banquo in the bathroom before First Lesson. He had the temerity and audacity to say, "Good-morning, Banks", whereat a huge mottled arm shot out, seized him by the scruff of the neck, hurled him beneath the shower while the other arm switched on a Niagara of cold water. Through the thunder and swirl of the icy torrent, Hugh distinguished a whisky-laden voice roaring, "Little man, when I think it is a good morning I'll tell you. Don't you tell me". Sadly, Banquo indulged increasingly freely, a fact very obvious to boys, who would set all the form room pictures swinging before he came in and who found that, from time to time, his First Lesson was largely occupied in leaning out of the window surveying the Severn. He retired in 1939 to St Mawes where he had long kept a boat, to disappear totally for many years and to be discovered, having lost a leg, by Joe Fison, then Bishop of Salisbury, who had been taught by Banquo. Those on the staff who remembered the good companion of former days put together some money to help with his keep in his last days. At Shrewsbury he had been for some years Adjutant of the Corps and will be remembered by many in that role, roaring out orders to the contingent, apparently seven feet tall with his drawn sword, towering over James West. Somewhere about 1936, Oswald Mosley came to speak at the

Shrewsbury Music Hall and one of his remarks was much enjoyed on the Site: "Most of the troubles of this country can be traced to the Banks".

In addition to those in the New House there were other lively members of Hardy's staff – the young Alec Binney, appointed largely to teach the violin; Patrick Childs, already starting to make his great contribution with the Rover Scouts who, over the years, turned themselves into an active and enterprising climbing club; Jim Pitts-Tucker, an addition to the immensely strong classical team in which Stacy Colman made so distinguished a contribution when he had decided not to be a don or a headmaster, though he tried both. Jack Grundy was not one of my favourite masters. He taught German – he had recently written a popular book, "Brush Up Your German" – and he would allow only German to be spoken in his lessons: "Auf Deutsch!". One day he wrote on the board "365 Tage sind ein Jahr: 366 Tage sind ein Schaltjahr", and asked me what *Schaltjahr* meant. I had a blockage and simply could not see the obvious meaning which was of course a leap-year. Grundy taunted me, made everyone else laugh at me and kept at it, trying to extract – unsuccessfully – the missing word. I never forgot this humiliation – the action of the bully – and never, I hope, in my own teaching did I victimise a boy in this way.

From time to time the staff produced plays; in 1936 *The Tempest* – a splendid partnership of Barnaby and Binney as Trinculo and Stephano, but most memorable were David Bevan as Caliban and Stacy Colman as Ariel. Then in 1937 *Much Ado*, again with Binney and Barnaby as Dogberry and Verges. Then there was *Twelfth Night* where Banquo as the sea captain had the expressive first line, "This is Illyria lady...", which rolled off the alcoholic tongue with greater alliteration than Shakespeare intended. Hugh Brooke was allowed to be Valentine, a Gentleman. He cut several of his ten lines but for years afterwards would delight in repeating them meaninglessly:

> But, like a cloistress, she will veiled walk,
> And water once a day her chamber round
> With eye-offending brine...

School drama only just existed and was concentrated in "the School Play" every Speech Day. George Simmons was in charge and gave many of us our first education in drama. We who participated learnt from George and enjoyed ourselves very much – there could not be anything but laughter and light-hearted enjoyment when George was about – but our standard must have been low. Startling however, in the context of the day, was the production of *Rope* by Patrick Hamilton, hinging on a most cold-blooded murder, starting on a darkened stage with the threatening hissed line, "Put out that light", which rocked the Speech Day audience in their seats and made Hardy sit up even straighter than usual. More usual were plays of the old Aldwych type, for example *Tons of Money* and *Rookery Nook*, in which performances I had the parts played by Tom Walls. Personally, I was greatly attracted by the stage and did not then realise quite how primitive our performances were. But if there was not much drama, there was an increasing interest in music under Johnny Johnson's direction and with Hardy's encouragement. The school orchestra was fragile, although supported by adults such as Mrs Wyn Corrie and Mrs Lock (widow of a master who had the rather splendid nickname 'Jimmy Click'), and by Mitford on the bassoon, Whitfield on the violin, and Kitchin on the double bass; Kitchin then owned a baby Austin and would take his double bass from Ridgemount precariously balanced on the car roof, held in place by a nervous passenger.

The subject of compulsory attendance at Chapel has been argued about for many years. We simply accepted it as part of the system. Every day we had a short service; there were two services on Sunday. Personally I did not gain much spiritual enlightenment, though occasionally preachers stirred a chord, particularly perhaps Eric Treacy (later Bishop of Wakefield), who was then our Missioner in Liverpool and who had startling stories to tell of life in Everton; and when Moore Darling from St Chad's crossed the river he commanded the attention of all. I am not sorry to have sung a psalm every day for five years of school life, nor to have become familiar with many hymns, sung with very full congregational participation, while Hardy's reading of the Old Testament in the Authorised Version seemed simultaneously to underline both the authority of Jehovah and headmaster, as the words rolled round the Chapel walls. Chapel was of course, as most other things, a disciplinary exercise and we all sat in allotted seats, to be counted as we left the building. Not that levity was entirely absent. The organ was occasionally played by an aspiring organ student, one such was Kershaw, in Ridgemount, who managed to play a heavily disguised version of "Love is the Sweetest Thing" as a voluntary, to be questioned by Hardy afterwards as to the name of that unfamiliar piece. At Christmas as we were singing "The Holly and the Ivy", suddenly every light in Chapel went out: chaos and darkness; at length Kitchin shone a bright torch up the aisle to reveal Hardy on all fours groping for the Chancel steps. So far as I know, no culprit was found, but it must have been Kershaw, sitting as he did adjacent to the light switches.

However, Chapel in our time was dominated by a new chaplain, following the quick disappearance of Wee Wee Crosse. This was the Revd A.L.E. Hoskyns-Abrahall, a name capable of variations, one of the kinder versions being Ali Ha Ha, Laughing Water. Hoskyns had been in the navy and was a muscular Christian, rather 'higher' than was usual in Chapel, with more than a touch of emotion in his ministry, a quality of which boys are always suspicious. Richard Cobb (in *A Classical Education*) pilloried Hoskyns and was himself a sore trial to the chaplain, ringing him up in the guise of God and asking for progress reports. Nor did Hoskyns go down particularly well with some masters who preferred the well-known words of the prayers in the Prayer Book to Hoskyn's 'variants': "O Jesus, the Master Carpenter...". I had a brush with Hoskyns when in my second year I had been detected in a peccadillo which was less important than it at first seemed. Hardy had me on the mat and dealt with it but Hoskyns, not knowing this, saw the opportunity of an intimate personal talk, asked me round and began by saying "You and I, Michael, must discuss this without reservation and talk more deeply than we ever have before...". I was able to cut him off and said that the Headmaster had already dealt with it, to the Chaplain's frustrated disappointment. Good qualities as he had in many ways, Hoskyns could not get on net with many boys. I remember little of my confirmation, conducted under his guidance, with housemasters also playing a part – a role which Sopwith did not enjoy. I was confirmed by Bishop Neville Talbot, who was a colonial bishop and must have been six foot six in height. I am reminded of a remark (which I have recently read), by a Victorian headmaster: "We try to produce Christian Gentlemen for to produce Christian Boys is an obvious contradiction".

There was an atmosphere of considerable formality in Chapel, the Headmaster and Chaplain in their stalls, the choir in the seats which had come from Manchester Cathedral, Johnny Johnson on the organ, which was all the time pumped by an invisible John, the masters in their special stalls, the ladies in the south transept (the 'hen coop') in their formidable hats. Sunday chapel was a focus of the community; we discussed what happened there and took delight in the very occasional unusual happenings, as when the John failed to pump the organ and the sound died with a despairing whoosh; when a boy was prayed for, being seriously ill, a dramatic hush descended; when Geoffrey Lane, Head of School, walked out during the sermon with a many-coloured face to be sick in the bushes, it was a subject for bedroom comment that night. Sermons were generally very long – up to half an hour or more – and seldom stirred us; Hardy deployed for our benefit a gaggle of bishops, headmasters, missionaries, men from the Gold Coast and India. The themes of King, Country and Church were intermingled: "Faith, Hope and Charity: and the greatest of these is Patriotism". Apart from Hoskyns and these visitors, other members of the home team preached to us. Joe Whitfield always glared balefully at the congregation; he had one sermon (well worn) which began, "I think it was Bishop Butler who said...". After hearing this several times Jimmy Street suggested to Joe that he really ought to look it up and actually find out if it was Bishop Butler. Also on the staff was the Revd L.F. Harvey ('Len' Harvey, after a well-known boxer of the day), one of whose sermons was long remembered. At that time dayboys were not esteemed as highly as they should have been by boarders, and Len Harvey took it into his head mistakenly to preach about the condition of dayboys in the school; boarders and dayboys alike, we sat in tense and uncomfortable embarrassment. Hardy himself was somewhat prolix in the pulpit, not knowing quite when to stop.

Before I left, the Revd F.L. McCarthy joined the staff, a biologist by trade and newly ordained. Here was a man for truth, gentle, patient and intelligent; his sermons were for the VIth form and needed intellectual effort compared to the brasher and more superficial Hoskyns offerings.

What did we acquire from these many hours in Chapel? Perhaps some slight sense of the numinous; certainly a familiarity with the psalms, hymns and prayers, not least that fine school prayer from the sixteenth century – "O most merciful Father and gracious God, without whose help all those studies, and all those things which we here learn are but vain; bless we beseech thee our labours and so plentifully water the same with the dew of thy Heavenly Grace, that as we daily grow through thy Goodness in Godliness, Knowledge and Understanding, so at the last we may become fit instruments for thy Church and Commonwealth..." The advance that we made in Godliness, Knowledge and Understanding may not have been very apparent but I think it was there, at any rate with some. And if being a Christian and a member of the Church of England are not necessarily the same thing, there are many of my contemporaries, as the records show, who have worked for the Church in various lay capacities, apart from the narrow but continuous stream of those who became ordained ministers.

CHAPTER VIII

'Farewell to Severn Shore'

On banks of Thames they must not say
Severn breeds worse men than they;
And friends abroad must bear in mind
Friends at home they leave behind
                                    Housman

In some play or film, in response to her husband's suggestion that
their son should go away to a boarding school, the wife angrily replies, "I
don't want him to be bullied, beaten or buggered". As I have already
indicated, I saw little evidence of bullying, except in the form of boys
occasionally ganging up against an individual, as tends to be endemic
when children are gathered together. Nor did beating figure prominently
in Oldham's. Where it happened at all it was accepted as part of the system
and was not, at that time, a matter of abuse by those in authority. Indeed we
would have smiled at the almost hysterical antics and propaganda of
the anti-beating lobby of a more recent age. Hardy beat occasionally I
believe, though I cannot remember any occurrence myself; Sopwith, my
housemaster, never used the cane; the monitors did so sporadically, perhaps sometimes unjustly, but we stoically accepted the practice without
comment.

But what of the picture, sometimes so dramatically painted – for
example in the novels of Simon Raven – of the Public School as a hotbed of
homosexuality? I never think that the word homosexuality is really appropriate, if it is indeed true that homosexuals are so mainly through genetic
inheritance rather than made thus by experience. But that the shallow wash
of strongly developing sexuality was a constant background to our lives
was certainly so. It would be strange if in a public school of that day, where
boys were almost entirely isolated from female companionship for nine
months of the year at a time of maximum sexual development, there would
not have been a strong romantic element in boy friendships. Physical
expression was, I believe, rare but there were plenty of love-sick boys
around the Site in a tangle of friendships (or hoped-for friendships) which

were constantly evolving and dissolving. Often there was an element of adolescent idealism mixed in with the emotions. (It is interesting to reflect that in the mid-nineteenth century under Dr Kennedy, one had to pay extra for a single bed whereas a hundred years later the sharing of a bed meant immediate expulsion.) We do not use the word adolescent now – 'teenager' has supplanted it – but the strains of adolescence were considerable. There were always boys keen to talk scandal; the School Shop was a great place for mixing with others, not always so easy elsewhere without exciting comment, and sometimes 'T notes' would be passed for, it was hoped, safe delivery.

The attitude of authority in this sphere was plain. Romantic friendships, if discovered, were ruthlessly suppressed; any indulgence, however trifling, was punished, often with expulsion. Few members of staff endeavoured to understand boys' developing emotions, but adult interest could itself be unhealthy. Basil Oldham thrived on emotional drama; he was himself homosexual, probably never expressed but repressed with difficulty; in his case, as with others of the Edwardian age, his homo-sexuality, unappeased physically, found its sphere in the mystique of hardship and bodily endurance, a creed shared by Baden-Powell with his doctrine of self-mastery which could make a man proof against sexual temptation and what he called 'girlitis'. This was his philosophy for the Boy Scouts.

An unusual member of the Shrewsbury staff, Frank Barnes, was the confidante of some boys in this sphere. He liked to be called Captain Barnes, having been an officer in the Rifle Brigade, though when someone unsportingly looked up his army record he was found to be a substantive Lieutenant. A fastidious man, with a profile like General de Gaulle, his life moved in a stately and unhurried manner centred on 40 The Schools, where he shared a bachelor house and lived in unassuming luxury. His teaching was decorous and in his form room there was a ritual of boys detailed to open the door, take his books, receive his mortar board, see that chalk was available and so on. Rather like an Evelyn Waugh character, he liked to look on himself as a gentleman who, having turned to teaching, had necessarily come down in the world. He was the careers master of the day but if an enquirer said that he thought he might take up teaching, Frankie discouraged him – "such a degrading profession". He did not speak of his war service save to say that he thought the men liked to be commanded by gentlemen. He interested himself in the web of romantic friendships and encouraged boys to talk about themselves, sometimes taking them for drives in his car (called William), to explore both the Shropshire hill country and the frailties of adolescent human nature. Not surprisingly he acquired something of a reputation, as these lines from a *Wollopian* show:

> If Mr Barnes
> Were given half a charnes
> He would get 40
> The reputacion of being naughty

Or in another parody of a popular song entitled, "You must say, Yes":

> You'll go a long ride in his car
> And all he'll say is "Most bizarre",
> And if you say black's white
> He'll just say, "Quite",
> You must say, Yes.

Lionel Birch, later editor of *Picture Post* in its heyday, wrote a novel at the age of twenty entitled *Pyramid* on the theme of romantic friendships at a thinly-disguised Shrewsbury. In the introduction he writes that "all the characters and all the communities in this book are entirely fictitious" but in fact names can be accurately attached to all the characters including Frankie Barnes. The book created a scandal and was said to have been 'banned' by the school, meaning, I believe, that the school booksellers were requested not to stock it. Boys competed for copies and read it avidly.

But Frankie was uncharacteristic. Most members of the staff and certainly Sopwith, my housemaster, kept well away from boys' emotions. He was particularly keen to distance himself from Basil Oldham's sexual overdrive which had so intensified personal relations with boys, often to breaking point.

That Shrewsbury in the 1930s was an intensely male community is obvious. The ideals of late Victorian and Edwardian England were only just beginning to weaken. 'Manliness' was not a word which we, as boys, would use but, implicit or explicit, it was a quality much encouraged and sought after by such as Basil Oldham and the older generation of housemasters. In his fascinating book *Godliness and Good Learning*, David Newsome has shown how in the late nineteenth century, muscular Christianity and the cult of games had displaced the old ideals of the pursuit of academic excellence and moral fervour. The influence of Charles Kingsley and Henry Newbolt was still being felt, though at far remove, just as the *Boys Own Paper*, though in decline, highlighted Adventure and Empire, as did the novels of Henty and Percy Westerman. In his autobiography, *A Shaft of Sunlight*, Philip Mason writes of being brought up with "a strong sense of commitment to duties, usually unpleasant and often dangerous – naval stories by Bartimeus and Taffrail, whose characters were always ending their leave and going off to the China station. Deep in middle class culture lay this sense of fate, of a real life of harsh male endeavour which was punctuated by a dream life of happiness and affection. The feeling that it was right to march stiff-lipped towards high adventure or a firing party, a throne or a scaffold, ran through all the books we read, *The Prisoner of Zenda* as well as *The Thirty Nine Steps*".

Manliness, Duty, Patriotism, Loyalty – these were the ideals set before us to which we reacted with some scepticism, especially perhaps in that redoubt of radicalism, Murray Senior's History Side. So emotions were contained and controlled, certainly never expressed in public for fear of one's being thought effeminate, hence our furtive and somewhat crude ventures into romance. Not that we had much time to pursue these forbidden paths, bound in as we were by the daily routine of a highly organised strenuous life, an unspoken comment on the dangers which leisure might bring. When Moberley, headmaster of Winchester in the nineteenth century, referred to "idle boys" he meant those who spent time playing cricket; when Warre, headmaster of Eton in the early twentieth century, spoke of "idle boys" he meant those not playing cricket. That a boy needs solitude and a sense of space in order to grow is an idea which a schoolmaster often finds difficult to accept.

Yet in his book *The Edge of Paradise* about Arthur Benson, David Newsome expresses a view which should not be met with scepticism or cynicism, though many might react in that way:

> Love is a noble passion; and no less noble for being the bond which may unite two persons of the same sex or of different ages. Such love might, at certain stages of history or civilisation, be considered unconventional but in itself is neither unnatural or immoral. Indeed the propensity to feel such a love, in a schoolmaster or a don, can often be the particular gift which he brings to his calling; and if such emotion were branded as ignoble or base, then it would remove from such professions the inner commitment or vocation which so often inspires them.

After a dramatic series of events had led Basil Oldham to resign from his housemastership in 1932 with a 'breakdown', he had established himself in a house on Kennedy Road, and, as I have already said, was keen to keep in touch with his old House. During my school years, I was the recipient of invitations to tea or to supper; I don't know why I, more than others, was thus favoured but I became a frequent visitor to that extraordinary study, filled to overflowing with books, ornaments, mementoes, *objets d'art* and, perched on the massive iron fender which successfully prevented any heat from the coal fire reaching his visitors, a mass of papers which were ultimately to result in Basil's learned books on bindings, laboriously written in his miniature handwriting. I once counted the pictures, calendars, maps, and photographs on the walls; they amounted to more than a hundred. On the mantelpiece were photographs of 'his' boys – a *corps d'élite* to which in due time I was myself added. It must have been irritating, to say the least, for Sopwith to see boys wending their way across the Common to receive J.B.O.'s hospitality, tacking back at a late hour full of sherry, claret and port. How Basil himself, had he still been housemaster, would have hated it! But he convinced himself that the role of 'step-housemaster' was a valid one and that there were things which a boy might tell him which he could not tell his housemaster.... So talk often ran into intensely personal channels in which I fought a dogged rearguard action of no comment.

After my final term, I stayed with Basil for the Shrewsbury Flower Show. His hospitality was, as always, generous, but there were hazards, one being the early morning cold bath, his use of the bathroom being carefully synchronised with mine. In the Quarry we listened to the bands, for by this time I had become a keen and knowledgeable bandsman and had started to learn the trumpet as an alternative to the bass. One day, dramatically, Basil asked me to come up to my bedroom. I do not quite know what I feared but there revealed on the bed lay a bright new trumpet which was Basil's farewell present to me. Soon after leaving I received one of the letters which he had been wont to write to 'his' boys. It ran to 3,000 words and had taken him five hours to write. Contained in it was his whole philosophy; emphasis on duty to others, high moral standards, the Englishman's creed of the stiff upper lip and *mens sana in corpore sano*; also, much emphasised, the temptations of women, of drink and of debt. How paradoxical that Basil should constantly harp on these themes, a man who knew nothing of women (his oft-repeated assertion, "I never had a woman" became a catch phrase in Oldham's), who was wholly dependent on whisky and who was in debt for almost all his life. Nevertheless I was grateful to Basil for generous hospitality, for the acquisition of much arcane knowledge, and for placing before me high ideals, unwilling though I was to accept them for myself and wrapped up as they were in verbiage which had a comical aspect. I became, as I believe, a good imitator of his speech and even today, on meeting an old member of the House, will easily drift into Oldhamese. I and a few others served as substitutes for his own boys whom he missed deeply and on us – his 'step-children' – he fastened those emotions, so deep and so frustrated which had been concentrated on the boys in his House. In the words of Sir Shane Leslie, "He loved the soft clay of boyhood, fresh from the mysterious and unaccountable potter, who planted the seed of such different flowers in the same-sized pots".

In my case however, at the age of eighteen, the soft clay of boyhood was hardening into something firmer as I reached my last term which was one of strenuous activity. Sopwith wrote on my report, "I doubt if any boy in the School has had a busier term in and out of school activities". The Band, my only really solid contribution to Shrewsbury, had reached a high point. We played on Speech Day, in our white flannels and straw hats. Hardy described us, with some poetic exaggeration, as "clothed in white samite, mystic, wonderful". At Camp we were asked to play in the officers' mess. I even gained a mention in Hardy's annual report to the governors. "In Camp, the Band covered itself with glory and was in demand by other battalions than our own for enlivening marches, and, though only two years old, was honoured by being asked to play one night at Mess, a task which I thought they performed admirably. Their success has been due to the remarkable enthusiasm and enterprise of one particular boy, M.L. Charlesworth, who deserves special mention". To my astonishment and pleasure, Hardy made me a praepostor for the last three weeks of the summer term so for a few days at least I was a 'tweak'!

Hardy himself had now had five years in office. Still unpopular with many of the staff, he was to us what one might expect a headmaster to be. As we became more senior, we penetrated the stern facade to the man within. On occasion I was asked to Kingsland House to enjoy the warm hospitality which was always in evidence there; and to play tennis with Hardy himself, a rather angular mover but an accurate striker of the ball; he did not bend easily and expected his partner to do much of the running. (He had a peculiar method of mounting his bicycle, using the step on the back axle to mount from the rear; rumour – quite untrue – said that he had been shot up in unmentionable places in the War).

In many ways Hardy might be well satisfied with his work thus far. The housemasters had been tamed; the school was full of boys, the highest total in his time being 539 in 1936; finances were on a sounder footing, enabling him to plan the erection of both a science building and a gymnasium; the Bursar had made a great difference to the administration; and, despite some adverse passages in the inspection report of 1935, 1936 saw eighteen awards to the Universities and forty-eight Higher Certificates – many more, for instance, than at Uppingham, Rugby or Malvern. He himself had been elected chairman of the Headmasters Conference. Hardy would much have liked to create the post of Second Master but he found no one on the staff whom he thought suitable for that position. So he had to put up with the housemasters he had and to comfort himself with the obvious energy shown by his own successful appointments. These men had not known the Sawyer regime and were content to accept Hardy as he was. Sporadic sniping came from Basil Oldham on the flank, working hard in the Library, largely unappreciated and for the nominal reward of £100 a year. When he asked the governors to give financial help to publish his work of very considerable scholarship on the bindings in the Library, they refused outright, only to receive the waspish response, "... I take it that you would raise no objection if it were produced entirely at the Librarian's loss".

People who have written about life in Public Schools seem to me to fall into two categories: those who thoroughly enjoyed the experience and were successful, generally in the field of sport, often academically undistinguished, recalling deeds of bravado, sporting feats and lots of jolly fun in the tradition caricatured by Harry Wharton and Billy Bunter at Greyfriars; and those who castigate the establishments which they hated and who dwell on beating and bullying, prejudiced attitudes, snobbery and philistinism, this latter group generally consisting of those who are articulate, artistic or literary. For me and perhaps for many, however, it was not a life of extremes; we accepted (perhaps too unquestioningly) the life which we had and we got out of it what we could.

That my education was limited is obvious: no science, no art and little music; minimal contact with 'normal' life outside the Site; no girls; bound into a tight social structure, deviation from which was not encouraged, living a communal life in which everybody did everything and choice was limited. Yet I valued much the guidance and later friendship of my urbane and civilised housemaster Sopwith; the teaching of Murray Senior, intellectually sharp, wide ranging and challenging; the contact with other members of the staff like Hugh Brooke and George Simmons who came more than half-way across the gap which then separated the teachers and the taught; being within the 'dome of consciousness' of McEachran; and the occasional contact with such as Jimmy Street, 'Kitch', Dick Sale and others. I do not think it is merely nostalgic distortion which suggests that they were a genuinely interesting and diverse body amongst whom to spend one's growing years. In a *Wollopian* produced in my last term, a scurrilous mock Fasti (calendar) ends with this entry:

> 27th July. Term ends.
> Work begins on the History Side.
> Housemasters leave for Bude and Harlech.
> Boys superannuated leave for good.
> Junior Masters leave for the Spanish Civil War.

And indeed to Barcelona went McEachran and one or two others, though what contribution they made to the Republican side is not recorded. Mac always had a habit of hitching his left shoulder, perhaps acquired in attempting to keep in place his ever lagging gown. A splendid boy rumour, which survived to the end of his days, had it that the habit came from hitching his rifle over his shoulder in the Spanish Civil War.

As a games player I naturally enjoyed all that Shrewsbury had to offer, even though disappointed in my ambition to attain the higher reaches; but there were some good moments in the plethora of inter-house matches, which took place on the Common or in the fives courts, then still guarded by the German guns captured in the Great War. There were also the regular school occasions which stay in the memory, bumping races on the river with every boy on the bank supporting his house boat; Speech Day with its formality, dignity, and deadly oratory; plays on the Alington Hall stage (I think I can claim to have faced an audience there in more capacities than anyone else in the school's history); the whole school watching school cricket or football matches, no doubt a waste of time for many but creating an exciting atmosphere; our domestic productions in Oldham's, dramatic performances which we thought stunningly funny; Bump Supper, at one of which I made my first public speech; and of course the Band, in whose evolution I had taken a leading part. Memory also retains country expeditions (we all knew our Housman), especially one in which we rode on the 'Criggion Comet' on the old 'Pots' railway line in its last days; and some historical occasions – learning to reverse arms before parading in the town on the death of King George V; being present again in uniform at the proclamation of the Abdication where the reader in the Square stumbled on the word 'abdication' and turned it into 'abduction', which was perhaps fair comment; the opening of the A5 by-pass by Princess Mary, a singularly dull occasion at which we lined the road and dutifully took off our straw hats as she drove past in her Daimler at 20 m.p.h.; the whole school going to see *Comus* in Ludlow Castle and the realisation that Milton was not such a dull old stick after all, as those splendid cadences bounced round the castle walls.

But more than anything I suppose, it was the many friendships I made which commend schooldays to me. It was perhaps rare, given the hierarchical structure, for boys of different ages to know each other so well as we did in Oldham's. Even as a doul I felt I was on close terms with the monitors; and when I was briefly a praepostor in all my supposed glory – was there ever again to be a position in which one exercised such complete power? – I knew well those at the bottom of the pyramid. Whatever the system under which one lives, it is the people who make or mar. I remember sitting in Headroom (the monitors' room in Oldham's) one winter evening and thinking that in many ways I was fortunate: my fellow monitors were good friends, our wind-up gramophone was playing *Night and Day*, later we would listen to Henry Hall on our battery-driven wireless, two Eton-collared douls were making toast in front of a roaring fire, from the walls looked down our predecessors in their regimented groups, over the fireplace was a miniature statue of King Arthur, given for some obscure reason by Archdeacon Oldham in 1911, and on the wall a small glass frame enclosed 'the first sod', cut by Oldham when the House was built – and periodically changed by succeeding generations – all these the symbols of a continuing, comforting and supportive environment. Soon the familiar rhythm would unfold – call-over, tea, top schools, dicks, and bed at 10.00 p.m. followed by uninhibited talk until sleep prevailed.

For five years, from 1934 to 1939, a group of Oldham's boys met in the holidays for a summer camp of a fairly shambolic nature, driving off in a variety of old cars (one could buy a decent runner for £25) to Dorset, Cornwall or Wales; twice we canoed down the Wye from Hay to Chepstow, using the Thornycrofts' lovely house overlooking the Wye outside Hereford as our headquarters. To these came Grey Thornycroft, who became an engineer at Loughborough, his brother Guy and Norman Field, who both entered the regular Army in which Lionel Parsons was already commissioned into Probyn's Horse in India (and what a *frisson* went round when we heard he had been wounded on the NW Frontier). Tony Howarth and Tom Ealand were on their way to becoming doctors as were John Ferguson and A.J.D. Rowlands (always known as 'the Brand' from a well-known advertisement for Monkey Brand soap); Rowley and James Hill were at the earlier camps, both destined to be parsons; John Lee, Brian Inglis and I were undergraduates and John Vaisey, with his attractive and stimulating personality, was prep-schoolmastering at Packwood. We were curiously innocent by the standards of today: a few smoked but we were more drawn to ice-cream sodas than beer; we did not find it odd that there were no girls; our occupations were fishing and shooting, walking and swimming; and never to be forgotten rabbit hunts at night when Grey would drive his Lagonda with full headlights across a field and we would spread out with clubs and kill rabbits by the dozen, a pastime that now slightly shocks me but which we all enjoyed more than did the poor old Lagonda. Our last camp on the Wye was only a few days before the declaration of war but the shadows lay lightly on us. It would not be very long before John Vaisey's bomber failed to return, before Grey was destroyed by a mine in North Africa and John Lee, after a brilliant career as a fighting soldier, was killed at Anzio. Talking to old Colonel Thornycroft, a First War veteran, at the conclusion of that camp, I remember making some brash and naive remark about war being an exciting challenge. He looked at me sadly. "If you've seen one war, Michael, you don't want to see another". I thought of that remark several years later. Of the five Thornycroft children, two boys had by then been killed, one was a POW and Guy was in the front line in Normandy; and Patricia had contracted a marriage which was in trouble. One of the happiest families I had known, whose hospitality I had so often enjoyed, was thus shattered.

My father's school bill at the end of my last term, summer 1937, was £72.10.6d. Value for money as far as I was concerned. I had, I suppose, learned some of the traditional things that a boarding school stands for: capacity to look after oneself, how to live with others and some idea of social responsibility. But beyond these things Shrewsbury had given me confidence and had given me friends. Memory tends to be selective. For those who enjoyed school, the bad things fade; for those who disliked it, sufferings become exaggerated with time. Most of school life is very

Father and me

Mother

Abinger Hill

Abinger Hill School 1932. M.L.C. (centre) sits between Henry Brereton (left) and James and Jo Harrison (right)

Oldham's 1937. S.S. Sopwith with monitors (sitting) left to right: James Arkle, Roger Bevan, John Lee, John Ferguson, S.S. Sopwith, M.I.C., Patrick Day, Peter Fowler

Oojah – my first car

My Talbot 10. Brother Richard at the wheel

ordinary and very dull. The sheer ordinariness of it all is shown to good effect in the *Diaries* of W.F. Ewbank (Ridgemount 1931–36), later Archdeacon of Carlisle, to which should be referred the enquirer as to what life was really like in the old-style Public School. Yet I can echo to some degree the words of Lionel Birch, written in later life when he was Mandrake in *The Sunday Telegraph*. ''. . . Mandrake was educated by, with, for, and, above all, in spite of that distractingly beautiful river at Shrewsbury. To Neville Cardus, for instance, the school Site was, quite simply, Arcadia. I, who was educated in classics, cricket and friendship at Shrewsbury between the wars, know what Cardus meant. I suppose there must be hundreds of people like me, who once studied the classics and to whom, like me, not more than one solitary line of Latin or Greek now remains. My own surviving line that has stayed with me through a very up-and-down life, happens to be in Latin: 'Et ego in Arcadia vixi'. I too have lived in Arcadia''.

CHAPTER IX

Home

The Youth, who daily further
From the East must travel
Still is Nature's priest,
And by the vision splendid
Is on his way attended;
                    Wordsworth

In my Abinger and Shrewsbury years, home naturally became more
remote but remained nonetheless much valued. When I left school my
father was seventy-two and my mother sixty – both quite 'old' considering
my own age, though neither of them suffered from any particular ills apart
from my mother's ongoing fits of depression with which she wrestled
unsuccessfully. How fortunate that this was the age – the last age – of
plentiful domestic labour. In 1932 when replacing a housemaid there were
no fewer than twelve to be interviewed. My father was happy in his narrow
domestic field of watching cricket and football, playing bridge, driving the
car, going to the club and enjoying the development of his children's
careers. He still retained something of his Yorkshire background and the
habits of his youth. He scorned the 'new' fashion of pyjamas and wore
nightshirts; he always wore boots. Strongly conservative in his instincts, he
was also Conservative politically, being a strong supporter of Baldwin.
"That man", he said to me once, "exactly represents all that I believe in and
feel", a sentiment shared by a solid body of English men and women which
made Baldwin, in Churchill's words, "the most formidable politician I
have ever known".

My mother, in her spells of restless energy, continued to play a major
part in the Maternity and Child Welfare world, both locally and in London.
It was with pride one day that I saw her pictured in the *Daily Pictorial*,
receiving the Astor Shield from Lady Astor, a trophy awarded (so far as I
remember) to the outstanding infant welfare centre. She was frequently in
London with her headquarters at the English Speaking Union, seeing plays
and attending meetings and conferences organised by such as the Rational-
ist Press. She travelled abroad, sometimes taking the older children and

sometimes with fellow freethinkers on some sociological expedition. My father used to retreat to Harrogate and see his Yorkshire relations on such occasions. Although there was discussion about moving house to somewhere in the country, a move which my mother ardently desired, my father's dislike of change prevailed. The house had some money spent on it. In 1932 electric light was installed and in 1936 certain rooms were altered and enlarged, my mother having met (on one of her tours) a 'modern' architect, Mr Basil Ward.

When my brother Richard left Oxford, he became a Traffic Apprentice on the London, Midland and Scottish Railway so the 1930s for him were a succession of railway jobs – at Tring, Wolverhampton and Preston – as he climbed the first steps in the hierarchy. At Oxford he had failed to marry Freda, his constant girlfriend, to her disappointment, and she married someone else. A greater power of decision would have saved much later pain. Freda divorced her husband and married Richard, at long last, in 1950. After Cambridge, Olive essayed to go into the social service field and was for some time in Bermondsey at what used to be called a Settlement, and later in a similar setting in Birmingham. She had the right instincts for this work but lacking confidence, particularly in meeting all sorts of conditions of men and women, she was never really happy and used to suffer from what was then called ' nerves', perhaps an inherited trait?

Being very short of relatives, there was little family visiting except rarely to the Yorkshire aunts, and many visits to and from Aunt May, my mother's elder sister. Her first marriage to a member of the Gurney family had lasted only four months before her husband's sudden illness and death. She married again in 1928, when she was fifty-three, but her husband, Dr Quartley, died after eighteen months of married life. Settled at Forest Row in Sussex, in her widowed state, she maintained an old-fashioned life style in a comfortable house, with a cook and housemaid (who were sisters), a gardener and a Rolls Royce and chauffeur. Having inherited some of the Noakes family money and, presumably, inherited from her two short-lived husbands, she was well off. I enjoyed her visits to Abinger as she swept up the drive in the Rolls. May and my mother were constantly sparring, May quick to sense imagined slights. Temperamentally different as they were, however, family ties bound them together in constant communication.

The 1930s decade is often decried and remembered for the great slump of 1930–32, unemployment and the misery of life in what an unimaginative government called 'The Depressed Areas'. But to a middle class boy from a reasonably prosperous family, life had much to offer. There was indeed the growing shadow of Nazi Germany but I cannot remember being unduly depressed about that. The value of money remained constant, indeed prices if anything went down; Woolworth's sold a wide range of goods for sixpence. After 1935 I had an allowance of £50 per annum which well covered my expenditure on clothes, travel and amusements. My first car, a splendid open bull-nosed Morris, said to be one of the first MGs, I bought from John Vaisey for £5 and after a year or two re-sold for £2.10s. A railway ticket to Austria cost £5, a gallon of petrol about one shilling.

Our pleasures were unsophisticated. Although my hut in the garden took less of my time as the years progressed, home and all that it held was always central. Our rough-haired terrier Cracker was delirious with delight when I returned for the holidays. For years I was a keen cyclist on my Raleigh. At the age of fifteen, sitting in boredom in Hans Pendlebury's classroom, I used to plan a cycle tour with the aid of a map on the classroom wall and on one holiday when we stayed at Barton-on-Sea, I returned from Hampshire by a circuitous route through Somerset and the Cheddar Gorge, Salisbury, Gloucester and Stratford. On the last day I covered 100 miles, arriving at midnight and sleeping in my hut so as not to disturb the family. The fact that a fifteen-year-old boy, alone, sleeping in various cheap Cyclist Touring Club hostels, could safely cycle for several hundred miles makes its own comment on the roads and the security of those days. In the garden we used to play endless games of croquet, much enjoyed by Mother, and strenuous deck tennis, perhaps the only game at which I was really quite good. (The championships of two P & O ships lay ahead!)

From an early age I was frequently with my father at the county ground, watching Northamptonshire play cricket, a painful experience for the club were permanently bottom of the county table and at one time went for three seasons without a win. Those were the days when amateurs were described as 'Mr' on the score card and the dominating influence in Northamptonshire during the 1930s was Mr V.W.C. Jupp, a friend of my father's, Captain and Secretary, an attacking batsman and spin bowler, eccentric in his behaviour, a short hairy man with long arms. Juppy was a controversial figure in Northampton but my father always stood by him even when he had to go, briefly, to prison for dangerous driving. His great day was in 1930 when the Australians visited the county ground. Before television, the actual sight of these great men – Woodfull, Bradman, McCabe, Grimmett – was to me wildly exciting, but nothing could be more thrilling than the match itself. Northamptonshire made a respectable 249, with the two best batsman, Bakewell and Jack Timms, sharing a prolific partnership, but the sensation was the dismissal of this fine unbeaten Australian side for 93. Caught on a wet wicket, Jupp spun them out, taking 6 for 32. The second innings was a different story with Australia well in command, but for the weakest county to make them follow on was unthinkable; Woodfull sat next to my father at lunch and was like a bear with a sore head. At a county match against Nottingham I met the great George Gunn who told me that he thought wicket keepers should be paid double.

During that match I saw nine runs scored off one ball: the batsman played it to mid-wicket and ran two; the throw was wild and no one backed up; the ball seemed to be going to the boundary and cover did not bother to chase it; it stopped a foot short and to the cries of the crowd, cover – who was Jack Timms – hared after it and threw so wildly and hard that the ball went for four on the far side of the field.

How important they were to me, all those forgotten Northants crick-eters! Bakewell, who played for England, the best close catcher in the country, Jack Timms with immaculate Brylcreamed hair and a scorching off-drive, the artisan pros like Bellamy the wicket keeper, Thomas the stock bowler, Frank Woolley's brother Claude, the mainstay of the batting for years, young Partridge, who bowled incessantly for many years and, for a time, the New Zealand spinner, W.E. Merrett, who used to coach me in my wicket keeping. Only sometimes present was the brilliant but tempera-mental fast left-hand bowler Nobby Clark, with an uncertain temper and bouts of insubordination, which caused him at one time to be banished to the Lancashire League; but he was a marvellous bowler to watch with his high swinging action and his ability to straighten the ball off the seam. How fervently I supported this indifferent side! How many hours I spent at the county ground, watching the great ones of the day – Hobbs, Sutcliffe, Larwood, Hammond, Duleepsinjhi and so many more. Occasionally we would go to a Test Match; I recollect watching Ponsford and Woodfull making an immense total at Lords; and I was present at the Oval to see Hutton complete his 364, the highest Test score at that time.

In the winter it was either rugger with the 'Saints' – Northampton played in the part of the town known as St James' End – or soccer with North-ampton Town, generally in the lower reaches of the old Third Division South, but given to occasional Cup runs which generated vast excitement. The 'Saints' on the other hand were among the best in the land, at one time boasting three or more members of the England side – Longland in the front row, Tom Harris in the second and Billy Weston (one of my father's old pupils) as flanker. To Twickenham we went from time to time, the finest match in my experience being the defeat of the All Blacks by England in 1936, the match always remembered for Obolensky's try; we were in the North Stand and I can still see Obolensky receiving the ball deep on one side of the field and threading his way through the entire All Black side to score in the opposite corner. On the other wing was Hal Sever, the only Old Salopian to play rugby for England, with whom I was to play some Saracens cricket at a later stage.

There were occasional ventures to London to see plays or to accompany my mother and sister in shopping expeditions to which they were prone. Once I went to compete over the hurdles at the Public Schools Sports at the White City stadium, an exciting but for me unsuccessful occasion. In 1936

Guy Thornycroft, John Lee and I went to play fives in the Public Schools
Fives tournament at Queen's Club. We stayed in a boarding house in
Notting Hill, I – the organiser – having manoeuvred the landlady by post
from charging 6/- B & B to 4/6d (23p) for which we had a room with a
double bed and a folding camp bed. It was the first time we had been free
'on the town' and our fives suffered as a result of staying up late to see a
different show every night, the most memorable being *Jill Darling* with
Arthur Riscoe, a very young John Mills and Frances Day; the tunes are with
me still. On the Saturday we saw the Boat Race in the morning, and Arsenal
in the afternoon.

The theatre then seemed to me to have a brilliance which I have never
found again. The classics flourished at the Old Vic and sometimes in the
West End, but it was the great age of the drawing room comedy often with
the almost obligatory French windows, cigarette box, telephone and drinks
tray, all to be seen as the curtain rose on Act I. In their prime were Gielgud,
Olivier, Peggy Ashcroft, Edith Evans, Sybil Thorndike, the Lunts; and no
star shone more brightly than that of Noel Coward with his mildly dissol-
ute plays like *The Vortex* and *Design for Living*, which amused and gently
shocked society. *Cavalcade* was for me a major dramatic experience, seen at
the age of twelve; I do not think I have ever seen a production which
affected me more or an English audience so deeply moved. We read avidly
the reviews of James Agate, W.A. Darlington, J.C. Trewin and Ivor Brown,
and decided what to go and see in the West End, choosing between
Bernard Shaw, Agatha Christie, John Van Druten, James Bridie, J.B. Priest-
ley and others; or we could go to the Palladium to see the Crazy Gang or to
the Aldwych for the latest Ben Travers farce with those familiar names –
Tom Walls, Ralph Lynn, Winifred Shotter, Robertson Hare and Mary
Brough. The plays of the 1930s and the general proscenium arch style were
widely derided twenty-five years later when the avant garde of Osborne,
Wesker, Brecht and Beckett finally killed off the French windows and
retired Brigadiers as the working-class protagonists with sociological
messages took over and denim replaced dinner jacket on the bare open
stage. A new brand of actor, with headquarters at George Devine's Royal
Court, swept away romance and farce alike, as the Method took over. But
for me those ridiculed plays of the 1930s and 1940s have never been
replaced by anything so enjoyable.

At home my family were great supporters of the local repertory company, in its charming Victorian theatre, which flourished, though often on
the edge of bankruptcy, with a different play a week for years on end.
Uncritical as I then was, the standard of acting seemed high and the
productions as polished as was possible, given the rehearsal time available;
and the Rep had one great asset, the scenic designer, Osborne Robinson, a
local artist full of original ideas and technical brilliance. A family friend,

Tom Robinson, was content to work in Northampton all his life and is rightly commemorated in the local art gallery. He did some work at Stratford but was not sympathetic to the ideas of Iden Payne, director at the Memorial Theatre, whose sets – according to Tom – were fussy, sombre and cumbered in contrast with the clean lines and uncluttered space which Tom sought, and which were so strikingly displayed in Kommissarjevsky's remarkable Stratford productions. Of those who acted at the Rep in the 1930s, Noel Howlett, Max Adrian, Curigwen Lewis and Vivienne Bennett went on to the West End, while Sarah Churchill, Winston's daughter, and Errol Flynn were notable figures though indifferent actors.

In these years the theatre became very much part of my life and part of me yearned to 'go on the stage' although I knew in my heart that my own performances, both at Shrewsbury and later at Oxford, were mediocre. Fortunately the war disposed of any possible decision which I might conceivably have made in this direction. These too were the great days of the cinema with a choice of half a dozen films to go to every week in Northampton, from Fred Astaire and Ginger Rogers to my great heroes, the Marx Brothers, each of whose films I must have seen a dozen times and would go to see again tomorrow.

In 1934 my mother noted in her diary that I had said, "I don't like parties; there are always boys there whom Mother would like me to know". Although secure in my strong Salopian friendships, I was wary of social occasions and avoided them where I could. When I was eight or nine I had become a Gugnunc – a club organised by Uncle Dick of the *Daily Mirror*, then the patron of the cartoon figures Pip, Squeak and Wilfred. Gugnuncs had a badge, an anthem and passwords. "Ick Ick pahboo" was to be answered by "Goo Goo pahnunc". Once I tried this on a boy on Brighton Pier who was wearing the badge, who answered correctly; we stared at each other in mutual embarrassment, not knowing what to say next – and fled. When I was about sixteen my mother, although very far from being a snob, was keen that I should go to parties, meet girls and generally grow up. She worked in infant welfare with Lady Henley of Watford Court (the name is still familiar as a service station on the M1) and accepted on my behalf an invitation to a New Year's fancy-dress dance in the Henleys' party. I was resentful and petrified, but to it I had to go, knowing no one, with only a rudimentary knowledge of dancing and dressed as a Turk. It was a miserable evening but a photograph of the party appeared in the *Tatler* and I garnered modest fame at school, never revealing what a dreadful experience it had been. My mother also knew the Spencers through her welfare work so to Althorp I went on several occasions, dining rather grandly and playing games but almost totally tongue-tied. At a dance there I remember desperately looking round the room wondering whom to ask to dance, and lighted on an amply-bosomed middle aged lady who I thought would be safe, only to have her react by saying that she would introduce me to one of 'the girlies' who thus had to suffer my clumsy monosyllabic conversation. Except on safe social ground either at home or with my school friends, I continued to tread a lone path, happy with books as companions, with music both classical and jazz – or 'swing' as we were beginning to say. There was also the pleasure of motoring – and it was a real pleasure when there was a tenth of the cars on the road that there are today. I had passed my driving test (it had quite recently been instituted) without difficulty; a more relaxed procedure than now. "Would your father like to come too?" said the examiner. I failed to back into the appropriate space but "Do have another try" he said. So I was able to drive the family Rover and later a succession of my own cheap bangers.

Family holidays were beginning to peter out as we tended to make our own separate arrangements but one summer we had a pleasant time at Portmeirion, then in its early stages, meeting Clough and Annabel Williams Ellis and interesting guests – Bertrand Russell, H.G. Wells and Gerald du Maurier. Aunt May twice took me to Glyndebourne in those days when white tie and tails were obligatory; going through a gate in the interval, I encountered a distinguished looking man approaching from the other side. "After you, Sir", I said. "Thank you very much", he replied. So ended my conversation with Sir Henry Wood. Twice Richard and I went to Austria to walk in the mountains and swim in the lakes. A train ticket to Vienna then cost £5. It was the time of the Anschluss, Austrian Nazis being recognisable by their white stockings. We heard "Heil Hitler" in the town streets but "Gruss Gott" up in the hills. A now forgotten English diplomat, Lord Runciman, was endeavouring to use his good offices on behalf of Neville Chamberlain which gave rise to a little rhyme:

> Wir brauchen keinen Weinachtsmann
> Wir haben unseren Runciman
> (We do not need Father Christmas, we have our Runciman).

By the time I was seventeen or so, my brother and I had become good friends and I had lost the 'little brother' status. We played squash and tennis; we walked; we sailed, on one occasion chartering a yacht on the west coast of Scotland together with John and Sam Malins, not a complete success as our hired skipper proved to be an explosive Scots-Irish mixture, not easy to control save when lubricated.

So for me life in the 1930s, my teenage years, was enjoyable; unemployment remained high, Hitler might threaten, there were the usual growing up tensions and uncertainties but I was lucky enough to rest on the secure foundations of Northampton and Shrewsbury – and now Oxford.

CHAPTER X

Magdalen

I have seen no place by inland brook
Hill-top, or plain, or trim arcaded bowers,
That carries age so nobly in its look
As Oxford with the sun upon her towers.

F.W. Faber

Fifty years after my father, I went up to Magdalen College, Oxford, in October 1937, when undergraduates were not yet students, wirelesses not yet radios and adolescents not yet teenagers. The formal social structure in which my father lived had long disappeared and the post-war Oxford bags and plus fours generation had introduced a more relaxed style (personified by the Prince of Wales during his unfruitful stay at Magdalen), but we were still constrained by a set of rules which the Second War would sweep away. Pubs were out of bounds, gowns had to be worn in the city in the evenings, hall breakfast was compulsory on four days a week, all had to be in college by midnight, weekend leave was granted grudgingly once a term, musical instruments were restricted to certain hours and "Undergraduates who are members of the Church of England are expected to attend Chapel at least once on Sunday". But to us, straight from the heavily supervised life of a boarding school, these restrictions did not seem unreasonable. We circumvented them when necessary (there was a regular route for climbing in late at night over the wall into our deer park) and otherwise lived happily within them. It simply did not occur to us to protest and demonstrate and confront authority as did a later generation. We were glad to enjoy all that Oxford had to offer on her own terms, as we cycled to our lectures through streets not yet thronged with traffic, wearing our sports jackets and ties, gowns flying in the wind.

I settled comfortably into my rooms (sitting room and bedroom – no bedsits in those days) in St Swithin's Quad, but to tell the truth my heart was still too much at Shrewsbury to enter fully into undergraduate life. Already at Magdalen was Brian Inglis, who was partly responsible for my being there, now very much at home in the college, sophisticated and sceptical in his Irish way. Going up with me were John Lee and Patrick Day, both from Oldham's. Magdalen undergraduates were mostly from the public schools but the dons of the day had a leftward tendency, seeking to attract 'the cream of the grammar schools'. ("More artificial milk than cream" as one tartly commented.) By the standards of that time we were a large college, perhaps 180 in all, consisting of some scholars but mostly of commoners paying for the privilege of being there. My first term battels came to £60. With an allowance from my parents of £300 p.a. and with a very economical attitude, I even managed to buy a dinner jacket and tails from Walters at 10 The Turl for £25 and still keep financially afloat. My neighbour Philip Profumo lived on a rather different plane as I deduced from the profusion of footwear which he put out for our scout to clean, ranging from hunting boots through golf brogues to patent leather evening shoes.

I suppose that it was the lack of structure that I found difficult. Mostly one's time was one's own, in a way enjoyable but also disorientating. There was the weekly tutorial; there were lectures to be attended, though only if one felt so inclined; games organisation depended on the relevant secretary and though enjoyable, lacked competitive edge. And then there were the dons. How did one treat them? Were they senior schoolmasters? Did one say 'Mr'? Christian names seemed too familiar. I was taught initially by Stephen Lee, already known to me as John's father, one of the politest and most considerate of men, perhaps more a schoolmaster than a don. All the dogsbody jobs in the college came his way as he was too nice to refuse. Very different was Bruce Macfarlane, a medieval scholar of massive erudition, in whose towering intellectual presence I felt wholly inadequate as I offered my puny essay on the 'Power of the Papacy in the 12th Century', while he stroked his cat Stubbs, who clearly shared his master's disdain. The President of the college was George Gordon, as big a snob as Sir Herbert Warren had been in my father's day, and remote from the ordinary untitled undistinguished undergraduate.

But there was one don who was exceptional in that he was really interested in the ordinary run of undergraduates. The Dean of Divinity, Adam Fox, became a lifelong friend – and long indeed was his life as he died in his ninety-fourth year. Adam had been Warden of Radley for a time, later teaching in South Africa, before his return to Magdalen. On the ship coming back he delighted to recount that a fellow passenger, on hearing that Adam was returning to become Dean of Divinity at Magdalen, said, "Ah yes, I believe they have had a good deal of difficulty in filling those posts". Short in stature, he had a puckish look, a large arched nose dominating the face, a firm mouth and deepset blue eyes, regarding the world around him with affectionate and amused detachment. He did not seek to display his Christianity but the sincerity of his belief was manifest in his lifestyle and in his easy relationship with all Magdalen men, whether they were clever, agnostic, hearty, shy, sophisticated or just plain dull. Though not outwardly paraded, there were elements of the poet and the mystic in his character.

Adam became a considerable influence in my developing religious thought, and I was struck by some notes on Chapel which he circulated during my first year and which included this paragraph:

> As far as I can tell, there is at present in college less agnosticism and indifference to religion than is usual in a student community. But people underrate the difficulty of going to chapel unless one has a rule about it. And they are apt to look for some excitement or some 'relevance' in chapel, which, I am glad to say, cannot be found in our chapel; where the services are sung and said to please God, and not to please but to sanctify the congregation.

I attended Chapel regularly, and began gradually to understand that sanctity of which Adam wrote, and the beauty of holiness which Magdalen Chapel so eloquently expressed.

During my time, Adam became Professor of Poetry in the University. A complicated intrigue lay behind this of which I forget the details. He was a very minor poet indeed but the election – voting was open to all Oxford MAs – was held on a weekday during ordinary working hours. To Oxford came flocks of clergymen, not bound by office hours, who voted Adam in, which many thought quite a scandal. I went to Adam's excellent professorial lectures on Wordsworth, which were enhanced by being held in the Divinity Schools, one of the most beautiful buildings in Oxford.

Apart from playing football, squash, fives and cricket, I also sought to develop two Shrewsbury interests – hurdling and acting. I joined the OUAC and used to go down to the Iffley Road track. It was a depressing experience. Oxford then had at least six high class hurdlers; one was Peter Knight, who later joined the Shrewsbury staff, another Rupert Powell, brother of Mike, another member of the Shrewsbury staff. When I sought some help, the then coach, who wore a bowler hat and was I think called Thomas, could only comment, "You'll never do it that way". Discouraged, I withdrew.

I joined the Oxford University Dramatic Society, again somewhat overwhelmed by the confidence and sophistication of my seniors. Very much the new boy, I was allotted a non-speaking part in *Much Ado About Nothing*, directed by Leslie French, which proved to be an undistinguished production. But in Magdalen we had a tradition of eighteenth century melodrama, performed on a tiny stage in the Junior Common Room, which was the greatest fun. The scripts were dug out of the recesses of the Bodleian. In 1937, we did *The Gamester's Curse* (or *The Wreck, the Miser and the Mines*) which was bloodcurdling stuff. Charles Rankin, a Salopian friend, was outstanding as the hero and Keith Joseph sinister as the miser; I was his nephew which caused him to write on my menu card at the Dramatic Society's dinner, "What a nephew! I wouldn't trust you further than my stick could reach".

At the end of my first term I took Pass Mods, a fairly simple examination which covered English, Latin and French texts. Having spent a lot of time acting, I was (as usual) apprehensive, though Adam Fox, who always sent a postcard to congratulate those who passed, wrote me a little poem which ended -

> Courage, dear Michael, on this other stage,
> Shall bring the picture postcard's painted page

The postcard duly came; I have it still.

My first year ended with the Magdalen cricket tour. We zigzagged up the Great North Road, playing against the Leicester Gentlemen, the Lincoln Gentlemen, Ampleforth, the Yorkshire Gentlemen at the lovely Escrick Park ground, and the Garrison at Catterick. The comfortable hotels in which we stayed charged less than a pound for bed and breakfast. We had a good side, winning all our matches save that at Ampleforth; although in a strong position at lunch, the wily monks did for us. After the port had gone round twice, we hazily returned to the field and dropped every catch thereafter. Where now are the carefree cricketers of 1938? Glen Balfour Paul, our captain, became an Ambassador; Colin Doran a BBC announcer in the news department; John Macdonald emigrated to Australia where he inherited many acres; Philip Pawson entered the Sudan Civil Service and later the oil industry; Keith Joseph was at the heart of Thatcherism in various ministerial posts; Alan Hamer returned to his native Australia and became Vice Chairman of ICI; Dick Hewitt became Director of the Royal Society of Medicine; our tall, willowy opening bowler, Robert Blake, now changed in figure after a lifetime of dining at high tables, is well known as an author and historian, and was one-time Provost of Queen's College; Colin Pitman and Peter Wells were killed in the war.

My second year, 1938–39, was the last year of the old-time Oxford but I cannot say that there was very much 'Après moi...' feeling, despite the political thunder clouds. By now I had gained in confidence and really began to appreciate Oxford, with new friends and new involvements. Having a tidy mind and an instinct for administration, I have always been the sort of dogsbody who finds himself appointed Secretary of something or other. So now I was Secretary of the Magdalen Cricket Club, Secretary of the College Dramatic Society, and Secretary of the Oxford Old Salopians. Another melodrama was extracted from the Bodleian, written by 'Monk' Lewis in 1797, and we persuaded Nevill Coghill to produce it, then one of

Oxford's foremost English dons, a man of much theatrical ingenuity and sophisticated charm. That year I even got a speaking part in the OUDS production of *The Duchess of Malfi*, again a rather ordinary production though we took it for one night to the Piccadilly Theatre in London and gave ourselves the illusion of having a London run. But I had by now realised that those who got on in the OUDS devoted themselves wholly to the theatre and hoped to make their living in it. There was little chance for fringe men like me.

I now had delightful rooms in Longwall Quad, neighbour to Richard Spilsbury, a man of compelling moral and intellectual integrity, eccentric in speech and action. He took a First in PPE, then studied philosophy and zoology, moving into academic life after the war but totally lacking in conventional ambition. Life was never dull in his presence. For reasons which are now obscure to me, we played a great deal of poker, often far into the night, though our stakes were minimal. Life was much brightened for me by the possession of a car which the proctors ordained should show a green light in front for recognition purposes. This was a gift from my mother and I can say that it was the most cherished possession that I had ever had, a Talbot Ten, a low slung, open touring model with the lines of a sports car. Thus I and my friends had access to the Oxford countryside pubs – the Rose Revived at Standlake, the Shaven Crown at Minster Lovell, Shillingford Bridge Hotel, and the Barley Mow at Clifton Hampden at which we were once 'progged'. A proctor and his bulldogs in their bowler hats moved in on this rural pub and solemnly took our names. A fine of ten shillings followed. It was the incongruity of the scene which struck us – a summer evening on the river bank and the bulldogs solemnly raising their hats to ask if we were members of the University while the proctor in his white tie stood by.

Those were expansive days. We had an excellent cook in Magdalen and I gave frequent lunch parties in my rooms, my scout, the amiable Johnson, carrying all the cutlery and food across from the kitchens several hundred yards away. Johnson was a tower of strength to Dick Spilsbury and me, with a splendid down-to-earth philosophy, typical of the scouts of that day, men devoted to the College where many spent their entire working lives. In a way they *were* the college, the constant element of continuity, a unique combination of servant and friend.

Although a member of the Union, I had no political ambitions and not much political interest, drifting along with many in support of Chamberlain as he sought to save the way of appeasement. The Left was strong in the Union, despite Edward Heath, Hugh Fraser and other future Tory politicians. In 1938 the University was enlivened and split by the famous Oxford by-election when A.D. Lindsay, the Master of Balliol, stood for the Left in opposition to the Munich agreement – against Quintin Hogg, now

Lord Hailsham. Lindsay, a popular man and a Christian socialist, had strong undergraduate support. I recollect a march round the City with the endlessly repeated slogan, "We want Lindsay: Hitler wants Hogg". On walls was chalked, "A Vote for Hogg is a Vote for Hitler" to which the reply was "Vote for Hogg and save your bacon". Hogg won by 3,000 votes.

I did attend a number of debates at the Union though I would rather have died than spoken. Anthony Eden made a profound impression and the socialist fire of Arthur Greenwood stays in my mind. On a different note, I don't think that I have ever heard speeches of such penetrating wit as in the Eights Week debates and anyone funnier than Ronald Knox. Moving the motion 'That This House Prefers to Travel With Its Back to the Engine', his first words were "Man is born free but everywhere he is in trains".

So that last peacetime summer term ended, the war now clearly discerned. For most it was to be the end of the weekly essays, of working in the Radcliffe Camera, rushing to lectures such as those by the young fiery radicals, A.L. Rowse and A.J.P. Taylor, spending too much money at Blackwells ('in whose booky house, half England's scholars come to browse'), wasting too much time in Fullers with their famous walnut cake, attending pre-London runs at the New Theatre (and always a Gilbert and Sullivan season), eating hotpot at the George under the improbable Indian punkhas, drinking in distant Oxfordshire pubs and never-ending talk in one's rooms. For me that last Long Vac started with the Magdalen cricket tour, again up the Great North Road, and was terminated by an enterprise which took much of my time and into which I stumbled quite by mistake.

This arose from my friendship with Eric Dehn, a Salopian who was at Worcester College. After the narrow world of Mitford's House at Shrewsbury, Eric had taken to Oxford with enthusiasm, particularly its social and dramatic life. Short of stature and sharp of wit, he never lacked for female company and his performance as Ariel in Worcester College gardens stays in my memory. It was through Eric that I was introduced to the Players Theatre, ('Late Joys'), where in a room in Covent Garden actors and actresses from the West End came on after performances to sing in Victorian music hall style. Here I first heard Peter Ustinov, Robert Eddison, Geoffrey Dunn, Hattie Jacques and so many others, under the chairmanship of Leonard Sachs. It was through Eric that I joined the fringe at the court of Rosa Lewis at the Cavendish. (Had she really been the mistress of Edward VII?). It was through Eric that I came to know those working at the newly built Playhouse in Oxford (where we had done *The Duchess of Malfi*) and particularly its director Stanford Holme and his beautiful wife Thea, leading actress in the company.

Under the auspices of the OUDS, Eric and Stanford had put together a cast to play *Tobias and the Angel*, by James Bridie, as a feature at the Conservative fête, which was a very large scale event in the grounds of

Blenheim Palace. Somehow I found myself as 'presenter' of this play but – much more – as the organiser of its prospective tour to Scandinavia, thought up by Eric but on which he was unable to go. So I spent time wrestling with ships, trains, accommodation and theatres in various Scandinavian towns, talking to cultural attachés and generally moving in an unfamiliar world. The enterprise was timed for September 1939; as the days wore on it seemed less and less likely we would go and after the sensational news of the German-Soviet Pact, we abandoned what would have been a fascinating tour though, in the light of later experience, I wonder if the cast would ever have stood up to the punishing schedule which I had arranged. David Tree (of a famous family) would have taken Eric's place and Caroline Bayley (Lady Caroline Paget) would have provided an aristocratic atmosphere, while Judith Masefield, daughter of the Poet Laureate, was responsible for the music. We had been told that some 'names' would be an asset.

For obvious reasons, the year 1939 remains fixed in the memory. I was at Glyndebourne in June, charmed by the Carl Ebert-Fritz Busch production of *Don Giovanni*; Kreisler played in the New Theatre in Oxford; I heard Beecham conduct the BBC Symphony Orchestra at the old Queen's Hall, soon to be erased by bombs; and I saw the most scintillating stage performance I had ever seen – *The Importance of Being Earnest* with John Gielgud, Edith Evans, Angela Baddeley and Margaret Rutherford.

On September 3rd I was at home, as were all the family, and we – and the maids – gathered round the wireless to listen to the fateful Chamberlain broadcast, his voice heavy with suppressed emotion. But somehow there was something satisfactory about the issue at last becoming clear cut, after months of hopes and fears. Undergraduates were invited to go to the Joint Recruiting Board at Oxford and thither I went with all my friends in Magdalen. After some fighting talk from Michael Maclagan, a Trinity don transformed into army officer, I took the King's shilling but we were all quite uncertain what we should do next. When would the services absorb us? Was it worth returning to Oxford in the meantime? In what service would we be placed? Most of us decided – wrongly – not to return. Academic studies did seem out of place in the welter of activity which the war brought. Ultimately I was told that I was selected for the Royal Artillery and that I was placed for call up in Category B. I asked a senior officer when Category B would be called up; he looked at me in some surprise and told me it would be after Category A and before Category C; my first taste of armyspeak. Little did I realise it would be eleven months before I was summoned.

At home I was busy with all the demands of the emergency – black out, cutting cardboard masks for the car lights and driving patients home from the hospital which was being cleared as far as possible to receive the expected heavy casualities. We all remembered Baldwin's words, "The Bomber will always get through". My one-time building skill was used in constructing a concrete air raid shelter in the garden, whither we on occasion repaired during that winter, generally on false alarms.

As the autumn weeks wore on, we gradually realised that the war was a phoney war. Normal activities were to some extent renewed including the Repertory theatre where there was a shortage of actors. Together with a neighbour, John Whiting, I volunteered. John was a rather morose person with whom I never got on very well but he was to become a playwright of note. His plays included *Penny for a Song* and *The Devils*. So I joined the Rep in an amateur capacity, and played small parts for those winter months. My contribution was minimal but I learned a great deal about the stage. In those days, though it seems hardly credible, the Rep put on a different play each week with two performances a night. As soon as a play was launched on Monday – and I recollect Osborne Robinson, the scenic artist, on stage still painting five minutes before the curtain went up – attention was turned to the next play; on Tuesday morning it was Act 1 Scene 1, lines to be learned by Friday with the dress rehearsal over the weekend. With such a punishing schedule it was astonishing that the performances were so good; and the plays were far from trivial. They included *Romeo and Juliet*, *Escape Me Never*, and Shaw's intolerably wordy *Geneva*.

At home we started 'open' evenings on Sundays when there would be coffee and gramophone music for any who cared to drop in. These became an institution and continued for the next seven years, bringing a wide variety of people into the house, some 'regulars', evacuees, Jewish fugitives from Europe and soldiers temporarily in the town. This social forum did much to sustain my parents in the long years of war when both sons were overseas and Olive was working at Bletchley Park.

By the end of the year, it at last became clear that I should not be called up until the late summer. So back to Oxford I went and there followed one of the happiest six months of my life. I lived in digs at 5 Longwall Street with Alan Hamer, an Australian Rhodes Scholar reading chemistry, and David Chapman, an Etonian, a keen squash and tennis player. Alan was an excellent all-round sportsman and the three of us played some golf at Frilford, a game which I have never really taken up and have always played badly but enjoyably. We had a very happy household, all working quite hard and being looked after by Mrs Chamberlain, a landlady of a type now extinct. There was about half the usual number of undergraduates, petrol rationing had remarkably reduced the Oxford traffic and, despite the blackout, it was a delight to have the free life of the undergraduate for the last time before the curtain descended. In Magdalen we were a compact but diverse group, which included Owen Darrell and Peter Ramsbotham, a Bermudian, destined to be our Ambassador in America and later Governor of Bermuda, an island which was to feature prominently in my life; also present was Cheslyn Jones, a senior Demy, later to be ordained, a Wykehamist of considerable but lightly-worn learning and of scintillating wit, with a gift for parody and a comprehensive knowledge of Betjeman's poems.

Encouraged by the absence of the galaxy of hurdlers, now absorbed into the Forces, I diligently applied myself to practise at Iffley Road and, to my great surprise won the OUAC event and found myself representing the University in the Varsity match at Cambridge where I did not, however, distinguish myself. No Blues were awarded and indeed the teams were certainly sub-standard. But I was pleased with this small success and pleased also to become a member of the Achilles Club, then of greater standing in the athletic world than now.

I felt now that I really belonged to Oxford and, for the first time, began to look closely at the buildings, to explore the colleges and penetrate the countryside (I had my much-loved Talbot Ten), visiting battlefields, memorials and churches. My somewhat nominal attachment to the Church of England developed now into something much more real, the influence perhaps of Adam Fox, of Cheslyn Jones and also of C.S. Lewis. I found myself tutored by him in political philosophy, the set authors being Aristotle, Hobbes and Rousseau. He wrote me a detailed letter before term with this advice: "Political philosophy can be practised all day long. Start from your own political views and regard every theory either as a welcome ally or an enemy you'll have to circumvent. When you hear people arguing politics, *listen*, and try to see what theories are unconsciously implied in their remarks ('that fellow is a pure Aristotelian though he doesn't know it')". Lewis had not at this time written anything on Christianity and he was certainly not one to proselytize. His Christianity was picked up by me in his general attitude to the subjects we discussed. As a tutor, he had a great gift of explaining complex issues and ideas by bringing them down to one's own level by metaphor and analogy without in any way oversimplifying; this comes out strongly in his books.

I also read quite a lot of theology at this time, though never at a very deep level. The result of this reading, the friends I then had and my aroused interest in church architecture, was to bring a genuine religious dimension into my life for the first time; I suppose too that the war itself made one think about the ultimate issues. In early April 1940, I walked alone along the Pilgrim's Way for a week, enjoying the spring sunshine, the quiet of the roads, the casual acquaintances, the pubs and their regulars discussing the war; and the opportunity to think. For a couple of days James Harrison joined me from Abinger. After a week's walking there was a great satisfaction in seeing afar the Canterbury Cathedral spires.

Meeting C.S. Lewis many years later in the Combination Room of

Magdalene, Cambridge, he recalled that we all worked very hard in that fateful summer; and indeed we did, while Europe was collapsing a few hundred miles away. The sun shone: we followed the war news closely but otherwise punted on the river, played cricket and tennis, and drove into the Oxford countryside to visit the pubs, play bar billiards and sometimes bathe in the river. This lotus life was hardly disturbed by Dunkirk and the fall of France, save that we joined the Local Defence Volunteers as soon as they were formed, soon to be the Home Guard. This was an extraordinary army in Oxford, with a sprinkling of Great War veterans, local businessmen and a variety of dons. I was in Stephen Lee's platoon, with Lieutenant Frank Pakenham (later Lord Longford) as company commander, while Maurice Bowra issued improbable orders from Battalion HQ. I was on a regular patrol which covered the then Oxford by-pass and at 4 a.m. was on my bicycle together with the son of a sweep and Georgie Gordon, the Vice Chancellor's son, looking for spies and parachutists. I have happy memories of those early mornings in sleeping villages like Hinksey, with memories of John Ruskin and his volunteer work force. At the time of Dunkirk it was a shock one day to meet Philip Pawson in his dirty battle dress and tin hat walking through the Lodge, straight from the battlefield and dumped in Oxford by train. We were just going down to the river to punt.

At the end of term we put on our white ties and did our exams – successfully – and said a reluctant farewell to Oxford life; though in my case there was to be a reprise. Most of us moved off to a forestry camp in the Forest of Dean where we laboured at cutting down trees for pit props, hard work compensated for by the bowling alleys and 'rough stuff' cider in the homely pubs of the forest. With Dick Spilsbury and Cheslyn Jones in the party, the forestry staff were by turns amused and bemused. And that was the end of civilian life.

CHAPTER XI

The Army and the East

Gracious Lord, oh bomb the Germans.
Spare their women for Thy sake,
But if this is not too easy
We will pardon Thy mistake.
But, gracious Lord, whate'er shall be,
Don't let anyone bomb me.

Betjeman

On 15th August 1940, with the newspapers and the skies full of the
Battle of Britain, I became 931026 Gunner Charlesworth at Bulford Camp
on Salisbury Plain. 'Going through the ranks' was a process common to
most of my generation and I will not dwell on it. After a boarding school,
one took barrack room life in one's stride, adapting as best one could to the
limited outlook and colourful language of one's fellow gunners. The
ponderous and circumspect way in which the army did things caused
irritation to those whose minds worked faster than average but humour
generally intervened and we all soon got used to the routine of PT at dawn,
square bashing, gun drill, lectures and occasional exercises on the Plain. Of
recreation there was little, though for me the rather fine garrison church
and library were retreats from grinding routine.

After some weeks, the potential officers were selected and gathered to
live in one hut. The POTS (Potential Officers Training Squad) were under
the loquacious and somewhat flamboyant Sergeant Porter, who enjoyed
putting us through remarkable manoeuvres and convolutions both on foot
and with the guns. Here was formed a small party of friends with whom I
was to live closely for the next year. John Thompson had captained Cambridge at cricket (he was later to play for Warwickshire), had read science
and was the son of the headmaster of Solihull School; Hay Colman was an
Australian from Geelong Grammar School, also at Cambridge, where he
had been captain of tennis; Christopher Fisher's background was Eton and
Balliol, an impressive mathematician – a great help to us in our trigo-
nometry which was the basis of gunnery calculations – and a good

musician. Christopher was physically ill-adapted to army life but met the tribulations of the day with a sharp sense of humour. Desmond Manners was from Malvern and Cambridge, a fine racquets player, who had married just before being called up; Richard Clarke was the youngest of the party, straight from Sherborne, small and lithe in physique, characteristics which enabled him to survive the first Chindit expedition to Burma. Charles Davidson was from Stowe (which he did not much enjoy) and Brasenose, Oxford. He was in some way related to our Colonel; this was to stand us in good stead.

Winter came early to Salisbury Plain that year, making life uncomfortable in our hut which was heated by one small coke stove. One day the POTS squad was informed that a number of cadets were to be taken to India to be commissioned into the expanding Indian Army and we were invited to volunteer. After a quick conference, eleven of us volunteered – India would at least be warm compared with Bulford. This quick and light-hearted decision was to seal our fate for the next four years and more. I had a more personal and rather absurd reason for volunteering. When very young, I used to look at the pictures in *The Nursery History of England*, a rather bad book but with – to me – fascinating illustrations. The last one was of King George Vth in India, surrounded by gaudily dressed Maharajahs and Princes, servants and elephants, soldiers and peasants. ''Perhaps you will go to India one day'', my mother had said. The scene had stayed with me; and now I was indeed to go to India.

So we finished our training, proficient in some degree in the science of gunnery, and the Indian draft waited impatiently to embark. Needless to say, there was endless delay, rumour and counter-rumour. It was now that Charles Davidson's influence with authority became important, for the Colonel decided that the simplest thing to do with us was to send us on leave. So it was that I spent a happy extended embarkation leave in the grim winter of 1940–41 when the Blitz was at its height. From Northampton one November night we saw the sky lit up over Coventry twenty-five miles away.

As a contrast to the Blitz and shortages of Britain, we soon began to realise, even in prospect, that life in India would be different, evidenced by the fact that we were each allowed to take three hundredweight of kit. It was suggested that we took our golf clubs and sports gear, though, it was explained, polo equipment could be more easily obtained there. Thus it was that when we finally assembled at Aldershot the eleven of us had sixty articles of baggage. Were we really going to fight a war or going on holiday? However, there wasn't much holiday at Willems Barracks, Aldershot, a vast gloomy set of buildings which had few amenities, twenty-five cadets in each barrack room and minimal washing and sanitary facilities. Here we spent Christmas, now a body of 600 cadets, mainly straight from school, whose first experience of the army this was. The eleven of us were, in comparison, seasoned warriors and we kept as closely together as possible, managing to have a Christmas dinner in a hotel where I first heard an ancient army joke in which a transient officer described Aldershot as 'the arsehole of the Empire' to receive the comment from a neighbouring lady, 'And I suppose you're just passing through?'

We were addressed one day by the GOC Aldershot Command, who told us that we were going to India at a vital time with the possibility of doing more in India than any body of men yet sent. Nothing about winning the war but a lot about not drinking until the sun was down, the importance of the topee and how to avoid malaria. We were accompanied in our draft by various dug-out colonels of the Indian Army, retired but now recalled to static jobs, who regaled us with stories of their time, of sport and shooting and polo, seasoned with anecdotes of fighting on the North West Frontier.

While at Aldershot all our kit was carefully marked with platoon and company codes and with symbols for 'wanted on voyage' etc. One night we entrained for our unknown destination which turned out to be Greenock on the Clyde, where lay a whole convoy of ships, amongst them the 14,000 ton 'Highland Chieftain', a name imprinted for ever on the memories of those of us who sailed in her, a converted meat boat normally running to South America. I don't think I have ever been in a situation where morale was lower than amongst those 600 cadets when faced with the awful reality of our living conditions. Below decks there seemed to be one enormous hold (though there must have been some bulkhead divisions) which would fit well into one of Dante's circles of hell. Row after row of fixed mess tables and fixed benches stretched out into infinity with scarcely room to squeeze between them. Above them were hooks for hammocks; at night mattresses were spread on the tables beneath. The night scene can be imagined – a mass of humanity swinging in hammocks while below them every inch of table space was taken up with sprawling bodies. When the weather became rough and sea sickness began, the confusion was complete.

Our massed baggage, so carefully marked and categorised, was lowered on to the deck in one vast heap, hundreds and hundreds of trunks, suitcases, kit bags – and golf clubs – which took days to sort out. Washing and sanitary arrangements were minimal, fresh water available only for a few hours of the day. Though there was a canteen, there was virtually no recreation space except the deck – and this was mid-winter. Life jackets and tin hats had to be carried everywhere in the day time; the black out at night created a steamy, misty fug on the mess decks, which drove us in the evenings to go on deck in the darkness, watching the vague outline of the convoy, the leap of the phosphorescent wake and the bright moon over all. In these brief moments of relaxation we exchanged intimate personal information, spoke of hopes and fears, made coarse jokes, indulged in amateur astronomy, laughed as others walked into unseen obstacles on the deck and felt the sad stirring in the stomach of unformulated desires, before descending into the 'black hole' and the smell of sweaty humanity sorting itself out into its hammocks.

One of the first things one was told in the army was 'Never volunteer'. I always reversed this dictum, generally, I think, to my advantage. Thus when the ship's Captain called for volunteers who could play the bugle, up went my hand, as did those of two others. We were then told that we were to be ship's buglers, dividing the day into three watches and playing the normal calls through the working day – Reveille to Retreat. I had never blown a bugle; but I could play the trumpet and as the mouthpieces were similar I reckoned I could manage, which indeed I did after some unfortunate first efforts. What a wonderfully privileged job this turned out to be! The buglers were excused all other duties – no cook-house fatigues, no guards, no submarine spotting, no mess duties; and we slept in a small 'private' hold which we had to ourselves. Admittedly we had to be up early to sound Reveille amongst the muffled oaths of the sleepers; and it was not easy to stand motionless on the bridge, while the ship rolled, sounding Retreat as the sun went down with all standing to attention. Otherwise, if on duty, one was attached to the Captain, accompanying him on his daily rounds and sitting on the bridge ready to sound the alarm in emergency. The Captain, a splendid old sea horse, one day said to me, "Do you know what you do if we get torpedoed?". "No, Sir". "Well, you stand by my side and you play the Last Post until the bubbles come out of your trumpet". "Yes, Sir".

Gradually the enormous gloom of our early days lightened. Life had a different aspect when we reached the tropics and could spend time on deck. We were kept fairly busy with PT, lectures by our colonels on the India they had known, Urdu lessons, boat drill, cleaning the ship and keeping oneself and one's possessions in shape; also queueing: queueing for fresh water, queueing for the canteen, queueing to read the sparse news bulletin posted daily. The most unattractive queue of all was standing naked for lice inspection; if lice were suspected or present, all hair was shaved from the body. Our convoy went far across the Atlantic to avoid submarines but we were never told where we were. Apart from a couple of days off Freetown – mysterious Africa briefly beckoned – we were at sea for five weeks before calling at Durban, a golden experience never forgotten.

As we went into the harbour we were surprised to find hundreds of people there to greet us, including the famous 'lady in white', Perla Siedle, who welcomed all convoys with patriotic songs sung through a megaphone. Once on shore people fell over themselves to welcome us. Hay

Colman and I were walking along the street when a man drew up and took us to his home for drinks, then drove us round the town. We were made honorary members of all the clubs; there was an organisation run by patriotic ladies to take us on little expeditions, on one of which I was whisked up to the beautiful Valley of a Thousand Hills. That first evening a group of us had an enormous meal at a hotel high above Durban; there were white tablecloths, servants and free drinks. As we looked out over the city with its myriad twinkling lights, the contrast to the crowded blacked out mess decks of the ship quite overcame us. And always these South Africans were telling us that we must come back and settle after the war, thus increasing the 'English' South African population. As we returned to the ship in Zulu-drawn rickshaws though the shrub-lined streets, the warm air filled with exotic scents and the incessant singing of the crickets, we felt strongly inclined to do so.

At Durban we said goodbye without regret to the 'Highland Chieftain' and transferred to the 'Windsor Castle' of the Union Castle Line. What luxury it seemed! Now we were in cabins with wash-basins and adjoining bathrooms. Although the ship was crowded, there was more deck space, a swimming pool and even space for a makeshift cricket net. We Bulford boys were still much together, playing a lot of bridge, talking of the past and speculating about the future. During these long weeks at sea we did not, of course, have any mail so were quite out of touch with our families though we wrote home copiously. Our correspondence was censored. Christopher Fisher's mother wrote to him later that various words like 'India' and 'Urdu' had been censored. She had no difficulty in reading them however.

On this long voyage I read a great deal. By now my religious faith, which had been focused during that last summer term at Magdalen under the unspoken influence of Adam Fox, C.S. Lewis and Cheslyn Jones, had strengthened considerably as I sought to make sense of the new life into which I had been thrown. On both the ships I managed to find some little-frequented deck space where, sitting on my life jacket, I endeavoured to read the Bible and to meditate and to pray – an activity I have always found (and still do find) exceedingly difficult. We had a small Christian Union-type of group on board and held periodic meetings at one of which I surprised myself by waxing more eloquent than I expected on St Mark's Gospel. The Captain of the ship was a thrusting Evangelical so our church services were lively.

After dodging into Mombassa for a couple of days to escape a U-boat – we dropped a few depth charges hopefully – we at last came to Bombay, seventy-seven days after reporting to Willems Barracks, Aldershot. There at last was the promised land, scurrying figures on the dock, cranes perpetually busy, vehicles, horses and railway sidings, shouts of encouragement, instruction and condemnation – our first experience of J.K. Galbraith's 'anarchy that works'.

Our home for the next six months was the School of Artillery at Deolali, a second-class hill station in the Western Ghats, a few hours from Bombay. Seventy strong, we were the first artillery cadets to arrive in the Sub-continent and we really could not believe our luck as we suddenly trans-ferred from the mass squalor of ship life, in which we had lived for ten weeks, to what seemed palatial quarters. On our first night I recollect one cadet from force of habit bringing his mess tin along to the Mess, not really believing that one could have an army meal without it. Instead we had a menu of brown soup; golden fish; roast beef; fruit salad and cream; dessert and coffee, all served by white-clad bearers on white table-cloths. We lived in decent bungalows – I shared a room with John Thompson – and had a bearer to every four cadets; laundry was done overnight; and (the ultimate luxury) I arranged to be shaved in bed every morning, a custom which I had read about in Winston Churchill's book on his early life. It was certainly a contrast to an English OCTU where sergeant-majors made life hell. Our Sergeant's first remark to us was "Now, gentlemen, we won't bother to march over to the parade ground but will go over in our own time". Gradually the realisation dawned: we were 'Sahibs'.

Although life was socially relaxed, we worked extremely hard at our gunnery. In fact we found even the instructors behind our own Bulford knowledge and we started by doing horse drill! The guns were obsolete 18-pounders. We soon became very fit, spending much of our days out in the hot, dusty, scrubby landscape, dominated by the Ghats, very geometric hills with names like Siva Donga and Bahoola Hill Fort which we used as reference points when laying out the guns. Colonel Lamb, who com-manded the school, was a cultured man of wide interests. He used to lecture to us on tactics and world strategy; and occasionally asked us to dinner. He saw to it that we were eligible for membership of the club, and that there were adequate facilities for games. Sadly his regime was rather too relaxed and for our last two months we had a fire-eating Irishman called McNichol who was only interested in gunnery and who made plain his opinion of our somewhat laid-back attitudes. Now we were marched everywhere. McNichol even resented our going over to a rather good golf course at Nasik on our days off: we should have been studying.

Being only seventy strong, we all knew each other well by the end of the course. Our Bulford friendships remained close in work and play. Tennis with Hay Colman or squash with John Thompson (both Cambridge Blues) were energetic experiences; Richard Clarke led the way at hockey; Charles Davidson taught me to dive in the club swimming pool; Christopher Fisher taught us our gunnery mathematics: Desmond Manners managed to find a salacious side to most situations. The club gave us a little social life though I should think that the times we spoke to a woman could be numbered on one hand. Still, we had all been brought up in boarding schools so this was no new experience. The club did have films from time to time – even a Marx Brothers film once – and there were occasional gramophone concerts and a radio over which faintly came the tunes of the time: *Don't Fence Me In, These Foolish Things, As Time Goes By*; but there was no one to dance with.

The months passed; the monsoon came; the parched landscape became green; we fired our guns and by the time Colonel McNichol had finished with us we were physically fit and knew a good deal about gunnery. I was pleased and surprised to pass out seventh out of seventy, much less pleased with my posting. Whereas all the others were joining regiments in groups of two or three, I was to go by myself to 158 Field Regiment, then training in the distant north among the Himalayan foothills. Our Bulford friendships which had sustained us through an eventful year were finally to be broken. I learnt later that I had been thus singled out because the Colonel of 158 had seen me conducting a shoot during a visit to Deolali and had asked for me; this was flattering but at the time my morale was low. Of our course, a number went to Singapore where they were made prisoners and some to PAI Force in Iraq and Persia where little happened for the next four years. So my posting was, in fact, a fortunate one.

Most of us went to the Taj Mahal Hotel in Bombay for some leave. It was there that we put up our pips on 4th August 1941 and very foolish we felt in our new guise – subalterns as green as you could find. Charles Davidson and I, both posted to the north, went off to Agra to see the Taj Mahal *en route*, but by the time we reached Agra I realised that I was suffering from a more than trivial stomach complaint. Thus I was admitted to hospital in Agra with dysentery. Charles continued on his way and there was I, feeling very weak, knowing no one, marooned in hospital in the hot weather, on my way to an unknown unit still 500 miles away where there awaited me (according to report) the fire-eating Colonel Gallaher who ate subalterns for breakfast. It was a gloomy time, a little enlivened by the Hospital Chaplain who drifted into my room of an evening in his white cassock, smoking a good cigar, ready to discuss theology or indeed any other subject; he lent me a difficult book, *The Spiritual Life* by Harton, with which I wrestled as strength returned.

So at last to Shinkiari Camp, tucked away in the hills behind Abbottabad in the North West Frontier Province, the tents spread over the green hillsides, the only flat space being the gun park. Here I met at last Colonel Gallaher, risen from the ranks, Irish, and now devoting himself with savage enthusiasm to training 158 Field Regiment, his first command. To my surprise I established a good relationship with him; only once did he go for me and then only from force of habit. So I tried to learn my job, anxiously going through that test of leadership which comes to every new

subaltern when he is faced by NCOs and men who are far more experienced than he, eagerly waiting for him to make a mistake. My four
Sergeants – each in charge of a gun – were called Kidd, Rumble, Wetton
and Randall. The names have never left me. Two had fought in the Western
Desert, Rumble was an old India hand and Randall an experienced Territorial. My troop had a number of men who had been long in India but most
had come in drafts from England.

Larry Gallaher was an absolute glutton for work; we were at it
from 6 a.m. to 6 p.m. except at the weekends when the senior
officers disappeared to Abbottabad, where some had their families,
and the juniors relaxed in the Mess. 'Chairs out' was the cheerful cry
and the servants would put the Mess chairs out under the stars and we
would drink and reminisce and sing songs and speculate. Soon I felt I
belonged.

My battery commander was John Branford, a distinguished horseman
who had won the great pig-sticking trophy, the Kadir Cup. Because the
changeover from horse to vehicle transport was very recent, officers were
each allowed to have a horse (or 'charger') on establishment and I was
invited to share a horse, an offer I accepted with well-founded anxiety, as
my evening rides often ended with a tussle of wills between the horse and
me. Very early in my time, Major Branford put me in charge of a night
scheme in a little village called Baffa, infinitely remote among dry paddy
fields. He and I went out in the early evening and I methodically went
through all necessary steps to ensure that when the guns arrived after dark
they could be correctly placed and laid, with necessary guiding lights and
all calculations completed. Having done all I could think of I sat down to
wait and despite my anxiety, I remember being struck by the sense of
space, the brightness of the stars, the cries of jackals, the smell of wood-
smoke and cowdung and the particular kind of dusk of an Indian evening.
Through the silence came the rumble of the guns and, to my delight,
everything worked well and the guns were ready to fire on a pre-arranged
target in a few minutes. I felt I had passed the test.

A welcome diversion from the grind of training was the Camouflage
Course for which the Colonel selected me. This took place at the Camouflage School at Kirkee, just outside Poona. So off on the Frontier Mail I
went, a forty-eight hour journey via Bombay to return to the country of the
Western Ghats. I enjoyed the course and worked quite hard; but an
additional reason for enjoyment was the hospitality of Brian Inglis's
parents who lived at Poona. He was a distinguished hydrodynamic
engineer (shortly to be knighted) and she an enthusiastic extrovert, much
involved in various activities in Poona, where she was librarian at the
Poona Club, and a prison visitor to the Congress leaders in jail nearby,
where she had a considerable friendship with the engaging Mrs Pandit,

later to be Indian High Commissioner in London. At the end of the course I found I was one of six who were awarded a 'D' (Distinguished) which surprised me a good deal. Ever since school days, the fear of failure had led me to work harder than others; it still did so.

In the cold weather of 1941–42 we moved down to Campbellpore, half-way between Rawalpindi and Peshawar. Here we completed our training with a firing camp at Nowshera. The cold weather of the Punjab was wonderfully stimulating, cold nights with occasional frost and bright sunny days with a brilliant blue sky. Our training thus far had had a twofold purpose. We were a reserve force ready to fight on the North West Frontier, whether against the tribesmen or the Russians or – conceivably – the Germans. The Khyber Pass was at this time being heavily fortified with tank obstacles, gun positions and pill boxes. So we learned picqueting, semaphore and heliograph signalling and what was liable to happen to you if captured by the tribesmen. We also had a role 'in aid of the Civil Power', a legacy of the Mutiny of 1857, whereby every unit had a task assigned to it. The pews in every church had fittings for rifles after the events in Meerut on 10th May 1857. But principally in training we thought of ourselves as fighting in the Western Desert and so learnt the sun compass and wide deployment in open spaces.

All this was thrown into the melting pot by Pearl Harbour in December 1941 and the implications, which only slowly dawned on us, of the astonishing Japanese advance into Malaya, the capture of Singapore and the conquest of Burma which brought the Japs to the Indian frontier. Suddenly all was activity and lethargic Indian attitudes were sharpened by the possibility, indeed the likelihood, of invasion. This flurry of excitement was not welcome to me for a private and personal reason. While at Campbellpore I had made contact with Lionel Parsons, late of Oldham's Hall and now of Probyn's Horse, who lived with his recently-wed wife in Rawalpindi. Having dinner with him one evening, I met a most delightful girl called Patricia Haylock, then aged I think about seventeen. Enormously attracted, my life so far having been deficient in attractive girls, I saw her again; and now, just as the affair was developing, we were to disappear into a distant jungle. But of course we would write; and we did ... for the next three years.

The Regiment was now mobilised; equipment poured out of the ordnance depots in Rawalpindi: we had new 25-pounder guns, new Chevrolet vehicles; such was the activity in the quartermaster's department that I was temporarily transferred there to be submerged by a welter of army forms without which nothing could happen. We tried to adapt our training for a type of warfare of which we knew nothing: the familiar TEWTS (Tactical Exercises Without Troops) became JEWTS (Jungle Exercises Without Trees). Soon we were off to an unknown destination, the guns and vehicles by road, the rest of the regiment, including the Colonel, by train – and I was made train Quartermaster.

The Indian railway system is one of the world's wonders. Gigantic steam locomotives snort across the endless plains, stations contain a microcosm of Indian society, bridges are major engineering accomplishments and the main stations, like Victoria Terminus, Bombay, could be taken for Gothic Revival cathedrals. But amongst the never-ending traffic on the system, troop trains take the lowest place. In peacetime they always carried coffins to cope with heat stroke casualties. We took a week from Campbellpore to Ranchi and were at least two days late on arrival. Rations were difficult to organise with constant revision of the timetable and the troops did not get much more than bully and biscuits with occasional vegetables for most of the journey.

At Ranchi we joined the new 23rd Indian Division commanded by Major General Reggie Savory, our divisional sign being the fighting cock. Soon we were on the train again, going up to Assam and again taking many days to get there.

The Japanese advance up Burma, driving before them the remnants of two British Divisions and countless civilians, had petered out as supplies became exhausted and the monsoon beat down. The only line of communication with our 'front' was a single line narrow gauge railway, broken at the Brahmaputra where everything had to cross the river by ferry, to Manipur Road station, then up a twisting mountain road for 120 miles to Imphal, the capital of the tiny Manipur State. Here we found ourselves in support of the infantry who endeavoured to cover the two roads which led to Burma and the Chindwin river where our retreating forces had had to leave all their transport to cover the remaining miles on foot. Up these roads and through the jungle paths came not only retreating soldiers in various stages of distress, but hundreds and hundreds of civilians who sought thus to escape the Japs, men, women and children, trekking through the jungle, soaked by the monsoon, many ill with malaria or dysentery, dying by the roadside in large numbers. It was an awesome sight to us inexperienced fledgling soldiers.

And then to me came a metaphorical bombshell. A sudden posting from GHQ to the position of Staff Lieutenant, Camouflage, HQ4 Corps, a legacy of my Distinction on the Poona Camouflage Course. I was very annoyed, the Colonel furious. He sought all means to block the posting but nothing apparently could stand in the way of a GHQ order. I found afterwards that he had me in mind to be Adjutant of the Regiment.

I had no idea what a Corps Headquarters was and very confusing I found it, a mass of officers and initials with a lieutenant-general at the apex. Once more the new boy. It was a chaotic life; the monsoon of 1942 was heavy though we were at least under cover in commandeered huts made principally of mud and bamboo. Not so the retreating Burma army and the civilians whom we attempted to help on their way. There was certainly no camouflage to do and I was occupied on sundry jobs such as checking the refugees for arms and confiscating anything found. We lived first at Dimapur at the foot of the Manipur Road, as hot and humid a place as one could find with the largest mosquitoes imaginable and a high rate of malaria. Later we moved to Kohima, a delightful change in that it was at 4,000 feet or so, but with the monsoon at its height, paths and roads became swamps, bridges were washed away and we lived on bully and biscuits amongst the Nagas, picturesque former head hunters, simple, enthusiastic and happy people.

After some months things changed for the better. Corps HQ was moved back to Jorhat and established in the buildings of the Indian Tea Association's research laboratories. At the same time my immediate superior was transferred and I was promoted to General Staff Officer Grade III and became a captain – and on Indian rates of pay. Before the war I had hoped that one day, much later in life, I might earn £1,000 a year; and now here I was already near that figure – and with nothing to spend it on. A further pleasure was the establishment at Jorhat of a contact which was a wonderful solace for the next two years.

Having had a bout of stomach trouble, I was somewhat frail when I arrived at Jorhat and this was noticed by a motherly English lady, Mrs Tunstall, who lived with her husband, a scientist who ran the tea research station, in a bungalow near our HQ. She invited me to stay with them for a period and she would feed me up! I wangled permission and thus established a home with the Tunstalls for several weeks before returning to the Mess. They were opposites: he talked incessantly and was always coming up with unusual ideas, walking into my bedroom one morning at 6.30 a.m. saying, "I've got it, Charlesworth, blowpipes!". Another Tunstall way to win the war, the Japs to be ambushed on narrow jungle paths by men armed with blowpipes and poison darts which he would manufacture. He periodically picked out promising Indian boys, paid for and supervised their education, and launched them into careers. He paid less attention to his own two children, far away at school in England, whereas his wife thought of them constantly. She was wonderfully kind to me, made me cakes, did my mending, wrote to my mother about me and really treated me as an adopted son. In all my travels in Assam I called whenever I could at Jorhat and must have arrived and departed at every hour of the day and night; she always had a bed made up for me and any companion I might have. She had done sterling work in dealing with the Burma refugees for which she was awarded the MBE.

I was with the Corps until early 1944 with my little unit – a clerk called Flett, a draughtsman called Tagg and a batman called Fudge. My work was to advise all Corps units on camouflage, to attend siting boards when units moved in and to organise courses for officers. So I was constantly on the move. I also had some training in air photo interpretation and the RAF supplied me with air photos of the whole area. We tried to fit our camps into the pattern of trees, tracks and paddy fields. After Jorhat we moved to Imphal and installed ourselves in native huts in a comfortable bit of jungle. We were only bombed on two occasions, after each of which my services were suddenly at a premium as everyone endeavoured to improve their camouflage. I really enjoyed the lecturing and organising demonstrations.

As in all semi-static formations we made ourselves as comfortable as possible and I acquired a portable gramophone with some records which was a great joy; also a tin bath instead of the unsatisfactory canvas bucket. At Jorhat we enjoyed the company of the tea planters and their families and the facilities of the Planters Club, when we had time to use them. This was not very often as our noses were kept very much to the grindstone by General Scoones, our Corps Commander, whom we all cordially disliked. However, as ever, I found congenial friends, particularly Robin Johnston, a Wykehamist and Lloyds underwriter, with whom I had much in common. In the Mess we played bridge, sang songs and drank whatever the rations provided; three bottles of beer a month, some bad whisky made at Nasik and worse gin made by Carew's. It was at this time that I wrote quite a lot of light verse of a topical nature which served to amuse the Mess of which, as always seemed to happen, I became Mess Secretary.

Occasionally, I got away on courses or conferences. It took three days to get back to Calcutta, so primitive were our communications, but once there the shops, the films and the social life transformed our lives after months of jungle life. One had only to sit in the foyer of the Grand Hotel for an hour and one was bound to meet friends, in fact all over India in the places I was stationed – or visited – Rawalpindi, Ranchi, Imphal, Calcutta, Poona, Bangalore, Bombay, could be found contacts. Once waiting in Calcutta for a fortnight while GHQ were deciding on my next posting, I met Robin Mellor of the Titaghur Paper Company, a friend's brother, who took me to lunch at the Bengal Club, the high point of Bengal social life. At the other end of the scale I found myself being taken by an Indian friend to a meeting of the Indian Friends of the Soviet Union where revolution was being plotted; and to attend, in mufti, the East-West Club, a body seeking understanding between the young of India and England, for this was the time of the 'Quit India' movement, sabotage and political unrest, with Gandhi in prison again.

Quite apart from the army, these were interesting years to be in India; I followed the politics closely. They were years of constant change. I was glad to have been present in the last days of the Raj (a word never used then), when the ICS ruled unchallenged, law and order was maintained, trains ran on time and the enormous bureaucracy plodded on under the time-honoured system – a pyramid with some carefully limited work at every level, checked by someone else. Indian history increasingly interested me and I read a lot.

I was never homesick. India soon became a second home. How fortunate I was to have two bases – when I could get to them – Lady Inglis in Poona and Mrs Tunstall in Assam, whose hospitable houses were always open to me and to both of whom I was a surrogate son. The nature of my work involved travel on those splendid Indian trains and the experience of life in different and contrasting places: the bare hills of the Frontier, the Punjab plains, the Assamese jungle, the well ordered tea estates, the austere Western Ghats and – later – southern India with its teeming villages and endless paddy fields. I had more than a passing acquaintance with the great cities – Delhi, Calcutta, Bombay, and with smaller stations like Rawalpindi and Bangalore. I enjoyed the great hotels – the Taj in Bombay, Maidens in Delhi, Laurie's in Agra, Flashman's in Rawalpindi, Dean's at Peshawar, Faldetti's in Lahore, with their herbaceous borders, immaculate lawns and equally immaculate bearers in white pyjamas and imposing pugris (turbans) with matching sashes. Here we sat out under the trees in winter consuming vast curry lunches or inside in lofty halls in summer, cool under the punkahs.

The old settled India of the Raj gradually disappeared with the onset of wartime shortages and dislocation. The Bengal famine of 1943 changed the face of Calcutta, brought home to me when, walking across the maidan one night in the blackout, I stepped on a dead baby. In that year American troops began to arrive in numbers with their distorted ideas of 'colonialism', their high standard of living, their bulging wallets and their sexual hunger. ("I've never had to *pay* for it before".) Prices shot up in every area.

Memory distorts. The sweaty discomfort, the incessant monsoon rain, the prickly heat, the stomach troubles, the low drone of the offensive mosquito, the leech which threaded itself through your bootlace holes – all fall into the background before the delight of bright cold days under the sun of the Punjab, the richness of the jungle, the exotic colours, the orchids growing round our jungle home, the welcome cool of the velvety evenings and the unexpected brightness of the moon and stars. India has both space and closeness; roughness and gentleness. I think with gratitude of the good feeling which – however loud politicians might shout – existed between Indians and the British, a not unhappy apartheid. As I said goodbye to our old mali (gardener) at Campbellpore, whose work I had greatly appreciated, tears suddenly stood in his eyes and unexpectedly my heart was touched. How much they wanted to establish friendly contact, these communist students in Calcutta. How inevitable the hospitable cup of tea in so many passing contacts.

In June 1943 I was sent on a refresher course at the Camouflage School in Poona; I came out top! What could it be that made me adept in a subject in which I was really not much interested? After this course I had ten days leave. My only leave in India so far had been ten days while in Campbell-pore which I had spent by myself in Delhi, absorbing the history, visiting the tombs and temples, admiring Lutyens's great concept of the imperial capital and living a luxurious but solitary hotel life. (There are seven past cities of Delhi, now all in ruins. When visiting New Delhi, Clemenceau, the French Prime Minister, was shown this latest capital and commented, "This will make the finest ruin of all!") Now I was going to Kashmir with John Cotterill, a 4 Corps friend. No one lucky enough to have had leave in Kashmir in those days is likely to forget it: houseboat living on the Dahl lake, exhilarating pony rides, golf at Gulmarg, expeditions and parties, bargaining with Suffering Moses and other sellers of shawls and papier mâché, and all against the backdrop of the mountains and lakes of one of the most beautiful places in the world. John and I soon got to know congenial companions, male and female. Srinagar was full of 'abandoned wives' and girls on leave.

It was difficult to re-adjust to life in Imphal in our jungly home. But my days with HQ4 Corps were numbered after nearly two years with General Scoones. It had been interesting to belong to a field HQ to which came figures of importance but I was eager for a change and there seemed no chance of going back to the regiment whose Colonel continued unsuccess-fully to try and get hold of me. I did not meet but had the opportunity to see Wavell, that brilliant yet unlikely Wykehamist soldier, whose anthology 'Other Men's Flowers' I carried everywhere, and to see Auchinleck, ad-mired by all ranks of the Indian Army whose finest traditions he embodied: both men badly treated by Churchill. Through our HQ went at one time Wingate and his Chindits, darkly lowering in uncertain temper when I saw him, and in Imphal I first met General Slim, commander of the 14th Army to which we belonged, 'the Forgotten Army' as we called ourselves, shut away on the far side of the world, bottom priority for everything, hardly heard of by the great British public at home. It was only later that Churchill was to praise the 14th Army "the like of which has not been seen since Xerxes crossed the Hellespont", and its commander, one of the very great captains, who welded together Indians, Pathans, Africans, Chinese, Gurk-has and soldiers from all over the British Isles into a force which fought the last great land battle of the war and inflicted on one of the great warrior nations its most crushing defeat. Without any of the mystique with which such as Mountbatten, Montgomery and Patten used to surround them-selves, Slim was the soldier's general, radiating confidence under his bush hat with his jutting jaw, unfussed and unfussy, terse and to the point. When

With the OUDS in The Duchess of Malfi

India 1942

On the Tirpitz

Dagmar. Hans Andersen's Mermaid?

White City 1947. Hurdling for Oxford

After the War. Father, Richard, Olive, Mother, M.L.C.

VIth form room at Geelong
Grammar School

Afghanistan. Jamie Learmonth,
M.L.C., John Sutherland

Tony Trench and Robin Moulsdale

wounded in Mesopotamia in the Great War, he had sent his wife an economical telegram – "Bullet Bottom Better Bill".

Before I left 4 Corps we had a quite successful entertainment which Tony Woodruff (whom I had known in the OUDS) and I organised, mainly song and dance with some topical sketches. Near Imphal were some massive phallic stones, rising to twenty feet or so. In fact a rest camp which was situated near them was known as Penis Park. This gave me the idea for the name of our dance band – The Imphallic Symbols – which contained some very good musicians. The show was an enormous success as hitherto there had been no entertainment for the troops of any kind; no ENSA parties penetrated to Imphal, no Vera Lynn came to assure us that we would meet again.

CHAPTER XII

Return – Release

Shout while ye journey home! Songs be in every mouth!
Lo from the North we come, from East and West and South.

C. E. Oakley

In October I left Assam, as I wrongly thought for ever, and had the good fortune to hitch a lift, with all my kit, on an American Dakota to Delhi. The American presence was now very considerable, flying 'across the Hump' from Assam to Chungking in the wholly unprofitable task of propping up the doomed Chiang Kai-shek. It was exhilarating flying along the line of the Himalayas on a clear day as I once more headed for the unknown. After considerable chaos, order and counter-order, I found myself posted to 33 Corps in Bombay and living in a remarkable Mess in the house owned by Lady Dinjabhuoy Bombajee, a rich and patriotic Parsee, where we used bathrooms with gold taps, although crowded six to a room. The house was fortunately very close to Breach Kandy, Bombay's best known swimming pool. My stay there was not long and I was directed by 33 Corps to join a 'secret' formation located near Poona which turned out to be a Beach Group.

At that time plans were in hand to invade Burma from the sea and certain formations were being trained for combined operations. The Beach Group was to land behind the assault troops and organise the beach head – traffic control, mine lifting, signals, supply and ordnance depots, with a defence company under command; it was a polyglot formation and my role was to control the camouflage and, if possible, mount a deception plan. In fact I turned into an extra staff captain on the Beach Group HQ. For weeks we practised our role, spending much time on the delightful beaches south of Bombay, sleeping beside the waving coconut palms under the stars and daily practising schemes. In and out of the landing craft we went with the infantry, goaded, encouraged and cursed by our CO, Colonel Jake Armstrong of the Royal Scots Fusiliers, who lived on a short fuse. Amongst other things I prepared an elaborate dummy beach dump area and photographed it from the air. It was meant to draw Japanese bombs; I at any rate thought it convincing. For some time we were at Ratnagiri, a small town on the coast with a Mahratta Fort on its hill top. This was my first contact with the Mahrattas, small, dark and wiry fighting men, who had given Wellington such trouble in the wars of the early nineteenth century. Now they provided numerous battalions to the Indian Army.

At Poona there was time for some social life and I got to know an attractive girl called Ruth with whom I went dancing at the Turf Club which maintained its pre-war magnificence and was the scene of my twenty-fifth birthday party in January 1944. Through Ruth I met Oliver Wakefield, then a well-known stage comedian, and through Oliver I found myself taking part in a film being made for the RAF. This was called *It Can Be Done* and featured Oliver as an RAF pilot who bailed out in Burma and found his way back to our lines by the gadgets provided for our pilots at that time such as compasses in buttons, maps on handkerchiefs, portable rations and so on. I had a part as a Wing Commander, Oliver's commanding officer. We made the film at night in the Bombay studios amongst the gorgeous sets of the Indian film makers. India made more films than any other country, almost invariably on the theme of unrequited love; until very recently kissing on film was not allowed so true love was always thwarted. Our film was, I believe, shown in RAF stations but sadly I never saw it.

Poona had become for me a very familiar station. Many times I bicycled from our camp to the hospitable Inglis household where there was always good civilian company and a meal. We were allowed to use the Government House swimming pool and squash courts where I played a great deal, generally with Guy Cooper, a member of our Beach Group medical team, who had been a Davis Cup tennis player.

By February we were all prepared to go, supposedly fully trained. Lord Mountbatten came to see us to wish us well and advance parties were already en route to Calcutta, the take off point, when one night I, as duty officer, received a message that the whole operation was cancelled! What an anti-climax. Years later I found out that the operation was impossible because of the shortage of landing craft which would have had to have come from Europe where they were fully occupied. As these craft would have taken weeks to get to India and as this must have been known for at least a couple of months, it is difficult to understand why our preparations were allowed to reach the advanced stage which they did, with some parties already travelling.

Hitherto my health in India, apart from stomach troubles from time to time, had been very good and amazingly I had avoided malaria despite living in one of the most notorious malarial areas. But in March I felt jaded, lost appetite and energy and was admitted to hospital in Poona with hepatitis. In no time I lost two stone and went yellow, building up again only gradually. The good Lady Inglis came to see me often and, as she did throughout my time in India, supplied me with books from the Poona Club library. Ruth, who was really very beautiful, sat on my bed from time to time; my fellow patients would have gone green with envy were they not already yellow. One day as we lay in our beds there came a distant somewhat muffled rumble as though of thunder. It transpired that this was the explosion of an ammunition ship in Bombay harbour, a hundred miles away. This major catastrophe – no part of the Bombay fire brigade, man or machine, was ever found – had for me a personal consequence. I had placed all my kit not wanted for active service in the care of Cox and Kings and it was stored in their sheds by the docks; thus I lost everything, including irreplaceable diaries and photographs.

After five weary weeks I was at length discharged from hospital and given a month's alcohol-free sick leave. Hearing of the delights of Ootaca-mund in the Nilgiri Hills I took the train – the Deccan Queen – for the south. Amongst the rolling grass-covered downs of that wholly delightful place I had such a leave as dreams are made on, much assisted in this by getting to know a beautiful girl called Elizabeth; golf, dinners, dances, tennis and walks among the eucalyptus groves filled the days and nights. "The best time I ever had in my life", I wrote ecstatically in my diary. So inspired was I that I wrote several pieces of light verse on the passing scene which were published in *Onlooker*, the Indian equivalent of *The Tatler*, which earned me ten rupees a time.

But what next? For three months I was a member of 33 Corps HQ established in Bangalore. This was a pleasant station with its social life based on the United Services Club. There were even a respectable number of girls, unlike the general Indian situation of a hundred men to a girl, for the WRENS had arrived and added some colour to the station. As the commander of the Southern Army, General Beresford-Peirse is said to have put it, "Up with the lark and to bed with the WREN". Certainly these girls fresh from England were a change from the rather hard-bitten locals to whom we gave descriptive nicknames – Winnie the Poonah, Betty, the girl who put the bang in Bangalore, and other names less repeatable.

Here as ever I met friends – Robin Johnston, back from the Chindit expedition, and a Shrewsbury friend, Noel Catterall, both in the Brigade commanded by Bernard Fergusson, that engaging and erudite Chindit leader with whom we discussed literature and played deck tennis. I discovered that Noel on his leave had been taking Elizabeth out at Ooty which made me very jealous! Also in Bangalore was Richard Clarke, a Bulford original, who had been awarded the MC on the first Chindit expedition which had experienced one-third casualties. Richard told me that he wondered whether he would have the strength to swim the wide Chindwin river on his return but in fact he floated across quite easily, weighing (as it afterwards transpired) only seven stone.

My work was to take a mobile camouflage training team to various formations in south India; a driver and batman and a vehicle full of equipment was my little command and we traversed the Deccan plain giving two or three day courses – lectures, films and demonstrations. I felt I was really getting quite adept at this sort of thing and have never had difficulty in speaking on my feet. Once when driving in a remote part of south India, my truck broke down and we had to stay the night in the vehicle. Around us inevitably gathered all the village children, shy but eager to communicate. One boy had a fair knowledge of English and recited for me a long forgotten though vaguely familiar poem, whose refrain was "Oh Mary call the cattle home across the sands of Dee". Looking across the wide sweep of the Deccan with its distant horizons, surrounded by Indians, their scrawny cattle and rice fields, it seemed extraordinary to hear this boy speak of the rich Cheshire landscape, its fat cows and the winding River Dee. What extraordinary ramifications the Indian Empire had. I took the boy's address and we wrote to each other until I left India.

Then came the next posting, this time to a formation called a FAMO – Forward Airfields Maintenance Organisation. This was the Beach Group transposed to a different medium. A FAMO was to keep close behind the forward troops to establish an air strip with great speed and thus open supply points immediately behind the assault. We had the same miscellaneous troops as a Beach Group with much the same function. For two months we trained at Visapur, near Poona, then off again to Assam and to Imphal. By now the great battles of Imphal and Kohima were over and the 14th Army was set to chase the Japs out of Burma in the cold weather of 1944–45. We were attached to the 19th Indian Division commanded by General Rees, a voluble little Welshman with superabundant energy, once found singing hymns with a group of Assamese Christians, he singing in Welsh, they in Khasi. We were a small and happy headquarters, Colonel Bertie Bayliss in command and Charles Cole as brigade major, a good friend for whom after the war I was best man. (I had already in India been best man to two friends; both marriages ended disastrously.) Also on the staff was Tony Hampton, a Highland Chieftain friend, with whom I had much in common.

After years of waiting, the reconquest of Burma took only three months. The 14th Army pushed on with great speed and we found ourselves constantly moving, depending on air supply almost entirely. This was provided by American Dakotas and by parachute drop. We established our air strips, occasionally under distant fire, and the C47s came churning in, load after load, sometimes, before the strips were ready, showering us with parachuted supplies. Fortunately the Jap air force was little seen though there was an occasion when we lost four Dakotas, caught on the ground in a night raid. A large proportion of the population of Burma was clothed in parachute silk by the end of the campaign. We saw 19th Div across the Chindwin, Pete Rees in the forefront wearing his silk neckerchief and urging his troops forward. Once we were visited by the Supremo, Lord Mountbatten, on one of his carefully organised informal visits. Driving his own Jeep with a small escort he erupted out of the jungle, an unlikely figure in full naval uniform with row upon row of medal ribbons and marmalade all over his cap. He gathered the troops around him, mounted the back of his Jeep and gave us a twenty-minute pep talk; it was a magnificent performance, direct and humorous, explaining the part we were playing in the world war scenario. One could almost see morale rising by the minute. Three cheers and he had disappeared in a cloud of dust to give the next performance elsewhere. Of Mountbatten, Denis Healey later wrote, "Few other officers shared his confidence in his own qualifications for the job". But we were not to know that.

When forces were gathering for the capture of Mandalay, there came to me that message which every British soldier awaited – report to Deolali for repatriation! Those who had completed four years of service in India were to return to England under a scheme called PYTHON. So I took my farewells in Burma from good FAMO friends, travelled to Calcutta where I met the girl to whom I had been writing for all these years, Patricia – not seen since Rawalpindi in 1941. We had a happy few days together but alas, there could be no future as her home was now Calcutta and I was home-ward bound. I just had time for a few days leave in Darjeeling to see that great spectacle, sunrise on Kachenjunga seen from Tiger Hill, before taking the train across India for the last time to join the transit camp at Deolali, now expanded into a large station instead of the cosy village which I had previously known. I had come full circle: it seemed an age since our arrival as cadets when I used to look out of the window as the sun beat down on Temple Hill and pinch myself to ensure the reality of my actually being in India. Now the Sub-continent had become my second home.

Here at Deolali were three of our original Bulford squad, Desmond Manners, Christopher Fisher and John Buss. I seemed to have had a more interesting life than they had had, Desmond remaining in a field regiment all his time, Christopher being repeatedly attacked by malaria and trans-ferred to administrative work, and John spending most of his time in an inactive regiment. Our voyage home through the Mediterranean was a contrast to the 'Highland Chieftain': much bridge was played, much Coca-Cola drunk; it was a shock to us to find that ships were now dry.

After four years and four months overseas, we looked with curious eyes from the windows of our slow troop train, bearing us from Greenock to Woolwich; a battle-scarred country, shabby and stretched, the people white-skinned and strained in contrast to the brown skins and perpetual sunshine we had left. A slow train took me from Euston to Northampton, wandering past places with remembered names – Bletchley, Wolverton, Castlethorpe, Roade, as I reflected on the four years and four months that had passed since I last saw Northamptonshire. Few events have touched me more deeply than that return home to the familiar surroundings of childhood. My mother was on the platform to greet me, my father at the front door of that same house where I had been born. They were both well; morale had remained high despite the absence of both their sons overseas. My mother was having one of her energetic periods in contrast to her heavy depressions; my father was now seventy-eight but reasonably fit. Their letters had much sustained me despite the seven weeks it took for them to arrive. I was fortunate to be home for VE Day but to those of us from the Far East, the rejoicing was tempered by the thought of the expected long campaign against the Japs. I have never been in any doubt that it was right to drop the atom bombs (but why two?) thus finishing the war at a stroke and saving millions of lives.

I had four weeks of unalloyed enjoyment, spent largely visiting friends and the families of those with whom I had served. Adam Fox was now a Canon of Westminster Abbey and I had a joyful reunion with him at the Athenaeum; also at the Abbey was Willie McKie, previously organist at Magdalen, who invited me to sit at his side in the organ loft whenever I managed to attend a service in the Abbey. In Oxford I met for dinner Dorothy Johnston, to give her news of Robin; and in Sheffield I stayed with Tony Hampton's family. I now had my much loved Talbot Ten on the road again with a special allowance of overseas leave petrol. But there was a dark side to this happy time. Often at the back of my mind were thoughts of those for whom there would be no homecoming. Hard to bear for me was the loss of my three closest friends with whom bonds had been forged in our happy days at Shrewsbury in Oldham's and with whom I had been in very close touch until war parted us. John Lee, as brave a soldier as any with a quite outstanding record with the KSLI, was killed at Anzio; Grey Thornycroft, most attractive of men, had been blown up by a mine in North Africa; John Vaisey's bomber did not return from its first operational flight. Every Remembrance Day they come back to me in those long two minutes silence.

One day a voice from the War Office came through on the phone; it was intended to post me as Staff Captain to a Liaison Headquarters operating with the Norwegian Brigade in Scotland; but I was not compelled to take this posting as they would soon be going overseas and I had the right to a home posting after my years abroad. I thought for ten seconds then agreed. Another few days and I found myself with my new immediate superior, Noel Lewis, flying in a Catalina to Tromsø in the Arctic Circle. The flight, from Shetland, took most of the day and was bitterly cold; Tromsø was under fog and we diverted farther down the coast to Bødo. Taxiing in across the fjord, we waved to those coming to meet us in small boats; rather furtively they waved back. Our first mistake; they were of course Germans, bedecked with swastikas. We were the first British soldiers into Bødo and objects of curiosity, more especially as Noel wore a kilt. Ensconced in a hotel, we wearily relaxed over a drink, thinking it to be about nine in the evening. We had reckoned without the midnight sun; it was 1.00 a.m.

Soon settled in what had recently been the Gestapo headquarters in Tromsø, we gradually realised the magnitude of the task which faced our small force. We became HQ Tromsø Zone, which covered all of Norway that lay inside the Arctic Circle, approximately 400 miles by 60 miles with only one axis road of communication. In 1944 the Russians had invaded Norway through the northernmost province in Finnmark and had slowly driven back the Germans who had carried out a thorough scorched earth policy as they withdrew. In our Zone were 130,000 Germans and 40,000 Russian prisoners-of-war. Our force consisted of a brigade of ex-anti-aircraft gunners, mostly elderly, and the Norwegian Brigade which had spent the war in Scotland, training for an invasion which had never materialised. We were outnumbered by the Germans by twelve to one. Fortunately they gave no trouble as they concentrated in Reservations to await evacuation.

To be controlling this large German force was a strange sensation for our small staff. The German infrastructure had to be maintained if chaos was to be avoided so, for instance, we used the German telephone system, road transport and even a couple of old unreliable Junkers aircraft which rumbled round our Zone. Fortunately an outstanding soldier was sent from Germany to command the Tromsø Zone, Brigadier F.W. Sanders, Durham Light Infantry, who had won the DSO in France. Of all the COs under whom I served, he was the best. Firm in decision, he was quick to cut to the heart of the many diverse problems which faced us; to his staff he was considerate and wholly relaxed in the Mess. We enjoyed his company and sought it – not always the attitude of junior officers to their commanding officers. We only numbered a dozen or so on the HQ staff and at first we worked for excessively long hours.

My own responsibility lay with the supply of the German army and its concentration in Reservations. In our Zone the Germans had 12,000 vehicles and 16,000 horses; what was to happen to them? We disposed of as many as possible to the Norwegians (under an Enemy War Material procedure), took what vehicles we ourselves wanted and gathered the rest into dumps which, later in the year, were covered with snow and rusted away. Having got rid of as many horses as possible, the rest were slaughtered and the Germans ate horse for the remainder of their stay. The total equipment of the German army was listed and stacked in enormous depots; it was a vast task over which I attempted to keep some control. Every day we had a formal meeting with the German staff officers, led by Major Hans, an excellent example of the German General Staff, immaculate in dress, correct in behaviour, efficient in execution of every order. I dealt with a Lieutenant Hahn, a one-time theology student. We had strict orders that there should be no fraternisation but it was difficult to exclude entirely the human element from our relationship.

It did not take long for us to realise that, as all German resources were ours, we could confiscate any items which we wanted for our personal use – with the complete concurrence of the Norwegian Government. We took over the vast German stocks of wine which were then sold in our Messes and canteens for a nominal sum; every HQ officer was soon driving a Mercedes; we each had a Leica camera, a pair of field glasses, typewriter, radio and a pair of skis. Accumulating so much loot, we needed the wherewithal to transport it home so I had the German carpenters make us large wooden cases – loot boxes; I still have mine. More ambitiously we all took to riding and set up a stable, manned by the Germans, and enjoyed evening rides round Tromsø island. Life in the Arctic Circle had its increasing attractions as we settled down into routine. My fellow staff captain, Hamish McGhie, a journalist, soon had the Tromsø presses rolling to produce a weekly newspaper, the *Arctic Times*. Although contact with the locals was very limited, another HQ officer, Ronny Buchanan, surprised us all by ringing up from Narvik, where he was stationed, to say that he had got engaged to a most beautiful girl called Elina Sundt – the first of several matrimonial casualties. Gradually people became aware of us in our northern fastness and we had visits from English journalists. One day we were visited by Wing Commander Tait who had led the flight which sunk the *Tirpitz*; he wore two medal ribbons, DSO with two bars and DFC with three. The *Tirpitz* lay upside down in the fjord and was the scene of several evening parties. We went out by launch and picnicked on her keel, popping champagne corks the while.

Meanwhile the main object of our presence was slowly being achieved as the Germans were sent home, passing through screening camps before entering the ships. They were allowed to keep only personal possessions, all extraneous things being taken from them. Thus their loot became our loot. Very early on we had ordered all swastikas to be removed; I had a small room filled with them. So they returned as anonymous civilians, a few with Norwegian wives. Repatriation was not an easy task. There were thirty nationalities in the Germany army and some stateless men with nowhere to go. Some were suspected of war crimes. The Russians, whom we found very difficult to deal with, scrutinised every German and detained many. We had been very relieved when the last of the Russian POWs was shipped off to Murmansk where, as we learnt, there were no welcoming crowds to greet their homecoming, but all were marched off to barracks under guard.

By September our task was done. What next? To our delight we were ordered down to Oslo to take over the Oslo Zone, all other troops being gradually sent home. When I flew off from Tromsø in a Sunderland flying boat, we circled the island for a last good-bye. By now the coming winter had already begun to take a grip. When we had arrived in May snow still lay on the ground; during the brief summer the crops had been planted, had grown and were already harvested, accelerated by sunshine for most of the hours of day and night. Soon there would only be four or five hours daylight.

In Oslo we took over from a large American force which included eighty officers. At first I, the advance party, was puzzled as to how our little headquarters could take on the responsibility of so many and it was only gradually that I realised that most of their time was spent on administering themselves. I was asked to the American farewell party which was on an unimaginable scale, every kind of delicacy, gifts for the ladies and ever-flowing champagne.

The three regiments in our Brigade established themselves in Oslo and its environs while we, the Headquarters, commandeered a delightful establishment, the Rose Hotel. We took the precaution of bringing a thousand cases of wine with us down from Tromsø together with our fleet of German cars – and the horses, soon established in a stable at Bogstad just outside the city. Overall Allied command was in the hands of General Graham's 50 Div, with whom we established very good relations, particularly with their General Staff department which included Iain Macleod, the man who should have been Prime Minister, one of the most amusing characters I met in the war. I still have the invitation to his birthday party which started: "Nov 11 is (a) Armistice Day, (b) my birthday. To celebrate sub.para. (b) a room has been reserved at the Frognesetter Restaurant. Personnel as shown in para. 3 will RV there at 1945 hrs. They are requested to bring (i) a bottle (ii) a girl: in that order of priority" (etc). Having already a reputation for statistics, he was appointed bookie for the race meeting which we planned but which had to be cancelled because of frost, in which post his abilities would have shown as clearly as they did later when he became Chancellor of the Exchequer.

Those four months of 1945 in Oslo were amongst the happiest of my life. Work was minimal as only a few Germans remained and the Brigadier very reasonably arranged that we should work in the mornings or afternoons but not both. Through Ronny Buchanan (engaged to Elina) we got to know a most delightful group of girls of unsophisticated charm and striking good looks. Oslo – and indeed the whole of Norway – was in those days given up to celebration after the long years of German occupation and

British stock stood high. We gave parties in our Mess, we attended cele-
bratory dinners and dances all over the city, we galloped our horses
through the fields and woods and, when the frost came, commandeered a
riding school where for the first time I learned to jump, falling off from time
to time without any serious damage. We skated on the lakes and played ice
hockey, we ordered skis from the German stores and began to learn to ski
in what became a winter wonderland in the hills outside the city. My
companion in all these activities was a beautiful girl, Ellen-Joanna Gran,
whose father had been on Captain Scott's ill-fated expedition. Would this
be more than a passing affair? It bid fair not to be – but in the end she
married my companion Hamish McGhie! When exhausted from too
much activity, we went to the cinema where English films were showing, to concerts by the Oslo Philharmonic, to *Peer Gynt* at the Opera
House and once to see a performance of Noel Coward's *Private Lives* (*Privat
Liv*).

Our stay came to a climax when we mounted a farewell parade for King
Haakon outside the Palace. Fortunately I did not have to organise this as
we had a composite battalion of the Guards under command (their daily
changing of the guard in Oslo attracted hundreds of spectators), whose
RSM organised the whole parade, my part being to provide fires in braziers
out of sight where bandsmen in turn could go and unfreeze their instruments. Privately my most poignant memory is of Christmas Eve when I
had the great privilege of being invited to a Norwegian home. Katrina Berg
belonged to our circle of girls, her father Arild being the owner of a
well-known glass works, her mother an official of the International Red
Cross. Like most Norwegians, Arild had been in the Resistance and a bullet
hole in a window of their apartment testifies to the danger he had under-
gone. He had already taught me to ski up at the family hut in the woods
where we had spent weekends and he had become a close friend. The
whole family was present and I was the only stranger. All the rituals of
Christmas Eve were gone through – the reading of a chapter from the bible
by the youngest son, holding hands in a circle round the Christmas tree, the
singing of carols, the giving of gifts, an enormous meal and the constant
toasts in aquavit. The first peacetime Christmas meant so much to all of
them and their deep but unexpressed emotion communicated itself to me; I
have never forgotten that night.

It did not surprise us that the army arranged our departure for Boxing
Day. It was time to go: the Officers Club in Oslo was down to a ration of 500
bottles of champagne a week instead of a thousand. We gave our farewell
dance in the Mess. Fortunately our Brigade Supply officer was an excellent
pianist and by this time we had written a number of songs which we sang
on party nights. Each member of the Mess had a verse written about him.
With some blushes I reproduce mine. (638 Regt referred to had been

dissolved and its remaining men sent to the other two regiments, a process called 'cannibalization').

Versatile Michael is Staff Captain Ack and Quack,
It's wiser not to write to him in case it bounces back.
He's haunted by ghosts of 638, whom he cannibalized to achieve a
    state,
Of time to skate and ski, most incredibly.
The ladies and liquor have tried to get him down,
But his knees are awfully strong because he got them frightfully
    brown.
If anyone sees a horse on skis come skating through the town,
On top you'll find the versatile Staff Captain.

Tune: The Stately Homes of England

On 27th December we sailed away, loot carefully packed below, while on deck we waved until sight of land was lost to those beautiful girls and that lovely city which had welcomed us so enthusiastically and in which we had led a life that none of us would ever experience again.

So home at long last, this time permanently. During a short leave the family were reunited for the first time in five years. My brother Richard had prospered in the Transportation section of the Royal Engineers and was now a colonel with the OBE. My sister Olive emerged from her secret work at Bletchley Park in the Enigma organisation with lips tightly sealed. My mother, after months of depression, had revived in 1945 and was full of energy and initiative, still involved with Maternity and Child Welfare. My father pursued his measured routine of playing bridge and watching cricket and football. The musical Sunday evenings had continued through the war and brought a great variety of people to the house. As a thank offering for our survival, Richard, Olive and I gave Mother a statue which she had much admired, a bronze of a boy looking upward, entitled 'And All the Trumpets Sounded'; it was by Lady Kennet, widow of Captain Scott of the Antarctic.

With six months still to serve, I now found myself in an extremely comfortable billet – Adjutant of Woolwich garrison. It sounded quite imposing as the garrison included the gigantic Royal Artillery depot, then seething with troops coming and going, many awaiting release. I soon found that our HQ proceeded on oiled wheels, largely staffed by civilian clerks, mostly elderly, who knew the answer to everything. The tone was set by our Commanding Officer, a brigadier at the end of his service, who was driven from his home in Kent to arrive in time for morning coffee, then mounted his horse for a ride round the garrison, retired early to the RA Mess for lunch and was on his way home long before 4 o'clock. The joy of Woolwich to me was its proximity to London. After five years overseas, the delights of the capital, even in its drab post-war format, were enjoyed fully. For the first time I discovered ballet, with Margot Fonteyn, Beryl Grey, Michael Soames and Robert Helpman at Covent Garden. The Old Vic company, then at the New Theatre, directed by Laurence Olivier, Ralph Richardson and John Burrell (a very remarkable Salopian, confined to a wheelchair from his boyhood), was having a brilliant season of classical plays. Olivier's *Oedipus* followed in the same programme by his Mr Puff in *The Critic*, left one alternately speechless with horror and with laughter. Then there were concerts with Beecham or Sargent; new films; and constant re-unions with old friends. I have always been a keeper-in-touch, aware of Dr Johnson's dictum that friendships have to be kept in constant repair, and I was a diligent letter writer. Remote in the Assamese jungle, I found I was writing sporadically to more than fifty correspondents; now, in London, there was a constant ebb and flow of friends.

As a member of the English Speaking Union, I was often in the club rooms in Charles Street and one day found myself sitting next to a delightful girl called Patricia, who had two tickets for the ballet and asked me to accompany her which I gratefully did. So began a happy friendship during these pleasurable months at Woolwich and we were constantly in each other's company. Was this indeed the beginning of what would today be called a relationship? Alas, no. She wisely saw that, as usual, I was distracted by too many things to concentrate on a serious relationship. Sadly, after some happy months, we parted. She would have been a wonderful wife ... but I as a husband?

In June I reported to a centre in Guildford to go through the business of release, an efficient process which saw me emerge with my civilian clothes in a cardboard box – grey suit, shirt, socks, shoes and a hat (never worn). Having some time to wait, I climbed up the hill to the embryo Guildford Cathedral and gave thanks for my safe emergence from nearly six years of army life.

In his autobiographical book *Changes and Chances*, Jimmy Street credits me with "a distinguished war record in Burma". Jimmy had an inventive imagination. My war record was wholly undistinguished. As is inevitable in the army, there had been long periods of boredom and discomfort but these had been balanced by the interest of travelling widely in India, of the unforgettable Norwegian experience, and the making of many friendships, some still enduring. In a sense six years of my life had been unconstructively consumed; but I have always been grateful for the experience. I echo Paul Scott's words: "There was a strange freedom in service life; always the uncertainty of tomorrow; the strange sights and smells of interesting places, the romance of distant lands, especially India where there was a life, an undefinable spirit, which was irrepressible and outweighed the faults and miseries and cruelties and corruption. That is why so many generations of the British have loved it and some of us will never get it out of our systems". I had been fortunate; unlike he of whom Kipling wrote,

> Two thousand pounds of education
> Drops to a ten rupee jezzail.

CHAPTER XIII

Oxford Again

Mente prosequamur grata
Regem et Reginam
Fautricemque amoena prata
Resonent Sabrinam.

The question of a career had never been more than a hypothetical subject but in the last months in the army 'after the war' discussions began to assume an air of reality. In youthful dreams I had seen myself on the stage, much as my mother had done fifty years before, but this romantic hankering had dissolved. As my army life drew to a close I had definitely decided to teach, partly influenced perhaps by my father's example, partly by the satisfaction I had had from teaching on my many camouflage courses, and partly by a feeling that I might be able to communicate with the young, in which the remembered happiness of Shrewsbury must have played a part.

So, at the mature age of twenty-seven, I decided to go back to Oxford and take a Diploma of Education, a qualification which I saw as an insurance, though it was not one which much impressed headmasters of public schools.

What sort of person had I become? What had I to offer the teaching profession? Gradually, rather painfully, I had evolved a basic Christian faith though without any Damascus Road experience; the war had certainly led one to question and think, especially when undergoing unexpected experiences in a strange land. I felt an affinity and loyalty to the Church of England and its comprehensiveness, its liturgy and its buildings. I had realised the value of friendships, though my contact with girls had generally been fleeting – they tended to give me up, detecting a superficiality in my feelings towards them. The army had obviously greatly expanded my experience of life. I had seen something of the sordid side; people do things when far away in wartime which home circumstances would inhibit. I was no exception. There had been a good deal of boredom and discomfort but little danger. My recreational interests lay in sport and in music, both curtailed by army life. I think I was more self-centred than many but had no very prominent vices; I had no temptation to overindulge in alcohol; I smoked a little, having taken it up to combat the giant mosquitoes of Assam; I leaned more to frugality than extravagance with money. All in all I was, I suppose, a fairly conventional not very exciting soldier-turned-civilian of whom several hundreds returned with me to Oxford to resume academic life, fortified only by a truncated, classless war degree which had left great gaps in my history knowledge, though I had read a lot while in India. (I remember covering the four volumes of Churchill's life of Marlborough while in hospital.)

In October 1946 my father died suddenly, without warning or illness. He was eighty-one. He retained his faculties to the end, living quietly in a long established routine, happy to see his children around him again, still going to the Club and still a member of the County Cricket Committee. Latterly he had only had two ambitions – to see the end of Hitler and to see his children survive the conflict intact. Both were achieved and he quietly took his leave. There were tributes from various of his former pupils, one from the editor of the local weekly paper, the *Northampton Independent*, who wrote of my father's little notes, periodically reminding him of some basic rule of English grammar when he had transgressed, or pointing out for instance that the word 'begin' was preferable to 'commence'. His high standards and insistence on accuracy had been communicated to several generations of Northampton boys. My mother was still a prey to intense depressions, lifting sometimes for several months, then falling again. My sister Olive, released from war work at Bletchley, now lived permanently at home, partly because of my mother's increasing decrepitude, and partly because she had no particular ambition to work elsewhere. My brother had now rejoined the railways, soon to be nationalised, and in 1950 married his one-time Oxford friend Freda, after she had obtained a divorce. My York-shire uncle and aunts were now dying or dead so, apart from my cousin Margie who taught in Portsmouth, there remained only Aunt May, still ensconced in her Forest Row house and looked after by a troupe of servants, though the Rolls Royce was no more, life having been scaled down to some degree.

Victor Gollancz writing of the summer term at Oxford in 1914 described it as having "a breathless quality of incommunicable magic". I would have used the same words of my last summer term of 1940. I had been warned that Oxford was not the same in letters from Dick Spilsbury, my next door neighbour in 1940, who returned to Oxford during the war from time to time. He wrote, *inter alia*, of Blackwell's bookshop where we had tended to spend too much time and money. "I will let the facts speak for themselves for no comment of mine could do justice to the enormity of change. While in Blackwell's one morning I was reading a pleasant book on the domestic virtues of mathematicians and about half way through I felt a tap on my shoulder and heard a voice enquiring if I wished to make a purchase. Now I can think of one charitable explanation of this; that the person accosting me was not a bookseller (I have often been asked to wrap up books myself) but a fellow reader who wished to read the book and frighten me off. If such was the case I am glad to think he failed. Still the suspicion remains".

If it was not the Oxford we had known, nevertheless it was a wonderful experience to be back again in that extraordinary year when the age range of those in residence included school leavers of eighteen and Wing Commanders of twenty-eight. Although I have seen it stated otherwise my own memory is of happy relationships between the generations. The physical conditions were bleak. Rationing was in full swing, with even bread being brought within the system, which had never happened in the war. It was one of the coldest winters of the century and fuel of every kind was short. Food in college was meagre. My South African friends would have dinner in college then immediately cross Magdalen Bridge to the local British Restaurant and have another complete meal. Those of us with Far East experience would fill up on chappattis and charcoal biscuits in the Taj Mahal Indian restaurant. Despite all this we thrived. I never heard of anyone who did not happily settle again to his books despite the years in between; there was a more than material hunger. Alan Taylor filled Magdalen Hall for his lectures in his own inimitable style, speaking for fifty minutes without pause, notes, or books. With total recall of dates, times, places and quotations, he held his listeners enthralled.

I lived in digs in Wellington Square with Noel Catterall, a Shrewsbury friend who had been a Chindit in Burma. We had – briefly – loved the same girl in Ootacamund. Our landlord was a man of goodwill who sometimes had surplus petrol coupons for us. My place of work was the Department of Education in Norham Gardens, conveniently close. Of the Diploma of Education there is little to be said. Our instructors were – to us – ancient and out of touch, regurgitating lectures of past days on the theory, history and practice of education without showing any sign that they had ever actually taught in a classroom themselves. I spent as little time as possible on these arid studies but spent time instead on reading and re-reading my history and going to general lectures by distinguished men of the day of which there were many. It was an exciting time: was a new socialist world really being born? In education, was the Butler Act of 1944 going wholly to re-shape the schools and presumably our careers? Was the implementation of the Beveridge Report really going to bring to the returned soldier the four essentials which he had been led to believe he would get – health care, a roof over his head, education for his children and benefits in time of trouble?

Taken up with the joys of return to civilian life, only dimly did we realise that 1947 was indeed a watershed year, the country half paralysed

economically by the arctic winter and shortage of fuel, the Attlee government pushing ahead with nationalisation but financially in desperate
straits until the marvellous lifeline of Marshall Aid. Above all the grim
realisation (apparent to politicians for some time but now obvious to all)
that the wartime alliance, the cosy figure of 'Uncle Joe' Stalin, the notion of
our Red Army friends, had been replaced by the Cold War which was to
last forty years. The private conversations which I had had with my
German liaison officer in Norway – against orders – in which he had
spoken of the Red menace and how we should soon be fighting it together
and which I had cheerfully pooh-poohed, returned to my mind as our
whole concept of the post-war world crumbled.

In Magdalen I resumed old activities with a few friends of pre-war days
and a cluster of new ones. We were soon involved in another Magdalen
melodrama. Playing a minor part was Ken Tynan who had arrived in the
college with a spectacular splash of self-publicity. He sat at the feet of C.S.
Lewis, for whom he had the greatest regard and who, to borrow a phrase
from James Agate, "looked more like a tobacco pouch than ever". I saw
quite a lot of Ken and did a service for him in rumpling his bed when he
spent a night out of college with whichever girlfriend was current. Brash,
confident and extremely intelligent, exotic in clothing and extravagant in
language, he certainly lightened the general scene of drabness in the
austere days of 'fish and Cripps'. His rise to becoming one of the best
known dramatic critics, to welcoming a new age in *Look Back in Anger*, to
personifying (or inventing?) the 'angry young man', to introducing nudity
on the stage in *Oh Calcutta*, was spectacular in the extreme, leaving behind
him a host of admirers and an equally large body of detractors. It was in his
later National Theatre days that someone described his voice as having "a
husky theatrical quality as if it had been smoked and bubbled through
gin".

But his influence did not yet prevail and, to me, one of the great joys of
peacetime was the enjoyment of the theatre after five years' abstinence –
the West End (*Ring Round the Moon* and the rising star of Paul Scofield),
Gilbert and Sullivan at the Savoy with John Reed, the Players Theatre (*The
Boy Friend*) and a revived Stratford (Robert Hardy – whom we had known
as 'Tim' at Shrewsbury – as Prince Hal). I think it was also at this time that
Paul Robeson appeared in *Othello*. Emlyn Williams's later comment was
'Look Black in Anger'.

Once more there was football in the not very distinguished college team
in which I again kept goal. As before we played the annual match against
Magdalene, Cambridge, for whom at that time played King Freddy, the
Kabaka of Uganda, destined for such an unhappy regal experience. Fortunately he had a considerable sense of humour, a favourite expression
being, "Well I'll be niggered!". There was also squash, in which game I

found myself the college No. 1, and there was hurdling on the old Iffley Road track where I had previously so failed to distinguish myself. But the situation had changed. I eyed my rivals: a South African who was reputed to have achieved an incredibly fast time in Johannesburg; an Australian of six foot eight inches to whom hurdles were as match boxes; a lithe sprinter from Marlborough; and other unknowns. We trained under Geoff Dyson, soon to be the chief National Coach, a man of many words, who was also coaching Maureen Gardiner, Britain's Olympic hope. She trained with us and subsequently won both an Olympic silver and also Geoff, becoming Mrs Dyson. To my great surprise I won the trials and became the Oxford first string, joining a motley team to face Cambridge at the White City, which included at one extreme 'Jaiker' Travers from Australia, a sixteen stone rugby international, and at the other the young Roger Bannister, who won the Mile in the first of his four successful races against Cambridge. At the starting blocks – but there weren't any for we dug holes in those days – I recognised in the opposition one F.R. Nicholson who had won the race in 1940 in Cambridge. We had both survived the war and here we were again. I got a good start but Nicholson gradually came up and beat me by two feet. My second string was Ray Barkway, a fine athlete who later represented England in the 1948 Olympics – but he never beat me! This has been a good line to shoot from time to time ...

The summer of 1947 was wonderfully fine for cricket on the Magdalen ground, providing one of the very happiest memories of that remarkable year. I have never played with such a happy or more varied team. Owen Hickey was the captain, a wily slow bowler, later the author of innumerable *Times* leaders; David Carr was the Carnot of the side – secretary and supreme organiser. He had been brewed up in a tank in Normandy, his right arm left without muscle. Painstakingly and with enormous application he had taught himself to bat with only one sound arm, becoming a really good club cricketer. Wounded in the face but now reshaped by plastic surgery was James Russell, the spearhead bowler sharing the attack with David Knight from South Africa. Also from Cape Town was David Philip (they were both at 'Bishops'), a mainstay of the batting. The former is now a lawyer, the latter a publisher and OUP representative, both in their native land. Evelyn Joll brought variety in more senses than one, change bowling and batting lower down the order; he is now chairman of Agnew's in Bond Street. Richard ('Round the Corner') Stewart bowled with guile. Willie Myers, most Wykehamist of Wykehamists, was a correct No. 3 and Mick Cudmore, from Adelaide, brought some solid sardonic Australian humour to the side. Only nineteen was Julian Bullard, bowling improbable leg breaks, later to be a Fellow of All Souls and a bright star in the Foreign Office. Keeping wicket amongst this array of talent meant keeping verbally as well as physically sharp. Our season ended with a tour in Devon. I have never enjoyed the companionship of the cricket field more.

The Dip. Ed. exams came and went without my really noticing. Cricket and social life were so much more important, especially as, during a winter skiing holiday, I had fallen in love with Dagmar. Working in London, Dagmar came from Oslo and was as beautiful a girl as could be found. She came often to Oxford, most memorably for the Magdalen Commem Ball, where she was quite dazzling. It was surprising that a ball of the old-fashioned type could be staged in 1947 but there was little lacking in what was – for me – the best dance ever. It was the final goodbye to Oxford, held in the most beautiful of colleges, surrounded by friends of all generations and in the companionship of the most beautiful girl in the world.

All that summer the sun shone and in the Vacation I went with David Chapman, my old Magdalen friend, and Dagmar on a long expedition to take her back to Oslo. David had a Jaguar and planned the route through the Netherlands, Germany, Denmark and Sweden. I suppose the most memorable part of this trip was going through Germany and seeing the devastation; it seemed impossible that Hamburg could ever be rebuilt. But the methodical Germans were busy sorting the rubble and picking the bricks from the bombed houses so that they could be used again. To drive into Sweden was an astonishing contrast, the Swedes bursting with health, the shops bursting with goods. So to Oslo, the hospitality of Dagmar's family, the renewal of old friendships with those delightful Norwegian girls of 1945 and with my dear friend Arild Berg, the glassmaker, still pouring aquavit. Oslo now seemed to me as familiar as Northampton. As David and I sailed back to England in that wonderful summer when the sun never ceased to shine, for the first time in my life I thought seriously of marriage, holding Dagmar in my heart.

My father was very conservative by instinct and cautious in practice; my mother was enterprising, interested in new situations and people and always ready to take the initiative. My own character includes both traits, with different emphases at different periods of my life. After the war the conservative instinct was uppermost. Home at last after six years wandering, I unenterprisingly turned to familiar pastures and towards the end of 1946 wrote to J.F. Wolfenden, now Headmaster of Shrewsbury, tentatively seeking a job. To my surprise, he invited me to see him and after some discussion and delay on his part while he worked out his staffing needs, I received a letter on 4th February 1947, which I remember opening in the Magdalen lodge, offering me an appointment as a second historian to Murray Senior, at the same time making it quite clear that this conferred no right of succession to Murray when and if he moved. I stood in the lodge in a brief trance of exhilaration. I had a job! And at Shrewsbury! Only in wilder moments of optimism had I expected this and I was in fact a beneficiary of a curious failing in Wolfenden, otherwise a very sharp practitioner. It fell to him to appoint no less than twenty-one new members of staff (nearly half the total) at a time when there was an immense amount of talent available, as five or six years' worth of potential teachers sought their first posts. There cannot have been a time when more ability was on offer, yet the Wolfenden appointments (with some exceptions) were thought by many to be an uninspiring lot. I think I owed my own appointment to the influence of my one-time housemaster, Sopwith. I have always felt that I was very fortunate. Wolfenden wrote that I would find his recent appointments "a pretty lively and enterprising lot". *Quot homines tot sententiae*. He also, with some reluctance, agreed that I could be inspected by the Oxford Department of Education during my first term. I should have had a practice teaching term during my year at Oxford which to many was the only worthwhile part of the course. But by persuasive eloquence I had managed to push the Department into letting me count my first teaching term as my practical experience, thus allowing me a free term in Oxford to attend lectures and do my own reading, while at the same time trying for my athletics Blue. It is a measure of those then running the Department that they could be thus bamboozled; I think they were a little apprehensive of the returned serviceman 'undergraduate'.

Thus I returned to Shrewsbury, ten years after I had left it. To return to one's own school to teach was indeed unambitious; but despite grave anxiety as to my ability to teach in the form room, wholly dependent on my inadequate knowlege, it was with pleasurable anticipation that I returned to the Site.

The school, though materially undamaged, had been much battered like the rest of the country during the war years. Particularly difficult had been the replacement of the twelve members of the staff who were in the services. Only one permanent appointment was made in the war, that of Guy Furnivall as School Chaplain. Toby Barnaby had a verse:

> Our great Headmaster, e'er he breathed
>   His tender last farewell,
> A Guy, Joe's comforter bequeathed,
>   A Furnivall.

('Joe' being the Revd J.O. Whitfield).

The school was kept going by the considerable labours of such as David Bevan (whose role was much as that of Kitchin in the First War), Stacy Colman, Patrick Childs and Jim Pitts-Tucker. The latter's skilful organisation deployed Salopians in the Shropshire fields and in harvest camps in greater numbers than any school in the country, according to the Ministry of Agriculture.

Hardy resigned in 1944 after twelve punishing years. In the war his merits shone brightly, his penchant for organisation and improvisation, his determination to sustain standards and to present to boys as normal a life as was possible. He was constantly concerned about numbers, both of staff and of boys. After the boom years of 1935–38 there was a sharp decline, mainly because all boys left at eighteen and in the later years at seveteen-and-a-half. The lowest figure was in 1943 when there were 433 boys, the highest in Hardy's time having been 535 in 1936. It is possible that Hardy's dictatorial attitudes to prep school headmasters and the considerable age of most of the housemasters had something to do with the decline. Hardy was stuck until almost the end of his time with the housemasters with whom he had started, save for Alan Phillips's appointment to Moser's in 1938. The blood was still not dry on the battlefields of the 1930s when Hardy had fought them to a standstill on salary and emoluments. But the proud barons of yesteryear were by now in reduced circumstances. Fewer boys meant a catastrophic drop in income. Mitford and Tombling were both in trouble with thirty-three and twenty-eight boys respectively. For them and others a rescue operation was launched and they became 'Managing Housemasters' on fixed salaries with bonus payment for boys over the number of forty-four and forfeits if the numbers fell below forty. It was decided to close Tombling's building, No. 6 The Schools, as being the most primitive, and to transfer the boys to Severn Hill where Mitford's House would be terminated, his boys opting thankfully for other Houses or staying gloomily to join Tombling's. Tombling himself was loath to leave the home where he had lived for fourteen years and once was heard to say that he never had much interest in his House in his three remaining years in Severn Hill before his retirement.

One of Hardy's major handicaps was his governing body. The Chairman, Offley Wakeman, was preoccupied with work in many areas of the county, Shrewsbury School being only one of his many responsibilities. F.J. Kittermaster, an Old Salopian, was the only governor with the interests of the school at heart, familiar with the Site and many of its inhabitants. Others attended rarely; meetings often numbered no more than four or five. To this body came in 1943 Duncan Norman, elected by the Headmaster and staff, himself an Old Salopian; a son, recently in Rigg's, had been killed in the Fleet Air Arm. Duncan was a businessman of genius; it was he who really established Owen Owen as a major store in this country and Canada. He was horrified at the lackadaisical attitude of his fellows – "the conduct of the Governing Body dismayed me from the start". Hardy poured out his heart to Norman: "What I have found at first very desponding, and latterly just maddening, is that hardly any (governors) pretend any interest in the School's affairs and only Kittermaster has seen the School in action at all..."; "A masterful Chairman who has the interest of things at heart would in fact induce Governors who do nothing to resign".

Hardy had been invited to stay until one year after the end of the war, but fixed his retirement for 1944. "To carry conviction these schools need to be in the charge of men younger in years and of more elastic minds than your present headmaster", he told his governors. Duncan Norman felt that Hardy was showing the strain of the war years. "Making full allowance for Hardy's good qualities, and taking the most charitable view, it almost seems that as the years have passed his passion for autocracy plus Rugby Uber Alles has got such a hold on him that his judgement is very seriously warped".

Discussion as to Hardy's successor waxed furiously both on the Site and in the committee of the Old Salopian Club, the latter pushing strongly for an Old Salopian to be appointed. Less interest seemed to be being taken by the Governing Body. George Kitson-Clark, a Salopian Fellow of Trinity, Cambridge, wrote ponderously that under Hardy, "Old Salopian tradition was persistently, almost contemptuously set aside". Alington, now at Durham, made his contribution: "It is very important that whoever goes there shall succeed in re-establishing the spirit which Sawyer left and if he is a good man he oughtn't to find it very difficult. (But I think he'll want some new Governors)". Sopwith drew up a long list of suggestions for the future on the theme that "it is the *spirit* that matters and it is the spirit that has been trampled on – and we *must* get that back". Basil Oldham joined in, his particular grouse being that the pictures left by Moser (Basil's house-master) to the school had been roughly dealt with by Hardy who had made the picture gallery into a writing room. He wrote of "the scandalous way in which our Housemaster's bequest has been treated, which made Freddy Prior so angry that he decided at once to leave nothing to the School and made another will". Basil had been working for years on the publication of his book on the bindings in the Shrewsbury School library, a work of major importance. When at last it was published to wide bibliographical acclaim he wrote that "the Headmaster and Governors have ignored the publication".

Roused to fury by the attitude of his fellow governors, Duncan Norman, a man of determination, energy and also temper ("I have a hasty and unreasonable temper which betrays me more often than it should"), travelled the country, questioning and consulting. Henry Kendall, an Old Salopian, first housemaster of Ridgemount and now Warden of St Edward's, Oxford, was thought to be the front runner but Rupert Martin, also an Old Salopian and now remarkably successful in reviving King's School, Bruton, was younger and in the end had powerful staff and Old Salopian backing. Walter Hamilton was considered but someone wrote from Eton of his being "silent, rather shy, doubt if he would be the man...".

Jack Peterson was also mentioned, according to Kitson-Clark "a very nice man indeed but a very dull one".

Duncan Norman drove down to see Rupert Martin and, with Governing Body assent, sounded him out. The job was his if he wished; but Martin felt he had been too short a time at Bruton and had other reservations. (His close friend Charles Crawford later speculated that he was hesitant about taking on the Shrewsbury Common Room.) But on that December day in 1943, he did solve the whole problem by suggesting Jack Wolfenden, the young headmaster of Uppingham. "Ring him up now", said Duncan in his typical thrusting way. Martin did; Wolfenden expressed himself surprised, said he had refused the approaches of three other schools but "Shrewsbury was different". He expressed himself "willing to be sounded", and in a few weeks was appointed.

Hardy went out in a blaze of controversy. The Governing Body had met Wolfenden in February 1944. Hardy was not present, and to his astonishment later read a minute of that meeting which stated that "The Governing Body in conference with the new Headmaster have agreed that in the best interests of the School, it is desirable that the Headmaster should return to the School House as soon as possible". And Kingsland House, Hardy's residence, should again be a boarding house of normal size. It is difficult to trace from where so astonishing a suggestion came – "absentee Governors, primed by some senior members of staff" – according to Hardy. Ignored and humiliated, he wrote in a private letter that not going to the School House when he first came, then yielding £2,500 a year to Canon Sawyer in profits, had cost him some £25,000, a far greater sum than any housemaster had had to forfeit after the 1930s battles. However they had never forgiven him; and he knew it. "After 25 years as a Headmaster", wrote Hardy, "I receive a Policy of £6,000 which will give me a pension of £210 a year. That is not an extravagant provision for a man who has been for three years Chairman of the Headmasters Conference and has some repute in the scholastic world. I was not talking loosely when I wrote that, in obedience to what seemed my duty, I was 'retiring into penury'. To do this humbly, after some words of civility, I might have contrived to do; but to have to do it, without a word of explanation or consultation, with my Governors relying on the views of certain few senior Staff members who have suffered financially with me, is more than I ought to have been asked to do".

Hardy could be brusque and insensitive. But to most Salopians of that day he was seen to lead the school with vigour and determination, working exceptionally hard to meet the bewildering demands of the war years. In 1940 he had been variously advised by well-wishers to lead a migration of the whole school to Canada, to retreat to a safe place in the UK, to send away all boys under sixteen, to continue the school through the holidays or to shut down altogether. But he carried on; his aim was always to give every boy as normal an education as possible. Through his connections, very many Salopians were guided into the Forces where they could best serve. He followed their careers closely; no Salopian was killed without his parents or his wife receiving a measured letter of condolence in the Headmaster's fine handwriting. It is now possible to see clearly how much he achieved in his early years – the school put on a sound administrative base with a bursar and staff, new buildings constructed and a more equitable salary scale. Though always gloomy about numbers Hardy, to his surprise, left to his successor 491 boys – a full school.

Nor had academic standards dropped. "Form Masters report to me every term (as they have for 25 years) that the standard has gone down even further and the boys as obstinately retaliate by getting more Certificates than ever before". So in what he called his "very painful duty of retirement", he greeted with wholehearted enthusiasm the appointment of Wolfenden ("though I was excluded from all consultation").

Humphrey Beevor, for four years School Chaplain, wrote a brief farewell poem. (Mrs Hardy, 'Joss', was a violinist; a psychiatrist was then known in slang terms as a 'trickcyclist'.)

> Our great Headmaster and his Bride
>   Together forth must roam.
> They can no longer stay inside
>   Their magisterial home.
> For Hartshorne soon will lock the door;
>   The Bailiff take the key.
> Whate'er the loss, Good-bye to Joss
>   And Harry H. Hardee.
>
> None will relieve their indigence
>   Nor take within their gates
> Whom the Headmasters Conference
>   Once excommunicates.
> So she for pence in taprooms must
>   Her fiddle strings untwist;
> He bread must win as an itin
>   -erant trick bicyclist.

CHAPTER XIV

Schoolmaster Apprentice

My brethren, let not many of you become teachers ... for we all
stumble in many things.

Epistle of St James 3.1

The academic year 1947–48 was for me full of interest and indeed
excitement as I took up my first teaching post. In the country in general the
situation was grim. The 'iron curtain' was now in place; we had not yet
come to terms with the fact that Britain was no longer a superpower; the
Labour government was in the throes of nationalisation and social legislation as it sought to fulfil the aims of the Beveridge Report; although there
was virtually no unemployment, the economic outlook was gloomy with a
40% rise in prices since 1945. Ration books did not finally disappear until
1954; we still carried Identity Cards. In 1948 the arrival of the first West
Indian migrants on the 'Empire Windrush', soon to register at Brixton
Labour Exchange, foreshadowed trouble. But to us, released from the war,
enjoying civilian life for the first time for years, these matters did not bulk
large. We enjoyed the revival of sport. Dennis Compton made 3,816 runs in
that glorious summer and you could join the 60,000 who thronged High-
bury every Saturday to see him play for Arsenal. We went to films in
greater numbers than ever before to see *The Third Man* or one of the Ealing
comedies. We listened to the reorganised BBC, laughed at *Take It From Here*
and appreciated Sir William Haley's attempt to smarten us intellectually
with the new Third Programme. Meanwhile the girls were adopting the
'new look' despite the disapproval of the clothes rationing authorities, and
though new cars were virtually impossible to come by, we admired what
seemed triumphs of British workmanship in the Jaguar XK series and in the
Comet aircraft. All that was optimistic was soon to be on show at the
Festival of Britain in 1951.

When appointing me, Wolfenden had made much of the new salary
scale which ran from £350 to £900 p.a. and, taking into account my war
service, generously placed me on it at point 4 – £400 p.a. As a staff officer in
India I had been getting nearly £1,000 but I was quite happy to manage on

this low figure. My married colleagues were less happy. I was most fortunate to find digs with Hilary Griffiths, a widow who had a large house in Kennedy Road called 'Braehead'. For the next eight years this was 'home' to me, starting with a bedsitter and graduating to two rooms, the bedroom being a sort of boxroom. Hilary was a splendid landlady and friend who looked after her lodgers wonderfully, despite the strains of rationing.

I was apprehensive as to my ability in the form room, though Murray Senior gave encouragement. Going round to see J.H. Tombling ('the Bling') who organised the timetable, I found him sitting in front of a vast sheet of paper in candlelight – there was a power cut at the time, not infrequent in those days – and marking places on the sheet with ear plugs which had been issued in the Blitz. Bling was a polymath, capable of teaching most subjects, and he explained that he filled up as much of the timetable as he could, and where stuck for a master pencilled in his own initials and taught whatever was required. My main area of teaching was the Lower Division of the History Side, a post 'O' level form which would today be the Lower Sixth. Wolfenden had appointed me because there was a growing demand for history, yet hitherto only one history specialist master. This demand was to expand enormously over the next few years. So I found myself facing a form of would-be historians, attempting to teach them in my halting, unskilled, inadequate way. It took me years before I began to see how to do it. In this I owed nothing to the Oxford Department of Education. In those early years I had some able boys – Brian Hutton, now Lord Chief Justice in Northern Ireland; James Adams, recently Ambassador in Egypt; Denis Henry and Richard Curtis, now High Court Judges; and, for a year, Jim Pfautz, an eighteen-year-old American who came to get a taste of England and, despite the shortages and austerity, enjoyed his year so much that he constantly tells me that it was one of the best years of his life, partly because he made good friends in his House, (Ingram's), and partly because he got on so well with James and Kay West, who became substitute parents. Jim has been a generous Old Salopian and rose high in the American Air Force to the rank of Major-General; forty years or so after his sojourn in my form he insists on paying for me to visit him in the USA where he is the most generous of hosts.

Wolfenden had become Headmaster of Shrewsbury at the age of thirty-eight, having already been Headmaster of Uppingham and played a major part in the organisation of the Air Training Corps which had given him an entrée to Whitehall and the Civil Service, among whose mandarins he moved smoothly. Having been a philosophy don at Magdalen, he had a sharp and incisive mind which, combined with considerable energy and a general urbanity, enabled him to lead with confidence. There was never any doubt as to who was in charge. To say that he in time became England's leading chairman would not be untrue, large claim though it is. On the platform on Speech Days, in the pulpit in Chapel, gently coaxing (and coaching) his governors, he was in his element, as also he was, in later days, as chairman of various Government enquiries (for instance the famous Wolfenden Report on homosexuality). On Mondays at Shrewsbury the school gathered in the Alington Hall for prayers and announcements by the Headmaster; on the rare occasions when he had nothing to say there was a real sense of disappointment.

His involvement in educational politics in London was known in Shrewsbury before he was appointed, and it was rumoured that Uppingham's farewell present had been a first class return season ticket between Shrewsbury and London. Notwithstanding his frequent absences – he was Chairman of the Headmasters Conference for four years during his time at Shrewsbury – he kept a tight hold on the school and all that happened in it, seen often around the Site idiosyncratically and ostentatiously wearing his mortar board (without gown). In wending his slow way back to lunch in Kingsland House from his School House study, he would wander round the fives courts in winter or the cricket nets in summer, seeing and being seen. At 7.45 a.m. his gaunt figure could be seen at the window of his study, seeing who was late for First Lesson, he having returned from London on the midnight train and with an hour's work on his postbag already behind him.

The problems of the Wolfenden years of 1944–50 were formidable. The deficit on the revenue account for 1946–47 was £13,000, for 1947–48 £20,000. A new bursar was appointed in 1947 and the fees went up from £210 to £236, with extra charges for medical attention and for laundry. Many believed that this big increase would threaten the school and a sense of crisis prevailed; housemasters voluntarily proposed giving up £100 p.a. of their salaries (the governors did not take up the offer), and S.S. Sopwith, who had been given an extension of two years, resigned, feeling that his salary was too big a burden for the school to carry. He was engaged by the extraordinary Canon Shirley at King's School, Canterbury (his old school) where in a short time he became again a housemaster! The King's School was known as 'Shirley's Temple' in those days. He was said to employ only young masters and retired hacks, both of whom were cheap, and to have sacked all those in the middle expensive salary range. Only Shirley could have coaxed Somerset Maugham, who had loathed his schooldays, back to Canterbury and persuaded him to endow a library.

Apart from wrestling with the economic situation, Wolfenden devoted time to what he called "the shape of the school", that is the number of forms, promotions, examinations, and the organisation of the various 'Sides' into which the school was then academically divided. The long academic ladder which had meant that a boy could be four years in the school and leave without taking 'O' level or the equivalent, was reduced and re-shaped. Time was also spent on discussing and introducing the 'Fleming Scheme'. By this local authorities were encouraged to place boys in public schools and pay their fees, the schools undertaking to accept a quota. Shrewsbury had as many as thirty or more Fleming bursaries at any one time. All fears that they would be 'different' or in some way ostracised proved to be groundless. A current London play called *The Guinea Pig* featured the anticipated social embarrassment. Few masters and no boys even knew who they were, and the scheme was a great success until the political climate changed and local authorities no longer wished to support such boys. One thing Wolfenden did not have to worry about was numbers; despite the rise in fees (up to £276 in 1951), there was no shortage of applicants. By the end of his time in 1950, Wolfenden saw the school back to normality, signified outwardly by the return to blue coat and grey trousers as daily dress. The governors even daringly took a step into the future when they authorised a refrigerator for every House! To the same meeting it was reported that the two school horses had died, an epitaph to an age now passed. The horses had been used to draw the school ambulance but had been living in retirement for some time.

In his autobiography, Wolfenden suggests that he made but little impact on Shrewsbury. "... it seemed at first sight, the Headmaster was at best a constitutional monarch intervening from time to time ... while the actual running of the school was in the hands of a highly competent body of masters and senior boys. A cruder way of putting it was that at Uppingham no boy was allowed to deviate from regulations (or even, they said, blow his nose) without express permission to do so, while at Shrewsbury everyone did pretty much as he liked until somebody, for some reason or other, told him to stop". In the chapter on his time at Shrewsbury, Wolfenden does not mention the name of a master or boy; most of it is taken up with extraneous activities. Yet this is not as Shrewsbury saw him. If for no other reason he is to be remembered for his appointment of nearly half the staff and the selection of new housemasters in all but two Houses. To the boys he appeared a larger-than-life figure. He instituted weekly praepostors meetings, discussing all aspects of school life with them so that they felt they were playing a major part. His masters meetings were formal and wide ranging, gowns were worn, punctuality insisted upon and subjects ranged from house stockings to what Wolfenden had said to the Minister on his most recent London visit. Certainly he had his critics, particularly amongst Old Salopians who – accustomed to the Sawyer-Alington traditions – saw Wolfenden as a climber, pausing only briefly on Kingsland. Was he too clever by half, like Iain Macleod? His habit of answering a question before you asked it was disconcerting. Was he over-effusive? Where was the human being behind the facade? On occasion he could get the atmosphere wrong. When a cleaning lady retired, his description of her back view, described one morning in the Alington Hall, was embarrassing to the boys as well as the staff. A forty-five minute speech, largely devoted to the country's educational policy, did not go well at an Old Salopian dinner. At a staff dinner – an innovation this – with Dick Sale in the chair, his speech, starting with the words, "Dick ... chaps ..." made his hearers cringe.

When he unexpectedly announced his resignation, he carefully orchestrated the announcement so that all should hear at much the same time. Letters to parents posted overnight, a late staff meeting, boys in the Alington Hall after First Lesson at 8.30 a.m. the next day. At the staff meeting Alec Binney rashly said that the boys already knew; Wolfenden was more than put out ("pen-throwing mood" whispered Brooke). I had to confess that I had that evening taken a party of the Forum Society to the offices of the *Shrewsbury Chronicle* where the boys saw the headline being set up in type. Black looks followed. He did not like departures from the script – his script. But Shrewsbury should look upon him with gratitude; after the war years, he re-vivified all those on the Site. There was a great sense of purpose and all felt that they had a place in what McEachran used to call the Headmaster's 'dome of consciousness', whether it was Hartshorne, the school porter, or the newest new boy. However much he may have discounted them, his influence and example counted enormously.

The senior figures of the Hardy years had now at last left the stage. Sopwith was in Canterbury where he was joined by Whitfield, still preaching his Trinity Sunday sermon; Mitford, softened in old age, taught part time and lived with his sister in the Kingsland House converted stables ('The Mitter and Mermaid'). He had an operation for the stone and kept the results in a match box on the mantlepiece asking his guests, "Have you seen the crown jewels?" Miss Mitford acquired modest fame by passing her driving test at (I think) the eleventh attempt. Mitford taught for so long that he was able to put on a boy's maths report "Better than his father but not so good as his grandfather". Kitchin's last years were sad; he was increasingly crippled by a wasting disease. Boys in Ridgemount pushed him in his wheelchair to the School Buildings: in his last two years neither he nor any adult entered the boys' side of the House, where discipline became lax. He gave a large farewell party to town and gown at the end of his last term, presiding from his wheelchair. No one knew that he had that day had a bad fall, fractured his leg and was in much pain. Tombling did not long live to enjoy his retirement; he suffered a complete mental breakdown. Dick Sale had betaken himself to a happy retirement at East Hanney, near Oxford, where he and Ray became thoroughly involved in village life. Dick was increasingly deaf and lame but played a shrewd game of croquet from his wheelchair. Hans Pendlebury rumbled off to even more involvement in Masonic affairs until his death in 1951. Jimmy Street and Russell Hope-Simpson, who had lived in the School House as tutor and housemaster for twenty-three years, were the elder statesmen, still very much about the Site.

Who then were the new housemasters who – most of them – were to guide the school through the 1950s? Alan Phillips was the most senior, appointed in 1939, short of stature, a man of abundant energy and general cheerfulness, as his nickname 'Bounce' suggested; a games player of high repute (he had played football for the Corinthians and for Norwich City), he and his wife Ethel ran a happy and civilised house, nicknamed the 'Happidrome'. Tom and Mary Taylor were in Churchill's, but when Hope-Simpson retired Wolfenden switched this formidable partnership to the School House as being best qualified to carry the heaviest responsibility in the school. Tom taught science and ran the football – he had been an amateur international. His approach to life was that of an athlete always in perfect training. He ran a tight ship and was not satisfied unless everything was in perfect order, devoting himself wholly to the work in hand, always running between the form room and the School House both to save time and to keep himself fit. His was a strong personality. To the boys his efficiency was astonishing; his humanity was less visible. None doubted that he and Mary were the people for the School House; few envied them their task. Mary's abilities as hostess and housekeeper shone forth abundantly – "though she cannot add up a column of figures" according to Tom whom figures obeyed instinctively.

James West (his real name was John), had been appointed to Ingram's in 1945 when he emerged from the war with red tabs and a bristling moustache, as a full blown colonel. He had been passed over when Alan Phillips had been appointed to Moser's and it was with some slight anxiety that Wolfenden appointed him to Ingram's, commenting to his governors that James was "a person who does not come within the category of 'non-controversial'". He had had a long exchange of shots with Hardy in the years when he was housemaster of the Dayboys, the Headmaster being dissatisfied with the discharge of his duties, writing of "many representations from parents of a certain negligence in the handling of business by their boys' Housemaster". There had also been controversy over James's remuneration, he representing that he was underpaid, Hardy that he was overpaid. Hardy would certainly prefer to have made another appointment but "I have never quite got to the point of relieving him of his job as Housemaster because I think it would result in a financial crash". Hardy was also a critic of James's editorship of the *Salopian Newsletter*: "the document ought not to go out with so many errors … in misprints and omissions: as regards opinions, I greatly deplore … that its editor even suggests opinions at all."

James had served in the first war and many saw him as a natural soldier; he had commanded the school cadet corps with style and efficiency. He brought his soldierly qualities to housemastering – he was firm, direct and straight. He was also unafraid of controversies and collisions and his imaginative qualities were not sufficient to comprehend all those for whom he was responsible or make allowances for change. On the staff he represented the traditionalist conservative view. Himself an Old Salopian, now housemaster of the House where he had been as a boy, he was well steeped in Salopian lore and custom and had written a short history of the school, "a much better book than you might expect" according to Fred Pritchard. He was a major figure in local politics, a member of the council and Mayor in 1952, also a Freemason and a dignitary in the St John Ambulance Brigade. With so many involvements, one felt that he never quite had time to do anything really well; his study was a mass of paper so that one had difficulty in finding a chair to sit on. He had had the courage to revise the school register in 1928; Basil Oldham took a rather malicious pleasure in keeping a list of inaccuracies and mistakes, running to four or five pages of his cramped handwriting. Good judgement was not among his virtues and there was astonishment on the staff when one September they found that a boy generally regarded as a crook had been made Head of House. James's pomposity was a byeword and he was imitated widely; but there was never a more devoted Salopian. At masters meetings he used to sit at the opposite end of the table to the Headmaster, a sort of counterweight. He was fond of such preambles as "Some of us have been thinking for some time, Headmaster, that . . .", by which he meant "I have been thinking . . .". Kay West was a Canadian. Devoted to home and family, she had no taste for public life but was kindness itself to the boys and to her guests. Though the House was kept immaculately, the mechanics of housekeeping and bookkeeping were outside her sphere; in this area many battles lay ahead.

By contrast, Hugh Brooke in Rigg's exuded a careless bonhomie, expressed in idiosyncratic phraseology, often surprising and sometimes startling, which concealed the very real care and concern he had for his boys. Dismissive of cant, appreciative of humour, with a fund of stories and rhymes (not always for the drawing-room), he was indeed a charismatic person (though he would doubtless affect not to have heard of that word). He pretended to be a philistine so far as the arts were concerned, though he had moments when he endeavoured to interest the boys in music, once explaining the leitmotifs in Wagner's operas to uncomprehending cricketers. His House was very successful in the games fields but he suppressed any trace of the arrogance which this easily brings. It was said that Rigg's ran on a three-year cycle of Cups, Christianity and Culture. He always had time for rebels such as John Ravenscroft, 'John Peel' the indestructible Radio 1 disc jockey, who was allowed to concentrate on the

Wedding 1958. Philippa, M.L.C., Joy, Bruce

Wales. Bruce, Philippa, Robin, M.L.C.

In the nets

School House Staff. With Freddy Mann, House Tutor: Matron, Secretary, Cooks, Gardener, Nanny, Maids and Dailies

Founders Day, Lawrence College. Joy (left); General Akhtar Malik, Chairman of Governors; M.L.C.;
Sir Morrice James, British High Commissioner; the President of Azad Kashmir

only thing he wanted to do – play and collect records. Many years later, he described Brooke in Desert Island Discs as "the greatest man I ever knew". Prospective parents were sometimes disorientated and indeed disenchanted by Hugh's unusual attitudes. I recollect one couple arriving just as Hugh, dressed suitably, was dashing out to Ashton Road to collect the droppings from a passing horse for his garden.

Hugh was one of the few housemasters consciously to develop interests outside the school. He had enjoyed the army in the war, though he had been invalided after a near fatal fall off a Welsh mountain. He is famously said to have told his troops, "I know a quick way down", to have lost his footing saying, as he disappeared downwards, "H.I.G. or Here I Go". He re-joined as a Territorial, spending an evening a week at the Barracks where he was a very popular figure. He also took up carpentry at one time, taking lessons at the technical college ("I must get off to my vice"). One of the results is still to be seen in the staff common room, a rather primitive rack for holding envelopes containing reports. In the classroom he taught modern languages, often to the less intelligent. Here he had a real gift for raising the morale of those who might otherwise wilt at being a 'sink' form of no-hopers. Teaching periods were full of interest and generally relaxed. He had a green and red light on his desk and when in good mood, allowing for diversion and some flippancy, the green light would show; but when red flashed on it was no milling and close attention to the task in hand. Many were surprised when he was ordained, and there were some comments about puffs of white smoke from the Rigg's chimneys, but those who knew him well were aware of the bedrock of belief and the Bible on which he was grounded. For some years he had been a Lay Reader, taking Evensong in obscure Shropshire villages. As a preacher he was famous for his seven-minute sermons, simple often to the point of being simplistic but remarkably effective in school chapels. He married Dorothy at the end of the war and they at first lived in a little house in Well Meadow Road. In the garden resided a fat pig, Claribelle, Empress of Copthorne, and Dorothy spent much time carrying fodder to Claribelle. With a young family to look after, Dorothy was somewhat overwhelmed by the responsibilities of housekeeping in Rigg's, a burden which never wholly eased.

In contrast to Hugh Brooke was Alec Binney in Churchill's, steady as a rock, painstaking and thorough in all he did. Problems seemed to dissolve when exposed to Alec's fund of common sense. He gave the appearance of never being in a hurry and at housemasters meetings expounded his views at length. Parents were delighted to have their sons under Alec's care and the boys equally had confidence in him and in his wife Heather with whom one did not trifle and who placidly sailed through the troubled waters of domestic organisation.

David Bevan has written of his own first experiences in Ridgemount and those unconscious of the responsibilities of housemastering should read his chapter on his first term in the House, when in the first week one of his new boys ran away, the cook failed to cook, a master who ate in Ridgemount announced dramatically that he was dying, and the Matron went mad. Slow of speech and with his idiosyncratic emphases, David with his wife Hilary and their small children devoted themselves wholeheartedly to Ridgemount. His book *Recollections* does not, I believe, show the real David, for much of it is taken up with their indigence and, as he believed, lack of support from the centre. With a non-conformist background, he had a strong sense of right and wrong, living out his belief in action rather than in word. Yet he was not a puritan and enjoyed to the full the more epicurean pleasures when on occasion they came his way. He served Ridgemount for eleven years and his influence, his enthusiasm and his humour permeated the whole establishment, while few wives worked as hard as Hilary. David ran the Corps, the boxing ("Well fought Red, Blue the Winner") and the Physical Training for some years. In earlier years he had played rugger for the town, always to be found in the midst of the scrum from where, on one occasion, a very Balliol voice was heard to say, "If you do that again, Sir, I shall be forced to retaliate".

In Oldham's, Bill and Helen Matthews had succeeded Sopwith, the House continuing on its even keel. In complete contrast with the days of J.B. Oldham, Bill communicated on the level of logic (which he taught) rather than emotion – there was solidity but no flamboyance. Stacy Colman took over Dayboys from Hans Pendlebury and for the first time (ever?), the boys had a housemaster who really cared for them and made an entity of what had been largely a collection of individuals. Stacy and Sallie were ideal in this position, which allowed Stacy to continue his sixth form classics teaching, sustaining the high standards on which the academic reputation of the school had largely rested for many generations, and in this, the last decade of the Classical VIth, his meticulous and scholarly teaching brought impressive classical awards to his pupils. Taught by Jimmy Street, then Harry Dawson (a fine and not always appreciated scholar) and finally by Stacy, assisted for a time by Tony Trench, the Classical Side could bear comparison with any of their predecessors in the golden age of Butler, Kennedy and Moss.

Somewhat out on a limb geographically were Patrick and Maud Childs in Severn Hill, where Patrick ran his House in his own way and managed by nagging persistence to get the Governing Body to spend money on badly-needed improvements. One of Patrick's main enthusiasms lay in mountaineering and hill walking. For many years he ran the Rovers thus awakening in a number of boys a love of the countryside and the hills, one such being Charles Evans, second in command to John Hunt on the 1953 Everest expedition and the leader of the 1955 Kanchenjunga expedition.

Patrick believed in the Roman virtues; he was often critical of the central direction of the school, resolute in standing firm on what he considered to be points of principle which others might call obstinacy. Maud was Mary Taylor's sister and had the same outstanding competence in matters domestic.

These then were the housemasters whom Wolfenden bequeathed to his successor, a diverse team of men who enjoyed happy relations with each other, contrasted though they were in personality. A number of Hardy appointments moved off to become headmasters in the post-war years. Alec Peterson to Adams Grammar School; Jim Pitts-Tucker to Pocklington; Harvey to Chester; Basil Deed to Stamford; V.A.L. Hill to All Hallows (a worthy, rather boring teacher whose initials inevitably gave rise to an unfortunate nickname), Murray Senior to Bury, then Monmouth, in both of which schools he had spectacular arguments with his governors, and Jack Grundy to Emmanuel; puffed with the pride of a lieutenant-colonel which he became in the war and assuming that a housemastership was awaiting him, Grundy had a passage of arms with Wolfenden, writing later that "Wolfenden seemed to regard war veterans as a nuisance".

Another man who had moved on was the Revd Frank McCarthy (later McCarthy-Willis-Bund), the school's first full-time biology master, an excellent teacher and a man of quiet Christian influence, not only with boys but with his colleagues, to several of whom he was a leading influence in their lives and beliefs. Few knew that he was up two hours before First Lesson every morning in order to have a period for study, meditation and prayer; he had a poise and tranquillity which were unusual, involved in the busy school life yet detached from it; 'in the world yet not of the world.' He was what was then called a Modern Christian with formidable intellectual powers, though his sermons reached only the most intelligent of sixth formers. He was considered for the headmastership of both Glenalmond and St Peter's, Adelaide, but went on to be a Fellow (and later Dean) of Balliol College, Oxford, where he played a major part in holding the college together during the excesses of the Sixties.

My first five years at Shrewsbury were indeed happy ones. Braehead proved to be a splendidly happy 'home' for those of us lucky enough to live there in Hilary Griffiths's comfortable Victorian house, so typical of the 'villas' erected on Kingsland in the last years of the nineteenth century. I shared the house with, at different times, four close friends, making a spirited and harmonious community, deeply committed (three of us for the first time) to the fascinating vocation of schoolmastering. Willie Gladstone had an all-too-brief stay. He taught history and threw himself into every activity with unbridled enthusiasm levened with considerable wit. It was he who instituted the Naval Section of the Combined Cadet Corps and Salopians saw with surprise bell-bottomed boys marching on the Common to Willie's encouraging, "Step lively on the deck". Even more surprised were the school ground staff on seeing Willie's bluejackets erect 'shearlegs' and lift a heavy roller to the skies. Willie was tempted back to his old school, Eton, later going on to be Headmaster of Lancing at a difficult time, before returning to the ancestral Hawarden Castle.

Youngest of the Braehead residents was Robin Moulsdale, just down from Cambridge, whose return had been urged by Tom Taylor, seeing Robin as his successor in running the football. Robin had switched from history and taught English. Both he and I fell easily enough into the Salopian scene, he having only briefly left it. We put a lot of energy into running and to a small extent endeavouring to shape the system, but did we have the originality to change it? In later years when, as he says, he started to think, Robin became one of the principal pioneers of a new Salopian age; but not yet. As a winner of the Kinnaird Cup (three times) he did much for the fives; he made an enormous contribution to the football; and was to the fore in the cricket world, then very short of coaches; he played golf when he could, having won a Blue at Cambridge.

Of a different generation was Mike Powell who had been at Shrewsbury since 1936, long-time house tutor to Hope-Simpson in the School House, still a bachelor and now incorporated into our close-knit community. Mike commanded the Corps and ran the rowing, succeeding the legendary Kitchin. He was ten years older than I was, twenty years older than Robin, but age was no bar in that congenial household. We had collectively an appetite for 'culture' and Mike was to the fore in visits to castles, houses and gardens in Shropshire, becoming quite an expert in architecture and just beginning to develop what was to be a very considerable skill and later in life a major occupation – painting. Mike also used to drive us in his Morris Eight to the Old Bush to which we would dash after evening lessons, to be refreshed by the landlord Mr Jones's excellent beer and entertaining conjuring tricks.

For three years Tony Chenevix-Trench was in Braehead. He and I had entered Shrewsbury as new boys on the same day and had returned to it to teach on almost the same day, fifteen years later. He had survived being a prisoner of the Japanese, returned to Oxford to take what was said to be the best First in Greats since Gladstone, won university prizes and been President of the Junior Common Room at Christ Church. Short of stature and slight in build – he assured us that as a new boy he could fasten a detachable collar round his waist – Tony would insert his own brand of originality and liveliness into any gathering, whether dons at Christ Church high table or Mission boys in Everton, adapting equally to either environment. Despite his formidable intellect, there was no trace of arrogance in his make-up and he never spoke of his own achievements, interesting himself in humble new boys as much as in classical scholars. It is worth quoting Colin Leach, one of the most distinguished of Shrewsbury's classical scholars in that rich crop of the 1950s:

> With Tony in the Classical Upper Sixth, all our potential was released. He treated us like grown-ups. He introduced us to textual criticism via J.D. Denniston's edition of Euripides's *Electra*. He integrated literature with history and philosophy ... and even started us on the road to understanding Greek pots. He was the sort of master who could say, after I had made a particularly outrageous suggestion for 'emending' Euripides, 'You know, Leach, you really are *bloody* sometimes'; and to whom one could reply as I did, 'Yes, Sir, I know, but it's rather fun ...'. It was easy to work for such a man. He was lax about returning our exercises, and often saw us at strange hours, but we knew that he minded – about us, about Cicero and Plato, about the school, about scholarship. Of the fifteen boys in that form ten got open awards at Oxford or Cambridge.

Of those awards Michael Townsend had the top scholarship at Balliol, David Peckett at King's and Colin Leach at Brasenose.

Tony's exuberance would at times carry him into that uncertain territory between truth and invention and one never quite knew about his many stories, for he was a skilled raconteur. The 'Six o'clock Express' was a favourite tale, recounted with flashing eye and expressive gesture. This purported to relate to happenings when Harry Dawson taught Tony and the Classical VIth in the last evening period. At two minutes to six, various quiet train noises would be heard as of an approaching express, coming from boys all round the room; gradually the noise would increase as the imaginary express roared nearer until as the clock struck six, the train would arrive at the station amidst the hubbub of porters, luggage trolleys, shouts of vendors and newspaper boys; then over all came the guard's whistle, doors would slam and with enormous puffs of steam the train would pull out, disappearing into the distance with faint hoots until total silence fell and every boy was working again at his unseen .... Did it really happen? Did Harry, rendered speechless and impotent, really go through this on 'Six o'clock Express' evenings? It made a marvellous story. Or again, there was a prep school story in which one night his friends, crawling in the roof space, lowered Tony on a rope through a trap door. "As the rope was lowered, I found to my horror that I was suspended about the Headmaster in his bath. I was beaten the next day for 'planned indecency'".

At the time of Wolfenden's departure to be Vice-Chancellor of Reading, I had coincidentally been writing an operetta entitled 'The Postors of Romance', which was performed by the staff at the end of his last term. To

the tune of 'When Britain really ruled the waves' from *Iolanthe*, I added
some verses the last of which was:

> We'll miss him here in every sphere
> They'll miss him on the London
>   train.
> He'll show his great diversity
> At Reading University,
> Our loss shall be their gain.
> But Salop never will forget
> The standards that he here has set,
> Our sun has not had brighter rays
> Since good Sir Philip Sidney's days

Singing in the Messiah at the end of Wolfenden's last term, some unruly
basses in the back row substituted "Wolfenden! Chancellor!" for
"Wonderful! Counsellor!" This was certainly how Salopians saw him. To
me he was the last Headmaster for whom I felt in the position of subaltern
to commanding officer, regarding him with awe.

There was a postscript to his Shrewsbury days when he was invited back
for the unveiling of his portrait in the presence of the whole school. It was
an appalling representation and Wolfenden resolutely refused to look at it
throughout the ceremony. Duncan Norman, who presided, somewhat
untactfully remarked that the portrait surely captured one side of Mr
Wolfenden's character – the look that told a governor with a cough to go
out and buy a cough lozenge before coming to a governors' meeting. Later
a copy was made of the Uppingham portrait which now hangs in the
Alington Hall, alongside Hardy who similarly had to be repainted after a
disastrous first effort. I bought the failed J.F.W. portrait for £1 and later
used it in School House shows. Having bored a hole through the mouth
and inserted a lighted cigarette and with a concealed small boy puffing
behind, the portrait – in indirect light – did indeed appear real.

There was, of course, intense speculation as to the identity of the next
headmaster. The Old Salopian Club, having endured Hardy and the disturbing and too clever Wolfenden, was agitating for an Old Salopian to be
appointed to revive the now rather distant ethos of Alington and Sawyer.
The governors deliberated in secret but a staff meeting presided over by
Jimmy Street was held to formulate a staff view, though no more than the
expected banalities emerged. The name of one of the candidates did leak
out, Ronald Lunt, who quite by chance was due to preach at this time; a
crowded chapel keenly attempted to assess his qualities. But it was also
known that Jack Peterson was being pushed forward as a candidate and
attention soon focused on him.

Jack had been in the School House and was Head of the School for two years, 1919–21, in Sawyer's time. He was the scholar-athlete par excellence; a scholarship to Oriel College, Oxford, a Double First in Mods and Greats, captain of the university soccer XI, a brilliant fives player, more than competent at cricket and golf and withal a Christian man of unaffected modesty. A contemporary at Oxford described him as "a golden youth, utterly unconceited, really loved, admired and respected, kind and thoughtful to all". It was typical of him that, although captain, he dropped himself from the university soccer match, being dissatisfied with his own form.

Some three years before being appointed Headmaster, Jack was at Deal for the Halford Hewitt; sitting on the bed of a Salopian friend one evening, he spoke for some time about headmastering and how he had no wish to be one. This same friend later wrote that, "deep down he never really trusted his ability to be a great headmaster or even a moderate one". This uncertainty may well have stemmed partly from the sad death of his wife while he was a housemaster at Eton. Inevitably it was Alington who persuaded a somewhat unwilling Jack to be a candidate.

The appointment was enthusiastically welcomed at Shrewsbury, particularly by senior men like Jimmy Street, who had taught him, and by James West and his Old Salopian friends (Gerry Sanger, the secretary of the Old Salopian Club, et al), and by Basil Oldham who struck a melodramatic pose and said, "To me it is Nunc Dimittis". Certainly no one could have had a better start, though the editors of *The Salopian* omitted any mention of the new Headmaster. Eton said goodbye with grace:

> At Shrewsbury your boyhood days
>   Non sine gloria were spent
> (Your modesty would look askance
>   At a straightforward compliment)
> A Shropshire Lad, as one might say,
>   In training for this greater day.
>
> Scholar and athlete, you must go
>   Where duty summons you, to rule
> (All Eton wishes you good luck)
>   Over an ancient, royal, school,
> An O.S. who deserves to be,
>   And is, by courtesy, O.E.
>
> You leave the Thames (no longer 'sweete')
>   To dwell by fair Sabrina's streams
> But we may confidently hope
>   That you'll remember in your dreams
> School Yard, the Field, the Chapel bell,
>   The Fives Courts where none played so well.

Eton has been in Shrewsbury's debt
  Since three and thirty years ago,
She 'borrowed' from her C.A.A.
  And, therefore, as a quid pro quo,
But with sad hearts, we now send back
  Her son, – affectionately, Jack.

CHAPTER XV

The Fifties

The Golden Evening brightens in the West ...
W.W. How

The years in which Jack Peterson was Headmaster, 1950 to 1963, were – in my view – the final years, perhaps the apotheosis, of the Public School. Some might think it a golden evening, long drawn out before the sun finally set; others might see the school as a declining institution in which the cracks became more and more visible. That Shrewsbury was a successful school in the 1950s decade there can be no doubt. Jack Peterson was embarrassed by the pressure for entry and reckoned in 1951 that there were 300 names down for the 100 places available. In contrast to Wolfenden's appointments, Peterson brought to Shrewsbury a number of men who were to make major contributions – John Stainer, Director of Music, Alan Laurie, Adrian Struvé, Laurence Le Quesne, Robin Moulsdale, Michael Hoban, Peter Gladstone, David Main, Arnold Ellis and others. Peterson himself made a sound start. "Jack Peterson has really got off on the right foot", wrote Jimmy Street, "His talk to us at his first Masters' Meeting could not have been bettered".

The 1950s saw a general easing of the country's financial problems culminating in the 'never had it so good' Macmillan years. Rationing and the forest of war time controls now disappeared enabling Shrewsbury to revert in quite surprising detail to its pre-war self. Tails and top hats did not reappear but boy-life as lived in 1952 was very similar to boy-life as lived when I entered the school twenty years previously – much the same dress, the same hierarchical system with monitors able to administer corporal punishment, an almost identical timetable (including First Lesson at 7.45 a.m.) and the academic division into 'Sides' – classical, languages, sciences, etc. Chapel was attended by all daily and twice on Sunday; virtually every boy was in the cadet corps, now called the CCF; the traditional games – football, cricket, rowing, fives and cross-country running were pursued with ardour, inter-school combats being watched by the whole school. As previously, a proportion of boys fell – temporarily – in love with each other. Stacy Colman's Classical VIth continued to produce scholars of the highest attainment, equalling and indeed surpassing the great classical record of past days. In 1951 the Headmaster reported that there were "not many good scholars this time" but the list contained Richard Ingrams, the future editor of *Private Eye*; Christopher Booker, author and journalist; Paul Foot, campaigner and crusader for the Left; Canon Christopher Hewetson, the Revd Patrick Duncan and John Hutchinson, pioneering headmaster of international schools. Willie Rushton, cartoonist and comic, entered the same term though his name does not occur on the scholarship list.

It was with enthusiasm that I threw myself into the Salopian scene, surrounded and supported by congenial colleagues. There was a coherence and a great sense of mutual support on the staff which did not then number more than fifty. Just as the boys attended all events so too – for the most part – did the masters; at least three quarters would be present at the chapel services, concerts, lectures, and house competitions. Yet despite this centrifugal professional life, off the Site one lived privately, there being no central provision for meals or for social gathering. Nor did the Headmaster, a widower who generally seemed to have housekeeper problems, impinge much on the social scene.

I had to work hard to keep up in my teaching but I enjoyed being a form master, seeing the boys for a third of their school periods and endeavouring to build a sort of club in which they all had a place, with tea parties and occasional expeditions; once I wrote a little operetta for the form – a parody of a recent visit by HM Inspectors. I was house tutor to Bill Matthews in Oldham's where I took Top Schools and 'Dicks' once a week and helped with the house games; Bill paid me, from his own pocket, three guineas a term, with which I was well satisfied.

Hugh Brooke ran the cricket in his own inimitable way but only five masters could be found who could coach teams and take nets in contrast with the eighteen who coached on the river. I had the cricket 2nd XI, partly old lags who would not get any further, partly up-and-coming boys of promise. We had a lot of fun and some happy times particularly at away matches when we had supper on the way home – a novelty then. My own cricket, never very distinguished, improved; there were the Saracens Devon tours, matches for MCC, the Free Foresters, Cryptics, and Shropshire Gents. For some years I ran the MCC match against the school and against Wrekin College on successive days. In the old days MCC teams for schools' matches were said to contain four gentlemen who were not players, four players who were not gentlemen, two qualifiers and one player borrowed from the home team. Things had, however, improved and one year I found, to my surprise, that I had three ex-county captains playing on my side. Every year Hugh and I would play a Sunday match at Horris Hill for

Monty Stow's side against Jim Swanton's Arabs, wonderful games to which 'Crusoe' Robertson-Glasgow brought his many talents and where for the last time one saw Ian Peebles's beautiful swallow-like action, full of the slow bowler's guile. 'Crusoe' himself said that he had stopped bowling except as a casual between the fall of wickets. His description of a rather staid member of our side was that he "had died young without ever quite admitting it". Having made sixty or so in one of these matches I received the ultimate accolade from E.W. Swanton, "Michael Charlesworth should certainly be playing for Northamptonshire". In fact I did play – once – for the Northamptonshire Minor County side, a humiliating experience amongst the young pros who constituted the 2nd XI, for I made 0, dropped a catch, did not keep wicket and was not asked again.

It surprised me that in my early thirties I played games so much better than in my twenties. I played a lot of fives and competed in the Kinnaird Cup. Once playing with Geoffrey Phillips, we were drawn against Peter and John May, Cup winners more than once. We had an excellent game which went on for a long time, had many fine rallies, took a lot of exercise – and scored hardly any points. Once more a lesson on playing above one's station. Again, surprisingly, I found myself playing for the Old Salopians in the Arthur Dunn Cup – surprisingly because this was a very good team and I was but a 2nd XI character, with no experience of good football. It was exciting to belong to this side, coached and collected by Robin Moulsdale, the inspirer of victory. It was never easy to assemble the best Salopian XI. Once we played at Lancing on the south coast to which players came from Edinburgh, South Wales, Oxford, Cambridge and Shrewsbury. However, Robin's boundless enthusiasm bound us into a team which included outstanding players like Dick Rhys, Miles Robinson, Johnny Clegg – all Oxford Blues – and Ken Shearwood, who was then also playing for the meteoric and dazzling Pegasus club which twice won the Amateur Cup. My feelings about Ken were mixed; his obstructive tactics in our penalty area sometimes resulted in penalties and he had a habit of unexpectedly passing back with a shout to me of "Yours!" as he accurately propelled the ball into the far corner of the net from where I was standing. After two seasons of nearly getting there – and some epic battles with the Carthusians, in one of which I let a penalty taken by Peter May roll slowly into the net, he having miskicked – we at length reached the final in 1952 beating the Etonians 6 – 1, and the next year having a more satisfying victory over the Wykehamists 3 – 1. The first time I handled the ball in that match was to pick it out of the net after Hubert Doggart converted a cross from the flying Tony Pawson. But we slowly fought back and won convincingly. Very few goals were scored against us in these seasons, largely because I was so well shielded by Miles Robinson and Harry Oxenham, delightful people to play with both on and off the field. How glad I am not to be playing now when black looks and condemnatory curses are exchanged by members of the same side. Goalkeeping is a great art; dramatic athletic saves which look so good are not really very difficult; but judgement in going out to narrow the angle, deciding when to go for the high cross – these were the really difficult situations; and in those days goalkeepers were not over-protected by the referee as today. I see little reference to the enormous change in the game brought about by the plastic ball. I was always a very poor kicker. Playing on Senior at Shrewsbury in the depths of winter on the heavy clay with a soaked leather ball was a great trial. I am reminded of the rather despairing cry during a school match, "Have it up the shallow end Shrewsbury!".

Athletics at Shrewsbury had been a very Cinderella activity, crowded into a few days at the end of the Lent term. Fired with enthusiasm arising from my own experience and feeling that there were many boys who were not distinguished in other sports but would enjoy athletics, I devoted time and energy to developing this sport. A new member of staff, Peter Knight, a most distinguished international athlete (also a hurdler), was in charge and having difficulty in asserting himself against other games' vested interests. Peter was most efficient – when he concentrated; but his enthusiasm was wayward. We were much handicapped by the March weather and by the lack of a proper track. When the grass was unusable we developed an ingenious system of running on the roads – the hundred yards down the Ashton Road, the half mile round the Common, the mile through the Quarry. After a year or two I took over from Peter and went on a summer holiday course run by the AAA at Loughborough in order to be able to coach the much neglected field events. Despite this training, such was my ignorance that I allowed spectators to stand far too near the circle in the first discus competition seen at Shrewsbury. Michael Kitchin – a left hander – threw first and winged a boy in Ingram's who was led away in dudgeon by James West.

To give athletics a fair deal it was at length decided to clear the last three weeks of the Lent term of all other games activity, save the 1st VIII outings. A Standards House Competition was set up to which every boy could make some contribution. It was typical of the attitude of the staff at that time that virtually every master helped to supervise this competition and vast numbers of races were held every day. At the same time a school team was built up and there were splendid contests against Malvern, Repton, Manchester Grammar School and, on occasion, Lancing, St Edward's and Radley. It was a great satisfaction to see how the general standard rose and a particular pleasure to coach two future hurdling Blues, Francis Glynne-Jones and Peter Pilbrow. I used every device I could to persuade the Headmaster and the governors that we needed a proper track. At this time Jimmy Street was raising the Fourth Centenary Fund and, largely through his own persuasiveness, induced an Old Salopian, Alan Stott ('Stotts of Oldham'), whose son George was currently captain of athletics, to present a track, small pavilion and groundsman's house. This marvellously generous gift transformed athletics. But I was annoyed as well as grateful. The Bursar, typically without any consultation, having had the go-ahead from the governors ordered a track from En Tout Cas and I arrived back one September to see the foundations already in place. I had clear ideas about the layout which would suit its intensive use by boys – three jumping pits for instance, both high and low, at least two shot-put circles and so on. But no one ever thought to ask me; I endeavoured to contain my disappointment. We opened the track with a match against Bradfield. I had asked Roger Bannister to open it but he could not and we had instead a demonstration from the Olympic 800 metres silver medallist, Dick Johnson. Sadly, as I write, athletics has moved down several categories. After thirty years or so of competition there is no longer a school athletic team.

In addition to activity on the games field by day and correcting and preparing work far into the night there were other occupations such as the Corps. All the officers had had war service so there was a certain professionalism about it, though the training had not significantly changed from pre-war days. National Service only ceased towards the end of Peterson's time, so there was some point in keeping our somewhat ponderous military machine going, massive inspection parades, river crossings by pontoon while David Bevan threw thunderflashes and mock battles over the Shropshire countryside amidst smoke screens and volleys of blank ammunition. For a time I ran an artillery section; for a time I was Adjutant. In retrospect it seems we had an unending supply of energy.

Holidays for me still centred on Northampton where my mother, looked after by my sister, was still reasonably active though slowing down. My romance with Dagmar had ended in 1948 – the closest that I had yet got to matrimony. There was, for a time, Elizabeth. Then the beautiful Fanny. I recollect taking her home to the village of Fitz one May morning as the sun was beginning to rise after a dance at Attingham and wondering if I was 'in love', whatever that should mean; I felt an upsurge of happiness. It didn't last. Two hours later I was in First Lesson. Many years later Fanny's sister-in-law reproached me for not asking Fanny to marry me. I still wonder why I didn't. Rather a different relationship was that with Barbara. We had met skiing and had several holidays with skiing parties in the Alps; she shared my tastes and enthusiasms; we corresponded freely, she stayed at Shrewsbury several times, her family became well known to me, though her mother was formidable. Was this at last the real thing? One day I drove slowly over the Malvern Hills to her home where I was staying the weekend, rehearsing my lines. In the evening I proposed. Barbara was very sympathetic, very sensitive; but she declined. And rightly, I now think.

Perhaps I was more in love with the idea than the person? Like other bachelor school masters before and since, there simply was not time to develop real relationships; no doubt a wrong sense of priority but that was how it was.

Since learning to ski in Norway, I had become extremely keen, going to the Alps once or twice a year and pioneering 'the school party'. It was at Easter 1949 that Tony Trench and I rather gingerly set off with fifteen boys for Scheidegg, the arrangements being made by Lunn's, then just starting the package holiday. We selected the boys we took and were no doubt criticised for being elitist, in today's jargon, for doing so. But we had no wish to be schoolmasters in the holidays and picked those whom we believed would be congenial both to each other and to us. This party and all subsequent ones were the greatest possible fun. Like much that he did, Tony's skiing was very individual as indeed was his après ski performance when he told his improbable anecdotes and made indiscreet disclosures with suitable panache, once trying to convince the solid Swiss that Chenevix-Trench was, in England, pronounced 'Shoe-Trees'. Tony and I had become close friends and had several holiday expeditions together, one to Norway where I was able to introduce him to my friends of past days.

The Fourth Centenary celebrations of 1952 were the high watermark of the post-war Salopian scene and on its momentum the school flourished unchanged for the next half-dozen years before stresses began to be apparent. The celebration in the summer was distinguished beyond all else by the Masque written by Paul Dehn. Seldom can any work have been written which better caught the atmosphere of the time or matched more suitably the occasion. In the intermingling of sentiment, sharp wit and studied understatement, Paul caught what I believe is a very Salopian characteristic. Allied to his words – and they were the words of a poet – was the delightful music composed by John Stainer, the production being in the capable hands of Arnold Hagger. Many things were good in that year but the Masque was particularly memorable.

In October the Queen and the Duke of Edinburgh spent a day on the Site. These were days of unquestioning loyalty, the first stirrings of what was thought to be a new Elizabethan age, the Queen herself in this the first year of her reign a radiant presence amongst us. The idea was that the Queen should see a 'normal' day with boys about their ordinary activities. Actually it meant a mad scramble as boys appeared and reappeared, as soldiers, as gymnasts, as fives players, as runners, in order to be discovered being normal. The royal party arrived by train, having spent the night in a cutting near Much Wenlock from where they sent for copies of Basil Oldham's recent history of the school in order to do some Top Schools; this sent Basil into a paroxysm of exuberant loyal enthusiasm as he signed two of his books with a suitable dedication, practising on half a dozen copies before he was satisfied that his spidery handwriting was calligraphically satisfactory. The royal visitors spent twenty minutes with Basil in the Library viewing the manuscripts, early books and bindings; no one will ever know what the Queen thought of the *incunabula* – pronounced of course as a monosyllable.

Altogether it was a memorable day – the mass PT display, the Guard of Honour, the opening of the Queen's Terrace, the Chapel service at which the singing of the National Anthem moved even the rugged Hope-Simpson. There was dignity but also light-heartedness; as the Queen walked down the high staircase of the School House after lunch, she accurately 'bombed' her husband, standing in the hall below, with her gloves. When Jimmy Street asked the Duke if he had ever done any rowing, he replied that he had done some pulling in the Navy. "Did you enjoy that, Sir?" "Hell" said the Duke. The Queen left at the Moss Gates (two boys cheekily but unavailingly thumbing a lift); such was our highly-charged enthusiasm that several of us ran all the way across the Site to the Port Hill gates for a final view of the slowly-moving Daimler. The Mayor of Shrewsbury for 1952 was James West who appeared quite magnificently garbed and splendidly pompous. As a postscript to this royal day, a group of boys, finding the sherry which the Queen and the staff had enjoyed unattended in the Moser Buildings, felt there would be no harm in joining in the general festivities with a loyal toast.

Tony Trench's stay at Shrewsbury had been temporarily cut short by his acceptance of the position of Mods tutor at Christ Church, a curious arrangement whereby he was treated as on loan but retained his place in the masters' list in the brown book – in brackets. ("...and I don't have to remind classicists that anything enclosed in square brackets is utterly corrupt", commented Harry Dawson). But in February 1952 the school was stunned by a tragedy. Tom Taylor, who had been playing fives, paused to watch another game and fell down dead. There had been no warning; Tom was only forty-seven and fit enough to outsprint most members of the 1st XI. He and Mary were making a very great success of the School House and who could replace them? Hope-Simpson was temporarily re-called to the colours. But Peterson now offered the position to Tony Trench and Tony accepted. In the same week he had turned down the offer of the headmastership of Charterhouse. (How remarkable for a thirty-two-year-old bachelor with only three years' teaching experience to be asked to succeed the renowned George Turner!) He was moved by the tragedy of Tom's death and attracted by the prospect of running his old House: *pietas* brought him back to the Severn from the Thames. His colleagues at Christ Church could not understand the decision and some, like Hugh Trevor-Roper, made their feelings plain. "My colleagues here feel quite certain that I am either mad or have been in some way duped into what they regard as a disastrous decision", wrote Tony. At Shrewsbury too, the appointment of so young and inexperienced a man did not pass without comment. Peter Knight discharged a sweeping broadside to Peterson, "this matter has disgusted me profoundly and it has greviously alienated a section of your staff: it is difficult ... to feel any assurance in one's future or to have any heart in one's work and it is difficult indeed to allay the very unpleasant suspicion of Old Salopian nepotism". As usual we went off skiing to Scheidegg where Tony soon rediscovered his *joie de vivre*. Sad it might have been for Christ Church but it was good for Shrewsbury to have Tony back with his enthusiasm, his scholarship and his wit.

Whatever else Jack Peterson did or did not do, he certainly assembled a good staff in the 1950s. Bill Cook came to bolster the classical side, Jimmy Street and Harry Dawson having reached retirement; the young Peter Hughes came to teach chemistry; Peter Gladstone added an unorthodox robustness to the common room and raised the rowing to new heights, the Crew twice winning the Princess Elizabeth Cup at Henley; the mathematical team of Hadland-Saint-Hagger would be difficult to beat in any school. In 1958 there arrived John Alford, David Gee, Mark Mortimer, Robin Trimby and Willie Jones – all to make major contributions – and also Vernon Armitage for an all too brief stay but one which left him with a lifelong love affair with Shropshire. In my own department – and I became head of the history faculty for a time by some odd chance – the numbers taking history after 'O' level rose to unprecedented heights. A glance at my 1955 brown book shows eighty names – and some interesting ones amongst them: Christopher Booker and Willie Rushton; Christopher Gill, presently MP for Ludlow; David Gilkes and Gilbert Rodway, long time residents of Hong Kong, the former a Fellow of the Chinese University, the latter a distinguished QC; William Cuthbert, whose premature death robbed Scotland of one of her leading citizens; Geoffrey Thompson, who runs much of Blackpool; Michael Abrahams, entrepreneur extraordinary (he was able to hold his own on a soap box in Hyde Park while still at school); James Mayall and Patrick McAuslan, Professors at the LSE; Douglas Bartles-Smith and Brian Lea, Archdeacons both, the former of Southwark the latter of Northern France.

Much of the History Side's success was owed to the inspirational teaching of Laurence Le Quesne, who exerted a very radical influence on Shrewsbury institutions, not without a certain measure of disturbance to the old guard but wonderfully stimulating to his sixth form. He soon became a close friend of Frank McEachran, united not so much by a common philosophy as by a common search for truth. Laurence was the master in charge of the *Salopian* magazine and a look through those old copies shows what a good magazine it was, full of quality, especially in its literature section under the editorship of Christopher Booker, Paul Foot,

Richard Ingrams and Willie Rushton – a rehearsal for *Private Eye*. As brilliant a contributor as any was Richard's elder brother, Peter John Ingrams, who had a considerable literary talent. As a prep school headmaster he never – to me – seemed wholly fulfilled; sadly he lost his life at an early age while climbing. The Ingrams household in Chelsea, where I sometimes stayed, was a lively one with four able and opinionated boys given to full self-expression. Laurence Le Quesne could never quite decide whether he wanted to be in Australia or Shrewsbury, so came and went and later came again. His place was taken by a man of equal stature, Michael Hart. With the young David Gee, Alan Laurie, Arnold Ellis and Roger Blomfield, we had a good team of historians.

In 1958 there were 550 boys in the school, an ideal number. This meant that Houses averaged 55, the School House having 100; the staff numbered 50. In a community of this size it was possible for everyone to know a large percentage of the boys and staff and for the school to be a cohesive entity. In this, the last age of the Public School, the strengths and weaknesses of these rather extraordinary institutions were apparent. There was much good teaching – some of it outstanding; there were 'diversities of gifts' amongst the extremely hard working staff; there was a good atmosphere between masters and boys; there were opportunities of high achievement in sporting activities. Many boys took advantage of what was on offer and flourished. On the other hand some found the constrictions of a tightly-organised, hierarchical society cramping and frustrating. They felt too bound by rules which seemed petty, too much controlled by conventions which seemed pointless survivals from the past, unhappy with an institution which valued athletic success higher than cultural activity. It is striking how differently contemporaries saw the school. It all depended so much on individual temperament, on the group of boys in one's year or House, on relationships with one's housemaster, on whether or not one established a sympathetic understanding with a master, as to whether there was opportunity to develop an individual activity or interest. Schools can, I suppose, be broadly categorised as 'good' and 'bad' but it is a generalisation I would seldom endorse. Is a school good or bad for a particular boy at a particular time? This is the real question. People are sometimes apt to look back on their school days and fit them to whatever philosophy they have subsequently adopted. Paul Foot would now be the first to condemn the Public School as he knew it; yet he was head of my House, a sympathetic and humane influence, a boy of much satirical wit but one who did well by and well at Shrewsbury. Michael Heseltine did not achieve much at school; Oxford saw the real development of his talents. He was indeed a noticeable presence but he was very ambitious and the school did not offer him scope for his undoubted talents – there was no particular ladder whose top he could reach. One minor activity in which Heseltine distinguished himself was high jumping. He was the school first string and practised with some diligence; I was his coach. When sports day came however, Brian Smallwood, a natural all-round athlete, who had not practised at all, won the competition. No Gold for Tarzan. But perhaps a useful experience for one who was to be Minister of Aerospace. Contemporaries remember his entrepreneurial instincts. Bottles of Corona were then popular, with twopence back on the empty bottle. Heseltine had a keen eye for bottles left about his House, compounding strays and claiming his twopences. In cold weather he hired them out as hot water bottles at one penny a night. His contemporary, Julian Critchley, disliked his stay at Oldham's very much indeed; a quiet, withdrawn boy, he made little impact except on his opponents in the boxing ring where he was a killer. He and Heseltine came down to the debating society after they had left and won a debate on the motion 'That this House deplores the Public School System' against the future Headmaster of Eton (Trench) and of Harrow (Hoban). The majority was ten in a House of two hundred. "A good humoured and controversial debate" recorded the *Salopian*, with boys, as ever, enjoying putting authority in its place, the proposers emphasising that what they sought was reform not abolition of the Public Schools. The aftermath was less good-humoured: the Press reported that Public School boys had voted to abolish their school – a fine opportunity for sensational and misleading headlines, enthusiastically taken up.

Stephen Jessel, currently BBC representative in Paris, was another who did not flourish, save academically. John Ravenscroft, 'John Peel' – indestructible disc jockey – survived because his housemaster left him to his records. Michael Palin had what he has called a straightforward 2nd XI career, without any particular distinction. C.J. Henty-Dodd, destined to have a meteoric rise in television as 'Simon Dee' (and as meteoric a descent), had a very brief career.

It is sometimes said that those who rise high at school do not flourish thereafter, having reached a peak too early. An examination of the careers of the twenty-four Heads of School in Peterson's time does not bear this out and also gives the lie to the oft-repeated complaint that public school boys favoured the professions and avoided industry and commerce. Of these twenty-four, twelve went into industry or commerce, four into education, two into farming or forestry, and one each into journalism, publishing, medicine, the Colonial Service, the Church and the Royal Navy.

In religion as in other areas, the conventions of the past continued placidly. One can never assess how much the religious aspect of his education meant to the average boy but outwardly Shrewsbury was a quite strongly religious community. Daily chapel for all and two compulsory services on Sundays might have been thought to be enough but the voluntary Communion Service on Sunday morning was generally attended by eighty to a hundred boys and many more went to evening Addresses which took place three times a week in Lent. These were given by members of the staff; names were never revealed in advance so there was the element of surprise – and sometimes considerable surprise – when the speaker stood up. At least two thirds of the staff were inveighled into giving these addresses – and nerve wracking they were. At one time after a sermon by James Hill, the School Missioner, who suggested that the time to pray was early in the morning, the chapel was opened at 7.15 a.m. and a number of boys prayed before First Lesson. Much was owed to the sincerity and humility of the Chaplain, Guy Furnivall. One boy at that time, who went on to be ordained, remembers that the sight of Guy saying his prayers in Chapel was in itself an inspiration to him. Jack Peterson's Christianity, unspoken and unassertive, yet very influential, had its effect on both staff and boys; it balanced the assertive certainty of the sermons of Michael Tupper, the assistant chaplain, while Hugh Brooke's seven minute talks added variety. Guy Furnivall was a keen games player with a strong urge to win; he played tennis, fives and cricket, at which he was said to attempt to do the double in May – five sermons and fifty runs. He suffered from asthma and at one time had to have a term off in a sanatorium in Switzerland. While there, to general surprise, he announced his engagement to a fellow asthma sufferer and so happily married Mary. "I knew he was ill but I didn't know he was *that* ill", said Hope-Simpson. In those days the singing in Chapel, encouraged by John Stainer and later Stan Lester, was remarkably good. Even those to whom what went on in the building was not of particular significance will remember the Stanford Te Deum in B Flat.

By and large, Shrewsbury was a very successful school in the 1950s, an old framework but containing much life and energy. Certainly for someone of my own characteristics and attitudes, it was a splendid place to work; but there were shadows. Before exploring those and the fundamental changes in my own life, both professional and private, which came in the second part of the decade, I must briefly record what was for me a challenging and delightful interlude.

CHAPTER XVI

Antipodean Interlude

I will go on the slightest errand now to the Antipodes
That you can devise to send me on ...
                                        Much Ado About Nothing II.i

Alan Hamer, with whom I had so happily shared digs in Oxford in 1940,
was now back in Melbourne working for ICI. We carried on an occasional
correspondence in which he urged me to come out to his old school,
Geelong Grammar School, on an exchange. The enterprising part of me
now being uppermost, I obtained Jack Peterson's blessing and it was
arranged that I should swap with John Barber, a bachelor historian, for the
year 1953–54.

Thus I found myself on the 'Strathmore', Australia bound, in August
1953, occupying the cheapest berth on the ship in a cabin for six, well below
the water line, at a cost of £85. Fortunately the occupants were congenial – a
Davis Cup tennis player who reckoned that his calling in life was always to
be beaten in any tournament's semi-final; a young New Zealand sheep
farmer; a veteran of Gallipoli; Jim Smith who had worked all his life at the
same machine in a Lancashire textile mill with the result that the fingers of
his operating hand grew sideways; and a totally anonymous student. Five
weeks on the ship, mostly in sunshine, was a delightful experience though I
was continually feeling I ought to be working in order to tackle a syllabus
which included Australian history of which I knew nothing (fortunately
there isn't much of it) and twentieth century American history of which I
knew little. But there was still time to swim and time to play a lot of deck
tennis at which I became champion of the ship!

In Colombo was Jeremy Syers, recently in my form, whose father was
British High Commissioner. They gave me a wonderfully interesting day,
with a large meal and sightseeing including a perharera – a Sinhalese
display of dancing at the roadside. While all the passengers were boarding
the ship in the evening, my reputation was much enhanced by sweeping
up to the quay in a Daimler with Union Jack fluttering from the bonnet –
only to resume my steerage life again.

I arrived a few days before term and was most hospitably received by Lex Spear, housemaster of Cuthbertson House, and his wife Dulcie. I was to be resident house tutor – in fairly primitive living conditions, sharing a bathroom with the boys though separated from them by a partition. I soon found that the boys had been used to playing tricks on John Barber, who was liable to absorb large quantities of beer and was also short sighted. Once they had parked a fully clothed dummy human figure (used in a play) on his lavatory seat; he kept attempting to go to his lavatory, stopped short on seeing the occupant, apologised and withdrew before realisation dawned. Another trick was to change all the furniture in his two rooms in every detail so that his bedroom became his study and vice versa and wait for his reaction when he returned late after a drinking session and blundered about uncertainly. I was an object of some curiosity as the boys tried to assess this English replacement.

Geelong Grammar (said to be "bloody English" by some Australians) was a really fine school and I quickly felt at home. It was, in its then format, really the creation of Jim Darling, now aged fifty-three and Headmaster already for twenty-five years (there were six more to come) and I would say unhesitatingly that of the nine headmasters under whom I have served he stands very high. Two particular qualities he had. The first was vision. He could and did lift his eyes above the routine and the mundane though he was a capable administrator. The second was his strong pastoral sense, shown in his ability to communicate with every boy, and by the balance that he kept between the disciplinary function of a headmaster and the openness and informality which characterised his personal relationships. Bill Lester, a colleague and Old Boy, told me an anecdote from his school-days. Passing through his form room between periods, Jim paused at Bill's desk, looked him quizzically in the eye and said, "And what will you have done for Australia in twenty years' time?" and passed on. It may sound trivial but Bill never forgot that challenge.

My own relationship with Jim was of the happiest. Often he would ask me in of an evening, prepared to talk on any subject, even implying that my views were of interest to him. His influence was everywhere, as much in Chapel as anywhere else, where he expounded simple Christianity in words that all could understand.

To my surprise, he disclosed to me that of all the schools in England (he was himself an Englishman), the only one of which he would have liked to be headmaster was Shrewsbury. He had accordingly applied in 1950 but the Shrewsbury governors had taken little notice, quoting his age as a disadvantage – he was fifty – and then appointing Jack Peterson who was almost exactly the same age. How *very* different would the story of Shrewsbury School have been if Darling had become Headmaster! As it was – in his own words – "I had to think of something else to do, so I invented

Timbertop". Here indeed was a seminal educational development, typical of Jim's creative mind. (At Repton he had been taught by Victor Gollancz and his penchant for radical thinking perhaps stemmed from that.) In Timbertop were incorporated Kurt Hahn, Gordonstoun and Outward Bound ideas, a hutted settlement in the bush in spectacular country, where a whole year's worth of boys would go for a school year, where academic studies continued as usual but where there could be no football or cricket or rowing, where the boys had to look after themselves, cut their own firewood, go for long-range expeditions, make their own amusements, learn bushcraft and self-reliance and live a life far removed from the hedonistic pastimes of city life. Timbertop was in its first year when I arrived and I spent a certain amount of time there on work camps.

I enjoyed the informality of the school, the forthcomingness of the boys, the uninhibited nature of their energetic pursuits and the opportunity to get to know the Cuthbertson boys really well, living as I did closely amongst them. The staff were kind to me, particularly Roger Blomfield and Ken Mappin, both bachelors, with whom quantities of sherry (at £1 a gallon) were consumed before that uncivilised Australian 'tea' at 6.00 or 6.30 p.m. I helped with coaching the cricket (taken very seriously indeed), and with the athletics. One day Jim Darling had a brainwave: "Now you are here" he said, "we'll have fives!" So an old ball court built for some defunct game was adapted for Eton fives, Jim having been a keen player himself. One day I received a note while teaching to ask me to go to the fives court; there were the Headmaster and the workmen who were then building the top of the front wall. "It's getting a bit expensive", he said, "do we really need the wall to be so high?" "No." "Stop!", he said to the workmen, who at once suspended action. So the front wall to this day looks like a medieval battlement. I taught a number of boys and they really enjoyed the game but I fear it gradually fizzled out after I left, though there have been times of revival. Nevertheless my great contribution to the Southern Hemisphere had been to build its first and only fives court.

Roger Blomfield and I both joined the band, a very formal, decoratively uniformed body, taught by the splendid bandmaster, Mr Barrett. I had long wished to try and improve my very basic trumpet playing and with Mr Barrett to instruct, I really got down to it; Roger meanwhile learned the bass. For reasons which I now forget I found myself actually running the band and therefore joining the cadet corps and putting on my Aussie uniform and slouch hat – familiar from Burma days. Despite the Australian taste for informality and willingness to take on things without (in English eyes) adequate preparation ("She'll be right..."), we did carry out some formal parades and marches, particularly on ANZAC Day, taken very seriously indeed, and once for the visit of the Governor-General, my old commander Sir William Slim, who was proving an excellent choice for that office. The band really came to mean a lot to me.

When Roger was not playing the bass, he was coaching (in Barber's absence) the 1st VIII. The Head of the River – attended by vast crowds and all boys of what were then called the six Great Public Schools – was a triumph for Roger, his crew winning handsomely. Sport was certainly taken seriously though Jim Darling was always ready to apply a pinprick of mockery to the overinflated keenness of some of his colleagues. He was a man who kept a sense of proportion, though he enjoyed praise and success ("I'm so vain", he would ruefully admit). He was delighted to receive a well-merited knighthood and was touched to be made an Honorary Fellow of his Oxford College at the age of ninety. Now ninety-three he still contributes a column to the Melbourne newspaper *The Age*. Looking back, I can now see how much of my own schoolmastering style was founded on J.R.D.

What has attracted many Englishmen in Australia certainly attracted me – the sun, the space, what seemed the infinite possiblity of development, the opportunities for the enterprising individual in a largely classless society, the sheep stations spreading over thousands of acres and the beach, social centre of so much Australian life. My base was in Melbourne where Alan and Margaret Hamer provided a home for me, but I travelled widely, covering thousands of miles in John Barber's Ford Anglia. Away from the big cities provision for travellers was primitive: simple hotels whose last meal – a couple of eggs on a steak – was at 6.00 p.m., which was the hour when the pubs closed. It was the time of the "five o'clock swill" – an hour's heavy drinking between work and closing time in bars empty of furniture, designed merely for elbow to elbow knocking-it-back. The 'New Australians' as they were then called, were only just arriving from Italy, Greece and other European countries, destined to transform Australia and make Melbourne today a city with the most varied and best restaurants in the world.

Another home from home was provided by Nevil Shute Norway, a great friend of Basil Oldham who had been his housemaster. Nevil had emigrated to Australia, having quarrelled with the Inland Revenue, and, finding in Australia a land of promise, was fired with enthusiasm for his adopted country. He had built a house near Melbourne and settled down to write in the mornings and farm in the afternoons, one activity compensating for the losses of the other. His novels had by now made him a rich man; he told me his income was about £60,000 a year and Australian taxation was low. Always a modest person, still retaining traces of the slight stutter which had handicapped him at school, he and his wife and daughters lived quietly though he travelled far, seeking material for his books. He was most kind to me and I recollect particularly a happy evening picnic on the beach on Phillip Island, seeing the penguins come out of the sea in their hundreds to feed their expectant families, waiting impatiently in their nests.

Working in a school does give one an advantage so far as contacts are concerned. I received many invitations and also made some Salopian contacts. In Sydney I stayed with John Douglas Pringle, then editor of the *Sydney Morning Herald* for whom I wrote an article on Timbertop; in Brisbane I stayed with my old Bulford friend, Toby Colman, busy getting engaged; I also passed some time in Canberra, still only partially built. I travelled by coach on a four day trip up the Queensland coast (and thence to the Barrier Reef) and endured the rigours of mixed and varied Australian company, sleeping in dormitory accommodation overnight, moving round the coach after every stop so as to meet everyone and sustaining the strain of community singing which was encouraged so that we should all be happy. In New South Wales I visited John Macdonald, an old Magdalen friend, on his sheep station and improbably played cricket for his local side, the Hunter Valley Light Horse. As yet the quality of the wines grown in this region was known only to the few – Australian wine in England still had the reputation of being cheap and nasty.

The long summer holiday I spent in New Zealand, hiring a Morris Eight, packing my tent, and with my primus and billy circumnavigating the North and South Islands, staying in eight homes and covering 2,500 miles. While there I coincided with the Queen who was on her first antipodean tour which was a stunning success in both Australia and New Zealand, she being the first reigning monarch to travel thus far. English stock stood high at that time, the youth and beauty of the Queen were very appealing, the Coronation not long past (at which my old friend from Magdalen days, Willie McKie, an Australian, played the organ), England had at last regained the Ashes and in the 'race of the century' Roger Bannister had beaten John Landy, a Geelong Grammar boy, having previously cracked the four-minute-mile barrier.

Stacy Colman had spent one year in Australia before the war as Headmaster of Melbourne Grammar School. This had not been a successful venture although in many ways Stacy was admirably qualified for the position – a very distinguished classical scholar, with experience of teaching both in school and university, a wide and humane outlook and a charming and beautiful wife. MGS was and is a fine school, on Manchester Grammar School lines, but it needed a different quality of leadership at that stage. Before he left Stacy deposited with his secretary a list of ten points defining what, in his opinion, needed to be done at MGS. Fifteen years later I found myself sitting next to his successor at a dinner of the Beefsteak Club in Melbourne. The list had been given to him by the secretary. "Tell Colman", he said, "that he was absolutely right; I tried to do everything that was contained in that list". It was through Stacy that I found myself addressing the Victorian Classical Association – an absurd situation for a non-classicist. It was run by a spinster lady whom Stacy described as being a woman of determined culture. Nor was this the only anomalous lecturing occasion; I found myself holding forth on Education to the local Association of Teachers, not to mention the YMCA and kindred bodies.

I carried on an immense correspondence with Shrewsbury during my time in Australia, with colleagues, particularly Robin Moulsdale, and with about thirty boys. Anthony Wieler wrote me a complete Fasti, week by week, of what was happening in the school and in his life. Michael Williams wrote long and sensitive letters; he, Johnny Pedder and Michael Gibbs were regular correspondents, all candidates to be Head of House – Michael Williams won. I was kept informed of the changing kaleidoscope of friendships and rivalries in Ridgemount by William Cuthbert, Gilbert Rodway and others; and that the 'in-word' was now 'squalid' which had ousted 'naive' and 'immature'. Peter Ingrams wrote of the debate in which he had moved that 'this House prefers Conceit to Gluttony' but that the opposition led by Richard had won – a typical Ingrams motion. Looking back on these letters now, it brings home to me what a tightly-bound social community the school and indeed every House was, full of energies and tensions, hopes and fears, friendships firm and friendships shattered amongst the fifty or so boys living so closely together. One letter which surprised me was from a senior master at Highgate suggesting that I might apply for the headmastership, soon to be vacant; the answer was obvious but I was quite astonished to be approached since headmasters to me were still, though not for much longer, beings on a different plane.

As the time to depart approached, I began to realise how deeply I had entered into Geelong Grammar and how difficult leaving was going to be. The names will mean little to those who read this but it had been good to serve with such as Roger Blomfield, Ken Mappin, Alan Cash (soon to be a headmaster), Bill Lester, a fellow athlete at Oxford, now stricken by paralysis, confined but by no means diminished by being in a wheelchair, Rolf Baldwin with his repertoire of music hall songs, Vic Tunbridge, the essence of Australian schoolmastering, Barney Hutton on whom Jim Darling unloaded the school administration, and John Brazier, musician extraordinary. These and others – John Ponder and Eyre Walker for instance – were good men to serve with. With some of the boys I kept in touch for a time and have renewed acquaintance on subsequent visits to Australia; Peter King was Senior Prefect; Bruce Rowe, Robin Ritchie (later chairman of the GGS governors) and Bruce Jeffcot were in my history class, as was John Paul whose knowledge of the Oxford Movement and developments in the Church of England surprised me; Richard Smallwood was to be a distinguished medic; Tim Murray, now Headmaster of Canberra GS; Ranald

Macdonald, whose family owned the Melbourne *Age*; James Cox, my fellow first cornet – these and others had become friends. I also taught Kerry Packer economic geography (of which I know nothing) but from which he has profited by becoming, so it is said, one of the richest men in the world.

My last days were hectic with farewell parties and my own valedictory contribution was what we at Shrewsbury called a band concert, really a variety show based on the band but including songs and sketches with the emphasis on Victorian music hall from the Players Theatre in London of which I had been a long-time member. The boys took to the spirit of the thing, never shy to have a go at something different and full of uninhibited energy. The rendering of "I do like to be beside the seaside" with white flannels, straw hats and canes was a furore. I was very touched to receive a book from the Common Room with the flattering inscription *Omnia quae tetigit convertit in aurum*. I left one evening and, fully packed, drove Barber's little car the few yards to the staff dining room for tea; having said goodbye I prepared to drive off – but no car. However, Peter King and the school prefects were hovering and led me back to the House where the boys had dragged the car and where there was assembled the whole school – and the band! As I approached there was a massive though ragged chorus of "I do like to be beside the seaside"; I drove off between cheering lanes of boys, my vision blurred. I had to stop on the Melbourne Road and have a good cry. Weeks later I received a letter from a sixth former, Roger Cook. "Those first days of August will always be a landmark to me. Because when you left, I realised all you had meant to me and to the school in this past year. Your going has left a blank gap in the life of the school". Can it be wondered that, as I drove to Melbourne, I kept turning over in my mind whether – much as I loved Shrewsbury – my place might not really be beside the lagoon at Corio where I had found such deep fulfilment?

Even before I left England I had been planning a return journey which would be unusual, though I told no one. While at Geelong I made some enquiries and read an old Magdalen friend's book on his car journey from England to India, *A Long Way South* by Geoffrey Dutton. I determined to return overland. Jack Peterson was sympathetically agreeable in allowing me a term off which was indeed good of him and I got down to detailed planning.

My main concern was recruiting companions. In the end I persuaded Jamie Learmonth and John Sutherland to come, both of whom had recently left GGS, and, for half the journey, Stewart Harris, a journalist (soon to be *The Times* Australian correspondent) whom I had met in Brisbane. Jamie was intelligent and quick, John was stolid and slow as befits a man of the land. Stewart was a seasoned traveller. There being four of us, we felt we needed space and so purchased a trailer with our Land Rover, a decision we were to regret. We were very fully equipped – tent, camp beds, six gallons of water, twenty-two gallons of petrol, mosquito nets, table, stools, and a Tilley lamp. The Doctor at GGS got very keen on the trip and also equipped us with a medicine chest of fearsome proportions, seemingly covering every known emergency. Jamie was the mechanic, John the practical camper, Stewart the cook, and I planned the route and handled the paperwork of which there was plenty; we were to cross thirty-eight frontiers and visas were wanted in almost all cases which involved waiting about in numerous embassies and consulates, filling in forms and passing through the intricacies of Eastern bureaucracy. The Afghan Government, for instance, required five forms per person with a photograph on each. There were plenty of muddles; on one form my 'colour of eyes' got confused with 'father's name', so that my father turned out to be a sinister character called 'Dark Brown'. Jamie's description of himself as a grazier proved difficult to explain and he was somewhat miffed that he, who had 22,000 acres and 8,000 sheep, should be described simply as a shepherd.

Having taken ship to Colombo, we had the marvellous advantage of staying with Cecil Syers and his vivacious wife in their newly completed High Commissioner's house where we lived in luxury for three days. In Colombo I had a full post bag from Shrewsbury including a letter from Mike Powell saying that he had married Hilary Griffiths! I nearly fell into the Indian Ocean. Having lived in Braehead for several years with no sign of any such event on the horizon, now that my back was turned there had been a whirlwind romance of less than six weeks and our whole domestic world was shattered! Mike had the solution – "the answer is for you to marry Fanny quickly". Robin was equally shattered and wrote that he had "absolutely no inkling ...".

Other news was that Tony Trench had given up smoking his pipe and taken to tapestry. (So that was what marriage did for you.) And Hugh Brooke had started Rigg's on a culture phase and had instituted a culture ladder so all his 1st XI philistines had joined the Concert Choir in order to score points.

So at last on 16th August we were awheel, to remain in motion until 1st December by which time we would have covered 14,300 miles and traversed fifteen countries. Five weeks were spent in India, visiting some old haunts of mine like the Nilgiri Hills of happy wartime memory, beautiful Kashmir and inevitably the Taj Mahal. In Delhi we stayed with the Director of Information Services and were entertained by the High Commissioner. Afghanistan was where the going got tougher, the roads appalling, no language in which to communicate, long stretches of road with no traffic or habitation, primitive rest houses and a general air of suspicion as far as foreigners were concerned. On through Iran and Iraq to Jordan and long days driving through the desert alongside the pipeline to Amman.

Jerusalem absorbed us for several days; and then the delights of that lovely country Lebanon, before the civil war. Slowly through Syria and Turkey, taking the route across the Anatolian plateau and so at last to Istanbul and Europe. Somehow the whole atmosphere changed as we crossed the Bosphorous and the East dropped behind. But there was Greece to experience before crossing into Yugoslavia from where we travelled quite fast for home.

What memories remain forty years later? The Taj, which I have seen on four occasions, cannot be omitted; the atmosphere of the Khyber Pass, now again a familiar place but then new to me, the dusty hills redolent with history and often tragedy; the blue mosques of Persia; caviar and vodka by the Caspian; nights in the Syrian desert, our camp a tiny spot in the stony wilderness under brilliant stars; the old city of Jerusalem; that finest of Crusader castles, the Krak des Chevaliers; Byblos, with remains from 2,000 years ago and every civilisation since; Baalbeck, romantically isolated in the desert; the mystical feel of Delphi, seen on a bright autumn day. Memories still linger.

We were scarcely pioneers but only met six or seven parties en route doing the same trip, for this was before the establishment of the hippie trail to India which did so much damage to British reputation. Apart from twelve punctures we had little trouble save with the trailer which tended to break away on its own. We had to replace bearings in wintry weather in the Sanjack of Novi Bazaar in Yugoslavia, a famous place in the Balkan Wars. Remarkably we lost little except the windscreen wiper which was stolen by the notorious Australian wharfies, though we lost bread and marmalade to plundering peacocks one night near Jaipur and a Persian pinched the side lights in Teheran. We made many interesting contacts, received generous hospitality, suffered no illnesses, maintained equable personal relations and found that the whole trip over nearly four months had cost us less than £500 each.

CHAPTER XVII

Housemastering and Matrimony

Oh tidings of comfort and Joy, comfort and Joy,
O tidings of comfort and Joy.

I did not find it difficult to settle again to life in England. My mother and Olive were both well, still in the Northampton family home. The Lent term 1955 started much as usual apart from my domestic life having a different pattern. The old bachelor Braehead was no more; Mike and Hilary Powell lived on the upper floors, Robin Moulsdale and I on the lower, looked after by various daily ladies. But not for long. Robin was soon in the process of getting engaged to the beautiful Julie Millen whom he had first met while skiing. And that term Tony Trench was appointed Headmaster of Bradfield. While I had been away he had married Elizabeth Spicer – the School House exerting its benign influence yet again in propelling those within it to the altar. Twins had recently been born to them to the surprise of all, including Elizabeth who was astonished to find herself the mother of two. Tony developed a typical Trench story about the unexpected appearance of four large ears, like his own, instead of the anticipated two.

The first bet in the Braehead betting book stated that "M.L.C. bets E.W.G (Willie Gladstone) five shillings that Tony Trench will *not* be headmaster of any school before 1965". How wrong one can be. Willie having left by 1955 I don't think he ever got the five bob. I realised then for the first time that headmasters are not a mysterious elite but elevated ordinary people. Few schoolmasters can have been so widely sought after as Tony. Robert Birley at Eton wanted him, Walter Oakeshott tried to tempt him into being his Second Master at Winchester, George Mallaby was sounding him with a view to his succeeding Wilkes as Warden of Radley and three Oxford Colleges were interested. So Tony and Elizabeth, the twins and their nondescript dog called Offley (after whom?), prepared to move off, to the great loss of Shrewsbury.

Who would succeed Tony in School House? I noticed that my colleagues did not discuss this with me and it slowly dawned that I was a possible candidate. Thus it proved. Jack Peterson casually one day, as was his wont, asked me if I would like "to go into the School House"; I didn't at first grasp that he was offering me the job but had no hesitation in accepting, feeling however a little awkward as several senior to me might have hoped for this position and also because Mike Powell, a dozen years my senior, had already been designated for Ingram's, but not until 1957. It seemed absurd that I should be a housemaster before him. James West, true to form had urged Jack Peterson to become School House housemaster himself, thus putting the clock back fifty years. Jack recoiled in horror.

I am surprised now that I was not more daunted by the task ahead of me. School House had a hundred boys; it was a very large building; and these were the days of house catering, a large potential problem for a bachelor. The private side of the House had been built on headmagisterial lines, the Headmaster having been the housemaster until 1932. I had one great and continuing asset; Freddy Mann was happy to continue as resident house tutor. Few people could be more fully devoted to their work nor more meticulous in its discharge. A deceptively mild exterior concealed a man of firm resolution, administrative efficiency (where he had compensated for Tony Trench's shortcomings), and unusual domestic skills – he could for instance turn his hand to making curtains.

The Governing Body in their generous wisdom had by now agreed to provide the carpets and curtains in the dining and drawing rooms but I had to provide everything else. I was determined to have a grand piano and, rather to my surprise, on the morning after a dance in Surrey, found I had bought one from a girl for £100. Fortunately my mother and Olive were happy for me to have a considerable amount of furniture from the family home in Northampton but it was nevertheless a financial strain to set myself up in School House; I was now earning £1,050 a year and had at last reached the salary which I had earned as a staff captain in India! My domestic organisation was less happy. The School House matron expressed herself willing to take the position of housekeeper; she had been in the House some time, knew it intimately and so it seemed a good appointment. It was however a not unfamiliar case of an NCO failing to make the transition to the rank of officer. An immensely hard and conscientious worker, she did not command the respect nor have the management skill to deal with the motley collection of staff – strong-minded cooks, maids from the South Wales valleys, girls from obscure Shropshire villages and rural Wales – who made up our twenty-strong domestic team. Fortunately I and several other School House housemasters had the ever reliable and willing Paddy Walsh and his wife Sarah who resided in the adjoining cottage, always rising to domestic emergencies of which we had many.

The principal of hierarchy in the running of the House still stood strongly, the monitors at the top with power to punish, the douls or scum at the bottom, and the years in between nicely graded and defined by small privileges. It was a system which was shortly to break completely but in its time it was not without merit *when working well*, though containing some absurdities and always liable to abuse. Tony Trench's charismatic personality and informal attitude had done much to break down the old green baize door division between housemaster and boys, though some of his unorthodox methods, particularly of punishment, were looked at askance by some. The difficulty of actually knowing well a hundred boys was considerable. Hope-Simpson said that he always feared that there were one or two obscure boys whom he would find that he had not spoken to for weeks at a time; and every housemaster knows there are always boys with whom he has no affinity, with whom he can find no common ground. But I was in the main very fortunate. This account must not become a catalogue of names but it was good to have a House with people of such diverse talents as Paul Foot, Humphrey Ward, Nicholas and Richard Barber, Andy and Chris Maclehose, Andrew Macaulay, Roger Willoughby, Simon Foster, Roger Nicholson, Michael and Patrick Balfour, Nicko and Peter Williams and the Wycherley brothers, to name but a few.

Apart from the threatening domestic cloud, never far away, these were happy years. Perhaps the most difficult aspect of the old system lay in deciding how much I should run the House and how much the boys should. It was a delicate matter of balance which I did not always get right. Another aspect which gave me much worry was the choice of monitors – then quite powerful people – and the sadness one felt in passing over perfectly good boys who were lacking in confidence and executive power. Yet to include them much weakened the system. Later and wiser housemasters in a different age included the whole year group as monitors, finding jobs for all according to talents. But by then the position of monitor had declined in importance.

School House, then as now, was divided into Headroom and Doctor's, keen rivals outside the walls, moving as one within them. Boys were ceremoniously placed in Doctor's or Headroom by drawing the new boys' names out of a mortar board on the first day of term. Jimmy Street always said that if you understood the School House you could come near to understanding the doctrine of the Trinity. In those years we had considerable sporting success which was good for morale. I also took some tentative steps into what was to be the future by holding the first house dance in term time, and by developing some liaison with Moreton Hall – even to the extent of playing cricket with (but not against) them. One inherited activity, which we developed, was the School House Sing Song at the end of the Michaelmas term. Originally songs round the piano with Bob Sawyer singing 'Abdul Abulbul Ameer', this entertainment became quite sophisticated with sketches and songs written by boys and a final item, such as a pantomime, which I wrote myself. All staff members were invited, dinner jackets were worn and refreshments provided.

Concentration on housemastering did not leave a lot of time for other activities but I was still a form master, still running the fives and the athletics, still in charge of the Old Salopian address list with considerable assistance from a recent Old Salopian, Richard Baylis. To this was added in 1957 a job which I had long coveted, that of editing the *Salopian Newsletter*, sent to all Old Salopians twice a year. James West had done this hitherto, again something which he never quite found time to do well. He also made some splendid blunders such as reporting that W.L.R. Carbonell had received the Most Honourable Order of the Garter ("that fool West has given Carbonell the Garter" commented Oldham) when he had actually been made CMG, ascribing a book of poems by W.H. Auden to an obscure Dayboy of the name H.W. Auden, and crediting Richard Raven's Oxford scholarship to his father the Revd G.E. Raven (1907–12). However I must not criticise too strongly; during my editorship I 'killed' two Salopians who were alive and well; they were both magnanimous about it. I felt considerably more could be made of the Newsletter, both in content and size, so that it might appeal to a wider readership of Salopians. I was to edit it for twenty-five years.

The Fourth Centenary Fund, almost entirely the work of Jimmy Street, raised in the end some £200,000; but nothing had been spent on the School House which, as a building, needed it more than any other House. Accordingly I started a campaign to secure radical improvement and after endless argument and discussion, major structural changes were made in 1957–58. This took much – too much – of my time but in the end we achieved a great deal, principally a splendid new dining hall adjacent to the kitchen. Hitherto all food had to come up to the main hall from the basement, and all washing-up was done by hand. We also had a completely new changing room to replace an unchanged nineteenth century structure, by now almost a period piece with its trough bath, holding six (Children Act!). The success of these alterations was largely due to Stanley Catterall, our Old Salopian architect, whose ingenuity and sympathetic understanding led to a wholly successful result – at a cost of £32,000, slightly less than the original estimate. Running the House while it was being disembowelled was full of hazard but normal service was maintained.

In the holidays I still took skiing parties, spent time at home, visited my brother Richard, working without much enthusiasm for British Rail, now living at Beaconsfield with Freda and a growing son, and occasionally travelled further afield, once to Gibraltar to stay with the Governor who had married Barbara – a wiser choice for her than I would have been. In fact matrimony seemed very unlikely now that I was in my late thirties: there simply wasn't time! Yet the unexpected happened.

Principal's House. Lawrence College

Cricket field. Lawrence College

The Burgage

1990. Alan and Gillian; Jane and Anna; Martin and Esther

Joy

Second Master

Cuthbert Brooke-Smith had been in Oldham's with me, though older; he was one of that congenial group of various ages which so happily kept some semblance of contact over the years. In 1955 he was promoted to command the 1st Battalion of the King's Shropshire Light Infantry after a solidly successful army career. I went to his predecessor's farewell ceremonial parade in the Quarry, by chance met Cuthbert and sat with him in the VIP enclosure. The battalion was under orders for Kenya to cope with the Mau Mau emergency and after the parade I wished him well in his new command. I never saw him again. Only a few weeks after the battalion was deployed in Kenya he was accidentally shot by his own men when visiting a forward post. Approaching this outpost from an unexpected angle, without warning owing to a signal having failed to get through, preceded by two black African trackers, fire had been opened; Cuthbert died almost immediately. His wife, Joy, with her three children was living in their Little Stretton house, about to proceed to Kenya. She was informed of his death by a telegram – surely a cold and unnecessary way of communicating such a tragedy.

I had met Joy once when visiting the family at Church Stretton but we did not know each other at all well. Now however the education of the children brought me in touch. Philippa (15), Bruce (12) and Robin (11) all had to be educated and this brought in my involvement as a trustee of the Shrewsbury School War Memorial Fund which had been subscribed so that children of Salopians killed in war could be assisted in their education. So Joy and I came to know each other and I spent a lot of time with the family. Joy, living on a tiny income, eventually obtained a job at Moreton Hall having timidly applied for the post of assistant matron but ordered (no other word) to be a teacher by the dominating Headmistress, Bronwen Lloyd-Williams to whom one did not readily say no. Philippa was given a free place at the Royal School, Bath, Bruce was given a free place at Moffats Preparatory School through the great generosity of John Engleheart, the Headmaster, and Robin went to Kingsland Grange, paid for by the War Memorial Fund. I had often wondered whether I would ever be able to devote myself with full commitment to the married state but doubts gradually melted away as Joy and I both realised that we could make our life together. So it was that on 1st August 1958 we were married by James Hill in Shrewsbury School Chapel, held a reception in the School House, had a brief honeymoon at Portmeirion and were soon off to Bermuda, with the children, to stay with Joy's mother.

Joy was herself a Bermudian, her parents having settled there after her father retired as a merchant navy Captain. In 1940 Cuthbert Brooke-Smith was posted there with a detached company of the KSLI to stay for only a few months before returning to Europe. He and the seventeen-year-old Joy made a compact: they would marry but the engagement was to be a secret until Joy's nineteenth birthday when Cuthbert would write to her father to ask for her hand. So in January 1942 the missive was sent – to the astonishment of both families who expected no such thing. Joy sailed in convoy to England, a country of which she knew but little, in wartime and in winter; they were married on a freezing day in March from the Brooke-Smith home in Suffolk. Cuthbert's father, himself a retired Captain, split the expenses of the wedding with Joy's father and the bill was two pounds, six shillings and twopence each. There followed a largely separate army life in the war – Cuthbert fought in the NW Europe campaign. In peace they had various postings which included India, Germany and – by lucky chance – Bermuda.

Granny Brooke-Smith's first words to me were, "You've got a treasure". It did not take me long to realise the truth of her remark. Having followed the drum for thirteen years, Joy was adaptable, resourceful and energetic. She also had considerable social gifts and could hold her own in any social gathering, at home with all sorts and conditions of men and women. We entertained considerably; these were still the days of formal dinner parties, with maids to wait at table. All her talents were needed during our School House years. My housekeeper, whom we intended should stay to share the work with Joy, soon had a virtual breakdown and Joy took responsibility for the domestic side of the House. We broke new ground at Shrewsbury by employing 'lady cooks' for the first time and had two resident girls for whom we were able to provide tolerable though not luxurious accommodation. When at full strength we had six resident maids, six dailies, a gardener, a part-time secretary and – soon – a nanny in addition to Matron and the Walshes. With Freddy Mann this made up a large contingent. In those days of full employment it was difficult to recruit any girls of quality to our domestic staff; they were a constant concern with their feckless ways, tempers and quarrels.

Joy was an experienced mother. One might have thought she would find three children enough but she enjoyed greatly another round of babies. Martin was born on 30th July 1959, Alan on 6th February 1961 and their arrival in the world brought us great happiness. Both were born in the School House and later christened in the big drawing-room. Brian Harrison, Head of House at the time (and a lifelong friend) was one of Alan's godfathers. We were fortunate indeed to have the services of nanny Pugh, semi-retired, but totally dedicated to her charges and one of the most truly Christian people I have known. She had started as a girl of fourteen in Kingsland House as nurserymaid to the Cock family.

The older children were soon all flourishing in their new schools. The position of step-father can be a fraught one. Just as I was aware that I could never be what Cuthbert had been to Joy, so I realised that I could never be the father they had lost. But, even before our marriage, I had established quite a close relationship with them which grew into one of much affection, enriched by the arrival of two little brothers of whom they were very fond. In fact Joy told me that if she hadn't married me, Philippa would have!

So I had suddenly made the transition from being a single housemaster to a man who had five children within two-and-a-half years of marriage, while Joy had had the courage to take on both an ageing bachelor and a full-time job. Looking back, I do not think I entirely appreciated what a tremendous task she had, with the babies, the domestic responsibility, our social life, and the older children. Certainly our holidays were very happy ones; we both enjoyed the School House as a building (despite the forty-five stairs to our bedroom and the nursery) and its garden; and for the children there were the facilities of the Site in contrast to a rather pokey suburban house.

At the time of our marriage I had no thought but to continue as house-master of the School House indefinitely. My perspective was soon to change, but the life I lived and to which I now introduced Joy was congenial to both of us, though the work was extremely hard. I am quite surprised that my correspondence files show that I found time to write numerous letters, largely keeping in touch with boys after they had left the School House; links continued for many years, some to this day. At our wedding the ushers were Andrew Macaulay, Christopher Maclehose, Michael Balfour and Nigel Hodges with all of whom I am still in touch. I did Nigel a good turn: by staying for the ceremony he met Fiona Peterson, the Headmaster's daughter, an encounter which was to lead ultimately to a very happy marriage.

These were still the days when boys had a deep sense of commitment to the school, living and moving in the community of the House – for better or worse – with the outside world far away. The actions and reactions of the hundred School House boys did indeed make up a world of its own. When the time came to leave some were delighted to move on; others found the parting painful. "That last week I was taciturn because, simply, I could not bear to go and could not drive myself to forced heartiness" wrote Paul Foot. Paul had been a critic of much that went on in the Public School of that day – particularly corporal punishment – but he loved the life of the community and the currents and cross-currents of friendship which ran through the body politic. We corresponded at length after he left. As a member of the Socialist Workers Party, he is now obviously opposed to independent education. But then he wrote, "I remember far more good than evil. Journalist, yes. Socialist, yes. But always an upholder of the Public Schools. We may find each other in that last ditch!" Oxford to him was the ideal world. "This is my idea of Paradise on Earth. It is extraordinary how the opportunities just sit there for the taking. I seem to spend most of my time in amazement at the joy of the place."

National Service claimed school leavers and they wrote from dim army camps up and down the country, from Catterick, from Park Hall, from Caterham, of the rigours of army life from which they would come on a '48' to stay at the School House and regale us with their experiences. To others also the University seemed a marvellous haven. Roger Willoughby and Andrew Macaulay wrote of the delights of Balliol. Chris Maclehose went to Worcester College after some uncertainty, at one time at odds with his father and trying his luck in Canada from where he still had time to be concerned about me: "It worries me, Michael, as to where you will go from School House".

There were some letters which I particularly valued such as one from the father of a largely undistinguished boy, "... it is to your sagacious handling of a youngster at odds with himself that I feel I owe the promising student, the self-possessed and enjoyable companion you have sent back to me". *O si sic omnes*. Faced as I was from time to time by boys or situations which I had handled badly, it was good to receive letters like these. I kept up too with Adam Fox at Westminster Abbey, a person who had influenced my life very much, unexpectedly showing considerable acumen as treasurer of the Abbey Appeal for £1 million. I was touched to find that I had a place in his intercession list.

A quite different series of letters came from Nevil Norway in Australia. Solicitous and generous, he was concerned for Basil Oldham, now in his declining years, whose financial condition was – by his own account – parlous, to the extent of lunching on a dry bun in town and not being able to afford a coffee, though he was given to over-dramatising his situation. Nevil established a bank account in Shrewsbury in my name which he replenished from time to time. I was to dole out the money to Basil entirely to be spent on holidays and whisky. I monitored this account until Nevil's death; it was in the form of a loan to satisfy Basil's *amour propre* but we all knew that it would never be repaid.

But it is time to turn from the School House microcosm and its busy life, which so absorbed Joy and me, to consider the school at large at the end of the 1950s and the strange crisis which overtook it.

CHAPTER XVIII

The Waters Ruffled

For violent fires soon burn out themselves
Small showers last long but sudden storms are short.

Richard II 2.1

Outwardly Shrewsbury was seen to be a very successful school as the 1950s decade drew to its close; in its final year there were sixteen university awards, academic results generally were good (though there were some weak subjects), matches were more often won than lost and the Boat Club under Peter Gladstone's charismatic leadership flourished abundantly. The staff in general was of high quality (though Peter Knight had to go – so good a teacher when actually there – but a careful account kept by boys showed him to be present for less than half of his teaching timetable). At a staff meeting in 1955 it was agreed that there should be as few special allowances as possible, thus maintaining the old theory – shades of Moser and Chance – that everyone worked hard round the clock. It was recognised that housemasters had a heavier responsibility but Heads of Faculties were paid a derisory amount.

In 1953, at the age of thirty-six, I was the youngest housemaster by some way. All, except Rex Connell, had been on the staff when I was a boy twenty years earlier, and they had collectively immense experience. Stacy Colman was in Dayboys, Alec Binney in Churchill's, Peter Hawkesworth in Moser's, Bill Matthews in Oldham's. Hugh Brooke continued to run Rigg's in his highly unorthodox but splendidly successful way. He had applied to be Warden (Headmaster) of St Edward's, Oxford, (his own old school), and had been confident of success. Frank Fisher was appointed instead and Hugh was bitterly disappointed. He had turned his attention to ordination instead, causing a considerable flutter at Westcott House by inventing improbable religious games – Biblical (B)Lotto, Heretical Housey-Housey, and a race game taking the Israelites from Ur to the Promised Land. Patrick Childs was running Severn Hill in his individualistic way ("It's a long way for little legs"). In Ridgemount, Rex Connell was finding the going hard, having succeeded David Bevan.

The strain of running the domestic side of the Houses was very heavy. Some wives were very competent, others found it immensely difficult, particularly Dorothy Brooke and Kay West. Practically every year there were large deficits in the Rigg's and Ingram's accounts. It did indeed seem extraordinary that in 1952 the Ingram's bill for fuel exceeded that of the School House which was twice the size. The governors made threatening noises and indicated that they would put in housekeepers if necessary; indeed in 1951 Peterson wrote to West that "unless expenditure can be kept within reasonable bounds, I may have to ask someone else to take over your House". A memo from housemasters in 1955 said that they viewed the future "with serious perturbation" owing to "the load of physical effort and nervous strain" on their wives. The firm of J. Lyons was asked to advise but their suggestion of appointing a catering supervisor to be responsible for staff, buying, meals and service was not taken up.

The domestic struggle was much exacerbated by the friction which existed in most quarters with the Bursar. Lieutenant-Colonel Bernard Alder MBE had been appointed in 1947. His predecessor had been amiable and incompetent, a believer in *laissez faire*. Alder was confronted with a mammoth task in difficult post-war conditions. By extraordinary industry he managed to get the school accounts and general accounting system into shape – the first time, so a governor said, that he had ever been able to understand them. I sometimes passed the Bursary late at night; the light would still be on as Alder toiled away. When Alder finally retired, Fermian Le Neve Foster, chairman of the Finance Committee, spoke feelingly of his "immense services to the school" and the "order and clarity" which he had brought to the accounts. Unfortunately his gifts did not extend to the area of personal relationships and management of people, particularly housemasters' wives. Members of the staff felt they were totally ignorant of the business side of the school and, with many things needing attention, were baffled by not only the lack of information but also the process by which decisions were made. At the end of one term at a masters' meeting it was decided to set up a small committee to choose colour schemes for the rooms in the School Buildings which were to be redecorated. As masters left the meeting, lorries drew up and started unloading the paint which the Bursar had already ordered without any consultation.

To try and bridge the gap, a General Purposes Committee had been set up, partly on my urging, consisting of the Headmaster, the Bursar, Tom Taylor, Basil Saint and myself. The atmosphere was frosty, Peterson ill at ease, Alder wholly defensive, Tom Taylor curt and scoring with a number of straight lefts. The committee achieved, I think, nothing. Stacy took Tom's place and wrote to me in Australia:

The General-Purposes Committee is to meet tomorrow!! (Will the

Bursar be there? How will the Committee fare while their champion is in Australia? Another long, gripping – and entirely futile – instalment of this endless and tedious serial will appear in our next issue. Order your copy NOW).

The governors appointed a Priorities Committee but as the members were Jimmy Street, Jack Bowdler, the Headmaster and the Bursar, no one reposed any confidence in it: admirable men no doubt, but gutters and drainpipes, heating and washing-up, furniture and fixtures were not their field.

Feelings ran so high that at one of my first housemasters' meetings James West moved a vote of no confidence in the Bursar, supported by Hawkesworth. Reluctant as schoolmasters are to push matters to extremes, the vote was lost. (Perhaps there was something basically inimical between a full colonel in the Rifle Brigade and a lieutenant-colonel in the West African Pioneer Corps!) David Bevan's resignation from Ridgemount before his time had spread considerable gloom; the school could not well spare a man of such proven housemastering ability. Although he said that he went because of the strain on Hilary and indeed on himself, he made plain that he felt they had been ill-supported by the central management of the school. "I cannot rid myself of the feeling that we have been treated with squalid parsimony".

What, it may well be asked, of the Governing Body and their involvement in these affairs? Broadly there were three groups; the Shropshire landed families – Offley Wakeman, Chairman for twenty-five years, Lord Bridgeman, Arthur Heywood-Lonsdale; the distant and distinguished – J.M. Wordie of St John's, Cambridge, Sir Charles Darwin, Sir James Chadwick; and Old Salopians who sought to be more closely involved – Duncan Norman, Dick Summers and Fermian Le Neve Foster, together with Stephen Lee. To these were added the Borough Council members, not generally carrying much weight, and the masters' representative, from 1956 Tom Bigland. Offley was a major figure in Shropshire, Chairman of the County Council and heavily involved in public work. He did his job as Chairman but was without any real knowledge of the school or close interest in it and the same could be said for all the governors except the group round Duncan Norman. Stephen Lee deserves a brief note: he was important in my life as father of my great friend John Lee, and as a don at Magdalen. He was the politest man I have ever known, thoughtful, generous and unselfish, devoted to Shrewsbury. In about 1946 I gave him a lift in my fast Talbot Ten from Oxford to Shrewsbury. He brought in an attaché case a thermos of tea for refreshment on the journey, a railway timetable in case we broke down and had to continue by train, and a folding stool in case the train was full and we had to stand in the corridor. This meticulous preparation for a hundred mile car journey mirrored his careful and punctilious outlook and his experience of wartime travel.

In 1956 it was at last found possible to move Offley from the Chair, a manoeuvre which involved difficult diplomacy. Duncan Norman succeeded. He had no illusions about the Bursar. He knew well that the staff had little enthusiasm for the Governing Body. Stacy Colman summed it up, "It is difficult to decide whether the habitual and total inertia of the Governing Body is worse than their occasional and wholly futile bursts of crazy energy". A good example of their havering lay in their long deliberations about James West and his position as Mayor of Shrewsbury which he held in 1952. If James was largely absent, there must be a substitute: who should pay? In the end James was to pay two thirds and the Governing Body the rest; then Peterson discovered that it wasn't necessary after all to pay for a substitute to cover James's teaching – a fact which might have been realised from the first. Offley's solution was an odd one: let him resign from Ingram's and be Mayor as it was "apparently agreed that he was unsatisfactory as a housemaster". Then no one would have to pay! One could not be more out of touch.

But it is possible to condemn the Governing Body too easily. During this period under Offley the financial position greatly improved, salaries were raised, the Fourth Centenary Fund – raised almost entirely by the personal labours of Jimmy Street – made it possible to build three masters' houses on Port Hill, Kingsland Grove was purchased, the running track laid and improvements made to Severn Hill, Churchill's and Moser's. And – a sign of the times – a ladies' lavatory was installed in the Alington Hall. A watershed indeed. Arthur Heyward-Lonsdale supervised the improvements to the grounds and Fermian Le Neve Foster (Chairman of Smith's Crisps) presented the football 'cage' before ill health caused his retirement (goodbye Mr Crisps). And, of course, there was the major School House improvement.

Back in 1951 on Duncan Norman's urging, the very well-known architect Sir William Halford was asked to draw up a development plan for the Site. He produced some interesting drawings: a central kitchen and dining hall for a hundred (staff and Dayboys) on what is now the craft centre site; a music and art building in the area of the baths; two masters' houses on Port Hill; a terrace in front of the School Buildings with a place for the Butler statue. (Had the latter suggestion been adopted at that time the Butler statue would have been saved from its horrid fate.) None of these suggestions was proceded with, constructive as they were, but the interesting thing is that no member of the staff had the least notion that these radical schemes were being considered. The Headmaster, Bursar and governors decided on the school's needs without consulting the people actually working in the place.

Duncan Norman approached his task in a very different spirit from Offley Wakeman. His enthusiasm for Shrewsbury knew no bounds; although running the firm of Owen Owen as Chairman, expanding now both in England and Canada, he made time to visit Shrewsbury frequently, wrote often and telephoned a good deal. He wanted to be wholly in the picture. Relations with the Bursar were not good. He contained himself with difficulty for he was a man given to passionate reactions, of which he often repented. He categorised the Bursar as being "short of skill, courtesy and common gumption in handling people". He condemned his choice of an assistant, one Captain McCunnin, a wholly anonymous man, whose "heel click was always audible and the only noticeable thing about him". McCunnin passed quickly into obscurity. At last in 1958 Alder moved on to be, eventually, a most successful bursar at Eastbourne College.

Duncan was in close touch with Jimmy Street, a relationship which later caused some adverse comment in time of controversy. But he also spent time with others. I recollect that back in 1951 he, alone of the governors, showed interest in what I and some younger members of the staff were thinking, coming round after a governors' meeting to my bedsitter at Braehead and talking to David Brown, Robin Moulsdale and me about our Rehoboam ideas. He tried hard to help housemasters' wives, once coming down to see each one in her home. But all suggestions for catering assistance, the installation of 'dames' on the Eton model, central cooking or professional housekeepers were not well received. Meanwhile in Moser's Peter and Felicity Hawkesworth were pointing to the future in employing 'dailies' and dispensing with resident domestic staff save for a cook. This was expensive. Governors gave grudging support – grudging because if the system became universal the fees would have to go up. In an attempt to make the shop more profitable, Gorringes were approached. Nothing came of this.

The new Bursar was Commander B.M. Edwards, OBE, RN, who had the easy manner of a naval officer and who was at once more approachable than his predecessor. It was only in later years that his manner was seen to be a good deal too easy-going for the financial health of the school. Of great significance was the appointment of Mary Taylor as Domestic Bursar in 1957. Since Tom's death she had worked in a senior post in the Owen Owen organisation; now her many talents were to be deployed on the Site and housemasters soon discovered who, in the Bursary, had the decisive say in matters domestic.

Jack Peterson had arrived in Shrewsbury on a cloud of good will. He had seemed to have every possible qualification for the position of headmaster of his old school and his staff soon came to admire his sincerity, his humility and his unobtrusive Christian witness, together with his warm humanity and sympathetic encouragement of things cultural. But as the years went on, undercurrents of dissatisfaction were becoming increasingly identifiable because of what many found to be a reluctance to take decisions, to face difficult issues, or to be seen as a leader. When I myself became a headmaster I determined never to say "Well at Shrewsbury we did so and so" in the way that Jack was constantly referring to Eton, a place which had set its mark on him; it was two or three years before he could consistently refer to 'terms' rather than 'halves', 'form rooms' rather than 'school rooms'. His other fatal phrase, so often repeated, was "Well, we do not need to take any decision on that yet". He seemed almost to make a virtue of humility and to exaggerate his lack of any business sense, causing Duncan Norman to write "in any matters of business he is often dangerously and exasperatingly humble". Indeed Jack was quite alive to his own weakness and wrote of "my notorious administrative incompetence". Another telling sentence was, "I think my critics would probably say that I have been too reasonable and perhaps too lax in my approach. I think they would be right". No one could be more frank or more honest. To some masters this very laxness gave them scope to do much as they wished without regard to higher authority and the wider picture of the school's needs; and they naturally were happy to have their heads. To housemasters and those close to the disciplinary framework, seeking common policies, the lack of decision was frustrating in the extreme.

Even during my absence in Australia as early as 1954, Robin Moulsdale had written of "the stray strands of complaint and frustration and despair that have undoubtedly increased lately and are increasingly voiced wherever two or three ... It amounts to a feeling that we are rudderless". David Bevan in a letter used the same metaphor, "We really are like the Queen Mary in mid-Atlantic with no rudder. The HM takes no initiative whatsoever". These feelings were kept below the surface. To talk to Peterson himself about them in terms of criticism or complaint was very difficult, for everyone admired his personal qualities. Hawkesworth put it well in saying that to remonstrate with Jack was "like hitting a woman". Those boys – sadly few – who came in personal contact with the Headmaster had the greatest admiration for him. Personally I saw a great deal of him, his study being in the School House; in fact I was sometimes a welcome port in a storm, reviving him with sherry after bruising housemasters' meetings. We shared many of the same interests and our personal relationship was close. But housemasters became increasingly concerned by what they saw as lack of decision and leadership. Patrick Childs was now senior housemaster and obtained Peterson's permission to hold preliminary housemasters' meetings at Severn Hill without the Headmaster in an attempt to make decisions and generally oil the school mechanism.

At this point a reference to the strange case of Dr A.V. Adams is not irrelevant. Adrian Adams, a doctor of medicine, was appointed to teach chemistry in 1956. He was one of those mavericks whom one encounters from time to time in the teaching profession. He gave himself completely to the teaching of chemistry, working all hours of the day and night. He once conducted a tutorial at 5.00 a.m. in his bedroom in his pyjamas (Children Act?) and at times would rush to the GPO at midnight in order to post corrected work back to boys who would get it with their breakfast. He was, in short, a fanatic. He thus ensured that many boys secured splendidly successful chemistry results; but at a cost, namely that the boys had not much time left over for other subjects, which brought a stream of complaints from other masters. He disregarded school engagements, by, for example, imposing afternoon chemistry papers in games periods, thus causing further friction. He also freely criticised the school and particularly the Combined Cadet Corps; prostitution and homosexuality featured in his teaching, also the properties of alcohol and its use. His end of term parties included three glasses of port for each boy, sometimes with foreseeable results. At least twice in lessons he used boys' bodies to demonstrate certain chemical reactions and badly burned the arms of his guinea pigs, one of them the son of Patrick Childs who, in his innocent dead-pan way, asked at a housemasters' meeting if it was in order for boys to be burned by members of the staff.

Naturally storms rolled around Dr Adams. (It was at this same time that another Dr Adams, the notorious poisoner of old ladies in Eastbourne, was brought to trial. Adrian Adams also lived in Eastbourne and his luggage, labelled 'Dr Adams, Eastbourne', did not pass without comment on the station platform.) While trying to support his excellent teaching, Peterson naturally could not tolerate his other actions. The Doctor soon retreated into a state of paranoia; Patrick Childs and he crossed swords dramatically and some other members of the staff came under the Doctor's whiplash tongue, particular Hawkesworth, "that Chinaman in Moser's". He expressed himself at enormous length on paper and wrote long screeds to boys in the holidays; for Patrick no words were black enough. He also detected a nefarious plot amongst the science staff to keep him away from the best teaching, the innocent Alan Phillips bearing the brunt of scathing criticism.

Peterson, always fair-minded, hesitated long but at length sacked Adams. In the next months he received a stream of self-justification from the Doctor mixed with vilification of his foes on the staff. Certain favourite boys, particularly in Severn Hill, also received letters which could amost be cited as encouragement to mutiny. When the Doctor threatened to visit Shrewsbury and stay at the Lion Hotel, the hatches were battened down, police consulted and legal advice sought. Flying pickets were to go down to the hotel and detain the Doctor (in conversation) to prevent his coming to the Site. Fortunately he did not come. Peterson received a 5,000 word letter – one of several of that length – as to his reasons. The cloud passed; but some thought that Peterson, once more, had been slow and reluctant to act. I had a hand in the battle, seeking to protect some of the School House boys. I was interested to read that Adams in listing those on the staff for whom he had a regard and whom he would miss, included "one half of Michael Charlesworth but not the other".

As may be guessed, Jack Peterson's methods and those of his Chairman, Duncan Norman, did not have much in common and Duncan became increasingly irritated, especially when dealing also with a bursar of whom he had become deeply critical. To a fellow governor he wrote that "Jack cannot maintain sustained and consistent authority over a man of Alder's type". To a man of Duncan's thrusting, impatient and sometimes passionate temperament the whole situation was understandably frustrating.

Towards the end of the 1950s the question of how long Peterson's tenure would last was increasingly the subject of speculation. When he had arrived, his strongest supporters had been Street, West and Oldham. Now Jimmy Street, 'retired' but still running the Fourth Centenary Fund, was hoping that Peterson's reign would not extend beyond 1960 when he would have completed ten years; and Jimmy had a direct line to Duncan. Later Peterson was to identify Street as the author of all the turmoil which was to come and to use condemnatory words which – for him – were strong. James West had retired but lived locally. "It is quite pathetic how Jack allows himself to be pushed around", he wrote to a friend. Basil Oldham – admittedly increasingly cantankerous – was waging war with Peterson over the vexed question of the use of the Moser Building, indeed he actually resigned as Librarian Emeritus until coaxed back by the governors. In fact Jack Peterson had been engaged for no fixed term, though his pension had apparently been arranged in terms which envisaged his retiring in 1967.

Matters came to a head in the summer term of 1959. It was a long and difficult term, for various reasons, and was remembered for a schoolboy prank which has taken its place in folklore. At Henley that year the 1st VIII, around whom the air of success had perhaps puffed up a certain inflated pride, were humbled by a school of which no one had ever heard – Tiffin (actually a very good rowing school). A couple of days after this debacle, coming to First Lesson at 7.45 a.m., the school found to its amazement that every chair from the School Buildings (perhaps three hundred) had been removed and placed upon the Common, spelling out the word TIFFIN. Peterson called for the culprits to come forward; they did not do so and punishment was laid on the whole school in that the Bump Suppers were cancelled. In many ways this jape was harmless but a serious view was taken of boys being out of their Houses at night. Hugh Brooke and others were adamant that mass punishments were always undesirable; and the loss of the Bump Suppers was not felt by the boys as in any way a heavy loss, though it was by Old Salopians who then attended in large numbers. The whole matter caused a considerable stir. (It was not until much later that the names of the culprits were known; they were in Churchill's.)

After the end of term, Hope-Simpson, the Senior Master, being much troubled by the events of the term (of which the Tiffin incident was only one), decided to bring together a cross-section of the staff to consider the situation. Those asked were mostly senior men but an effort was made to bring in masters on the circumference as well as those at the centre – George Simmons for instance. There was a good deal of gloom and doom about the state of the school and the lack of leadership. It was, of course, a very bad time to hold such a gathering, the end of a long and difficult term when most were very tired. It was then that I learned of a similar meeting held five years earlier with the same agenda at which it had been decided that nothing could be done except soldier on. Feeling that something must be done this time but not knowing quite what, it was decided that Hope-Simpson and Alec Binney should go to Duncan Norman and Tom Bigland, the masters' representative, and give them the flavour of the discussion, at the same time expressing the hope that, *if it could be done honourably* (my italics), the Headmaster's tenure should end in 1960. It was stressed repeatedly that the meeting had no *locus standi*, nor did it represent the staff as a whole; it was an expression of opinion by fourteen senior men.

It was, in retrospect, foolish to take this action rather than go to Peterson in the first place, by then on holiday in Harlech. He was naturally upset and prepared to fight back. The participants had agreed to keep the meeting entirely confidential but Peterson broadcast the event to others so that highly-distorted versions were soon in circulation – that the meeting purported to represent the staff, that it was a deliberate stab in the back, that it was a clandestine intrigue planned in advance, that it was a deliberate attempt to stir disloyalty, that Duncan Norman was pulling the strings and so on. Actually fourteen rather weary men, baffled and frustrated, decided on the spur of the moment to take a certain (and mistaken) course of action for lack of any other ideas. The fact that the emissaries were men of such patent probity and integrity as Hope-Simpson and Alec Binney should have silenced the more exaggerated versions.

What then were the real complaints? They are best summed up by Alec Binney in a letter to Jack Peterson:

> ... owning to certain inherent qualities in you as a man (delightful qualities, if I may say so) – your dislike of autocratic methods and of laying down the law, your reluctance to think ill of or to offend anyone, and your dislike of the trivialities of administration – you were becoming overwhelmed with an accumulation of unresolved

problems, a situation which seemed to threaten the school with potentially dangerous relaxation of discipline and administrative tangles which might well sap its efficiency.

The aftermath was unpleasant. Charge and counter-charge were made. There was a strong rally to support J.M.P., represented as a lamb led to slaughter, against the intrigues and the plotters of whom I was represented as one of the foremost; indeed I never changed my view – nor does time change it – that the school would be best served by having a new head-master in 1960. Jack asked for the loyalty of the fourteen: he got it without question – though some felt they had been too loyal already for too long. At a common room meeting Hope-Simpson called on all to bury the recent past. Duncan Norman resigned from the Governing Body, his relations with the Headmaster having been entirely destroyed; Patrick Childs re-signed as housemaster; Peter Hawkesworth prepared to leave; David Bevan had already gone. I decided that the time had come to go too. I resigned from the staff on 23rd October 1959 and at once got in touch with Sopwith at King's School, Canterbury, to see if there was a chance of employment there. He reported a favourable reaction from Canon Shirley, the sort of man who was not averse to picking up discards from important schools.

But it was not to be. Tom Bigland arrived to persuade me to stay, having been briefed by Peterson; conversations with two people whom I much respected, Alan Laurie and Michael Hart, arrested my perhaps too precipi-tate decision. So I stayed, but determined to look elsewhere as opportunity offered. It was sad to see Duncan Norman departing from the scene in such controversial circumstances, having been heavily criticised by at least two of his fellow governors. Hope-Simpson wrote a letter of gratitude from the staff: "you worked to close the enormous gap that existed between the Governors and the Masters – you were the first to take the trouble to know the men individually". United by devotion to Shrewsbury, in both cases service given unstintingly, the contrasting personalities of Norman and Peterson made it impossible for them to work together.

The scene changed on the arrival of Sir Fred Pritchard as Chairman of the Governors. An outstanding High Court judge, promoted early in life, he had been felled by a stroke and was physically handicapped; not mentally so however, with a sharp and analytical mind which lacked exercise though he was now in charge of the Council of Legal Education. He was looked after by his wife with embarrassingly thorough devotion. Fred loved Shrewsbury with a total and complete devotion. He and Jack Pe-terson had much in common as did Graham Heath, the secretary of the Old Salopian Club, all three steeped in the Alington-Sawyer tradition to which they constantly looked back, and all much the same age. The Headmaster now had a Chairman who gave him total and unfailing support but it was to an astonished common room that it was announced in 1960 that the governors had unanimously asked Peterson to stay until 1967. In fact Jack settled for 1963; but his triumph over his critics was complete.

Behind all this turmoil there were deeper stirrings of which we were as yet only dimly aware.'The Sixties' and all that we associate with that decade, had already started in the late Fifties. Macmillan made his 'wind of change' speech in 1960 but to Bob Dylan 'The times were a-changing' already: the Teddy Boy and the Angry Young Man had made their appearances, *Look Back in Anger* and *Absolute Beginners* were being read by VIth form boys, CND was beginning to exercise its influence and the pop world and teenage culture were arriving. Public school boys were not isolated from these social changes and many seized on them with enthusiasm. I remember my own surprise when I came across a boy in his study making the most elaborate charts of the popularity of the pop songs of the day.

I do not think that Jack Peterson greatly enjoyed his last two years. He stood for the principles on which he had himself been brought up and they were indeed unchanging and right but they had to be applied in a rapidly changing world to which the *modus vivendi* of the school had to be adapted. In 1962 he wrote that "over the last two years there has been an extraordinary landslide in standards of decency, morality and behaviour. It has taken me by surprise...". He wrote also of being quite out of touch with his VIth form. To the father of a troublesome boy he commented with disarming honesty: "I really don't understand these boys". Perhaps the combination of Peterson-Pritchard-Heath was just too cosy an Old Salopian package. He wrote of the possibility of excluding the boys with atheist parents: "the damage that these boys do is incalculable". At the time when corporal punishment was being questioned and was soon to be abandoned he expressed himself as "sure that you cannot run a House containing boys of the normal Public School age without the stick in the background". In 1962 he had hoped, needless to say under pressure from James West, that there would be a revival of Paul Dehn's 'Masque' which had so delighted audiences in 1952. This was strongly and almost unanimously opposed at a masters' meeting, the feeling being that it was utterly out of tune with the current generation. Peterson was more than disappointed: "I was absolutely amazed". Then there were battles with the editors of the *Salopian* who were not allowed to publish articles on religion or on the Corps. In his last Speech Day address he spoke feelingly of the importance of an all round education, of which he himself was so excellent an example, and the necessity of maintaining standards at school and in the home which were not incompatible.

After he died one of his Heads of School wrote, "I have always championed his headmastership, but it is not his successes or failures as

Headmaster that I remember. Sufficient it is that the spirit and achievements of the school during his reign – and particularly the spirit – do not
suffer by comparison with what went before or came after''. That was a
timely reminder that though there might have been rough seas in the
common room, the boy world with all its day-to-day activity went on
largely unaffected.

Despite all the arguments, my personal relations with Jack Peterson
remained in good repair. I salute him as a man of tolerance and compas-
sion. His excellent portrait done by Edward Halliday in the Alington Hall
(one of two which stand out in an indifferent lot), splendidly catches the
quiet charm and serenity of his nature with a hint of the spirituality which
lay behind the facade. Joy and I saw him several times in his retirement
home in Wiltshire. But long before he left Shrewsbury, I was perched on a
hillside in the Himalayas with headmastering problems of my own which
made insignificant those which arose at Shrewsbury.

CHAPTER XIX

Return to the East

An' I'm learnin' 'ere in London what the ten year soldier tells
"If you've 'eard the East a-callin', you won't never 'eed naught
else".

Kipling

One evening in the Michaelmas term of 1960, I was idly flicking
through the pages of *The Times Educational Supplement* before going to bed,
when I came on a full-page spread which described a new school to be set
up in Iran. With the blessing of the Shah and the British Government, the
idea was to establish a British-type boarding school for Iranian boys, the
staff to be half British, half Iranian. Plans had been drawn up by a London
architect and the Headmaster elect was J.W.S. Hardie, then Headmaster of
Canford. The British Council, who was handling the project, was seeking
British staff. Without much thought I sent off a postcard the next day
asking for further details, having a general interest in overseas matters
after my Indian experience. Hardie was on the phone to me at once, full of
questions and information, asking me to go up to the British Council in
London and talk to him. Rather dazed by his speed and keenness, Joy and I,
having discussed the matter, saw no harm in making further investi-
gations. The result was that before I quite knew it, I had been appointed as
Deputy Head of this putative school in the Elburz Mountains north of
Teheran to which Hardie was soon on his way to supervise construction
and find staff.

All this was part of a scheme called Educational Co-operation in the
Commonwealth, then being pushed by the Ministry of Education,
whereby it was hoped that British teachers would serve overseas to help
developing countries. The fact that Iran was not in the Commonwealth did
not seem to matter. Governing Bodies were being urged to make this
possible by seconding teachers. Having discussed this fully with Jack
Peterson, the governors were approached and agreed to second me for
three years; I was and am eternally grateful to them and to Jack for this
permission. I waited with interest to hear from Hardie, out in Persia, as to

progress in both the building of the school and in his recruiting Iranian staff. Strangely, I heard nothing at all. At Christmas he returned: he was totally disillusioned. The buildings had not started, the Iranian Ministry was uninterested, the possibility of recruiting suitable Iranian staff was non-existent. He gave up the project. Summoned by the Director General of the British Council, Sir Paul Sinker, I was urged to take the position of headmaster and continue the scheme; he pointed out that the Shah, the British Government, our ambassador and the Minister of Education were all keen on this important plan which could have wide implications for Anglo-Iranian relations. But I refused the bait: if Hardie found it impracticable, who was I to contradict him? So Heserack School disappeared without trace.

So there was I, all set to jump off into the Third World, with nowhere to go. The British Council looked about them to see what they could find for me. The answer was Lawrence College, Ghora Gali, Pakistan. I consulted Joy on the telephone as to whether she wanted to go to Pakistan: "No", she said, "It's too far". I pointed out that it was only a couple of hours flying time further than Teheran and that we had entered the jet age.

Always holding that it was a wife's duty to follow her husband's career, wherever it led, she agreed. All that was required was for the Pakistan Government to sign my contract; it took them ten weeks to do this by which time it was March 1961 and essential that my going was publicised before the end of term. In fact the announcement was made before confirmation arrived. Had I known what I later knew about government in Pakistan, I would not have been so sanguine in announcing my departure, which had been kept entirely secret, my only confidante being Brian Harrison, Head of House. Along with our many preoccupations at this time, we had a steady stream of visitors. Lord Attlee stayed a night when visiting to address the Forum Society. He was as terse as one had been led to expect but happy to talk indefinitely about politics. The achievements by which he would like to be remembered, he told us, were the establishment of the National Health Service and the independence of India and Pakistan. Small in stature, he practically disappeared into one of our large armchairs; it was difficult to imagine him talking on equal terms with Stalin and other world figures. Another visitor – whom Joy was prepared to dislike, not having much sympathy with the Labour party – was George Woodcock, General Secretary of the TUC. He was one of the most charming and delightful of visitors and won all our hearts.

Those last two terms in School House were, as ever, over-full of activity. Alan was born in February 1961. He was two weeks early, born at seven in the morning; though the doctor had only a few hundred yards to come to the School House, he arrived late and the midwife supervised. All went well. With two small boys and the full responsibility of housekeeping and catering, Joy's skills of organisation were now tested to the full, as was her power of endurance. She confessed that, for the first time in her life, she felt tired. For this reason, if no other, it was time to make a change.

My last Heads of House gave much support – Richard Barber, Patrick Balfour, Brian Harrison and Athol Cornish-Bowden. Everyone was delighted that my successor was to be Michael Hart. He and his wife Dabney were close friends of ours – Dabney was Martin's godmother – and none doubted that he would make a major contribution in School House, as indeed proved to be the case. Dabney was well able to take on the domestic responsibility and also to provide much for the House and the school in intellectual stimulus. Her school production of *Twelfth Night* in 1962 was outstanding.

Looking through the Fasti for our last summer term reminds me of how very unchanging the general pattern was; and in those days the summer term was actually in summer – beginning on 9th May, ending on 28th July. One of the preachers that term was the Revd Robert Runcie: followed by the Revd R.H.J. Brooke on the next Sunday – the sublime and the unusual perhaps. There were still two-day 1st XI cricket matches, Ascension Day was a Whole Holiday, Speech Weekend stretched from Thursday to Sunday night, ending with a late Evensong at 8.15 p.m. The four nights of Bumping Races were in the penultimate week, followed by a week of exams. Right at the end of term was Up River Swimming, now a long forgotten event. In my first Shrewsbury summer term in 1932, the Fasti was similar.

I was sad to leave the School House boys though I knew that they would be in good hands and Freddy Mann was continuing for a term as house tutor. Thirty-three boys were the sons of Old Salopians, most of whose fathers had some personal connection with me. It is curious that when I first went into School House, there were seven boys called Williams (Nicko, Wobbly Will, Nicotine Bill etc.) and about the time I left there were seven Thompsons including two pairs of twins. Bump Supper was for me quite a moving occcasion. Headroom were, of course, Head of the River again, Russell Hope-Simpson's phenomenal run continuing. Anthony Barton (now Professor of Art in Halifax, Nova Scotia) produced a suitably illustrated menu-programme with the verse:

> The best of friends must part,
> So do not look so glum.
> The time has come
> His work is done
> So cheer up Man – take Heart!

The photograph of our full School House staff, taken at the end of term, now has an almost Edwardian look: House Tutor, Matron, two cooks,

Nanny, Paddy and Sarah Walsh, Gerry the gardener, the resident maids in their uniforms, the faithful dailies including Nancy Beastie who served the House for forty years. What was not reflected in the photograph was the time and trouble it took to assemble such a team. When Joy died twenty-six years later, two of the maids came to see me; married and with children, they told me that they had based their housekeeping entirely on what Mrs Charlesworth had taught them. It was in fact the end of the old system. Dabney Hart decided on a radical change and managed without any resident maids; soon their bedrooms were to be bed-sitters. The end of house catering itself was not far away and the the new dining hall on which we had spent so much time and money was to have but a brief life.

My departure coincided with other major changes in the school. Jack Peterson had for some years been anxiously turning over in his mind the appointments to five Houses which would fall vacant in 1961–63. This has always been a matter on which it has been difficult to look ahead; appointments to headmasterships and other unforeseen changes unexpectedly remove likely candidates. Peterson's plan in 1958 was for Hagger to go to Severn Hill, Laurie to Oldham's, Hoban to Churchill's, Tupper to Rigg's and Saint to take over Dayboys from Colman. In fact Laurie went to Severn Hill, Tupper to Oldham's, Mann to Rigg's, and Struvé to Churchill's, only Saint going as planned to Dayboys. Michael Hoban had by then gone to be Headmaster of St Edmund's, Canterbury, and Peter Hawkesworth had swept off in a flurry of critical umbrage to become the squire of Sutton Hall in Yorkshire. He was succeeded by Robin Moulsdale. A new team for a new age.

The logistics of our change of life were formidable. As a home base we bought a house on the Port Hill Road, 'Cotmandene', which would be headquarters for the children. Thither went as much furniture as could be fitted in, some going into store and some lent to the Harts. We decided that Joy should stay for six months in order to see the children settled; Philippa was about to go to the Birmingham Art School, Bruce was leaving HMS Conway and would go to sea, Robin was in his last term at Kingsland Grange and about to enter Severn Hill. We were all starting in new spheres. Separation would be hard and in fact proved harder than we both anticipated; but it would give me a chance to concentrate on the job and prepare the way before Joy and the babies arrived. We were both used to army life in which travels and separations were commonplace.

After a delightful holiday with the whole family in Portmeirion, I set out for Liverpool to sail on the 'Circassia', leaving a tearful family. There was no denying that morale dipped at this point; what had I let myself in for? What was I doing to my family of six? As ever, Joy's confidence and courage shone through.

Ship life was much as usual – the last kick of the old P & O: soon ships on regular passage would be no more. There were on board the usual wide range of passengers, the old colonial types, the intrepid deck game players, the romantics, the Indian chatterers – subdued until Suez, increasingly loud thereafter – the rather uncertain mixed marriage partners, the missionaries, the hosts of unruly children. I tried to enjoy it all, was again ship's champion at deck tennis, but recorded in my diary 'sad and lonely'. One good friend sustained me, Arthur Iliff, a missionary doctor, who was also travelling without his family, returning to his hospital at Bannu on the North West Frontier. Port Said was not what it had been; the Simon Artz Emporium had many empty shelves though the gulli gulli men and the pimps were as numerous as usual. No longer did De Lesseps's commanding statue point the way down the Suez Canal. The Red Sea was an oven. The importance of travelling POSH (Port Out Starboard Home) was really apparent.

At Karachi I was looked after very well by the British Council and also by a parent with a boy at Lawrence College, Mr Shakur, who worked in the Customs and cleared my mass of baggage with extraordinary speed. It was from him that I first heard the refrain that I was soon to be heartily sick of hearing, namely that Lawrence College used to be a fine school, that it was in bad shape, that other schools were better BUT now Mr Charlesworth had come everything would improve....

So, after twenty-eight hours in the train – how good to be on a train in the Sub-continent again with the massive steam engines, the crowds on the platforms, the shouts and apparent chaos – I found myself at Lawrence College, Ghora Gali, immediately and totally immersed in my new life and not knowing a single soul.

Founded in memory of Henry Lawrence, killed at Lucknow in the Mutiny (I now had to remember that it was the First War of Independence), the College was the oldest school in Pakistan, founded in 1860. Originally the Lawrence Asylum, it had catered for boys and girls of British soldiers, many of them orphans, giving a decent Christian education in a healthy climate to children who would otherwise just kick around the Lines in garrison towns. By 1947 it had long since lost that image and was a boarding school and teachers' training college of good standard, educating domiciled British, Anglo-Indians and a few Indian children, run by the Government and the Diocese of Lahore. After Partition the British children and teachers gradually left, Principals came and went (I was the seventh in fourteen years) and the College gradually subsided into an administrative muddle. The trouble was that it was tied to the Education Department in Lahore which knew nothing of boarding schools; and Pakistani teachers of calibre were rare.

An attempt to straighten out the school had led to the appointment as Principal of H.L.O. Flecker in 1955, recently Headmaster of Christ's

Hospital, aged fifty-eight and a man of considerable educational experience (and the brother of James Elroy Flecker). He had laboured hard with
only moderate success, not through any failing on his part (though having
been a headmaster for twenty-five years his autocratic ways did not oil the
wheels) but because the Government never gave him the support he
required. Flecker had been taken ill in his last week in the College and was
carried out, a dying man. So dilatory were the Education Department in
deciding what should happen next that it was a full three years after
Flecker's departure before I arrived.

In the interregnum the acting Principal was Sheikh Muin-ud-Din and it
was he who welcomed me and on whom I leant for those first difficult
months. Muin was from the Doon School in India, a good teacher, understanding well the ways of boarding schools. His wife Mahmuda was a lady
of considerable personality and an excellent teacher of the English
language. The Government might well have appointed him as Principal
but he had too many enemies in the administration and he had become
reconciled to rejection. In the circumstances his welcome to me might have
been less than cordial but the opposite was the case. Within twenty-four
hours of my arrival I had had tea with the 'Heads' Committee, a buffet
supper with the staff, tea with the prefects and had addressed the whole
school at Assembly. I was thus launched on a sea which, the more I saw of
it, looked increasingly stormy. I was conscious that all that I did and said
was under close inspection from eyes and ears, seen and unseen. I had
wondered before my arrival how many people would be resenting me – an
English Christian Principal of a wholly Pakistani and Muslim School.
There may have been mutterings but none reached my ears, indeed during
the whole of my stay, I never encountered hostility from anyone. Shaky as I
felt my position to be, uncertain as to whether I could manage a job of such
greater magnitude than I had expected, the staff, the boys and the parents
seemed to be confident that I must know all the answers: behind my name
were the magic letters MA Oxford; Dip.Ed. Oxford. They never knew that
it was a classless cobbled-together wartime degree or that education was a
subject of which the Oxford department, in my day, knew little.

Strung out along the Himalayan foothills, the site of the College was very
remarkable indeed. Footpaths wandered amongst the pine trees, connect-
ing the Senior School on one level with the Prep and Junior School a
hundred feet higher; staff houses and other buildings were pitched where
flat space could be found. There were only two playing fields – a grave
disadvantage – heavily over used. The views were breathtaking; the Pir
Panjal range of mountains in Kashmir could be seen in the distance; Nanga
Parbat was sometimes visible and from the neighbouring town of Murree
one could see K2. The dramatic beauty of the place astonished visitors and
could not but cast a spell on those who lived there.

The Principal's house was delightful but, curiously, constructed as one might build a bungalow on the Plains, with very high ceilings to cope with the hot weather. Thus it was exceedingly cold in the winter. The kitchen was, as was the Indian custom, detached from the house; I took care never to go there and was content merely to eat the food that came out of it. There was the inevitable wide verandah and a lawn, a rarity in the hills. There was no water-borne sanitation so the sweeper emptied the thunder boxes. Nor was there running hot water, though the British Council did later give me a water heater. All was on the good old Anglo-Indian pattern – primitive luxury; primitive as regards how we lived, luxurious in that we had six servants with carefully circumscribed jobs. I was not wholly surprised when I heard a rat running round in my chest of drawers on my first night; I killed it there and then.

I spent many hours with Muin, trying to understand how everything worked. The problems were really twofold, one external the other internal. The College was caught in the grip of slow-moving bureaucratic control from Lahore. The rules were as for day schools: masters could leave on giving a week's notice; the Principal could spend no more than Rs100 (£8) without confirmation from the Education Department; the appointment of staff was in the hands of the Public Service Commission whose meetings the Principal could attend but at which he had no vote. To construct a building meant making one's way through a bureaucratic obstacle course of seemingly infinite length and complexity. It had taken Flecker two years to build an extension to the Prep School. It was rumoured that a Board of Governors might be set up, to act independently of the Education Department. This was obviously essential if I was ever to have the power to do what I hoped. But the chains linking us to the Government were many. The staff were paid and various other activities financed by a Government grant; parents paid fees which covered boarding but not much else. It was vital that this grant should continue, yet independence was essential. How was I to set about motivating the Education Department?

The internal problem was that the staff were riddled with discontent and internecine strife. Muin was a man of many virtues, but he was not able to command the loyalty of a divided staff. Only slowly did I stumble into this tangled area. When Muin told me that he was applying for a head-mastership in Peshawar, I was devastated to think that the only man of real ability was leaving me. But as I understood more and more about the level of intrigue, I realised that a clearing of the air would be helpful, even though I should be left with no experienced adviser. Not that I was short of people who sought to advise me, indeed some members of the staff made a dead set at me, coming to my office one after another to sell themselves and their abilities. One who was particularly persistent was Mr Quraishi, the physics teacher; sly and calculating, he had a good mind and was a good

teacher; but he was at daggers drawn with the Establishment and submitted a long document to prove by esoteric argument that he should
really be the Senior Master. One thing I did know and that was never to
commit myself on paper if at all avoidable; so I replied to him *tête-à-tête* as I
made a habit of doing with all who wrote. It is more difficult to be rude and
critical in personal confrontation than it is when writing at length and at
leisure. Quraishi kept up his pinpricks though lavishly praising me and my
efforts and bringing gifts; these I declined. I knew enough of the Sub-
continent to know about gifts and their consequences. Fruit and flowers
yes; all else no. But Quraishi did get one over on me. Every year a complete
audit was made of all school equipment against ledgers in which everything was recorded. I was supposed to supervise this and indeed I did
make spot checks in various departments; Quraishi's science equipment
was all present and correct. What I did not find out till several years later
was that he had himself copied out the complete ledger and destroyed the
old one, various items being omitted from the new version which became
his personal property. He had a sad end. After leaving the College and
becoming Headmaster of a small school he had a violent dispute with a
contractor and was murdered in his bed.

But there were of course some good and conscientious members of staff
also, striving to do a good job in difficult circumstances. Munir, who ran the
Prep School, was a man of real integrity and dedication; Mrs Rifat Ali, head
of the Junior School, was experienced though without much drive; the
energetic and likeable Mushtaq had the makings of a very good housemaster (which he was not); Ashsan Elahi, an Old Boy of the College, was an
excellent teacher, a considerable personality and was the only member of
staff who appreciated (or understood) my sense of humour. Naseer was a
really good maths teacher and had a proper rapport with the boys. These
and others gave me encouragement. Hospitality abounded. I was asked to
party after party all of which followed the same pattern, the men sitting in a
half circle, the women (though some wives never appeared, being in
purdah) in another half circle. No words were exchanged between male
and female; in fact not many words were exchanged at all; the conversational ball was permanently in my court. The women put on their saris
and best finery and were redolent with scent but not with words. The curry
menu was always the same, the very sweet sweets did not vary. Naturally
there was no alcohol in the College – so far as I knew.

It took me some time to get near the boys; they were friendly but
suspicious, unused to talking to senior staff other than within a formal
framework. Mahmuda, Muin's wife, suggested that I ought to do some
teaching which I was indeed happy to attempt; I say attempt because I
found myself teaching English language and this included grammar; could
I recollect the difference between a noun clause and an adjectival clause? It

was a strain but Mahmuda was a great help. Gradually I began to know the senior boys, assisted by my own interest in sport. I think I really made it with the boys when I made 40 batting against the 1st XI. I also kept goal and occasionally wielded a hockey stick.

Sadly the school seemed stuck in the ways of English schools as they were at the start of the century. Prefects had enormous powers of inflicting punishment through 'fatigue' – compulsory PT. Bullying was common – and expected – and I found out what a knuckle-duster was when I confiscated several which boys had in their lockers. I later found out that two boys had been kept at the school who were aged about twenty and should have left long ago, to act as gauleiters; their principal interests lay on the games fields so they were happy to stay though their academic future was nil. Certainly some members of staff were frightened of the senior boys and the prevention of 'incidents' and the enforcement of discipline were high on my agenda. One night, returning from Murree in his car, Flecker had had a bullet through his windscreen. I heard from an English friend who knew him that Flecker went round the College at the end of the school year counting the number of broken windows. He gave up when he got to a thousand.

In my first months 'incidents' kept occurring which took my attention away from the serious matter of reorganisation. On the day I arrived there was a notice in the *Pakistan Times*: "LOST. Shaukat Aziz age 16–17 years. Colour grey. Student of Lawrence College. Rs100 reward for information." Not a very good advertisement for the school. Shaukat had been knocked about by the Headboy and had had enough. He was soon found. One morning I found twelve dhobis (washermen) sitting on my lawn, refusing to work unless their wages were raised. A medical crisis arose because the laboratory attendant had been drinking meths. An enquiry had to be made because one of the matrons had been falsifying the tailor's bills, apparently needing a gross of greatcoat buttons (in July) for the boys' needs in the middle of summer; actually she had been buying knitting wool for herself. Rumour reached me that the Bursar's servant was stealing wood for him from the wood store, a hole having been made in the barbed wire fence. More damaging was a complaint from a parent that a woman was having an abortion in the College hospital; this proved to be only too true – and the woman was one of our own nurses. When I was asked to sit in judgement on a servant who had attempted to elope with another servant's daughter, I felt that really I had seen everything that could happen to a Principal.

But my worst crisis was to come. The biology master was a young and hot-headed man called Shami. One evening when supervising roll call, he had a dispute with the Headboy, Sultan, who was equally hot-headed. High words were exchanged. By chance I met Shami as I returned from my evening walk; he was in tears and temper, storming off to the doctor's bungalow, the doctor being at the centre of the party warfare which prevailed. Shami demanded there and then that Sultan should apologise to him in front of the whole school, otherwise he would resign and go in a week's time. He was the only biologist and external exams were approaching. What to do? There is a word in Urdu – izzut – which means repute, 'face', esteem, honour, regard, status or any similar word. To have your izzut dented was serious. I was determined Sultan should not apologise in front of the whole school; it would make his position impossible as well as over-dramatising the whole thing. I sent for him and told him straight that he would have to apologise to Mr Shami in my presence which he reluctantly agreed to do. This offer Shami refused. I let the days pass, hoping time might be a healer; it wasn't. Finally I had to do something. I sent for Shami and told him that he should accept the apology, using every means of persuasion I could think of – his duty to the boys doing biology, his responsibility to the College, to his country, to his religion (I even threw in Allah), even to me. I felt I was losing all the way along the line but then suddenly he broke. If Sultan apologised there and then, he would stay; I sent for Sultan immediately, he apologised and they both more or less fell on each other's necks. Biology teaching could continue.

The great sports fixture of the year was against Aitchison College, Lahore, and in October we went down to play them at cricket, football, hockey, tennis and athletics on successive days, these five games forming the 'rubber'. Aitchison was an eye-opener to me, a most beautiful campus in the middle of Lahore, wonderful sports fields, impressive buildings and a seemingly dedicated staff and smooth-running administration. I stayed with Shah Sahib, the Principal, whose wife was in purdah so I never met the family, immured in their side of the house. There were four or five British staff. We were well entertained; but the games were humiliating to a degree. They were watched by the whole school, not backward in their vocal support, I and Shah Sahib placed in prominent positions. I kept a fixed smile on my face as we were thrashed at every game. In the five tennis matches, each the best of three sets, not only did we not win a set but we only won in aggregate four *games*! In athletics, five points for each event, our total was two points! Only at soccer did we manage to save face by drawing, one-all. We returned to the hills thoroughly chastened. One good thing came out of this visit, namely my meeting with Mohammed Akram, Aitchison Bursar and Vice-Principal, who became a fast friend. His bungalow became and still is my home in Lahore and I benefited greatly from his advice.

To bolster authority, Muin had invented a Committee of Heads consisting of himself, the Bursar, the Heads of the Prep School and the Junior School and the school doctor. It was a mistaken idea, in my view, and I did not call it again after a couple of meetings. At the last a flaming row took place between Muin and the doctor whom he accused of not being willing to treat his wife; I moved into my customary fire extinguisher act, mentally deciding that the doctor must go. On my next visit to Lahore, I sought out the Director of Medical Services expecting to be told of a long and bureaucratic procedure. To my surprise I found the Director not only sympathetic but ready to take immediate action. He had a complicated card index system worked by knitting needles of which he was very proud, and promptly produced the name of a suitable successor and posted our doctor to some god-forsaken area in the Frontier Province. The orders were at once issued; I returned to the College and told the doctor to pack. He was thunderstruck. Unable to contain his indignation, he at once asked for four days' leave to visit his sick mother; this I refused as I knew he would be off to Lahore to make trouble. In a few days he had gone and a major trouble-maker was thus removed. My reputation rose . . . .

Autumn in the hills is the most beautiful time, hot sunny days and cool nights with a touch of early frost. This was the time of one of the most extraordinary events – the Marathon. The course was down the twisting road from Murree, four miles with a drop of about eight hundred feet. The seniors ran the whole distance but each age group had a shorter course down to the five and six-year-olds who ran about four hundred yards. The races went off at different times. Spectators clustered at the finish as wave after wave swept in. The actual finishing line was chalked across the road on which was written in large letters STOP. It meant FINISH of course; how difficult the English language is.

So winter wore on to the climax of examinations. The Cambridge Overseas O level was for the senior boys the target which opened the way into the Army, into the professions and into Colleges. Elaborate precautions were taken to get the papers to the examination desk without anyone seeing them. They came to Pakistan in the diplomatic bag, were delivered to me in person by a member of the High Commission, and reposed in a locked tin trunk under my bed until taken by me personally to the examination room. The results would not reach us for three months. I felt sorry for the boys; it was very cold indeed and almost impossible to raise the temperature of the examination hall to any reasonable degree, though we had fires burning at different points. Balaclavas and mittens were often worn.

In the first week of December the term finally came to an end. Now at last beginning to feel that I belonged, I remember climbing up the hill one evening and looking down on the estate just as it was getting dark; there was the Junior School with the little boys safely indoors trying to keep warm; there was the Prep School, the boys just finishing their tea; from the Senior School came raucus shouts as the boys returned through the pine trees from evening prayer in the mosque building; and there were the servants quarters, smoke rising from the cooking fires; in all perhaps 1,500 people in this my kingdom in which everyone looked to me for leadership and guidance. I looked on the scene with a curious mixture of pride and humility, of determination and doubt. There was no turning back, nor indeed any standing still; I was committed to the future of Lawrence College for a considerable time: 'Come what, come may; time and the hour run through the roughest day'.

CHAPTER XX

Himalayan Foothills

And the end of the fight is a tombstone white with the name of
  the late deceased,
And the epitaph drear 'A Fool lies here who tried to hustle the
  East'.

Kipling

Democratic government had never taken root in Pakistan. In 1958 a
revolution had brought the army into power in the person of Ayub Khan,
President while I was there. His benevolent despotism worked well until in
the end it ran into the deep waters of corruption. But in my time a real effort
was made to clean up government; individuals in all government institutions were screened and many dismissed. Ayub himself, the very model
of a Sandhurst-trained army officer, was firm, honest and approachable. I
met him several times and always felt that if I got into an impossible
position I could appeal directly to him and would be listened to.

Corruption was indeed the great brake on progress. It was not so much
direct bribery as the use of influence, the application of pressure by the
powerful on subordinates – pressure in the awarding of contracts, pressure
in appointments to positions, pressure from political parties or from family
groups. I was not exempt. Far more boys than I could admit were attempting to get into the College – about five applicants for every place – and the
high and mighty did not scruple to use every means to get their sons
admitted though admission tests were meant to be the sole criterion. I stuck
to this as closely as I could but common sense suggested a certain prag-
matism. It was a nice judgement as to when to bow to pressure, when to
resist. It was an advantage that, being an outsider, I had no relations, no
politicians and no influential friends to please. It was assumed that no
Englishman was corrupt.

Terms at Lawrence College were as nowhere else. The year was divided
into one term of nine months and one holiday of three months. A nine
month term! No one at Shrewsbury could even imagine it. The weather
dictated this arrangement; whereas the summer was beautiful, the

temperature sometimes in the 80s, the winter brought freezing conditions with frequent falls of snow. Everyone fled the estate except the office staff, the chowkidars (watchmen) and the Principal. It was a strange life, living up in the clouds, sometimes literally cut off from civilisation by the snow, the estate deserted and the jackals seeming to creep nearer the house every night. But in that first winter I had plenty of work to do, frequently visiting Lahore for a dispiriting round of the Government offices, seeking to push my reforms through the administrative machine – principally the formation of a Board of Governors.

The Director of Public Instruction was Dr Jehangir Khan who had written his name into the cricket record books. When bowling for Cambridge at Lords he had hit and killed a sparrow which can still be seen – stuffed – in the Long Room. He was polite and understanding but little action resulted from my interviews with him. He was the father of the Pakistan cricket captain, Majid Khan. After weeks of trying, I managed to see the Education Secretary himself, Mr Sharif, a very able and hopelessly overworked man who was wholly sympathetic to my case. A Board was set up, to function in 1962. But another hurdle had to be overcome if real independence was to be achieved. All salary scales were laid down by Government and promotions governed entirely by paper qualifications with no regard to merit in actually doing the job nor any recognition of the heavy responsibilities of boarding school teachers, so different from day schools. All were Government servants who could not be sacked. Then it was discovered that the Lawrence College staff were a separate cadre which could be dissolved and their status abolished. Was this possible? It would certainly be very unpopular. At last I managed to see the Minister for Education himself, an engaging lightweight called Enver Adil who went from ministry to ministry and finally sank to Family Planning; one could not go lower. He supported the dissolution of the cadre but this could only be done with the concurrence of the Governor of West Pakistan, Malik Amir Mohammed Khan, a dominating rajah, the very essence of autocratic landlordism, who looked all of seven feet tall when wearing his high pugri (turban). Having at last secured an audience and accompanied by Enver Adil, I put my case. He nodded. In two minutes the Lawrence College cadre was dissolved. I was free to build my own castle and to reorganise the College from top to bottom – provided I could carry my governors with me. On the whole they proved docile. The Chairman was the local divisional commander in Murree, General Shaukat Ali Shah, with whom I had the happiest of relations. Others were also predominantly military and thus tended to take orders from the General. I set up a new salary scale, increased the pay of almost all, got the right men into the appropriate positions, manoeuvred Mr Quraishi out of housemastering and created a new position for him as Head of Science ("I can certainly do both, Sir''. You certainly won't). I remain grateful to Malik Amir Mohammed Khan: that slight inclination of his head made life possible for me. He had a dramatic end. While breakfasting in bed one day, his son came to see him, a dispute started, and he whipped out his revolver which he kept under his pillow. Too late; his son fired first and Dad was dead.

If my professional life changed in the early months of 1962, my private life was transformed by the arrival of Joy and the little boys at Karachi in March. The Principal's house was now made into a real home. Joy simply loved being in Pakistan and wrote to her mother ''how happy I am to be in this remote, quiet place''. The simplicity of our life appealed to her and the children were soon entirely at home. At this time we acquired a wonderful bearer, Zardad Khan, equal to all occasions, a dignified Punjabi, prepared to work hard and soon very much attached to Martin and Alan, as indeed were the other servants. In the car park, where all entered the College, the chowkidar was Karam Din who would always greet the children on their walks with elaborate courtesy, ''Salaam Martin Sahib, Salaam Alan Sahib''. We also managed to find an Ayah of reasonable competence and were thus able to leave the children occasionally and go off down the mountain to Rawalpindi, sometimes to shop, sometimes to parties, not that they were very numerous. But it was pleasant to be treated as persons of some importance and asked to occasions the High Commission arranged, such as the Queen's birthday celebration, or a gathering to welcome touring politicians like Barbara Castle, Duncan Sandys, David Eccles and various ministers concerned with overseas development. British ex-patriates belonged to our branch of the United Kingdom Association, Pakistan, and functions were arranged by them from time to time. I was soon elected to the committee and ultimately became chairman, a role which was later to have a more serious purpose than I anticipated. Our High Commissioner, Sir Morrice James, soon became a friend. At one time he asked me to accompany Sir Charles Arden-Clarke, the last Governor of Nigeria, on a visit to Swat, a small semi-independent state in the mountains whose ruler, the Wali (or the Akond?) with whom we had lunch was both enlightened and energetic; schools, pharmacies and even a university blossomed in Swat, one of the most beautiful places in the world. We also knew well the Bishop of Lahore, Laurie Woolmer, a CMS man who had devoted most of his life to the struggling Pakistani Church.

With Joy arrived Tom Walter, appointed to the College as housemaster and English teacher for three years. Tom had taught at Shrewsbury and had gallantly accepted my suggestion that he might apply for this post. He proved a tower of strength both in teaching English, in housemastering and in running various games. The idea was that he should set a standard of housemastering which others might follow; unfortunately Tom was just too successful and it was not so much emulation that was inspired as jealousy. Tom's temperament did not always enable him to contain himself when under strain, which sometimes set me yet another problem of man management. After two years Tom went home on leave, determined to find a wife. He got engaged to a charming girl in the remarkably unromantic circumstances of a motorway cafe and Dorothy, with great courage, came out to this unknown country to marry him. Joy and I arranged the wedding in our College church followed by a reception on our lawn to which came a splendid assortment of friends, Christian and Muslim. So Dorothy started her married life as the only English woman in the College apart from Joy. Soon after Tom came David Broad, a Salopian eighteen-year-old VSO volunteer. I had asked for David, whom I knew well. In his last year at school he had been an intelligent, awkward, bolshy questioner of most establishment things. He taught in our Prep School and was a huge success, undertaking all manner of tasks with cheerful energy. I smiled when he commented to me after a few weeks that what the Prep School needed was more discipline – extra lessons for offenders etc.; a change of attitude indeed. I was very grateful to David, now in the Foreign Office; and I was lucky too in his successors, Salopians Richard Best from School House and Peter Renshaw from Churchill's and other non-Salopians. I also had VSO girls to help in the Junior School, all successful except one whom I soon got rid of.

My greatest coup however lay in persuading Miss Norah Glegg to return from retirement in England to run the Junior School. This section consisted of little boys between the ages of five and nine – all boarding. To English ears boarding at this age sounds horrific but with good food, a healthy climate, good discipline and teaching, we did much more for these little boys than they could expect in most homes. Pakistani families are large and by the time a boy was five there would have been another baby and child care was generally in the hands of unskilled male servants. Certainly it gave the boys a splendid educational opportunity especially in learning English. Many of our boys spoke quite excellently when they left – and what a long time that was! Coming at five some boys would stay until they were eighteen and so would have spent most of their lives at the College. It is small wonder that the experience had so deep an effect and stirred such enduring loyalty. The return of Miss Glegg strengthened the Junior School immeasurably. Herself educated at Lawrence College Girls School, she had, after training, worked there all her life. She knew all there was to know about the education of little boys and was supremely confident and authoritative in the exercise of her powers as Headmistress – a little too confident for some parents which caused occasional ripples to reach my office.

Soon after Joy's arrival I received news of the death of my mother at the age of eighty-five. Though this was not unexpected, the inevitable sadness seemed exaggerated by my remoteness and inability to be with Richard and Olive at this time. For the last several years of her life she had been a shadow of the energetic and enterprising person she had been when not afflicted with the depression which overshadowed her so often. An atheist for most of her adult life, she had many of the virtues which we associate with Christianity and constantly worked for the good of others in her concern for babies and children. Although I did not have a very close relationship with either of my parents, at a deep level there was mutual love, perhaps not often enough expressed.

I have written at some length of my first year as Principal. The years that followed can be more briefly passed over. As things could not have been much worse they must have got better. But I could never feel that I had a smoothly running machine under control. The chief difficulty was in finding staff who were good enough to teach lively and able boys. I was constantly recruiting and from time to time felt I had brought someone of real ability into the College; but I was generally disappointed with the calibre of people presenting themselves. Not that there was a shortage in quantity: absurd and wonderful applications arrived; one man in his CV under sporting achievements listed "Second in College pillow fight"; not even first!

After the Board of Governors had taken over, I had liberty in the appointment of staff and was able to chose a Senior Master or Vice-Principal. Mr Naqvi had been doing this work under Muin, a serious, conscientious man, a good teacher of Urdu (he came from Lucknow where the best Urdu is spoken) but a man entangled with the politics of the past, lacking in pastoral sense where the boys were concerned and without any sense of humour. I was determined to make a change though I knew he would be deeply hurt. I chose Mr Abul Nasr who taught French (unlikely as it may seem) and played tennis well. He was essentially a gentleman whom no one could dislike, though not a strong personality. Recently married to a lady who was the ultimate in saris and perfumes, he was quite outside party politics. So I chose him, well aware that he was not strong, but I had already determined to run the Senior School myself. The appointment caused a frisson of considerable proportions. Naqvi withdrew to his house and would not come out for three days; he was, I fear, a broken man. *Izzut* had taken a severe shock. I was sure I was right but it was a painful time; a headmaster is paid to be a cad as H. H. Hardy used to say.

The general attitude of a Principal in Pakistan was to sit behind an immense desk and dictate to the world. At a neighbouring school at Abbottabad, the Principal, Mr Rehman, did just that, moving on a level remote from the boys. He was wonderfully self-satisfied and well-tuned to the arts of PR. I recollect one of his school magazines which had on the front his full-page portrait over the caption 'Our Beloved Principal'. Later I found out who was the author of the caption – himself. Playing games against that school was tricky. If they lost, their boys would not turn up for tea and would shout abuse at the departing coach. The British Council sent Rehman on a tour of English schools. On his return he assured parents and guests (of whom I was one) on Speech Day that, having been to Winchester, Rugby and other English schools none was in any way superior to the Abbottabad Public School.

Having made it abundantly clear that nothing mattered to me except devoted work for the College and that no other criterion would play any part when it came to promotions or pay, the staff gradually settled down and – I think – the divisons of the past to a considerable degree evaporated, though I was constantly dealing with ruffled feelings, hurt pride and 'incidents'. My own temperament is reasonably calm and I was determined never to show anger, never to force an issue if conciliation was possible. I eased the incompetent out by degrees; and had to get rid of two men after homosexual offences. Owing to the separation of the sexes and the fact that in most families no boy could consort with – or meet – a girl even in the most innocent way, homosexuality was very prevalent. Egged on by the boys I did approach the Headmistress of a girls' school in Murree with a view to arranging a dance but her enthusiasm was faint; she would have to write to the parents of every girl to obtain written permission; the plan petered out. One lady did cause me a great deal of trouble, a matron in the Prep School whose incompetence was such that she had to go. Being well-connected, she took me to court. I consulted my great standby, the Bursar, Mr Butt. "We must find a good liar, Sir" was his reaction. The difference in pronunciation between 'liar' and 'lawyer' in Pakistani-English is fine drawn. Fortunately we did get a good lawyer and won the case. The matron had used all her arts of persuasion on me, bringing in God, Allah and Jesus and telling me that out of respect she always sat in her bath facing the College church.

Shortly after I arrived I was asked if I permitted boys to visit masters in their homes. "Yes, certainly", I said, puzzled by the question. I had not seen the implication which was that if a boy visited a master it could only be to arrange some mischief at the expense of another member of the staff. Competition to be seen to be successful was intense.

As time went on I took on more teaching and so began to understand the boys better. At the top there was some good academic ability but the generality was intelligent enough if well taught. The academic criterion was the annual Senior Cambridge result. After a dreadful first year, results improved until in my last year they were the best ever achieved by the College – a hundred per cent passes. About ten per cent of the boys were Pathans from the Frontier, attractive, lively boys with much spirit. If on your side they never let you down; if against you then keep your powder dry. They did not take kindly to discipline and there were some early struggles. A major crime was to go up to Murree at night to see a film, returning sometimes in the small hours. Persuasion, argument and threats did not prevail so I instructed my peon to cut some canes from the trees and then administered corporal punishment, resorting to this method of keeping discipline from time to time. This had a very salutary effect. I also wrote to the boys' parents occasionally, threatening expulsion. One Pathan father exploded with such wrath that his son virtually went into hiding for three days lest his father should arrive with a gun.

Smarting after the sporting slaughter at the hands of Aitchison College in my early days, I determined to get the games organised and properly coached. We got better and better until in 1964 we defeated Aitchison and won the rubber 4 – 1. Great was the rejoicing and I received letters from Gallians from far corners of Pakistan. (Old boys were called 'Gallians' from the name of the local village, Ghora Gali.) The occasion was memorable for me because the Principal of Aitchison at this time was Mr Abdul Ali Khan, a fearsome Pathan who had rowed for Balliol and who, on appointment, had made a clean sweep of the administration, sacking amongst others my dear friend Akram, the Vice-Principal – given a week to get out. Ali Khan and I watched all the games, he jumping up and down, shouting encouragement (and I think abuse) in English, Urdu and Pushtu. I sat with true British phlegm and stiff upper lip, inwardly seething with excitement. But when victory was won my rival was magnanimity itself and personally presented the cup to our boys. I don't think there has ever been a sporting encounter which I was more pleased to win.

The big events of the year were Sports Day in June and Founder's Day in September. We sent out invitations to the five hundred parents: about thirty replied and six hundred came. Sports Day was studded with ceremonial; first a march past by the whole Senior School accompanied by a bagpipe band borrowed from the army; then the Olympic oath taken in Urdu, English and Bengali; a gorgeous tea party; the victory stand; and the presentation of prizes by our chief guest followed by the lowering of flags as the band sounded Retreat. Founder's Day was equally impressive, starting with an address by the Principal to all three schools and the whole staff arranged in a hollow square on the playing field and followed by a presentation of far too many prizes by a minister, general or ambassador. Everyone – particularly the ladies – put on their best and these occasions were very colourful. Joy and I also attended each year the Passing Out parade at Kakul, the equivalent of Sandhurst; and very like Sandhurst it was – the adjutant on a white horse, the band playing 'Over the Sea to Skye' during the inspection and the march off to 'Auld Lang Syne'. People in the West dislike and distrust military rule but in Pakistan the army, to which many of the best of our boys went, is a stabilising influence in the floating world of unstable politics.

Although detached in part from the Government in Lahore, I still depended on it for money and indeed for the necessary permission to build. I had all sorts of plans but principally one for a new boarding house. Fortunately I managed to lay my hands on some Aid money from Canada; I engaged a British architect, John Terry, and planned the house with him, to include a master's house as part of the building. One winter this large building was completed, freeing accommodation elsewhere for other activities. I also resolved to build a College mosque. As the College had been a Christian establishment, there was a large Anglo-Gothic church. This the handful of Christians on the estate used on Sundays; Joy played the harmonium and I took the service with a congregation of eight or ten. But there was no mosque, only a large room which inadequately served the purpose. I set about fund-raising from parents and College friends; it was a powerful appeal – every good Muslim should respond in the name of Allah: and they did. With some help from the Fine Fund I raised enough rupees and an attractive mosque was built to universal gratification. (We used to fine parents for the misdemeanours of their sons such as returning late after an exeat; the Fine Fund grew so large that I was able to buy a bus from the proceeds.)

I trod warily in religious matters. I was after all in a strange position as a Christian Head of a wholly Muslim establishment; but the common ground between Christianity and Islam is considerable. I read prayers at the daily assembly which were God/Allah centred except on Fridays when the Second Master took the assembly. I took care that all activity was avoided which could be classed as un-Islamic. I never drank alcohol in the presence of Muslims; we never ate any products of the pig. I saw to it that the boys attended their sunset compulsory prayer. I was never conscious of any criticism on the score of religion. I was expected to get on with my own religion in my own way, they got on with theirs.

No account of the College would be complete without mention of the servants. We employed about one hundred and twenty men. There were few machines; everything was done in the traditional way and I doubt if the College kitchen had changed in any respect for the past fifty years or so. In some ways the servants *were* the College; most of them served over many years, their homes and families were in the College or in Ghora Gali or Nimbal, the neighbouring villages. Labour-saving devices were anathema – it was important to provide employment, not to reduce it. I learned a salutory lesson in my early days by deciding to buy a lawn mower for the Principal's lawn – virtually the only lawn in Murree. Previously the grass was cut by a team of men each with a sickle. When the lawn mower arrived, a simple machine which had to be pushed, it was regarded with some doubt. Soon however it was decided that it should be worked by a team of three, one steering, two pulling; a team of three required a reserve team of three to take over; they sat in the shade until required; any group of six needed an 'in charge' to direct them and so in the end the lawn mower had a team of seven to cut my grass. Old principles were thus upheld.

I was able to do quite a lot for the servants. Although the voiceless and neglected part of the establishment they were nevertheless fine people. Despite their comparative poverty and frugal lifestyle, they were a happy community, I suppose illustrating what is certainly true elsewhere in the world that the simpler the lifestyle the happier, on the whole, people are. I received a petition early in my time praying for better conditions of service and an increase of pay in the prevailing conditions of inflation; the phraseology was apt – "our present pay is so meagre that we cannot meet our both ends". Pay was increased and medical provision provided, also some system of holidays, so that gradually their lives become easier though always hard. It was pleasing to receive in my third year an unsolicited letter: "We the servants of Lawrence College express to you our most humble and grateful thanks and we pray God to bless you and your family always for all the benefits you have done for us. Some of us have served in the College for 20 years and we all say that never before has anyone taken such interest or done so much kindness in all these years as you have".

After four years it is fair to say that a wholly new administrative and educational structure had been established; but there were still many weaknesses, particularly in staffing. I continued to be concerned that we provided so little for the boys – a desk and a bed, teaching and games but not enough really to stimulate or challenge. Though there were exceptions there were too few either boys or masters with a proper pastoral sense; leadership was still a question of orders and punishments. I spent my life as much as possible out and about on the estate, climbing up to the Prep School and the Junior School on most days, trying to keep an eye on every activity, bowling in the nets, teaching the little boys to swim, visiting the boys in their Houses. In all this I was greatly helped by the first Headboy chosen rather than inherited, Khalid Aziz, whose sound common sense and realistic approach saved me from many errors; and his successors gave me equal support. Thus I did not have to face 'strikes' or demonstrations such as were common amongst students elsewhere and I made as much war as I could on the common practice of cheating. There were some peculiar hazards: for instance how to establish a boy's age in a country without birth certificates where many boys did not know their ages. This made things difficult when awarding scholarships which were limited to certain age groups. Boys used to present themselves for admission to the Junior School with bass voices and moustaches; Miss Glegg used to inspect their teeth to get a reasonable estimate of age. I found myself in difficulty compiling an alphabetical school list when boys had two or three names, any of which might be the name by which they were commonly known. I puzzled over two brothers born six days apart: a biological miracle? In fact – and obviously – two mothers with a common husband but it took me some time to see it.

While still in Pakistan I managed to persuade the Governing Body of Shrewsbury to admit a Lawrence College boy each year without fee on my recommendation into the VIth form for A levels. All these boys did well. Salahudin Imam (a Bengali) is now an international banker; Zafar-ullah Bangash lives in Canada and edits a very fundamentalist Muslim journal; Khalid Nazir went to Oxford and is an engineer and businessman; Changez Sultan, poet and painter, runs tourism in Pakistan. One of my first meetings with Changez was when he appeared one evening on my verandah, his shirt soaked in blood, complaining bitterly of his treatment by a prefect. It was good to see these boys take the opportunity presented and good, too, for Shrewsbury to have some contact with the Orient. With Changez I am often in touch still and his son is shortly coming to Shrewsbury.

Our family life was extremely happy in these years, despite the absence of the older children. Joy entered into College life with zest. Generally wearing shalwar and khamiz, she taught music in the Junior School, where she introduced a percussion band, taught boys in the Prep School to sing the very fine Pakistani national anthem properly and played the piano at the Senior School daily assembly. Hitherto a matron had played 'Roll Out the Barrrel' as the boys marched in – a singularly inappropriate tune in a teetotal Muslim country; fortunately no one knew the words. Joy also improved her Urdu and was thus able to cope with the purdah wives who were invisible to me. She had parties every month in the Staff Club, making different ladies provide the tea and organising simple games like hunt the thimble. These parties were red letter days for the purdah ladies whose lives were so circumscribed. Both Martin and Alan went to the Junior School when they were old enough, Alan before he was five. Here they seemed to flourish, two little fair heads amongst a hundred dark ones. When the time for the Marathon came round (the Juniors' Marathon being about four hundred yards) Alan surprised me by telling us that in the practices he was first, second or third on occasion. It was some time before I grasped that he was counting from the back.

Murree being the only Pakistani hill station, to it came floods of visitors in the summer to escape the heat of the Plains; we got to know a number of the missionary community who had a language school in the summer months. With some of them we had pleasant social evenings, often musical, for Joy was now starting to practise the violin seriously, and we had inherited a piano. We also had friends to stay; one of the pleasant things about an ex-patriate community is the way people are drawn together and are happy to entertain each other, not a difficult thing in a land of large houses and servants. Occasional visitors from England arrived: Richard Baylis, Martin's godfather, stayed some days, as did Andy Maclehose and Brian Harrison, both School House boys, Andy on his way to Australia, Brian with a medical research group from Cambridge. Richard Barber, also ex School House, came and taught for several months.

Philippa, Bruce and Robin all came out as often as possible, Robin regularly in his school holidays. He was flourishing at Shrewsbury, very keen for some time on athletics, though his enthusiasms waxed and waned. His running was very successful. "I am the happiest boy in England", he wrote. After Bruce went to sea with the Royal Mail Line we saw him in Pakistan no more. Phil was at Birmingham School of Art, not far from Shrewsbury where friends – particularly Michael and Dabney Hart – were very good to her and the boys.

Our own school holidays were memorable: when there was snow in Murree there was warm sunshine on the Plains. Several times we stayed with our dear friends the Dost Mohammeds in Peshawar and travelled through the Khyber. I took the children to Kashmir, having to go 750 miles through India, where they enjoyed houseboat life, a trek in the hills and the wares of Suffering Moses and Subhana the Worst. One Christmas we spent with Charles and Rosemary Brooke-Smith on their beautiful tea estate in Ceylon, later staying with John and Alison Webb at Vellore where John ran that great medical school and hospital. We were sometimes in Lahore staying in Aitchison College, sometimes in Rawalpindi where once, as Chairman of the United Kingdom Association, I received the Duke of Edinburgh. Once we went to the oil fields of the Attock Oil Company where Denis and Marie Barber entertained us, they having twin children of Martin's age. Agra and the Taj Mahal, New Delhi and its fort were visited one holiday. Ajmer another. Sometimes we drove home up the hill after these expeditions to find the College covered in snow and the road impassable. Then our servants would meet us and we would walk in single file through the pine trees in moonlight, the servants carrying the children and the luggage.

Although 1965 brought better days as far as the College was concerned, there were private sadnesses. One day in June I was going through the mail, dictating to my secretary, when a cable was brought to me: it was from my brother Richard telling me that Olive had taken her own life. I remember absorbing the news and quietly getting on to dictate the rest of my letters before going to tell Joy. Olive had, it later appeared, been suffering from anxiety neurosis for some time and had been having electric shock treatment for it. None of us knew this. After the death of my mother, she had found life purposeless; although she had a group of good friends and various activities including the Citizens Advice Bureau, she felt she could not go on. She had visited us the previous year and seemed in good health. Naturally it was a profound shock, made worse by separation.

It was in 1965 also that Philippa ran into a crisis. She had announced her engagement the previous year to a fellow student. We were delighted and all seemed set for the wedding in the summer for which Joy would return early with Alan and to which I and Martin would go during the August break. But as the date grew nearer and the banns were called, Phil found she could not go through with it; her doubts overwhelmed her. So all was cancelled with wide emotional repercussions. Our absence had been hardest on Phil who lacked family support at a time when she needed it.

But our family concerns sunk into insignificance before a major crisis of a quite different kind. Many will have forgotten the twelve day war between India and Pakistan in September 1965, the cause inevitably being Kashmir. Suddenly we found that all the paraphernalia of wartime conditions were upon us – black-out, air raid precautions, censorship, rationing – all imposed on a country ill-adapted administratively to cope. I was fortunate in having as my Chairman the GOC in Murree who was conducting part of the war but whom I was able to see and from whom I got instructions to carry on as normally as possible. Only three or four boys were taken away, for Murree was as safe a place as any. But the imposition of the black-out was extraordinarily difficult. Every night I went round the whole estate to check for lights and to supervise our ARP. We followed in the newspapers the tank battles outside Lahore, the air dogfights, the front near Sialkot where in happier days I used to buy our sports equipment. I was appointed Warden of all British residents in the Hills, was summoned to conferences with the High Commissioner and discussed plans for the evacuation of women and children for whom a Hercules aircraft sat ready on Rawalpindi airport. Twice I drove down to Rawalpindi for conferences at night, driving without lights down the twisting mountain road; fortunately the moon shone. At night the bombers droned over as they made for Kashmir.

My personal position was not an easy one. I naturally did everything in my power to assist the war effort and to keep up morale but as a foreigner it was difficult to be closely involved in someone else's war about which the boys felt so passionately, longing to go and kill Indians rather than do maths. In some quarters too I was suspect. Had not I been to India twice? What else was I doing with my little torch at night as I went round the College but signalling to Indian planes? In the bazaar there was a graffiti 'Principal is an Indian spy'. All fantastic but truth is an early casualty in war. A day was fixed for the evacuation of Joy and the children, going we knew not where, with a baggage allowance of fifteen pounds per head. But on the day before they were due to leave a cease-fire was signed, largely through the efforts of Morrice James, our High Commissioner. We repaired to his house for a celebration but it was a sober one. The cost of the war had been high, not only in casualties (three old Gallians had been killed and were proclaimed martyrs) but in confidence and in general dislocation of the economy and way of life.

Nothing was quite the same after the war and I decided that the time had come for me to leave at the end of the school year, thus giving my governors six months to find my successor. I had already extended my original contract. I knew that Joy had reached the stage of wanting to be with the family, especially after Philippa's troubles, and it was time for Martin to go to an English school. Thus the most interesting and challenging years of my life came to an end. I will draw a veil over the prolonged, touching and somewhat painful leave-taking. I was presented with an inscribed scroll on which are recorded my supposed achievements.

Without doubt this was the most productive period in my life. There were many problems and troubles but there are so many happy memories: tea on the lawn in summer brought out under the acacia trees by Zardad with Joy knitting and Martin telling us in his beautiful clear voice what he had been doing at school; the tremendous monsoon rains and thunderstorms such as I have never met elsewhere; the wonderfully clear skies and intoxicating air of autumn; our simple family life in winter; the friendliness of the servants; the many friends we made, both Pakistani and British; and beyond all, the boys in their great variety, their robust energy and willingness to follow a lead. I am proud that one of my successors named the main road through the College 'Charlesworth Avenue'. And proud too that an Old Gallian, now a Brigadier, should say to me twenty-five years later with slightly misty eyes, "We shall never forget those years with you, Sir".

CHAPTER XXI

Home Again

Where the Severn's waves enfold
Pastures green and fields of gold.

We came home the long way round, circumnavigating the world. In Thailand we stayed with a Pakistani World Bank parent; in Singapore with an Old Salopian, Malcolm Shaw and his wife Pauline, also visiting Nigel Hodges, late of School House, and his wife Fiona, Jack Peterson's daughter; and we stayed with my old army friend of 'Highland Chieftain' and Bulford days, Richard Clarke and his wife and increasing family (they were to have seven children), stationed at Seremban in Malaysia. Thence to Australia to visit Alan Hamer and his family in Melbourne and to renew acquaintance with Geelong Grammar School. Jim Darling having at length retired (after thirty-two years as Headmaster), Tommy Garnett from Marlborough was Headmaster. Although I did not know him, he asked us to a meal and surprised me by suggesting that I join the Geelong staff again, with a view to becoming Master of Timbertop; he had clearly been doing his Top Schools. Gratified as I was to be thus remembered in Australia, I declined. We also visited Stewart Harris, now *The Times* correspondent in Canberra, fellow traveller on our great Land Rover epic of 1954. After a short stop in Fiji, we flew to Bermuda where Joy's mother, whom she had not seen for five years, was continuing a life of great activity; thence to New York where Clyde Sanger and his family were ensconced in a large house in Connecticut and to Halifax, Nova Scotia, to see Joy's sister Jill and a flock of cousins. Jill was now divorced and struggling to bring up her seven sons without a husband. We had been on the move for ten weeks when at last we reached Shrewsbury. Martin (7) and Alan (5) were excellent travellers, nonchalantly taking in their stride the planes, trains, buses and cars by which we had travelled and adjusting easily to the various homes in which we stayed, Martin's first question on arrival at each new house being "Are there any toys?"

We had already bought 'The Burgage', in Kennedy Road and it was deeply satisfying to establish our home in that lovely house with its large garden after five years' exile. Martin and Alan went to Meole Brace School; Robin had just completed five very successful years at Shrewsbury and was soon to go to Durham; Bruce was home sporadically, when the sea released him. Philippa's life had had its difficulties but she had now completed her art course and had become engaged to a young architect, Tony Goodall. They were married in the School Chapel. Altogether this, the summer of 1966, was an eventful time for us all, with the World Cup thrown in. Stacy Colman quite surprised me by asking me to go with him to see Korea play Spain in Manchester. And one day there came a letter from the Foreign Office appointing me an OBE.

I was so pleased to be home and to see so many friends again that I had not seriously thought of my own future beyond assuming that I would rejoin the staff as an ordinary teacher, without any special responsibility. If my life was in tension between outward-going enterprise (the legacy of my mother) and conservative home-based instincts (the legacy of my father), it was the latter characteristic which was now in the ascendent. Family life in the Burgage and involvement in Shrewsbury School was all that I sought after the rough and tumble of Pakistani life. Only faintly did voices in my ear question whether this would be enough. I had already had a letter which suggested that I might be a good candidate for the headmastership of a well-known school, soon to be vacant. Some years previously I had had a most mysterious communication from the Colonial Office which invited me to apply for the headship of a new school in Iringa, in what had been Tanganyika. (Only much later did I find the hand of H.H. Hardy behind this invitation.) Did I want to be a headmaster? Should I take a different line entirely and join the state system? I had rather desultory talks with the Headmaster of a new Comprehensive in Telford, the Abraham Darby School, who was seeking a Deputy Head. But conservative instincts and my attachment to Shrewsbury remained predominant. Although I would not expect to be a housemaster again, I hoped to find a role in which I would be fulfilled. My headmastering in Pakistan had been a wonderful and unique experience. Reasonably untrammelled, I had had the chance to re-make a complete school and at the same time to fulfil a role, not unlike that of housemaster, to two hundred boys. But headmastering in England would be different. If one was a schoolmaster because one enjoyed contact with youth, if the boys were the purpose of life in and out of the form room, then headmastering put formidable barriers in the way – administration, finance, parents and prospective parents, mountains of correspondence and paper generally, committees and conferences; how much time was left for the boys, how much for the form room? I did not feel this was a field in which I wanted to compete. But of course my future at Shrewsbury would depend to a considerable extent on one man – the new (to me) Headmaster, now completing his first three years in that summer of 1966.

While in Pakistan, I had carried on a considerable correspondence with friends at Shrewsbury. Robin Moulsdale and Stacy Colman wrote regularly and at length so I was not without knowledge of developments on Kingsland. It is through them and others – particularly Peter Hughes – that I knew of those early years when Donald Wright burst like a whirlwind on the Site when – to some at any rate – "Bliss was it in that dawn to be alive"....

Although I was far away, it is interesting to seek to recreate those early years of the new regime. Donald came from Marlborough out of the John Dancy stable, where he was said to have been a liberal and energetic housemaster. There was an air of high expectation before his arrival which was certainly matched by the dynamic – almost frenzied – activity of his first months. His first masters' meeting started with prayer of a distinctly informal character and term ended with an Assembly in which he played a short classical piece on the piano. To one of those present he seemed "twice as large as life, full of ideas and, with the latest educational jargon, as different from Jack Peterson as Wilson from Hume. He was 'forward looking', a great phrase of the Sixties. He was quite obviously a Tab and not an Oxford man". The comparison with Hume and Wilson is apt, for, at this same time, a man standing for the traditions of the past and of the old order was replaced by a Prime Minister who had all the trendy liberal ideas of the day and whose 'white heat of the technological revolution' was matched, *mutatis mutandis*, by Wright's subjection of Shrewsbury to a barrage of new ideas. He made no secret of his opinion that Shrewsbury was in decline and that he had come to revive it.

A symbol of the new age was the enlargement of the footpath down to Kingsland House from the Common into a proper road to bring Kingsland House into closer touch with the community. The contrast with his predecessors is interesting: at lunchtime Jack Wolfenden had made his leisurely way home on foot wearing his mortar board, seeing and being seen; Jack Peterson had cycled unobtrusively in his old mackintosh hoping not to be seen; Donald Wright drove at a furious speed, not a moment to be lost, along the new road soon labelled the M1. He had a reputation for speedy driving and there was a distinct reluctance to ride in the Headmaster's car. Returning from a trip to Liverpool, David Bevan was heard to say, "whenever I dared open my eyes the needle was hovering between eighty and ninety – I just prayed the whole way".

The improvement of the teaching facilities was a first priority and ancillary matters like the supply of books were the subject of radical reorganisation. Slide tapes and overhead projectors were all the rage and a language laboratory was to come. 'Subject centres' were in fashion so there began a long and tortuous debate about buildings and their uses. The curriculum was totally overhauled, the old division into 'sides' abandoned, the choice of A level subjects widened and the knell of the great classical tradition sounded. Arnold Hagger was appointed as Second Master to oversee all this – a mistaken title as the job he did was that of Director of Studies and there was already a Senior Master. Arnold brought all his very considerable administrative ability to this gigantic task and soon a whole new nomenclature had been invented. (David Bevan staring short-sightedly at the notice board found he was teaching DR6 in X: "Can anyone crack the code?")

The turmoil into which Shrewsbury was thrust was not due solely to the influence of the new Headmaster. Not only in politics had a new age dawned: Lady Chatterley, Profumo, the Beatles, the Bishop of Woolwich, Carnaby Street, had in their different ways made in-roads into the old order. Philip Larkin's oft-quoted verse suggested that sexual intercourse began in 1963; the pill and the miniskirt rendered girls all legs and liberty. The permissive society opened its arms to welcome the young; the advertisers – realising that youth had money – invented a teenage culture which was not easy to reconcile with the traditional ways of Shrewsbury School. Old Salopians played their part: Christopher Booker, Richard Ingrams, Willie Rushton and Paul Foot launched the immensely successful *Private Eye* and contributed to *That Was the Week That Was*. Jack Wolfenden had made an unsuspecting contribution with his report on homosexuality, which led to a change in the law and added the expression 'consenting adults' to the language. All this against the background of the distant rumble of the Vietnam War, protest marches and draft-card burning in America; London was now the most 'swinging' city in the world, inhabited by brilliant playwrights, irreverent film directors, uncensored novelists and TV presenters, with a motley gang of fashion designers, hairdressers, cookery experts, discothèque owners and colour supplement men. Drugs, until now known only to a tiny minority, were encountered and purchased in hitherto 'respectable' social circles.

How would the Public Schools reconcile themselves to the new age? Some, like Harrow, clung limpet-like to their traditions, putting up barriers against this disturbing new world, not recognising that adolescents had become teenagers and were part of it. Some, like Marlborough, attempted a sweeping adaptation, abandoning the old platonic vision of enlightened social, moral and political leadership, which lay at the heart of the Public School ethos, and turning instead to the concept of responsibility and of individual achievement – now more important than public service. Even the Plato-brought-up-to-date philosophy of Kurt Hahn at Gordonstoun and elsewhere (Timbertop!), was under pressure, though Hahn had softened the old prefect/leadership philosophy by calling his prefects Guardians or Helpers. So came the in-word Meritocracy, perhaps best illustrated in practice by Eric James at Manchester Grammar School: merit would rise from a sea of equality of opportunity. The old ideals of the Chapel, the sports field and the OTC/CCF were superseded by individual achievement and success in competitive examinations. T.S. Eliot had already warned against losing the transmitted culture of a society, pointing out that equality of opportunity would lead to greater inequality, in which elites were not equipped to lead, thus repeating the message of a book written many years previously, which I recollect reading in India: *The Idea of a Christian Society*. In the new age of the comprehensives, equality and individualism were to be uneasy bedfellows.

Apart therefore from seeking to reform the academic work of the school, which also involved plans for new buildings ('plant' was the word), Donald Wright had to consider how to deal with this teenage counterculture which gradually seeped into the school. His leadership here was to be put to a severe test as were the attitudes and capabilities of his staff. Who were they?

By the time of my return in 1966 a completely new generation of housemasters had been appointed. My successor in School House, Michael Hart, had played the part of Grand Vizier in Jack Peterson's last years, separated from the Headmaster only by the School House study door. He was making a great success of housemastering at a difficult time, liberal in attitude, authoritarian in practice but, beyond either of these, efficient in all that he did. His was a whole-hearted commitment with his wife Dabney playing a full supporting role. Having no children, Michael's concentration on the School House, and school matters in general, was complete. Donald Wright was not slow to draw on his abilities, particularly in the administrative sphere, and he managed to continue the role of Grand Vizier undisturbed by the change of Headmaster. But the real trend setters in this new age of housemastering were Robin Moulsdale in Moser's and Alan Laurie in Severn Hill. Both were Liberals in the political sense (Alan was for some years a Liberal member of the Borough Council) and both were prepared to meet the new age on its own terms. They were inheritors, too, of the old Henry George philosophy which had been so popular with Murray Senior and a group of masters in pre-war days, Frank McEachran, then as now, being the father figure, still the inspirer of a legion of boys, still reciting Spells (two books had by now been published) and having an influence which, in the case of many Old Salopians, has never been effaced. It was somehow wholly in keeping with the air of myth and mysticism which hung around him that he should have celebrated his sixty-sixth birthday on the 6th June 1966.

The major social change of the Sixties in the school, was the almost complete disappearance of the hierarchical structure. This was not in any way 'abolished' from without; it crumbled from within. Significantly, it was the School House which took the initiative in abolishing corporal punishment and 'douling' (fagging) and the reforms quickly spread to other Houses. Soon boys did not want to be monitors or even praepostors: the exercise of authority was to some distasteful. The cult of individualism – 'doing your own thing' – became fashionable. The essence of the new housemastering, as I understand it, was to recognise this and not seek to preserve a tottering structure. The secret of the Moulsdale and Laurie way was to emphasise responsibility as opposed to authority, to seek to get boys to look after each other rather than command them, to make the whole of the senior year monitors and to allocate to them responsibilities which lay within the capability of each; the boys without confidence or drive could at least run the library. At the same time privileges and unnecessary rules were jettisoned but a firm structure of basic rules maintained – rules which were clearly designed for the good of the body politic. Robin managed a wonderfully laid back and casual air; but this could be deceptive. There were strict boundaries and when boys came up against them they knew it. Irritating to him as it was, administration was necessary. "It's fundamentally all about dustbins", we would say, meaning that however relaxed an atmosphere one tried to create, the basic groundwork of emptying dustbins and general infrastructure had to be maintained. One future housemaster who tried to run his House in the relaxed and liberal Moulsdale way failed to realise the necessity for a solid core of rules as a base; his House soon became chaotic.

This method of running a House required much from the housemaster himself, and both Robin and Alan devoted an enormous amount of time to seeing boys individually and in small groups; herein lay the secret of their success. But stamina and a co-operative wife, fully involved in running the increasingly difficult task of house catering were also essential. Alan gave up after eight years; Robin, despite domestic difficulties, went on successfully for fourteen and did as much as anyone to shape the very different Shrewsbury School which was emerging. 'Caring' was another in-word of the time, soon heavily over-used to the extent of becoming a cliché, but it was indeed appropriate for Moser's and Severn Hill which became, to a considerable degree, 'caring' communities.

Other housemasters followed the Moulsdale-Laurie-Hart lead to a greater or lesser degree. Even the most conservative – and there were such – found it impossible to stand still. Freddy Mann, in Rigg's, had a rough ride for his first years; Hugh Brooke – more Brookeish than ever in his last phase – was a difficult man to succeed, especially by one whose character was in total contrast. The admirable Mike Powell had to negotiate some difficult waters in Ingram's, as did his successor David Main. In Churchill's Adrian Struvé's four years were overhung by tragic ill-fortune in his family life, leading to his premature retirement. Michael Tupper, always sure of the answers, presided over a very black-and-white regime in Oldham's.

There were a number of casualties. After a considerable amount of mayhem in the preceding year, Peter Gladstone sailed into Ridgemount, both barrels blazing, retailing every detail of the terrible scandals and lurid incidents he had discovered. Early in 1966 he uncovered a robber gang who were said to have cut keys to every building in the school. Peter's domestic arrangements were unusual: visiting parents might find themselves sharing the drawing-room with almost any kind of wild fowl. In Dayboys Basil Saint had succeeded Stacy Colman. This responsibility, together with being head of the very successful maths faculty, proved to be too heavy and after five years he handed over to Arnold Ellis.

The senior names on Page One of the Brown Book were now more or less redundant, some happily, some resentfully so. Brooke at any rate was happy, writing to me, "Whilst you are in Conference with the Governor of Waziristan, I am cutting a Masters' meeting with the Headmaster and whilst you are drinking laced coffee with the Begum of Bhopal, I am sipping warm syrup of figs with Mrs Pendelbury. And I'm delighted with my garden; my second name is now 'A.G.' or 'Asparagus Genius'. We've sold the 'C in W' or 'Cottage in Wales'." Hugh had lately conducted the marriage of Noel Surridge, late of Rigg's. Noel was – and is – a considerable friend and I was able to send a cable "May Brooke Bond lead to all Happiness". Alec Binney on the other hand, was somewhat irritated on his being asked (as Head of English) to submit a report on that subject and, having taken time and trouble to produce a reasoned document, to be told that it was now redundant. The game had moved forward a couple of places since the report had been commissioned. Stacy Colman commented, "I am too old and stale and square and set in my ways to learn new tricks, and, badly as we all need shaking up by Wright, it is disagreeable to be shaken up in one's last three years as an usher". John Woodroffe was eased out of the position of Head of Science, to be succeeded by Peter Hughes, who was moving firmly in step with the new regime, which John was not. Easing out Rex Connell from Ridgemount was another Wright tactic as was easing out George Riley from the Gymnasium. Meanwhile the new appointments were to be 'fizzers', men with a thoroughly Wright outlook. The word 'fizzer' was attacked by Willie Jones in Wright's presence as a dangerous metaphor in that once a fizzy drink was opened the fizz soon disappeared. Willie later thought that Wright had never forgiven him for this seeming attack, though Willie was talking about metaphors not men. Graham Garrett was the first of the 'fizzers', hung around with the aura of the 'new maths'. Another was Barry Pitt, and the school suddenly found itself immersed in Physical Education as opposed to the old PT, accompanied, needless to say, by a new layer of jargon.

Of the older men, David Bevan alone remained, now in the position of

Senior Master, a figurehead of stability and experience, "frisking the corridors of power" in his own phrase, a man universally respected but not one who made any attempt to keep up with Wright's headlong reformist zeal. The future apparently lay with the fizzers.

CHAPTER XXII

The Sixties

We shall not all sleep, but we shall all be changed,
in a moment in the twinkling of an eye.

I Cor. XV

I am told that each common room meeting seemed to produce a bomb-shell of some sort in those early Wright years, some masters at once adjourning to the New House, where gin was poured and the Head-master's statements eagerly examined for the expected crop of solecisms and trendy jargon, particularly by Mark Mortimer with his acute sense of intellectual integrity. His occasional verses pricked many a balloon and sometimes needled the Headmaster, who used to reprimand him for sailing too close to the wind and make suggestions about packing him off on a sabbatical – suggestions always refused. There were some notable statements, such as that in which the staff were congratulated on the Oxbridge results, described as a "meretricious performance". Later, firms which had subscribed to the bursary scheme were thanked for their "patri-mony". But these things did not take away from Wright's general popu-larity and support for his aims.

Discipline certainly provided problems for all at a time of changing standards everywhere. Robin Moulsdale wrote to me, "I don't feel the old-fashioned way in which we ran Houses works any more. The boys have no real standards to follow and they are ready to question any presented to them by authority, so I think you have got to get right in among them to show them what you believe and why". In a circular to parents in 1964, Wright wrote of his increasing concern in this area, particularly centred on a minority of boys who constantly flouted the rules. Suspension, rustica-tion and gating became common forms of sanction and if all else failed there was the Tavistock Clinic which became well known in these years. One boy is reputed to have said, "What is wrong with me? I'm the only boy in my year whom the Housemaster hasn't phoned Dr Miller about."

What place would I find in this new developing Shrewsbury? Donald Wright inherited me in brackets at the bottom of his brown book staff list, exiled to the remote Himalayan foothills, and must have wondered at receiving back a man who had been a headmaster longer than he had. His welcome was genuinely warm but I could detect an undercurrent of uncertainty as to how to deal with me. It was not till many years later that I found out why. The Secretary of the Old Salopian Club was at this time Graham Heath, a solicitor operating from the impressive address of 1 The Sanctuary, Westminster. Graham was a pillar of the ecclesiastical establishment, Registrar of two Dioceses and Chapter Clerk of St Paul's Cathedral. A lawyer to the fingertips, fastidious, thorough, industrious and loyal – he was a man of complete integrity who devoted himself whole-heartedly to his work for the Old Salopian Club, being also a keen member of the Old Salopian Lodge. A traditionalist, his school days had been spent under the influence of his housemaster, Basil Oldham. His younger son had been a boy in the School House with me, intellectually sharp and critical, with whom my relationship had not been easy, though in the end he became Head of House and went off with an exhibition to Cambridge. But he had not followed his father's course of extreme loyalty and enthusiasm for Shrewsbury School.

Wright treated Heath with great respect and looked on him as representing the view of Old Salopians in general; nothing could be further from the actuality. Graham was firmly rooted in pre-war days and in, for instance, a long correspondence with Wright about religion and worship in the Chapel, showed that he had little understanding of the difficulties of the Sixties, the questioning attitude of the current boys and the need for the new approach which Wright was painfully developing. Holding me responsible for his son's failure to be a loyal Salopian, Graham Heath submitted a barrage of comment, almost entirely derogatory. Certainly I do not think I was clever in dealing with the younger Heath but the range of adjectives with which I was belaboured was sweeping – "unimaginative", "unintelligent", "authoritarian", "not the slightest idea of how to cope with the intelligentsia". And, of course, there was my part in "the deplorable conspiracy" against Jack Peterson which had been "inaugurated by Duncan Norman". Graham Heath naturally had an interpretation of those events which differed markedly from the facts which I have earlier endeavoured to describe.

No wonder then that Donald Wright had his doubts about me! However, for the moment, there was no necessity for him to make any decision. There being enough historians on the staff, there was not an obvious place for me so far as teaching was concerned, and I expressed myself very ready to do any other work inside or outside the school for a year or so. It so happened that the Priory School at that time had rather suddenly lost its Head of History to a headmastership and so was looking for a temporary historian. So I became Head of History at the Priory for one year while a replacement was sought. The Headmaster was Cyril Peckett, one of the wave of grammar school Headmasters who had emerged after the war, a classicist and musician, with a concert pianist wife and an excessively brainy son who had been a Dayboy at Shrewsbury School. Standards at the Priory had risen in Peckett's time and it was a thorough-going, well organised grammar school of the old type. It was a pleasure to join this very welcoming staff, which included a nucleus of men of quality who had spent many years at the school. It was a novelty for me to walk across the Kingsland Bridge after breakfast, plunge into the non-stop day school activity, both in and out of school, and to be home for tea at 4.30 pm. I enjoyed my teaching, which ranged from A level down to the lowest form, and soon felt part of the act, though I had to work hard in the evenings to brush up my rusting history. I was actually in a strong position: if the A level results were bad I could shrug my shoulders and say that one could not do much in a year, while if they were good, I could (at least in theory) preen myself and happily take the credit for what was actually largely the work of others. In fact the results were rather good. From time to time I meet former pupils in the town – now lawyers, businessmen, accountants and doctors – in whose education I am happy to have played a tiny part; they include two vicars of Shropshire Parishes.

Another responsibility came to me in the summer of 1967; that of Director of the Friends of Shrewsbury in the last days of its Appeal. It had been decided in 1964 that Wright's ambitious building programme could only be financed by an Appeal, run professionally. Hooker & Craigmyle were the firm chosen and for two years the campaign, as it was called, was carried on from an office in 15 Ashton Road. Enormous energy had been put into this endeavour, not least by the Headmaster himself, and it had achieved considerable, though uneven, success, notwithstanding a somewhat shaky start. Now the professionals moved out and the campaign was to be carried on in its last phase by me and by Patrick Childs, the treasurer. So I had a new sphere of activity bringing me into contact with many Old Salopians up and down the country. This last phase brought in £60,000, so it was reasonably successful; the final figure raised was about £285,000.

Venturing a little further in giving me responsibility, Wright asked me to run General Studies and to supervise the use of the newly re-ordered Moser Building, the school library. One of his criticisms of Salopians had been that their academic studies were too narrowly focused and he accounted for this partly by the lack of private space to study. Passes in the general paper at A level were fifteen or twenty per cent lower than at comparable schools. Hence the emphasis on the Moser Building and the drawing up of numerous ever-changing plans for its renaissance. Not everyone agreed with the treatment of the ancient library – Stacy Colman certainly did not – but out of the rebuilding did emerge facilities for study far in advance of what this very underused building had previously offered, though there was a curious contradiction in including a tape room equipped with powerful loud speakers, cutting across the idea of silence which was encouraged in the main rooms. In reorganising General Studies, I was able to visit a number of other schools to see what they were doing, including, I remember, a very stimulating evening with Oliver Van Oss at Charterhouse.

After I had been back on the staff for a year, I began to see where I might be useful and find a position which would give scope to such talents as I have, namely as Senior Master or Deputy Headmaster. Hitherto the man who was top of the seniority list in the brown book acted as the Headmaster's deputy if needed but this was an *ex officio* position without any duties. Before he arrived, Donald Wright had corresponded with Jack Peterson about the possibility of an appointment which would have definite responsibilities. He was not the first headmaster to think in these terms. A.F. Chance had acted as Deputy Headmaster to Sawyer in all but name; Hardy had wished for such but never found a candidate who would suit him; Peterson wrote to Wright that he was inclined to think that "the appointment would be a good one if only one could find a job for him to do". My relationship with Wright, despite his early misgivings – and the lurking influence of Graham Heath – had developed very happily, and in 1968 he invented a rather indefinite position for me which was entitled 'Assistant to the Headmaster'. In 1969 I became Senior Master, a title which I managed to have changed after a few years to 'Second Master', which had a proper historical pedigree. Wright quickly assigned various areas of administration to me, particularly that of entries to the school. His whirlwind activity was such that he certainly needed a deputy. It was said that for an ordinary member of staff to see the Headmaster a couple of weeks' notice was required. Reinforcements were soon to arrive in the secretarial department, where Dorothy Jones, used to the slow pace of the Peterson days, was struggling to keep up.

Before taking over this new role, however, I had a different experience. Wright was a great man for sending staff on courses and conferences, also secondments and attachments. Peter Gladstone, for instance, had a term off, to study birds and whales in the Falkland Islands. He was also keen to give housemasters a sabbatical break after they had done some years' service. So it came about that the Moulsdale family were given the summer of 1969 off and made their way to Kenya. Joy and I moved into Moser's to deputise. This was a fascinating experience for me as I adapted myself to the Moulsdale method of running a House. I was impressed by the way in which he had created an informal but purposeful atmosphere in which each boy had a part to play, and even more impressed by the way in which the senior boys sought to look after the junior ones and by the ease with which communication between the different year groups – and with me – took place. I was fortunate to work with a very pleasant group of monitors (the whole year group) and especially with Allan Kerr, Ian Jones and Brian Argyle, the praepostors. I knew something of the boys because I had already acted in a Moser's play as Jack in *The Importance of Being Earnest*, in which Willie Jones gave a fine performance as Lady Bracknell and Ian Jones and Mark Bingley were quite outstanding as Gwendolin and Cecily. Moser's had for many years had a dramatic tradition and had been the first House to attempt a full-length play in the Alington Hall, four years previously.

I had few disciplinary difficulties in that co-operative atmosphere but Joy had to work hard on the domestic side. This was the last term before central feeding and, though we had two splendid daily ladies in Joan and Roub, who seem to have worked in Moser's for ever, cooks and matrons were as difficult as always. One cook had to leave in mid-term and the matron was off for half the term with a bad back. Joy, in her usual confident way, filled in while even I was deployed as matron on occasion. It was a happy term, finishing with the last Bump Supper of the old type. Even our cats contentedly made the transition to Moser's; Teddy – an adventurer – enjoyed being near the Site. His presence at Assembly in the Alington Hall, however, was not appreciated and he had to be restrained from attending Chapel. The fire escape was his usual way into the House; I now forget which boy it was who soon became reconciled to Teddy arriving on his bed with a thump in the middle of the night.

Sir Fred Pritchard was still Chairman of the Governors when Donald Wright arrived. He was a devoted supporter of the new Headmaster, just as he had been of the old, and his loyalty and interest in the school did not waver. But change in the governance of the school was not long in coming. Wright's ambitious plans involved spending large sums of money; despite opposition from some governors, the Hooker & Craigmyle campaign was launched but the whole question of finance was now under review and scrutiny. The gross deficit on the year's working in 1963–64 was £25,599. Was it right that the budget for the next year should aim at a surplus of only £650 on expenditure of £245,000? Uneasiness amongst the governors, not unassisted by the pessimism of Richard Summers, Chairman of the Finance Committee, led to the calling in of accountants Layton-Bennett, Farrow & Co to report. Of this firm K.L. ('Pat') Young, an Old Salopian, was a director; so there came upon the scene a man who was to transform the whole of the school's finances. He became first financial adviser, then financial controller to the Governing Body from 1965 until his sadly premature death in 1979 at the age of 62.

Pat Young had an immensely successful career, taking part in various mergers of accountancy firms which led to the establishment of Dearden

Farrow of which he was senior partner. He was a director of twenty-six companies and chairman of fourteen of them, yet he found time to devote to Shrewsbury School, always ready to listen, never afraid of difficult decisions and with a directness of approach which some found disconcerting. The report which the governors had called for did not make pleasant reading. The school's finances had been allowed to drift for many years and there was no doubt that the Bursar must go – on that all were agreed. Fred Pritchard was a very fair man and convened a special meeting to give the Bursar a chance to speak but also to tell him of the firm decision of the governors.

Thus a new system of accounting, of a much more rigorous nature, was instituted, an accounting machine bought (this was before the age of computers) and, most important of all, M.M. Jones was appointed Bursar. Micky Jones had been Head of School in 1944; he was a Chartered Surveyor and had been Bursar at the Dragon School in Oxford. A man of considerable personal charm and of broad humanity, which was soon recognised by every employee on the Site, he brought a thoroughgoing professionalism to the Bursary, well backed by the contribution of his wife Alison who entered into school life with infectious energy and gaiety. This type of bursaring had not been seen at Shrewsbury before. His relations with Pat Young were of the happiest; they fully understood one another and worked as a partnership. Micky Jones was assisted by Mary Taylor, Assistant Bursar, who handled with great competence the workforce and domestic matters without number. Thus was the foundation laid which stood up to and facilitated Wright's ambitious plans and sustained the school even in the fearful inflationary days which were soon to dawn.

Pat Young was keen to bring the staff into the picture and, at a meeting in 1965, the financial position of the school was revealed for the first time. A grim picture was disclosed – as was the fact that the Bursar was leaving. Economy was to be the rule and all were asked to help. Micky Jones inherited a sum of £997 in the school account when he took over. Delving amongst minor accounts in forgotten ledgers he came across one in which the last entry was for the funeral expenses of the Reverend Rigg who had died in 1872.

Apart from the advent of Pat Young and his refreshing vigour, there were other changes on the Governing Body which put life into a somewhat moribund and aged group. Fred Pritchard had given notable service but was beginning to fail. As Offley Wakeman had been in former time, he was persuaded – with reluctance on his part – to resign from the Chair. For fourteen years from 1969 the school had the advantage of an experienced, wise and witty Chairman in Walter Hamilton. At one time a don, Master in College at Eton, then Headmaster in turn of Westminster and of Rugby, he was now Master of Magdalene College, Cambridge. To me – and I saw a good deal of him as will be seen – he was the ideal Chairman; never a man to interfere, he nevertheless gave steady support when needed, could be decisive when required and had a deep fund of experience on which to draw. Donald Wright has put together a fascinating series of essays on Walter which well describe a man who was essentially shy, had few of the characteristics normally associated with headmasters ('more Max Miller than a Minor Prophet'), lacked any sort of vanity and will be remembered by many for his wonderfully lugubrious voice, once described as being "like a depressed bloodhound". There is an oft repeated, probably apocryphal story, of how he proposed to his wife: "Would you like my name on your tombstone?". Many Shrewsbury parents will remember his three-minute speeches which terminated the Speech Day proceedings: a combination of sincerity, sentiment and wit.

Shrewsbury was lucky indeed to have the combination of Wright-Hamilton-Young-Jones; few schools were as fortunate. The other notable newcomer to the governors was Sir Paul Sinker. At one time a don at Cambridge, he had risen in the Civil Service to be First Commissioner and then Director General of the British Council. He had retired to Shrewsbury and was soon Chairman of the Executive Committee of the governors. I had met Paul when he offered me the post of Headmaster of the ill-fated school in Iran and I had remotely served under him when in Pakistan. He and his wife had a great love of India; Joy and I had several happy evenings at their house in Berwick Road, largely discussing the affairs of the Subcontinent. Other new governors were Jock Burnet, Bursar of Magdalene and a governor of countless other schools; Peter Bowring, most loyal and generous of Salopians; Alan Booth, nominated by the Lord Chief Justice; and Reggie Lloyd, elected by the Headmaster and staff, replacing Tom Bigland. The latter had not been entirely happy with the new Headmaster. Fred Pritchard was keen to point out that Lloyd should regard himself as "merely a member of the Governing Body and not a sort of champion of the Masters' cause".

The troubles of the Sixties were at their worst during the first part of my time as Senior Master, particulary during the years 1968–73 which will be remembered everywhere as years of student unrest. It seemed that everywhere institutions were being attacked, accepted standards ridiculed, 'permissiveness' breaking out in all directions. The Little Red School Book preached subversion. How far was Shrewsbury affected by all this?

I have already mentioned that the old hierarchical social structure had largely collapsed. How were boys to exercise authority if there were no sanctions? Persuasion and example were the right methods but it is asking a lot of a seventeen-year-old to have the force of personality to lead without a disciplinary structure to support him. Consequently, the offices of praepostor and monitor lost a good deal of status and dignity. There were, of course, boys with strong qualities – and there were some good Heads of School at this time – Edward Armitstead, Peter Saltmarsh, Andrew Eddy, Ben Duncan and Tim Lamb come to mind; but for those with lesser responsibilities to discharge in the study or bedroom, life was not easy. Inevitably the staff, particularly housemasters, were drawn closer to the boys and the last shadow of Houses being boy-run republics behind the green baize door disappeared. Masters too lived in a less hierarchical atmosphere. No longer were they 'capped' (an apparent scratching of the ear purporting to be the removal of a non-existent cap) and in the form room the dais and high desk disappeared; gowns were only worn on ceremonial occasions.

My answer as to why Shrewsbury survived these turbulent years with so little trouble lies in the many networks that criss-crossed the school, networks of personal relationships which cut across boundaries of age, status or the academic form structure. A sophisticated VIth form tutoring system brought almost all the staff into play, the vital element being that boys could themselves choose their tutor – not necessarily a man who taught them but someone whom they liked, possibly through sharing common interests. If you didn't get on with your housemaster, there was always someone else to talk to. Thus was built up a network of close – and often confidential – relationships, which took the steam out of much of the unrest which characterised schools at this time.

Such a system could not work without masters able and willing to work it, which meant a considerable degree of commitment. Such men were on hand. New housemasters with new ideas were taking over; Richard Raven in Severn Hill, Roger Blomfield (an architect of the tutoring system) in Churchill's, Geoffrey Phillips in Rigg's and Arnold Ellis in Dayboys. In the Common Room there were no diehard reactionaries; the average age of the staff was thirty-eight. Willie Jones was a man of great sensitivity and wide influence, who feared lest his influence should seem authoritarian, declining, as Head of English, to sit at the top of a table lest he should seem to impose. (Meetings had to be held at round tables.) Willie taught with enthusiasm, produced plays, ran the Hunt and enjoyed the confidences of many. David Gee, in addition to presiding over the flourishing history department, deployed his abundant energies in many fields, as did Robin Trimby, successful coach to the 1st XI for many years. And there were those considerable contributors who did not seek the centre of the stage – John Alford in the Art School, Adrian Struvé, the main link with Shrewsbury House in Everton, and Lawrence Edbrooke, ever willing workhorse in the less spectacular and less popular activities. In 1967, Alexander Mackinnon, Michael Eagar, Michael Hall and Anthony Bowen arrived, all of whom built up confident and constructive relationships with boys. When Arnold Hagger retired from the post which was really that of Director of Studies,

Peter Hughes brought his many talents to this central position. By these men, and others, Donald Wright was well backed in the new Shrewsbury he was trying to create.

But of course there were problems. Drugs appeared in most schools at this time. Shrewsbury had, I think, three cases where drugs were brought into the school. The real question to ask about drugs is not whether a school has them but how soon one finds out about them. In these cases the news was almost immediately known to the authorities and action taken. The threat of drugs was always in our minds but never a serious worry.

More superficial, though more irritating, were constant arguments about length of hair and 'mod' clothing. The radicals maintained that these things were indeed superficial and not worth expending energy on. Was not the school motto *Intus si recte ne labora*? But, unfortunately, the world – and prospective parents – thought otherwise, judging outward appearance to indicate inner character. Regulations were made and amended. The blue coat, hitherto uniform for everyday wear, was replaced by the choose-your-own-sports jacket. Perversely, the boys in Rigg's, most traditional of Houses, refused to wear any other than the old blue jacket – for a time. Casual dress – jeans and jerseys – was allowed in off-duty times. Most boys looked reasonably smart but some looked pretty dreadful unless constantly chivvied. A boy in Ridgemount whose hair grew upwards and sideways but not downward was able to stay inside the rules though he looked like Strewlpeter.

Pop music invaded the Site, along with machines to relay it at a high decibel level. How much television should boys be allowed to see? Now that bounds were relaxed and the school was starting to look outward, what about the inward influx of girls? Mr Wilson had introduced the franchise for the eighteen-year-old. If boys were legally 'of age' what limits, if any, should a school impose on their behaviour patterns? Should there not be a Club where drink could be obtained and girls entertained? The dissident few were ever ready with questions which started, "Why do we have to …".

CHAPTER XXIII

The Death of the Public School

There are nine and sixty rules for running Public Schools
And every single one of them is Wright.

Donald Wright, faced by difficult decisions, was always prepared to give a strong lead, distinguishing between matters where it seemed right to change – often radically – and where there were principles at stake which had to be sustained. Shrewsbury certainly deserved its reputation as one of the most liberal of the great schools but, through it all, standards that really mattered were maintained. Academic results improved considerably and boys found themselves involved in a new range of activities, such as the Craft Centre, 'Basic Year' (outward-bound training for all), the 70 Club, where beer was on sale and a disco could operate, bee-keeping, expeditions to plays and concerts, and weekends at Talargerwyn, the school's cottage in Snowdonia. Some senior boys, in their last term or two, became 'out-boarders' and stayed with members of staff, living a more relaxed and (it was hoped) studious life away from house responsibilities and restrictions. Joy and I had, in succession, thirteen outboarders, all of whose company we enjoyed – except one!

In two areas there was anxious thought: the Combined Cadet Force and Chapel. The CCF became increasingly difficult to run once National Service was abolished. Was the training relevant to anything apart from the past? Where were the officers to come from? The army was slow to change and standards in the CCF were eroded as restless boys wondered why they were putting on khaki on Thursday afternoons. Was not this the age of flower rather than military power? Were they not enjoined to make love, not war? After some difficult times it was at length decided that the Corps should be voluntary and an alternative found in other occupations on Thursday afternoons, in which the accent should be on service. Hence the rise of Social Service or 'granny bashing' as it was known. So, one term there were at a stroke only thirty boys in the Corps instead of five hundred. It is true to say that the Army did at length see which way the wind was blowing and, by offering a number of attractive alternatives, the voluntary Army and Air sections have sustained a flourishing military life for a sizeable minority.

In the prevailing atmosphere of criticism of institutions and general scepticism, Chapel and the religious life of the school came under attack. Shrewsbury is a religious foundation; hitherto Chapel and the teaching of Divinity were accepted as part of the expected package of public school education, however lukewarm many of the participants. But the Sixties brought the questions. Was not this indoctrination? How could one be 'forced to believe'? Was not this an entirely personal matter for the individual? Donald Wright, a very fully committed Christian, boldly faced these challenges, determined that the presentation of the Christian religion should continue, but prepared to rethink the Chapel services and their content without in any way abandoning the central doctrines. Guy Furnivall, the Chaplain, a man of personal piety and deep Christian integrity, retired in 1966 after twenty-five years' service; in his last years the going had been difficult, both in Chapel and in the form room, where an atheistic minority was not reluctant to express opinions. In his place came Alistair Conn, with a background of Cambridge, Hartlepool and Uganda, whose theology was tempered by the new thinking of Tillich, Bonhoeffer and Quoist with a touch even of Bultmann. So, Chapel was launched into an experimental phase, sometimes involving the boys in the conduct of services. Realising that the run of the mill missionary/bishop/general could no longer hold the boys' attention, Donald Wright was selective in choosing visiting preachers, bringing to Shrewsbury some outstanding men like Tony Bridge, Dean of Guildford (who was bold enough to preach on the theme of *Lolita*), Dennis Nineham, Stuart Blanch of Liverpool, later Archbishop of York, and W.J.P.M. Garnett, Director of the Industrial Society.

Typical of Wright was a long weekend conference which he held in term time at the Lake Vyrnwy Hotel, taking all the housemasters and the Chaplain (and leaving me to run the school single-handed!), to discuss the whole question of Chapel. (The boys called it a 'love-in'.) So was gradually evolved the pattern which exists today: namely, a Sunday service and one week-day service for every boy, with voluntary services at other times.

With typical zeal, Wright also set about brightening the Chapel building itself. The walls were painted, the stone mullions disappeared, the chancel roof became blue and the Victorian reredos was covered by a curtain. New furniture, of indifferent design, was acquired for the chancel. A new portable altar was placed in the sanctuary. Thus disappeared the old choir stalls, which had originally stood in Manchester Cathedral; heavy and unmovable, their departure was not regretted. Not so the stalls in which the Headmaster and Chaplain had formerly sat, graceful and beautifully carved and designed by Kempe to fit with his windows and panelling. The stalls were *given* to St Mary's where they now stand. Three succeeding Headmasters have tried to get them back without success; how easy it would have been to have made a loan agreement instead of an outright gift! Relations with St Mary's were, however, soured by an astonishing act of vandalism. A statue of the great Headmaster, Samuel Butler, which had stood in St Mary's had been given to the school some years previously; not finding a place for it in the redesigning of the Moser precinct, Wright had it broken up – an outrage remembered and resented at St Mary's to this day, thirty years later.

The Chapel was indeed lightened by the new look. But the obscuration of the reredos – on the grounds that it was an inferior Victorian work of art – destroyed the Chapel theology which Moss, Headmaster in 1882 when the Chapel was built, had conceived: namely, that the virtues shown in the glass of the nave windows should lead up to the crucifixion scenes in the East window which should, in turn, lead to the resurrection scene (the road to Emmaus) portrayed in the reredos. In more general terms it was really impossible to make the Chapel otherwise than what it is – a straight-forward example of Victorian Gothic. The next Headmaster had the curtain removed but the two coping-stones above, which had been taken out because they protruded above the curtain and which, according to Wright's contemporary statement, had been 'safely stored', were never found. At great expense new stones had to be carved. Also at this time appeared some strange altar frontals, one of which, according to Fred Pritchard, was just like a Field Day map.

Courageously, Donald Wright took on, and solved, one of the most difficult and contentious issues in the school, that of catering. For years housemasters' wives had struggled with this heavy responsibility; some were good at it and some ladies of the older generations had in particular coped wonderfully; Mary Taylor, Ethel Phillips, Maud Childs, Helen Matthews and Heather Binney come to mind. But the newer generation of wives, often with small children, operating in an age when domestic servants had more or less disappeared, had found house catering a heavy burden. So, after much discussion, central feeding was decided upon. Kingsland House (from which he and his family had moved) featured in many Wright plans: a prep school? a boarding house (again!)? a senior students' house? Now it was to be the central feeding centre. Already a forward-looking architect, of the correct 1960s posture, had been found in Michael Greenwood. His design for Kingsland Hall has been generally accepted as a success. Not so the advice of the catering consultants who guided our thought. They had been responsible for the catering plans on the *Queen Elizabeth*; that ship had little in common with KH. September 1969 saw the changeover: that Michaelmas term was the worst I can remember in my long experience. Wright had given me the responsibility for the organisation of the front of the house and all that concerned the boys; Micky Jones had the heavier responsibility for the kitchens. The kitchen staff did not harmonise, some of the equipment was inappropriate, the food was of poor quality, the boys did not like the change in routine. No-one seemed to have foreseen that we had to give six hundred boys their lunch in half an hour; we did not even have trolleys on which stacking of used plates and cutlery could take place. They had to be made in Sheffield and rushed down at half-term. I found myself down at Kingsland Hall for virtually every meal; Micky Jones bore much more worrying burdens; his wife Alison was soon played in as a manager, which much improved the organisation. But it was several terms before we had what could be called a smooth-running operation.

This is not the place to summarise all Donald Wright's building schemes and achievements; these can be found elsewhere. But one central problem overhung his time and that was the School House. The control of a hundred boys in this large and rambling building, at a time when rules were relaxed and more liberal standards generally prevailed, posed a considerable problem to a housemaster. Michael Hart's excellent regime had ended on his appointment as Headmaster of Mill Hill in 1967. Graham Garrett had committed himself no less fully to the School House but, in times of change, his regime of keeping the boys tightly bound by rules had meant a number of collisions; the House became known for producing groups of dissidents who, if not very numerous, served as irritants on the body politic. Whoever the housemaster might be, the control and smooth running of this hundred-strong community was bound to be extremely difficult. All were agreed that there should be change. But of what sort? Plans were discussed and discarded; financial estimates made and revised; ultimately there came a solution which was no solution.

Alexander Mackinnon and his wife Cleodie succeeded the Garretts when Graham moved to be Headmaster of Wellingborough in 1973. They were an attractive couple: both intellectually sharp with wide-ranging interests; both sensitive and outward-going; well able to communicate with the boys, particularly those academically minded. Many boys of that era will look back on Alexander as a guiding figure for whom they had the greatest respect.

By now it had been decided that School House should be divided and that there would be two housemasters. My opinion was asked and I said that this could only work if there was a *total*, vertical, physical division, possible only if a large-scale building project was undertaken. Mackinnon went in with the promise that this would be achieved; as a purely temporary measure a second housemaster would occupy make-do accommodation in the House so that Headroom and Doctor's could each have their own housemaster pending a permanent division. Sadly there followed months and years of planning and discussion as the Headmaster and governors wrestled with the finance that this plan needed for its fulfilment – all this at a time of rising inflation. Hindsight also suggests that Michael Greenwood – good at new buildings – was not the man to modify and adapt an old one; was his eye entirely on the ball? When it was realised that to achieve the goal of separate Houses would cost £100,000 more than the estimates suggested, everyone concerned had to fall back on compromise.

Meanwhile, Adrian Struvé and his wife Brenda – they had been Mackinnon's choice – had taken over Headroom. Thus two Houses, mixed up together, were being run by housemasters who, it was soon painfully clear, had very contrary views, in a building which was being assailed by the builders on all sides. When the work was at last completed there was increased accommodation but the two Houses still shared common facilities. Without the essential vertical and complete separation, it would have taken wholly angelic attitudes by all, together with total unanimity of outlook and policy to make the compromise work.

The Mackinnon-Wright correspondence file was more than twice the thickness of that of any other member of staff. Mackinnon felt hard done by, constantly promised what was not delivered, and his letters are full of complaint. Wright did what he could to keep the temperature low but did not find it easy. "It is almost as if, unless he can have all he wants all the time, life becomes something to complain about." In truth, Mackinnon, for all his virtues, was not the right man for this difficult task. School House could not be run without a much firmer structure than he was willing to impose. "I simply have not the time to check up on who is cutting periods, to guess who is slipping down-town after lunch, or who takes seventy minutes to get back from the Music School in the evening". Yet, without such checking, the whole social structure must slip – and slip it did. It was the question of dustbins again. In the end Mackinnon was bitter and his correspondence with Wright tart. "How it has come so low on your priority list that you have let it (School House) ride ten years before action I do not know – compared with School House the vast expenditure on the new Science Building seems of purely ritual importance". "I do not see myself soldiering on for ever out of a sense of duty just because my predecessor was mad enough to do the same".

Meanwhile the patient Struvé was making the best of Headroom in his typically low-key and undemonstrative way. The Wright-Struvé file of correspondence was slim.

Donald Wright's energies were formidable. Apart from the radical reformation of the school internally, in his early years he devoted much effort to introducing a bursaries scheme in an endeavour to widen the social group from which Salopians were drawn. Working with local authorities and seeking support from industry, he had some success and engendered a good deal of publicity. ("The 13 year-old son of a cotton worker has been picked to study at a top Public School . . ."). Hailed as breaking new ground (though it was really a development of the old Fleming Scheme), it was difficult to sustain the flow of money needed to keep the plan afloat.

Another area in which he took the leading role was in the rebuilding of Shrewsbury House – the old 'Mish' – in Liverpool, at the same time extending and widening its role. Several schools and colleges which had sustained 'missions' in the slums in pre-war days now closed them because the welfare state had so changed conditions. It would have been easy to close Shrewsbury House on the grounds that its original purpose was no longer relevant to modern circumstances. But Wright, assisted by Stuart Blanch, Bishop of Liverpool, and in partnership with the local authority, gave the leadership which heralded a new and useful age for the 'Shrewsy', and it was a proud moment when Princess Anne opened the new premises.

Always in the foreground of educational politics in the Sixties was the question of the future of the Public Schools and, specifically, what the Labour Government would do about them. The answer was , as so often, to set up a Commission. It is difficult now to remember how important this body and its deliberations seemed to us at that time. Everyone was talking about 'integration' and 'boarding need' and the figure of a certain Dr Royston Lambert, never heard of before or since, hovered over the scene, a sort of *eminence grise* whose researches and solutions were for some reason thought to carry deep significance. He was a bachelor don who knew nothing about children and had never been to a boarding school.

Donald Wright had soon established himself as a leading and influential liberal headmaster, forming with Ian Beer, who was transforming Elles- mere, and John Thorn, who was failing to transform Repton but was on the road to Winchester, a trio of forward-looking, powerful Midland head- masters. John Thorn later wrote of Wright as "a man revered by us all". Over several years the Commission laboured while the Headmasters Con- ference huffed and puffed. At length there came the report and the re- commendation, amongst others, that over a period, fifty per cent of public school pupils should be composed of those with a 'boarding need' – another way of saying 'deprived'; a grotesque piece of social engineering! No one ever actually managed to identify these many thousands of children who had 'boarding need'. The report still gathers dust somewhere; no one has ever taken any notice of it. "Of all the futile committees on which I have sat none equalled the Public Schools Commission", wrote Noel Annan.

I have dwelt at some length on Donald Wright's work and on the tumultuous Sixties for I think no one has yet written about this interesting period. Where did I stand in all this? In general I was only too happy to be a firm supporter of all that was being attempted at this time. As Second Master my sphere of action ranged ever wider as the Headmaster became more and more involved in his multifarious activities, his feet rarely touching the ground. A price was paid in his domestic life. In 1970–71 he was Chairman of the Headmasters Conference in which he had become a major figure. He was away for about a third of the time in what was not an easy year with poor leadership from the senior boys. Then in 1972 the governors agreed to a sabbatical and the Wright family vanished for nearly six months, some of it spent abroad, leaving me as Acting Headmaster.

This, on the whole, was a happy experience though there were times of anxiety. I enjoyed the responsibility, as I had at Lawrence College, and at my right hand was Andrew McFarlane, Head of School, a good friend then and now. We did however make the mistake of appointing a crook as second in command on the assumption that he would become a non-crook; this did not quite work out. For Speech Day I invited Robert Blake, my old Magdalen friend, to be the principal guest; Roger Sainsbury, Warden of Shrewsbury House, where he was doing impressive work, preached. As ever, Joy was a tower of strength having all the gifts that a headmaster's wife should have.

1973 was a good year; as I recollect it the school had begun to pull out of the uncertainties and difficulties of the previous half-dozen years; we had a crop of good boys at the top, led by a determined Head of School in David Fitzsimmons. Donald Wright was more relaxed, partly as a result of his sabbatical when, in his own words, he had got to know his family again and partly because even his furious pace had to slow down sometime. The buildings had been built, the Appeal had been successful in the main, Kingsland Hall was functioning, the Science Building was open. A new Chaplain seemed to promise a new approach, a promise however not fulfilled. Ten new masters were appointed about then. Five were good appointments, five were not. One – a scientist – did not last long and found to his own surprise, while sitting in the audience at Speech Day, that the Headmaster was saying that they were sorry to lose him. In the matter of successful appointments, Hardy and Peterson were well ahead of Wolfenden and Wright, a matter which, however, does not rest only on the ability to choose but also obviously depends upon the choice available. Before the war thirty per cent of Oxford graduates went into teaching of one sort or other; to-day (1993) the figure is two per cent. In one area however, an enormous mistake was made. When Micky Jones made his much-lamented departure for Radley – Radley! – he was succeeded by Trevor Dixon, before whose arrival I filled another interregnum, this time in the Bursary where I was Acting Bursar for a term. In reality, Jill Hurdman, the Bursar's admirable secretary, knew the answers to almost everything. I do not think I would like to be a bursar and I soon understood why Micky had seldom been seen in the Common Room; virtually every member of the staff seemed to have a need or a complaint. I have said earlier that Shrewsbury bursars come in two categories, alpha and gamma: Trevor Dixon was not an alpha. As a soldier he had no doubt been competent but he lacked the skills for this bigger and more complex job. Fortunately he stayed only two years.

Not a scholar himself, Donald Wright always felt the need for Shrewsbury to move with the educational times. To this end he appointed a part time teacher/tutor from Keele's education department to sharpen up the teaching of the staff. For someone to come in from outside to tell fairly intelligent and experienced schoolmasters what to do in the form room and get away with it was bound to be a tall order. We did try very hard to take Dr John Gilbert seriously. But when it was realised just how theory-ridden and jargon-soaked he was and that he hardly ever seemed to have been exposed to the full rigours of form room work, nor seemed to have much idea of what made boys tick, his cause was lost. He disappeared without a trace, to be sighted many years later in the *Times Educational Supplement* as the winner of the award for "the most pointless piece of research of the year" – 'The Role of the Telephone in Educational Research'. He was now apparently entirely immersed in jargon: "Within a framework which includes a review of the comparitive strengths of questionnaire and interview-based research and of the use of the telephone within both traditions, an account is given of an apparently innovative technique used to evaluate the trials of an educational database".

In the last year of the Wright regime we all felt as though we were in the cast of *Waiting for Godot*. Donald had clearly shot his bolt, an exploded volcano. He had done ten years hard labour, faced and overcome many problems, ridden out the Sixties and brought the ship into the quieter seventies. But what do headmasters, who are comparatively young, do next? The answer for Wright when at length it came was that he would be an Inspector of Schools. "I know only too well that it is time to leave", he said to his governors. He recognised that by his very success in encouraging a wide range of activities for the boys, he had perhaps taken the edge off intellectual sharpness – both for masters and boys. He hoped that his successor would be firstly "a scholarly teacher"; and that the school "[would] become more intellectually distinguished but no less happy".

What was not fully realised at the time – and many have been slow to realise it since – is that the Wright years saw the total demise of the Public School. In an earlier chapter I have suggested that the traditional Public School derived from elements of St Benedict, HM Prisons and the Versailles of Louis XIV. Where were these elements by 1975?

Whereas religious observance had been central, if only because all boys were gathered in Chapel eight times a week, now there were only two compulsory services. Whereas house 'dicks' in the evening had always consisted of prayers and maybe a hymn, now they were well on the way to being purely secular assemblies. Whereas many boys had once knelt by their beds in prayer, this was now unheard of. Whether there was more or less 'real religion' (whatever that might mean) in the school is naturally impossible to say. But outward observance had shrunk dramatically.

Greater freedom had meant that bounds were relaxed; more boys went down town, parties travelled far and wide to plays, concerts and lectures. Conversely into the Site from outside came parents much more frequently, visitors of all kinds – and girls! It had once been virtually a beatable offence to talk to a girl. In the sexually-relaxed climate of the Sixties, girls were constantly about the Site, took part in plays and concerts, cavorted at Saturday night discos and became girlfriends to senior boys. House-masters braced themselves for house dances and sighed with relief when they were over. One housemaster had an oft-repeated rule, "No horizontal snogging". Shades of the prison house did not begin to close upon the growing boy but rapidly dissolved in the teenage years.

I have referred earlier to the small pink book which listed in a few pages the school rules and in many pages the privileges. At one stage Donald Wright held this small book up at a housemasters' meeting and asked if anyone was interested in its continuance: no one was. But in fact this was a non-question put to the wrong people. The boys were already deciding that the whole hierarchical and elaborate social structure with the privileges and punishments which supported it should go; step-by-step demolition took place. Gradually too the slang words went out of use. Slang is the product of a closed community; it does not flourish in an open one.

Add to the above the demise of the compulsory CCF and it will be seen that the Public School, after a hundred years existence, was no more. For better or worse Shrewsbury was now a new type of independent school. What did this mean? Those interested will find in Colin Leach's book some long extracts taken from Bloxham Project reports. The one on 'Hartfield' refers to Shrewsbury. In a searching questionnaire filled in by the boys it emerged that Shrewsbury "was markedly different from all other boarding schools" in the degree of satisfaction with the school that was expressed by its pupils. I think that Donald Wright would like to be remembered by those 'Hartfield' judgements, reflecting the kind of school which he and his staff had sought to create.

He had expressed his philosophy in 1968. "I am convinced that there is nowadays only one ultimate authority whereby a boarding community of boys can retain stability and develop purpose, and that is the respect which boys have from knowing that there are men about them who really care and who enter into discussion with them; thereby there comes about an understood and appreciated atmosphere which makes it unreal for boys to identify masters only with authority".

It was a philosophy in which I wholly believed and which made my partnership with Donald, as his Second Master, a happy one. When Chairman of the Headmasters Conference he had sent me an advance copy of his big speech. "I think I should let you see it because without your encouragement and daily help it would certainly never have come about". Kind words for which I was grateful.

A book much quoted by Donald was Paul Tillich's *The Shaking of the Foundations*. The four hundred year-old foundations of Shrewsbury School were not shaken by Donald but the superstructure was quite radically re-shaped. He found a school of 523 boys; he left one of 634. Fees had been £147 per term; now they were £500. He had made seventy appointments to the teaching staff and had selected all the housemasters except one. He had appointed one good Bursar and one dud one. So much for figures. His real contribution cannot be thus measured; in these pages I have tried to give at least an indication of what it was.

CHAPTER XXIV

Second Master

Much may be made of a Scotchman if he be caught young
Dr Johnson

'The Burgage', Kennedy Road, proved to be a most happy family home and a centre for the children, now mostly elsewhere. Philippa was in Birmingham where she had various jobs under the 'Arts' umbrella and was soon the mother of Jasper and Jessica. Sadly her marriage disintegrated, though she and Tony lived near each other and harmoniously devoted themselves to bringing up the children. Bruce did not find the sea a career to sustain his interest and after a short essay into commercial life joined the RAF and became a helicopter pilot, soon to be married to Barbara – another wedding which we organised, Barbara's father being a widower. Robin had a successful university career at Durham, spent a year in Malawi on VSO, flirted with journalism and finally settled for teaching. Martin and Alan both went to Abberley. It was a great wrench; but they settled happily after the initial shock. Abberley as run by Ronnie Yates – a master of improvisation – was chaotic but happy. They then went to Malvern where I did a swap with the Headmaster, Martin Rogers, who sent his sons to Shrewsbury. I am still uncertain whether I was right not to have them at Shrewsbury. I feared that, as I played a central part in the school, it might have been embarrassing for them and possibly for me. I am no doubt prejudiced but I think that Shrewsbury was at that time a better school than Malvern; but both boys did well, Martin going to Oxford and Alan to Durham. Martin must be one of the few who, being asked to be Senior Chapel Prefect (Head of the School), declined; for good reason in my view.

Joy displayed all her usual energy in various fields, particularly in music where she not only quite transformed her violin playing through the teaching of Kato Havas, but also learned the viola and, later, the double bass. Active in the Shrewsbury Orchestral Society of which she became secretary, she played in other ensembles and went on orchestral playing courses at Attingham, in York and elsewhere. We were both members of St

Chad's church, where I was on the Parish Council, then under the immensely stimulating leadership of Christopher Spafford, the Vicar. He urged me to be ordained but I knew I had not the depth of commitment to take that step. However, I did become a Lay Reader which involved writing essays for a Lichfield canon. When I became Headmaster for the second time, I could not find time for this and told the authorities that I must postpone my appointment for a year. Bishop Stretton Reeve was on the phone in a trice; he didn't actually say "to hell with the essays" but bad me come to Lichfield to the next service of licensing. Stretton was a splendid bishop of the old sort, running his diocese as a man both with authority and under Authority, not afraid to take decisions, towering over lesser men and preaching with powerful conviction, every inch the rowing Blue that he was. To me he was an inspiration. When some years later I went to see him on his deathbed and he took my hand and asked me to pray with him, I felt a great spirit was passing from us.

Hitherto in my life in Shrewsbury, I had limited my activity to the school side of the river. Now I wanted to get more deeply into the local community, hence my involvement in St Chad's. Also I became chairman of the Civic Society whose president was George Trevelyan. I had always been interested in architecture and in the splendid heritage of Shrewsbury, bruised as it had been in my Pakistani absence by demolitions and the coming of some brutal architecture, the product of the late 1950s and early 1960s, particularly the hideous market hall and tower which so disfigure the Salopian scene. The Civic Society had been founded to fight such monstrosities, to attempt to protect what was good and to act as an independent non-political voice in the affairs of the town. I was chairman for eight years (in two spells).

At the behest of the famous Bronwen Lloyd-Williams, the archetype of the unmarried proprietor – headmistress, I became a governor of Moreton Hall. Bronwen had turned the school into a Trust but still dominated the Board of Governors; on the whole we all sat round and said yes. I did not then realise how closely I should be involved in the years ahead when Bronwen was no more and rocks would have to be negotiated. Another preoccupation was a governorship of the Royal Normal College for the Blind (as it then was), situated in rural Shropshire where Alan Laurie was now the Principal. This brought me into a quite different world; I soon found myself chairman of the Education Committee.

We had many visitors to 'The Burgage', some official, most not. Boys I had once taught now had sons at the school and would come and stay, as would friends from former days. Such were William and Caroline Cuthbert, Claude and Anne Boys-Stones, John and Alison Webb, whose youngest son was at Abberley: watching him play football in the garden with my sons I remarked to John on what a powerful kick Jonathan had for a boy of his age; a perceptive remark, as Jonathan became the record-breaking England full back. We also had two visits from Gary Karr and Harmon Lewis, Gary being perhaps the greatest double bass player in the world and also one of the world's great humourists.

Twice we visited Norway in the holidays, keeping up with my old friends from war-time days, the Brinkmanns and Dagmar Collett, as she now was, fast producing children, all of whom came over at different times to stay with us. My connection with these two families has been one of the happiest outcomes of those wartime years. How greatly pointed up and memorable are holidays when children are at boarding schools! We had some splendid times both at home and abroad, once going to Bermuda again to stay with Joy's mother, once to Halifax, Nova Scotia to stay with Joy's sister. But I have always had that itch to pack a small bag and push off by myself into unknown lands, a taste which India had encouraged. Joy was understanding enough to let me disappear for six weeks in 1974 and Donald Wright – as everyone else seemed to be having sabbaticals – allowed me leave of absence. So I went to Kenya to visit the Vasey family, to Pakistan to see Lawrence College again, to India to see two places I had never been to – Simla, with its still tangible air of Mrs Hauksbee and the Raj, and Lucknow where the Residency is still untouched from Mutiny days; I crawled all over it, reconstructing the famous siege which had always fascinated me. *Pietas* led me to carry away a loose marble chip from the grave of Sir Henry Lawrence.

I had resumed editing the *Salopian Newsletter* on my return from Pakistan. It is not easy to make this publication into anything other than a factual record of the school's successes (with oblique reference to its failures). I sought to enliven it by dealing with the unusual as well as the usual, and to interest former generations by introducing anecdotes or references with which they could identify. I had also been the keeper of the address list of Old Salopians since 1949 and so developed a considerable knowledge of the Salopian community. Unlike in some other schools, there has never been conflict (in my experience) between Old Salopians and the school or governors; the OS Club has always played a major part in Appeals and has sought to back the Headmaster of the day in whatever scheme was afoot. I remember Donald Lindsay telling me of his gloom when, shortly after he had become Headmaster of Malvern, the chairman at an Old Malvernian dinner ended his speech with the words, "And so, gentlemen, I think we can congratulate ourselves that Malvern is virtually entirely run by Old Malvernians". The decision of the governors to subsidise the *Newsletter* and of the Friends of Shrewsbury School to pay for a part-time, later full-time, secretary in the Old Salopian office illustrates well the commonality of purpose between school, Friends and Old Salopians. That the wheels turned smoothly was in large measure due to Peter Dixon, who had succeeded Graham Heath as Secretary to the OS Club, and who for twenty-one years gave his unstinted services with enthusiasm and efficiency. How often it is true that in clubs and associations, success or failure generally depends upon one key person, be he the chairman, secretary or treasurer, who is willing and able to carry the main burden of responsibility.

There were, however, Old Salopians who were disenchanted with the changes of the Wright regime. Those who thought of the school as unchanging and whose vision was of the short-haired blue-suited Salopians were shaken by the long-haired, jeans-and-jersey modern boy. Wolfenden used to say that Old Salopians managed to hold in conjunction two contradictory views, one that the school was the same as it had always been, the other that things had gone to the dogs since they left. There were not lacking those of the second viewpoint who seemed unaware of the pressures in society which were bound to be reflected in Salopian youth. However the proportion of Old Salopians sending their sons in no way declined during those years.

My duties as Second Master I found increasingly congenial; I enjoyed contact with all parts of the school, made it my business to know the name of every boy, endeavoured to assist new masters in their early stages and kept closely in touch with the praepostors. My teaching was largely to the second year boys, the Fifth form as it then was. I was a form master in the old-fashioned way, teaching history, English and Divinity, sometimes to VA, the top Fifth form, more often to VB. Also I found myself in charge of the fives again for a spell – a good time to be so as the powerful pair of Nick Pocock and Peter Worth won the Schools Championship. Peter was, I think, the most able ball games player that I can recollect.

In 1969 I had a very able VA, mostly scholars and intellectually sharp. There developed a remarkable *esprit de corps* in that group which made it a delightful year for me and, I hope, them. The names of Richard Hudson, Christopher Prentice, John Shawe-Taylor, Charles Bird, and Gerald Wilson come to mind. At the end of the year all declared on oath that they would meet again in fifteen years time notwithstanding the Works of the World, the Machinations of the Devil, the Requirements of Mammon and the Responsibilities of Matrimony (if any). So in 1984 a dinner was held and there round the table was every boy; they had been aged fifteen; now they were thirty. It was an occasion when I felt I was fortunate to have chosen schoolmastering as my profession. In 1970 I again had the year's scholars. To my disappointment the group never gelled or developed the togetherness of their predecessors. Such are group dynamics.

1974 took Joy and me to Churchill's in the place of Roger and Jan Blomfield, off to Australia on sabbatical. It had been through me that Roger had come to Shrewsbury, for we had been colleagues at Geelong. He ran Churchill's very well, though like some other members of the staff, had not always found it easy to keep in step with the Headmaster. As I later told him, I could see why he had chosen this particular term to be away. The Head of House and monitors were entirely anonymous, pleasant enough but with no drive or ability to control; so I had a more strenuous time than expected though there was always the support of Michael Hall, the resident tutor, to fall back on.

Naturally speculation was rife as to Wright's successor but in the Shrewsbury Common Room little was known of possible candidates. The short list was of three – the Revd Peter Pilkington, soon to go to King's Canterbury and afterwards St Paul's; M.S. Scott, Second Master at Winchester; and Eric Anderson, Headmaster of Abingdon, who got the vote. However, there had to be an interregnum in the 1975 summer term so once again I established myself in the Pentagon. Donald Wright left in a happier state of mind than might have been expected as the Archbishops of Canterbury and York had asked him to be their Appointments Secretary. So Donald vanished into the dim religious haze wherein he joined the ecclesiastical elite and laboured mightily in the conception and delivery of bishops.

I enjoyed that summer. Head of School was David Chance with whom I worked in close harmony. Apart from the School House where things were not good, the school faced no particular difficulty. That term was as summer terms always ought to be – the sun shone almost throughout. Speech Day was the old traditional event, stretched over three days with an attendance of ninety-five per cent of parents, a number of whom brought their caravans or tents and established camp round the running track. Our guest was Sir Richard Southern, President of St John's College, Oxford. On the morning of Speech Day he rang to say that owing to rail disruption he could not arrive until 11.40 a.m. Speeches began at 11.30. So when I took the stage with the governors there was a vacant chair beside me. How relieved I was, as I drew to the end of my speech, to see Sir Richard standing in the wings, having been rushed up from the station by Peter Hughes. He spoke brilliantly, setting the stamp on a memorable day. He wrote afterwards, "the impression which the school made on me on that lovely day has left a memory which I shall always cherish – it was like a scene from an ideal world. I expect it is not always like that, but to be capable of being so is an achievement of high quality".

That term the cricket XI was undefeated and the 1st VIII won the Schools' Event at Henley. It was pleasant to glide behind the winning crew in the launch and to commiserate with the opposing headmaster ("I thought your chaps rowed awfully well ..."). So fine was the weather that several times I had Chapel out in the Masters' Garden, the six hundred boys sitting round the old First War memorial from which I took the service. Another event was the Sounding of Retreat by the massed bands of the Light

Infantry on the Site, a stirring spectacle after which we entertained five hundred visitors to drinks.

As the term ended I could not but help thinking that Eric Anderson was fortunate indeed to succeed to a school with housemasters of the calibre of David Gee, Geoffrey Phillips, Roger Blomfield, Robin Moulsdale, Richard Raven, Michael Eagar, Robin Trimby and Arnold Ellis, with the academic guidance of Peter Hughes, and the wisdom of Walter Hamilton to fall back on. In fact in that term I had no communication with Walter save socially. He believed in letting a headmaster get on with it. So much had I enjoyed the term that I almost – but not quite – wished I had answered differently to a question Walter had put to me six months previously when Wright's resignation was made known. He asked me if I would like to be considered for the post of Headmaster, intimating that several governors had suggested to him that I would have their support. I had no hesitation in giving a negative answer. I felt confident that I could run the school but was certain that the new headmaster should be a bigger man than I was and should come with outside experience. I had long since discarded the idea of headmastering which so cut one off from the boys and burdened one with paper, parents, finance and committees. In my own role as *inter rex*, I had managed to keep these demands to a minimum and spent my days out on the Site, while for those who raised awkward policy questions, I had a practised answer, "I am so glad you brought up that point but it has wide ramifications which I am sure must be left to the future Headmaster to deal with".

Any lingering thoughts I might have had about being headmaster were entirely banished by the arrival of Eric and Poppy Anderson. He was a big man in all senses with a touch of Scottish ruggedness and a certain initial shyness but confident and, when need be, decisive. A scholar himself, where Donald Wright had been hesitant, he could take on the eggheads of the staff on their own terms. Whereas some had categorised Wright as being a trendy liberal/ideas/committee/media man – on the whole unfairly in my view – none of these epithets would fit Anderson. Not that he was without ideas – far from it – but his general stance was conservative; he was really a pretty tough educational pragmatist. During his time Margaret Thatcher replaced Wilson and Callaghan and, as Laurence Le Quesne has pointed out to me, there was a remarkable parallel in Anderson replacing Wright; there was certainly "a smack of firm government" and sometimes a touch of *ex cathedra*. This upset some of the liberals, particularly in the first years. Robin Moulsdale muttered darkly of Hardy *redivivus*. It took Anderson some time to adjust to the Salopian *modus vivendi*, in which there was a good deal of flexibility not to say looseness. One might at Shrewsbury echo Walter Hamilton's reported statement to the assembled freshmen at Magdalene, "We don't have any rules at Magdalene but if you break any of them I shall certainly send you down".

The arrival or rather the explosion of Poppy Anderson on the Salopian scene could not go unnoticed by any denizen of the Site, exalted or humble. Her energy and participation in all sides of life had not been seen in a Headmaster's wife since the days of Hester Alington. Well able to cope with all situations, she was the ideal complement to Eric. Humour was never far away. Visiting a bedsitter in Oldham's which was in an even more chaotic state than boys' bedsitters generally are, she remarked, "What you want in here, Guy, is a good woman."

It is small wonder that the Andersons found the Headmaster's house on Canonbury unsatisfactory in its remoteness from the school; it was a pleasant suburban house that might have been anywhere. So the Ashton Road house was purchased, close to the action. Whereas some headmasters like to be remote, the Andersons liked to look out of the windows and see boys. As soon as they arrived they launched a large-scale programme of entertainment; all the new boys came to tea at different times; in that first year there were 282 guests to dinner and innumerable visitors to coffee. Very soon their knowledge of the community was extensive. Eric found time to be out and about and was less study-bound than his predecessor, nor did he get involved in the HMC world and its committees and commitments. And there was time too for local involvement in the town and with local schools. He soon gained a reputation as a speaker which led to invitations to dinners and other local functions.

Particularly impressive to me was the trouble he took with staff appointments. It is an exhausting process and, as I had found myself, all too easy to get into the position where one says, "well, not exactly what I was looking for but he's the best of the bunch and will probably do". Eric never did this. He was prepared to be patient, to temporise and advertise again; he always was careful to consult his Heads of Faculty and his Second Master. As a result he made some excellent appointments, bringing Jeremy Goulding, Stewart Roberts, Gordon Woods, Robin Case and Hugh Ramsbotham to Shrewsbury, all to be successful housemasters; finding Mark Williams to run the fives and cricket (but not the fixtures) with superabundant energy and Mark Dixon to run the football. How fortunate Shrewsbury was to have a man of Mark's calibre, with his background at Eton and St Luke's, Exeter, when in other schools the football had fallen into the hands of much lesser men. Another good appointment was Simon Funnell who came as Head of English. He replaced Willie Jones, whose offical spheres of activity had been the English faculty and the Hunt but who will be remembered fondly by many Salopians for what he was – an enthusiastic, sensitive, open and vulnerable man of complete integrity. One was fortunate to be counted amongst his friends. Willie's going was mysterious. Just as Basil Oldham's coming to the staff is always said to have been because, having been a temporary master, no one remembered to tell him not to come back, so it seemed that no one had quite told Willie to stay. He was appointed Head of English at Haileybury, cancelled the appointment for a trivial reason, was next heard of taking the qualification for teaching English overseas at Edinburgh following which he, whose most ambitious journey so far had been a bus ride to Hereford, flew off to teach in Japan where he has been happy ever after, in his spare time compiling a lengthy autobiography in verse whose successive volumes periodically thunder through the letter box.

Under Wright so many activities and alternatives had been developed that the School was in danger of becoming a series of disconnected organisms with little in the way of a unifying force. Long gone was the day when, for instance, every boy watched the school's football matches; now the XI played with its customary skill, but watched by perhaps fifty or sixty fans, others being busy elsewhere, ignorant of the matches or the results. It could well be argued that this was as it should be – each to his own activity – but it did mean that the school tended to lack a centre. I do in fact recollect Donald Wright quoting the well known lines of W.B. Yeats, "Things fall apart, the centre will not hold ..." when addressing the staff. The truth was that the school had become *à la carte* rather than *table d'hôte*.

Eric and Poppy Anderson provided a strong focal centre. The edges became focused and there was a tightening of discipline. The Headmaster was now living at the centre of things; Poppy was in the bookshop, not far away. Donald Wright had built the 'Pentagon' as a headmaster's study where, like the captain of the ship, he could look out in all directions through its angled windows. The corollary was that everyone could look in and Anderson withdrew into an inner study, at the same time providing me with what I had so far never had, an office near him, which I shared with Peter Hughes and, when Peter left, with Lyn Duffield who, however, never used it, his interest in the school being carefully circumscribed around his essential work.

Anderson did not waste time before tackling immediate problems, the foremost being the School House now in its second year of divided control. Before Anderson came, Adrian Struvé in his typically unassuming way had quietly mentioned that I should remember when discussion took place that "the Struvés are expendable". It says much that he could thus express it, having been brought into what was in any case a most difficult situation which, through no fault of his own, had deteriorated. Anderson was in no doubt; the School House must go back to being a unity, thus confirming what I and others – Joy and Mary Taylor among them – had instinctively felt, namely that if there was not proper physical vertical division, the House would defy any attempt at partition, an illustration of what Thring of Uppingham had called "the influence of the almighty wall".

But who was to be housemaster? No candidate on the Site commended himself and so Anderson, boldly, looked outside and lighted on Tom Wheare, then teaching at Eton, aged thirty-two, a bachelor, self-confident, energetic, clear on the essentials of schoolmastering, though given to imaginative unorthodoxy, and undaunted by the prospect of taking on the biggest job at Shrewsbury without any Salopian background. Eric gave Tom two years to get things sorted out; he gave him a first class resident house tutor in Richard Field and together they set about a 'back to basics' approach. I played a tiny part in that Tom asked me to be one of his house tutors, an interesting role for a former housemaster. I was able to help in another way for I was still dealing with entries: any boys of quality without a house designation on the general list I steered in the direction of the School House. Thus it was, if my recollection is correct, that School House greatly benefited from having such as Mark Wormald, the Robarts brothers, Richard Goldsborough, the Reakes-Williams brothers, Clive Hayward and others. "It is vital that Mr Wheare succeeds" said Anderson to his governors. He did. Particularly strong in drama and music, Tom was a broad-brush man and covered a wide field. But the influence of the School House got him in the end. Like others who had gone before, matrimony overtook him.

Anderson found the Chapel services 'dreary'; and a chaplain who was not in tune with the boys. After one sermon he asked me if I could find any meaning in what we had just heard; gloomily we came to a negative answer. So there must be a change and Eric was unafraid of confrontations when his mind was made up. But, as all headmasters know, the field from which good chaplains are drawn is narrow indeed. There are plenty of applicants, eighty per cent of whom are men who have found no niche in the Church of England and are restlessly seeking pastures new, having failed in previous appointments. Few men of quality seek school chaplaincies. Searching in my mind, I suddenly thought of David Allcock who had been a curate at St Chad's, and was now a school chaplain in Somerset. Protocol about contacting him had to be carefully observed; his headmaster was of an explosive disposition. But I was able to bring together Eric and David; they liked each other; the appointment, after devious but legal manoeuvres, was made. David brought a new approach to the Chapel. It took time for him to settle, time for him to communicate, time to have an effect on that restless, uncooperative element in the congregation which had been contained, but no more than that, for ten years or so. David, not a product of the university but of the textile mill and Mirfield, brought sensitivity and imagination to the services and developed into an inspirational preacher, fired with the Holy Spirit. An individualist and a perfectionist, he did not find it easy to work with any of the assistant chaplains who came and went. It was an idea of mine that we might get an assistant chaplain who would also be a curate at St Chad's, thus carrying on his work on both sides of the river to the benefit, I hoped, of both communities. I still think it was a good idea but, to my chagrin, it quite failed to work. Ian Browne was appointed and got so interested in schoolmastering (which he seemed to think he had discovered), that he had little time for the town.

Anderson had no hesitation in restoring the Chapel itself to what it had formerly been, in so far as was possible. The reredos was again exposed, the hanging cross removed and – an innovation this – the choir stalls were put down to congregation level; but nothing could extract the clergy stalls from St Mary's. True to his Presbyterian background, Anderson had a feeling for decency and order in worship. By touches here and there, Allcock pushed the services a little higher up the candlestick in the Mirfield direction: candles appeared by the dozen! Never had such illumination been seen at Shrewsbury. Another innovation was to appoint an Organist and Choir-master – a separate post from that of Director of Music. This has brought a succession of younger men, Denny Lister being the first, who have contributed greatly to the Chapel services.

Less happy were his appointments to the post of Director of Music. The standard of much of the music was high under Stan Lester but the higher the standard the fewer boys participated. It was a fine achievement to perform the Verdi Requiem or Beethoven's Ninth, but the number of boys in choir, orchestra and audience was tiny. Music had little impact on the school as a whole. John Yarnley as Director was more a man for the masses and struck a few sparks but soon departed. Colin Edmundson struck rather fewer and also departed after a brief stay.

Another departure, not unanticipated, was that of Bursar Dixon; the job was beyond him and in his stead came Ron Harrison, who had been Bursar at Abingdon, ex RAF, a man well up in the alpha class. On first meeting Ron one was not necessarily impressed. He spoke a good deal with his eyes shut or looking out of the window. But gradually his qualities were revealed – sympathy, understanding, integrity, business sense and an even temper. Soon all employees, high and low, realised that they had a bursar of real stature. Before his coming there was another short interregnum, so I found myself once again at the Bursar's desk, hoping that I understood the content of all the pieces of paper I was signing. Among other things I learnt a lot about parents and fees – particularly reluctant payers with their ingenious arguments, subtle excuses, and devious avoiding actions. Another area where Eric Anderson took firm steps was in establishing Dayboys in the old Sanatorium, impelled thither by the never-failing energy of David Gee, a move which enabled two houses to be formed soon containing sixty or so boys each.

Many years later, Eric Anderson would say to a group of aspiring headmasters that it was a good experience to have a first class crisis early in one's time at a new school. He certainly did. A few days before the beginning of his third term, Geoffrey Phillips, housemaster of Rigg's, went off with the wife of another member of staff. Although the intrigue had been known to a few, it burst with startling suddenness on the many, including the Headmaster and me. These things didn't happen in establishments like ours. I volunteered to go into Rigg's as a temporary housemaster, an offer which Eric at once accepted and the bewildered parents found that they had lost their housemaster only a couple of days before the summer term of 1976 began. It was not an easy assignment. Betty Phillips stayed in the House to run the domestic side, really because she had little alternative, and bravely saw the term through. I lived a split life, having some time off to be at home. The boys, as boys do, quickly accepted the situation, and the rhythm of school life soon absorbed them, but I found that the senior year were split into two antagonistic groups and had been since they first arrived as new boys. Their late housemaster's attention being not wholly undivided, this situation had never improved, so as a temporary housemaster I had some difficult diplomacy on my hands. We got through the term all right but it was the least enjoyable of my housemastering experiences in the four Houses where I have held that office and I was glad to deliver Rigg's into the safe hands of Richard and Caroline Auger who soon got things sorted out.

CHAPTER XXV

The Seventies

Westward on the high-hilled plains
Where for me the world began,
Still, I think, in newer veins
Frets the changeless blood of man.
Housman

After three years, Eric Anderson could write, "1978 has been a year in which schoolmastering has been particularly enjoyable". He was beginning to see some of the results of his attempt to sharpen the academic performance, particularly that of the more intelligent boys. In 1975–78 there were forty-three Oxford and Cambridge awards, the best results since the last Peterson years, 1959–62. His endeavour to attract more clever boys seemed to be succeeding, partly through initiatives with prep schools and partly by the institution of a Junior Scholarship scheme. We had a good Bursar in place, able to cope with the appalling inflationary pressures – the fees doubled in Anderson's time – and able too to fight off NUPE and other trades unions who were uttering threats of strikes. It was at this time that plans to sell the School Library, under consideration for many years, were finally laid to rest, Walter Hamilton declaring that as he could not have defended the sale it would be advisable to have a new Chairman who could, should the sale take place. Vandalism it might seem to some; others argued that this considerable asset – hardly used by the school and in effect a museum – should be turned into cash and the money used for academic purposes where the need was great. In the shadowy background for some years had been the figure of Dr Feisenburger of Sotheby's whom the governors had periodically consulted about the value of the library. RIP therefore the ghost of Basil Oldham.

An Anderson innovation was the institution of the Harvard Fellowship, through which a carefully selected Harvard graduate joins the Shrewsbury staff for a year, to teach, to participate and to be American. This excellent concept has flourished greatly and brought to Shrewsbury periodically the Reverend Peter Gomes, the black Professor of Theology at Harvard who has selected the Fellows with unerring discernment and has brought much wisdom and laughter into our lives. Another from afar who featured on the Site at this time was Mr Semaan of the Middle East and of deep pocket. He arrived unannounced one day wishing to enrol his eldest son immediately. It was the middle of a term and the school was full. Shown round Churchill's to convince him that there was no space, he at once offered to build a wing on to the House to enlarge the accommodation. This was not taken up – but was carefully noted. In fact, his three sons, Hadi, Fadi and Nagi all came to Churchill's in due time, the eldest, Fadi, playing in the football XI. Choosing his opportunity on the touchline when Fadi had scored a fine goal, the Headmaster reminded Mr Semaan of his offer to build for the school but said that squash courts were what were most needed. Fired with enthusiasm on account of Fadi's success, Mr Semaan showed an interest which Eric Anderson carefully nurtured: and four Semaan squash courts ultimately materialised. It was at one time suggested they might be called Hadi, Fadi, Nagi and Daddi.

If Eric Anderson felt that he was much enjoying schoolmastering by 1978 and that he had by now the measure of Shrewsbury, I too would say that I was much enjoying being his Second Master. Our relations were of the happiest. By about this time I felt that the school was settling down on the Wright foundations and beginning to find the balance between liberalism, which could easily degenerate into licence, and the old authoritarianism against which 'youth' had so often rebelled. As I have said previously, the key was the network of personal relationships which criss-crossed the body politic both through the formal tutoring system and in so many other ways, based on shared interest and activities. I think with pleasure of my own three or four tutees every year who had chosen me and with whom a sympathetic understanding developed. These relationships, spread over the whole school, and seen in the still continuing form master structure in the Lower School were what really kept the show on the road so successfully. The general air might seem laid back, even casual, but below the facade was much achievement and striving for excellence.

Tom Wheare and Richard Field were winning in the School House. Eric had a good set of housemasters (with one exception) and the senior staff contained people of quality. In the Biology Lab was Bertie Fowler, widely-read, sceptical, private, always with a band of devotees who learned far more than biology in his teaching periods. The old Science Building, now wonderfully transformed into a splendid art centre, saw John Alford running, in his own quiet way, a department increasing in both size and quality, still finding time for his own delightful painting, examples of which decorate the walls of so many Kingsland houses. After several departures and arrivals, Laurence Le Quesne had settled at Shrewsbury to add his touch of brilliance to the history department in which Michael Ling had dropped anchor for the duration. The Welsh hills had long been echoing to the cries of encouragement, instruction and witticisms of Michael Hall, whose creation of the Basic Year – the compulsory outward-bound type training of the second year boys – has been one of the really outstanding achievements of the last twenty-five years. When it is said, "There aren't any 'characters' on the staff any more", one need look no further than F.M.H. and Mark Mortimer, guardian of the Royal Shrewsbury School Hunt, wit and versifier, whose comments on the passing scene in English or Latin have punctured pretentiousness and sometimes needled his colleagues, drawing occasional headmagisterial reproofs. Another who added his skill away from the central spotlight was Chris Etherington, whose tact and firmness made him an ideal warden of Tudor Court, refuge of sixth formers who wished to leave their Houses for one reason or other, a jazz enthusiast and performer, supervisor of the Tudor Court bar and guru to the discontented who restlessly looked for sympathy. Then there was the patient and efficient labour of Simon Baxter in any field to which he was called; Roger Blomfield's ability as River Master ('Sophisticated Scholars with aplomb, / All bow before Sabrina's idol, Blom'); the infectious enthusiasms of Wally Marsh; the erudition of James Lawson on all matters appertaining to the Library or local history; and Martin Knox's careful coaching of cricket and football, interspersed by long-distance pilgrimages up and down the country to cricket grounds and opera houses. These, with those more recently appointed, made for an enterprising and co-operative staff.

In 1978 Nick Bevan launched another rowing spectacular (having already taken the 1st VIII to Australia) by arranging a visit to South Africa which he invited me to join. These were the days when sporting tours to South Africa had ceased and feelings ran high. Eric Anderson was however prepared to sanction the tour, feeling (as I did) that nothing but good could come of contacts on this level, whatever might be the arguments at the international level. So we slipped away quietly for three fascinating weeks in which, apart from rowing, we endeavoured to gain as wide a view of South African society as possible. Our hosts being white and of English stock, we naturally saw things from their point of view but in various ways we had contact with Blacks, Coloureds and Afrikaaners, spent a day in Soweto, were entertained in Parliament by two opposition MPs, saw how the gold mines worked and were the recipients of a bewildering variety of political views.

I broke away from the party at times as I wanted to see Martin who, now having a GAP year, was working in the Transkei in a psychiatric hospital for Blacks run by a wonderfully dedicated and experienced missionary doctor, Guy Danes. Martin had dropped into the role of hospital general handyman without difficulty. With him I visited Cape Town to stay with

David Philip, a Magdalen friend and a member of that splendid cricket team of 1947, and also to meet a third member of that team, David Knight. We spent a happy time with them and their families and visited the famous Bishops School from which so many Rhodes scholars and others had come to Oxford.

We were in South Africa for Easter and I visited several churches; one in a white suburb which was indistinguishable from, say, Surbiton; on Good Friday I was in a multi-racial church at a three-hour service taken by Beyers Naudé, the heroic Afrikaans pastor who had been head of the Christian Institute and was one of the few Afrikaaners to denounce apartheid. Under house detention, he was permitted to come and take the service but not to have any personal communication with any of the congregation. It was an uplifting occasion. The hymn book was in four languages, English, Sotho, Afrikaans and Zulu so each sang in his own language; the result was not at all unpleasing. On Easter Day I was in Johannesburg Cathedral with a vast concourse of all colours. I also visited a USPG missionary parish priest near Pretoria to whom I had been sending periodicals for some time. He had a difficult parish, largely of Coloureds, amongst whom drink was the major problem. So through many personal acquaintances I came in contact, at least superficially, with various sides of African life.

Having some knowledge of the 'Old Commonwealth' countries, Australia, New Zealand and Canada, I was interested to compare South Africa. If – and a big if – politics could be discarded, there is no doubt where I would prefer to live: in South Africa, though preferably in the Cape and not on the high veldt. I thought it was a most splendid country, in climate, in scenery and in pleasant living – as a white of course!

By 1980 my sons had gone to universities, Martin to Oxford after his GAP year in South Africa. He enjoyed Exeter College and his Second in History was not all that far from being a First. Evangelical Christianity was his guiding enthusiasm. Alan meanwhile had taken off for a year as a jackaroo in the outback in Queensland and courageously survived that harsh baptism into a wholly new type of life. Thence he went to Durham to read General Arts. Both boys met their future wives at their respective universities.

Joy and I had numerous guests at 'The Burgage' and tried to entertain as freely as our commitments allowed. Music continued to occupy Joy but it was at this time that she became converted to 'born again' Christianity, joining the Bayston Hill evangelical parish church. Her energies were increasingly absorbed in evangelism. We had two splendid holidays about this time. Robin had married Diane in 1975 and after a period teaching in Darjeeling, had joined the British Council and was stationed in Tanzania. We visited them and saw something of that country and Zanzibar. Another foreign trip was to Gibraltar where Bill Jackson, an Old Salopian friend, was Governor. He invited us to stay and we had a most delightful ten days at the Convent where I had stayed some twenty years before. It was a luxurious time; Gibraltar is, I believe, the only place where the Governor's House still has footmen. There is also a Governor's cottage, high on the Rock with a fine view of the shipping in the Straits, isolated and private: here we spent some mornings watching the passing ships, reading and writing, the footmen bringing lunch in the Land Rover. It was idyllic.

It was at this time that the old plan of founding a boys' boarding school in Iran was again advanced, a matter of interest to me who had been offered the headmastership of the putative school in 1961 which never materialised. Again the British Council were asked to present a plan and they turned to Eric Anderson. So it was that he and I with Peter Hughes, Tom Wheare and the Bursar from Charterhouse (where a lot of recent building had taken place) found ourselves on the plane for Teheran for two weeks' study and recommendation. We were well looked after, stayed in fine hotels, consumed mountains of caviare, saw various officials and ministers, and were entertained by our ambassador and the Prime Minister. We also worked hard, producing – as we thought – a highly practical plan with a recommended site on the Caspian (good for rowing!). These were, of course, the days of the Shah, who apparently warmly supported the idea of the school. Did we but know it, these were the very last days of his reign. This we could not in any way detect. Naturally we, as casual visitors, could only form superficial opinions, but from none of the many people we met did we ever gather the slightest hint that there was instability or any uncertainty as to the future. Yet shortly after our visit the whole structure began to tremble and shake. Was the idea of a British-type boarding school just too much? Had we been the straw that broke the camel's back? Was the Ayatollah's first action to consign our report to the anti-Western flames?

As the Seventies came to an end, the Salopian ship of state seemed to be rolling steadily forward. Despite rocketing fees – £1,000 a term at the end of the decade in contrast with £225 at the beginning of it – the numbers had gone up over the same period from 547 to 643. Walter Hamilton was still Chairman, Ron Harrison had a firm grasp of the economic levers, educational politics carried no immediate threat, and Shrewsbury had escaped damaging scandals concerning drugs or other misdemeanours which so excited the popular press. At this point a heavy blow fell. Michael McCrum having come to the end of his time at Eton, speculation became rife as to the identity of his successor, Eric Anderson's name being freely bandied around. I spent a long whisky-filled evening with Eric talking it through, but I could sense that he was eager to go – and for a man of proper ambition it was a unique chance. His hesitation was caused by the shortness of his stay at Shrewsbury and the feeling of letting the school down. I had no hesitation in urging him to allow his name to be put on the short list, saying that Shrewsbury would manage without him, realising that if he allowed this chance to pass by it would never come again and he might reproach himself indefinitely for the opportunity missed. Eton wrote to four existing headmasters – Dennis Silk at Radley (who was not interested), Peter Pilkington of King's Canterbury and Ian Beer. Eric was chosen. It was sad to see him and Poppy go, for they had totally absorbed themselves in the Salopian scene and obviously felt fully at home in it. Their leaving dinner was in one way sad, but in another a joyous culmination of so much that had been successfully achieved. Punctilious about small things, Eric had insisted that notices should be attached to notice boards by four drawing pins. His leaving present to the Common Room was a small brass urn containing several hundred pins; it is in use still.

Once more there had to be an interregnum: once more I found myself on the stage of the Alington Hall addressing the school as Headmaster. Through my memory passed all the roles I had played on that stage – an alto in my dickey in the Concert Choir; an actor in various comedies; tuba player in the orchestra; imitating Jack Buchanan in straw hat and white flannels; conducting the School Band; author of skits and parodies; organiser of concerts for the 'Mish'; even once playing a two-piano item with Peter Ingrams; more recently taking a favourite Gilbert and Sullivan role, that of the Judge in *Trial by Jury*; and now again as Headmaster in what had become a familiar role.

This time my headmastering was in the Michaelmas term. Before it began I played a joke on *The Times*. Shrewsbury then, no longer now, inserted a notice concerning the beginning of term, in those ridiculous columns in which schools reveal to an awaiting public who is Captain of Lacrosse and who is Keeper of the Pancake. My notice said, *inter alia*, that M.L. Charlesworth would be 'Acting Headmaster for the Michaelmas Term notwithstanding which Term will end on 13th December'. Two days later *The Times* was on the telephone. I answered with a wry smile: I had been rumbled. But the sub-editor only wanted to say that they preferred to spell 'headmaster' without a capital letter. So they published my notice intact. I was fortunate to have James Cross as Head of School, out of the Yarlet and Oldham's stables and bound soon for Magdalen as a Choral Scholar. He was succeeded by Andrew Berry, son of 'Sam' Berry, noted Salopian geneticist and ecologist and the best expounder of a Christian view of Creation I know. With experienced housemasters and a strong team of praepostors, the term passed quietly enough, a contrast to the somewhat jumpy situation back in 1973, during my first spell in the Pentagon. In particular, the School House now contained a really good set of boys and the anxieties which had surrounded that establishment were forgotten.

My relations with the Governing Body were very cordial, Walter

Hamilton still being Chairman, though nearing retirement. A great loss had been the premature death of Pat Young in 1979; for fifteen years he had been the linchpin of the school's finances, working closely with successive Bursars and Headmasters. No school could be better served. About the same time Tony Chenevix-Trench died, in his last year as Headmaster of Fettes. I had not seen much of Tony in recent years but I felt his loss keenly. Our names stood next to each other in the school register and we had shared much – and hoped to do so again in retirement. I had been in Pakistan during his time at Eton which had not been a success. He was ill-advised to accept that position. His great powers were as a teacher, as a personal communicator, and as a friend who radiated intelligence, wit and charm in a delightfully informal way. In a small school like Bradfield these qualities were sufficient, so long as someone else was keeping an eye on administration, and Tony had John Moulsdale to do that (though there was a time when Tony had offered the succession to a certain House to two people). But the direction of a school like Eton, with its hierarchy, its social position and its magnitude, called for formality, for delegation, for administrative competence and for the dignity of a figurehead. The boys soon called him 'Chummy'; well-intentioned as his friendliness was, the attitude was not appropriate. I wonder if one can be Headmaster of Eton without being at least six feet tall, preferably six feet four or five. Tony in retirement intended to write a book about his experiences – *Four Loves* – covering Shrewsbury, Bradfield, Eton and Fettes; it would have been good reading. Another death about this time was of Mrs Sawyer, widow of H.A.P. Sawyer, Headmaster from 1916 to 1932. She had expressed a wish that her ashes should rest beside her husband's, below the Sanctuary tiles in the School Chapel. One day her ashes arrived in a tube in the Headmaster's office, to the great distress of my secretary who would not touch them ('Oh Mr Charlesworth'!!). Mr Rogers, the school builder, and I then repaired to the Chapel and started taking up the Sanctuary tiles. The first thing we came across was the casket containing the ashes of J.B. Oldham. If there was one person Mrs Sawyer could not stand it was J.B.O. and the black joke of uniting them in death did pass through my mind: we struggled on with the tiles. Alas, we never found Canon Sawyer, but knowing roughly where he must be, we laid Mrs Sawyer to rest – and as far away from Oldham as possible.

At this time there had reached Shrewsbury the influence of the Bhagwan Rajneesh of Poona. David Brown had found his way to the ashram and become a follower, the last development in a career on the staff which had taken him gradually from conformity to radicalism. (It was he, for instance, who had suggested that the time had come for boys to stop 'capping' masters.) David had flown the lone and somewhat forlorn flag of Geography for many years; he had become interested in art and had been instrumental in organising an annual Speech Day exhibition of London artists. His house at Nesscliffe doubled as an art gallery. Now it became a staging post for followers of the Bhagwan – indifferent soup and bed on the floor, said to merit two stars in the The Good Guru Guide. David, with his bristling black beard, had decided that the time had come to part with Shrewsbury School, and with his wife.

Robin Moulsdale, still on the staff though no longer a housemaster, followed David's trail to Poona where he spent a sabbatical and was thus transformed into a disciple of the Bhagwan, growing a beard which made him look at least ten years older and wearing bright clothing which made him an incongruous figure on the Site which he had adorned for so long; his separation from his much loved wife Julie, far advanced with MS, caused anguish to their friends, as did a BBC broadcast some time later in which Robin described his spiritual aeneid and its consequences. As Headmaster for the moment, I took the opportunity of suggesting to Robin that parents might be doubtful of paying the fees for their son to be taught by a Rajneesh disciple. I hoped thus to spare embarrassment to the next Headmaster. Robin took the point that the time had indeed come to leave Shrewsbury and so, after some negotiation, he went off to pursue his interests elsewhere.

In January 1981 Simon and Diana Langdale arrived. A boy at Tonbridge, he had been a housemaster at Radley and Headmaster of Eastbourne College and was thus well experienced. Simon was a man of considerable personal charm and sound sense, but took a little time to adjust to the esoteric Salopian ways of doing things. What did Shrewsbury need at this stage? A firm hand at the helm, a steady course and no shaking of the foundations. This is broadly what Simon provided while Diana, once she had discovered that life north of Watford was possible, embarked on a breathless whirl of activity both in the school community and outside it.

Langdale was able to benefit from the excellent Anderson appointments when it came to selecting a new generation of housemasters. Thus he was able to give the two Dayboy Houses, Radbrook and Port Hill, separate housemasters in Stewart Roberts and Gawen Harvey, to appoint Jeremy Goulding to Oldham's when Robin Trimby moved off to be Headmaster of Prestfelde, and to unleash the manifold energies of Richard Field on Ridgemount. Peter Morris, now risen far above his PE origins, was re-called from Dorset where he had been teaching for some years, to be housemaster of Churchill's. When Tom Wheare moved on to be Head-master of Bryanston, Hugh Ramsbotham took on the heavy responsibility of School House which he has so admirably discharged over the years.

The conversion of the gymnasium to a theatre was by far the most successful building project of recent years. Built originally by H.H. Hardy, that devotee of Physical Training, realm to many of Sergeant-Major Joyce, a brilliant transformation was effected resulting in a delightful 250-seat theatre, almost entirely within the shell of the old gym. More controversial was the erection of the new gymnasium (or sports hall to use the jargon), which – practical as it may be – has been an aesthetic disaster so far as the Site is concerned. I suggested that we should get Robert Hardy, actor son of H.H.H., to open the new theatre, symbolising in the change in function of the building the contrasting interests of father and son. He came, and much enjoyed seeing the Site again and his old home, Kingsland House.

Numbers being buoyant, investigation was made into improving and enlarging the existing boarding houses, now overfull. Instead a bold decision was made to build another boarding house – the first since Oldham's in 1911. This, The Grove, has been a success, both architecturally and in practice, in the hands of its first housemaster, Peter Fanning, building up from difficult early days to full functioning in a surprisingly short space of time. But alas for the wisdom of the planners! Whereas The Grove was meant to be followed by a phased reduction in the numbers in the other Houses, the decrease has been negligible.

Langdale did not long have the guidance of Walter Hamilton who retired from the Governing Body in 1981. He had enjoyed his years as Chairman and always said that Shrewsbury gave him less trouble than any other body of which he was a member. His visits to the Site were always congenial social occasions; he was one who enjoyed the chatter and gossip of the community ("The trouble with me is that I haven't got any Big Talk"). He was succeeded by a man of a different type, Sir Peter Swinner-ton-Dyer, of formidable intellect and total efficiency but one who confined his interest to the meetings which he chaired with such competence; no time for chat or indeed for tea. But Shrewsbury has continued to be well governed. I was glad to play a small part in bringing to the Governing Body two Old Salopians of quality, Nicholas Barber and Jim Sanger.

Although in 1981 I was sixty-two years old, no one had said anything to me about retiring but I felt the time had come to leave the centre of the stage. I had been Second Master for twelve years and was always conscious of how I used to feel about old men staying on too long; Richard Raven was at hand to succeed to the position and was to put his own particular stamp on it. Joy and I had done what we could to see the Langdales established. But my retirement was gradual; I continued to teach for another couple of years, kept on editing the *Newsletter* and continued my work in the Old Salopian Club where now we had a professional secretary, Dee Dakers, to whom I was able to delegate more and more and to whose devotion and industry all Old Salopians owe a considerable debt of gratitude.

The year 1982 was the centenary of the move from the town. I had been thinking for some time as to how we might celebrate this; obviously a time for Old Salopians *en masse* to be invited, with meetings, dinners, exhibitions and so on, as there had been in 1932. But what extra could we do? What could we do which was different? It was Tom Wheare who supplied the idea. Looking out from the Pentagon where we were having a meeting, he sketched the idea of a pageant with the backdrop of the School Buildings. At once I went to work on this: but more than a pageant. We could take a leaf from *son et lumière* and have a pageant in darkness with sound and music and lighting – scenes from the school's history. So came about *A Most Uncommon Site* (or *Move Over Mr Moss*); I wrote the book which was then scripted and directed by Robin Case with great flair and competence. Marshalling his forces, working with lights and music and arranging such dramatic scenes as the School Buildings fire of 1905, took all his ingenuity. Simon Langdale had asked former headmasters to the celebrations and Joy and I had dinner at the Headmaster's House with the Wolfendens, Wrights and Andersons, before progressing, in evening dress, to witness the performance. The drizzly rain fell steadily; I sat next to Jack Wolfenden in the front row under an umbrella, he by now quite aged; I wished to sink into the ground; obviously we should be in for a fiasco. But Robin Case had courage; he decided the performance should go ahead, the rain cleared and we saw a very fair likeness to what I had had in my mind for months.

At the Commemoration Service in the Chapel next day, it fell to me to preach. The lessons were read by Jack Wolfenden and Donald Wright, the prayers said by Eric Anderson. It was a gathering, with Simon Langdale, of four headmasters, a unique occasion. I was pleased when Jack came up to me after the service and said, "I give that sermon alpha, a mark I have seldom awarded". Perhaps at last he felt justified in appointing me to the staff all those years ago.

Those celebrations were to me the climax of my Salopian life. It wanted only a few weeks to the fiftieth anniversary of my entering the school in my Eton collar, frightened out of my wits.

CHAPTER XXVI

Retirement

Is there no bright reversion in the sky
For those who greatly think or bravely die?
Pope

"Michael will never retire", Walter Hamilton had said once at a governors' meeting and in a sense I never have. I was made an Honorary Member of the Common Room and I owe it to the kindness of Simon Langdale that I received a small 'retainer' partly because he wanted to be in a position to ask me to do things from time to time and partly to give substance to my continuing involvement as Old Salopian Club representative. I cannot remember how many years ago it was – certainly twenty – that I started my lectures on the history of the school to new boys and these still continue on the old Shrewsbury principle that no one has told me to stop; each boy listens to me for three sessions during his first year. This has enabled me to see all the new boys, many of whose names are familiar. Also I have continued to have Confirmation groups to prepare, as I have had for many years.

But my main involvement in these last dozen years has been outside Shrewsbury School from which I have been happy to be free of responsibility and executive function while yet retaining an interest. With other schools I have been closely involved. At Moreton Hall we governors had to face difficult decisions after the suicide of Bronwen Lloyd-Williams. Unwisely and against a vocal minority of which I was one, we appointed Janet Norton, the existing second-in-command, as Principal. Janet was a longstanding friend who had devoted herself unstintingly to Moreton over most of a lifetime. But, as she knew in her heart, she was not cut out to be Principal. By what I considered sharp politics, Arthur Gem, the Chairman, rallied a majority to support Janet. After two years I, having succeeded to the Chair, had the delicate task of unmaking the appointment; in fact Janet was ready to step down to her old position and so we advertised for a Principal. Jim Cussell, then head of the International School in Geneva, was our choice and an excellent choice he turned out to be. Moreton might have withered at that point; but Jim immediately involved himself not only in stabilising the present position but energetically planning for the future, launching what seemed an impossibly ambitious building programme, which made me, as Chairman, shudder. However, we had the inestimable help of our financial adviser, John Knight, to whose wisdom Moreton owes so much. After a series of testing lunches with bank managers, loans were raised and Jim's plans went ahead. I learned from these experiences. Boldness is all. One has to bank on a full school which will provide the surplus to pay interest on loans and go ahead. If one waits till one has the money, the school may disappear in the meantime. Jim was not a great communicator with the pupils; but as an architect of a growing community he was excellent and our financial position and general repute grew stronger, in contrast to my early days as Chairman when once I had to ask the staff to postpone pay increases for some months as we simply didn't have the money to pay them.

When Yarlet, the Staffordshire prep school, became a Trust the Head-master David Carr asked me to be a governor. David had been the secretary of that happy Magdalen cricket team in 1947 and was now proving a quite outstanding headmaster of this small but flourishing school which had and has a delightful atmosphere allied to high all-round standards. I was a governor for twenty-two years and Chairman for twelve of them; no governor could have had a smoother ride. We had a good Board mostly of local Staffordshire worthies, a wonderfully co-operative staff and a full school, enabling us to view our annual balance sheets with satisfaction. There were of course occasional hiccups. On arriving for a meeting once I was greeted by David with the words, "Matron's in prison". A startling statement but I could only laugh.

At a later stage I became a governor of Prestfelde where Robin Trimby was conducting a thriving prep school. Here I encountered for the first time the Woodard Foundation, of which, in its spiritual and religious work, I am a strong supporter. Not so of its cumbersome administrative structure which, to me, verges on the scandalous. Above the normal school Govern-ing Body with its Headmaster and Bursar, there towers the Woodard Corporation proper with its imposing array of members in London and, nearer to hand, the Midland Chapter with thirty-three members (or Fel-lows), which is administratively responsible for the seven schools in the Midland Division. This Chapter has a full-time Provost (a clergyman) and a full-time Bursar, each with his office, secretary and car. Thus the governors of Prestfelde and the other schools are not masters in their own house; they can neither, for instance, appoint the Headmaster nor control his salary. In certain areas decisions can only be made by the Chapter. I find it difficult to see why these schools cannot be governed as are other schools, by a good Governing Body and a full time bursar, capable, with the Headmaster, of taking all necessary decisions. Thousands of pounds are annually sucked out of the schools to support a totally unnecessary administrative super-structure, largely consisting of people who have little experience of edu-cation. All that is required, as it seems to me, are the services of say a retired bishop as Provost on a very part-time arrangement, and a firm of account-ants to handle such financial matters as there are in common between the schools.

Another characteristic of the Woodard Corporation is paranoia. There was a moment when it was suggested that I might be a member of the Chapter; I was not particularly keen, having enough governing in my life, but was willing to be elected if that was the wish, as it was, of the Prestfelde governors. But no; I was not acceptable to the Chapter on the grounds that I was already the Chairman of Yarlet which must be seen as a rival school. What skulduggery was envisaged I know not. A lady who was living in the Weald of Kent was appointed instead. On another occasion we invited the wife of a local headmaster to join the Prestfelde governors as she had particular experience which we needed. But no; her husband's school was seen as a rival so she too would presumably carry away secrets and sabotage Woodard. Yet the Headmaster of Shrewsbury, clearly the local rival school to the Woodard Ellesmere, sits happily on the Prestfelde Board. To paranoia add hypocrisy.

Will Woodard one day get into the twentieth century before the twenty-first century dawns? But I must not let my antipathy to this unnecessary bureaucracy blunt my enjoyment of being involved with Robin Trimby and Prestfelde at a successful period for the school.

My other educational participation was with the Royal National College for the Blind which moved from Shropshire, where it was awkwardly situated on two sites, to Hereford. The redundant Teacher Training College was an ideal site on which to develop and expand this unique institution, the only Further Education College for the blind in the country. With the coming of new and sophisticated technology, the potential employment prospects for the blind had been greatly enlarged and the students reached remarkably high standards both in academics, in business techniques and in piano tuning. The college was well led by Lance Marshall, the Principal, and by the Bursar and it was interesting to meet a new group of both sighted and blind people, most of them active in the world of the blind. I was for some years Vice-Chairman of the Board and Chairman of the Education Committee.

Since Oxford days, the Church of England has always played a major part in my life, though I can point to no Damascus Road experience nor to any spiritual highlights. The flame of belief has sometimes burnt high, sometimes low. But I have seen godliness in people I have known who have much influenced me – in Adam Fox and in C. S. Lewis at Magdalen, in

Cheslyn Jones, then a monk in the monastery at Nashdom in Buckingham-shire, where I used to go and stay, in Christopher Spafford at St Chad's, in Stretton Reeve and his later successor at Lichfield, Keith Sutton – these and some others have shown me the Christian religion as lived in the world. Of the Church of England I have a Betjemanesque view being influenced by all those material things which contribute to the beauty of holiness and which succeeding generations have created to the glory of God and which give me some sense of the numinous. With my function as Lay Reader I was never wholly happy; once one puts on a cassock and surplice one feels that one should be a better person than one is and I have always been conscious of an atmosphere of faint hypocrisy, knowing my shortcomings only too well. I endeavour to be a follower of Christ but only as a rank and file member. So I gradually ceased my Reader functions.

But as, in retirement, I had more time, I was available to serve the Church in whatever capacity seemed useful. I was encouraged by some words of Archbishop Ramsey, "Where exciting charismata are seen, there is the Spirit. But where hard work is done with patience and exciting perseve-rance, where pain and sorrow are borne with quiet fortitude, where schol-ars pursue the truth with patience ... here too is the Holy Spirit, here too is the charismatic Christ". To one wholly uncharismatic in the accepted sense these were encouraging words. 'Hard work done with patience' I could perhaps contribute.

So it was that I became heavily involved in not only St Chad's parish, but also in the Deanery Synod, the Diocesan Synod and ultimately, the General Synod to which in 1980 I was elected as one of the lay representatives for the Lichfield Diocese. I was an archetypal backbencher but I enjoyed the experience if only for the sense of being at the centre of decision-making, seeing and hearing the leaders of the Church both clerical and lay. Bishops have not had a very good press over recent years ('episcopi Anglicani semper pavidi') but I thought they were rather an impressive group; I particularly admired Archbishop Runcie whom many have undervalued. At a time of considerable tension between parties within the Church, he kept the show on the road with skill and his own speeches were weighty and wise. Others whom I admired were John Habgood, later Archbishop of York, whose intelligence cut through much verbiage (which did not make him popular with some); Stuart Blanch, before he retired from York, whose writings for the layman have been a great help to me; Hugh Montefiore of Birmingham, sometimes splendidly original, sometimes chasing hares; and John Taylor of Winchester, a leader of learning, moderation and humanity. These were to me the outstanding figures.

Hensley Henson, Bishop of Durham half a century ago (of whom it was said that "he was brought up to speak the truth, especially when it would displease"), used to open his Diocesan Synod with the prayer 'that we may do no harm'. Experience of the General Synod showed me the point of this prayer. I had not realised how strong ran the feelings in the two major groups, the Catholics and the Evangelicals. A very middle-of-the-road Anglican myself, my sympathy lay with the Open Synod group who were the liberal voice in the assembly. But I had no real party affiliation and voted as I thought fit, guided though by the senior cleric in our Lichfield Group, Bernard Maddocks, a good friend: when I saw him heading for the Ayes lobby I knew I should be in the Noes, and vice versa.

I only spoke once and that was on the question of multi-faith worship; I was able to tell the Synod that I believed I was the only member who had built a mosque. I was keen to speak in the debate on Freemasonry but was never called. For some years I had been a Mason, a member of the Old Salopian Lodge, but the activity had not appealed to me and I withdrew. The Synod, in its typical nosey-parker way, took it into its head that it must investigate Freemasonry, a good example of how money was often wasted compiling reports which few read and none acted upon. There was a great deal of earnest discussion about what Masonry was, whether it contained seeds of heresy and so on. I wanted to tell the members that there were in practice only three strands of Masonry to the average Mason – it was a club whose companionship they enjoyed, it was an ethical society proclaiming moral standards and it had a strong emphasis on giving to charity. Not many people knew or cared about its tangled esoteric philosophical background and many Masons were active Christians, as had been Archbishop Fisher. But these simple truths were not enough for the Synod: an investigation was set on foot and ultimately a Report published. I don't know how many read it but resulting action was negligible: a good example of pointless and expensive activity.

One of the major shortcomings of the Synod is that its *modus operandi* makes it almost impossible for lay people with full workloads to be members. Thus those without employment, the retired and the semi-retired predominate, many of them senior citizens. How far they actually represent the laity of the Church it is impossible to say. To me there seemed to be too many people, both clergy and lay, with axes to grind. Although not without sympathy for the Anglo-Catholics, having been brought up in St Matthew's, Northampton, their representatives depressed me; looking at the trio on the bench of Synod leaders, the grim-visaged Venerable David Silk, Canon Peter Boulton and Oswald Clark, all clothed in un-relieved black, was a depressing experience. By contrast there were some interesting personalities: Colin Buchanan, the cheekie-chappie of the Synod, later to withdraw in disarray from being Bishop of Aston; the self-publicising Michael Saward; Canon George Austin, another given to too much eloquence and later to make wholly unnecessary comments on the Prince of Wales; Canon Bennett from Oxford, whom I found myself sitting next to, a wintry man who later released his bile in the Crockford preface and committed suicide. Often criticising the Synod with his Welsh eloquence was Ivor Bulmer-Thomas, whom I came to know quite well. His wife's Bulmer relatives had been at Shrewsbury and I was asked to convivial evenings at their home in Edwardes Square. Few people can have had more varied lives – Parliament, journalism, the classics, athletics and in his later days, devotion to the Friends of Friendless Churches. He worked to the last days of his long life, acknowledging in long handwritten letters my not very substantial contributions to the Friendless Churches.

An offshoot of membership of the Synod was my co-option on to the Council for the Care of Churches, the advisory body in the Faculty System whereby all changes in the fabric of a church or in its fittings and furnishings have to have the assent of the Chancellor of the concerned diocese, the object being to encourage high aesthetic standards, prevent destruction and curb misdirected zeal. Thus the Council had to give judgement on the aesthetic and liturgical merits of the various schemes referred to it and also to give opinion in regard to plans for church redundancy. Meeting monthly in the Council's offices on London Wall, I got to know a group of clergy, architects and experts in various branches of ecclesia, whose guiding lights were the erudite Peter Burman, the secretary, and Archdeacon Eric Evans in the chair, knowledgeable, experienced and courteous in the conduct of business. Some years later he was to find himself catapulted, I think to his surprise, into the uncomfortable seat of Dean of St Paul's, perhaps as a gesture towards orthodoxy after the fireworks of Alan Webster's tenure. Amongst these learned pundits I liked to think I represented the man-in-the-pew in the average parish, perhaps a little more aware of the practicalities of parish life than some of my colleagues but wholly lacking their high level of expertise.

Apart from these activities in London, I became more deeply involved in the affairs of the Diocese. Prompted by the Archdeacon of Salop, Bob Jeffrey, the Bishop asked me to be Chairman of the Diocesan Advisory Committee whose function was to examine and recommend to the Chancellor of the Diocese the requests for Faculties which emanated from the parish churches of our vast diocese. As churches never seem to tire of advancing schemes large and small, to move a pew or knock down the chancel, the work is brisk. The committee is large and includes the three archdeacons, four architects and various experts on matters like textiles, heating, lighting, archaeology and so on, together with representatives of amenity societies such as English Heritage. Fortunately, the secretary, Canon John Howe, is extremely experienced and David Ashton, assistant secretary, extremely industrious. In the ten years I have been in the chair, the work has expanded greatly, extra staff have been deployed and we have become highly computerised. More and more responsibility has been laid upon the committee by Act of General Synod. I have enjoyed the work and the contact with clergy and laity through the diocese, as we have sought to keep the balance between the practical schemes advanced by parishes for good pastoral reasons and the aesthetic, historical and liturgical considerations relevant to so many of our parish churches which have five or six hundred years of history behind them. Of course we want to support parishes in their desire to worship and use their buildings as seems fit to them; but we have a rich inheritance which we must pass to succeeding generations, unspoilt by passing whim and fashion.

Kenneth Skelton had succeeded Stretton Reeve as Bishop of Lichfield, a man of impressive intellect who had been Bishop of Mashonaland and acquired notoriety by standing up to Ian Smith's UDI – 'Red Skelton'. His speeches and addresses were outstanding and he was in the forefront of liberal theology, arguing for the ordination of women and trying, unavailingly, for a change in the laws concerning the marriage of divorced persons in church, in both of which campaigns I was one of his minor lieutenants. It was he who made me a selector on the Advisory Council for the Church's Ministry, the body charged with the heavy responsibility of selecting candidates for ordination. Selection boards, which are residential, were held over four days with five selectors (laymen and clergy) and sixteen or eighteen candidates. We lived closely together for those days of communal discussions and prayer, each selector having forty minutes with each candidate and ending up, the candidates having departed, with the great summing up and decision making. I found it a most exhausting process. But it was remarkable how unanimous were the selectors; I can hardly remember any disagreement. And the whole process did open one's eyes to the wide range of people who were thus testing their vocations, some of whom should never have got so far. But the general calibre of those we recommended seemed to me to be very high.

It was Kenneth Skelton who gave me a tip I have remembered. I was complimenting him on what I thought was an outstanding opening address to the Diocesan Synod. "I write it out", he said, "then I go through it and cut out most of the adjectives". Since then I have tried to do likewise.

In 1983 Joy, to my astonishment, said that it was time to move house; she was of course right. We were living in a house too big for us, the family having grown up and fled the nest. Philippa was still in Birmingham, bringing up Jasper and Jessica with Tony's separate but closely involved help; Bruce had left the RAF on the completion of his commission and he and Barbara with Jonathan were now established in Cornwall where, however, he found work hard to find; Robin was teaching in Bristol but soon to join the staff of Shrewsbury School; Martin had married Jane in 1982 and, after teaching and a short stint of commercial life, also was now in Shrewsbury, a salaried Christian evangelical leader in the recently established Barnabas Church Community; only Alan was nominally at home though about to start the grind of chartered accountancy examinations, and soon to marry Gillian. So for the first time in our married lives we were alone. The day after Joy's suggestion that we ought to move, I was driving past Woodbank Drive on Port Hill and saw a 'For Sale' sign. I took Joy round to look at No. 2 and we agreed that it looked suitable; a phone call to the owner, a look inside and we bought the house within a fortnight. It took rather longer to dispose of The Burgage but that was ultimately achieved and we moved in the summer of 1983 – sad to leave a lovely family home, but happy to be established in a small but comfortable modern house.

In these years Joy devoted herself to charismatic 'born again' Christianity, espoused with all her abundant enthusiasm and energy, a supporter of local and national crusades, of Billy Graham and David Watson and a member locally of Christ Church, Bayston Hill, an expanding charismatic congregation. Prayer groups, study groups and evangelical endeavours filled much of her life. At home she read nine – later six – chapters of the Bible every day.

This was ground on which I could not follow her. By contrast my own religious beliefs had become more agnostic; I found myself in sympathy with the Bishop of Durham though disliking the way he 'approached every problem with an open mouth' and seemed to delight in firing off controversial artillery on the eve of major festivals, thus attracting maximum publicity and unsettling many. But if one concentrated on what he actually said as opposed to what the media said he said, he was suggesting no more than has been matter of discussion for years. Not for him the dislike of intellectual argument and the uncritical fundamentalism which the charismatic movement seemed so often to display together with its seeming rejection of the fruits of the past century of painstaking biblical criticism. He does not, for instance, deny the resurrection but points out that we really can know little about what form the risen Christ took, while accepting as fundamental that he appeared to the disciples and others.

His uncertainty concerning the virgin birth certainly found an echo in me. It seems to me a matter of little import and rests on very slim biblical authority – seven verses in Matthew, repeated in Luke – and never referred to by Paul or in the early church. The essential fact is of the incarnation. Much of the teaching in the Old and New Testaments is by story, poetry, analogy and metaphor, which was the Jewish way.

Similarly the fuss about the Three Wise Men seems trivial. Here is a much-loved myth – a story expressing important truth but only a story. St John's gospel has no need of the stable, the wise men or the shepherds but uses the infinitely more powerful though mysterious language of the Word becoming flesh. The truths of the Bible are not about facts; they are about the spirit. Nor do I find the least difficulty in reconciling creation and evolution which are so often posed as opposites. It seems perfectly reasonable that we are spiritually created by God but genetically related to the ape.

On these and similar matters, Joy and I went in different directions and attended different churches. I have attended church services in many contrasted places – early morning celebrations of Communion amongst the gum trees of the Australian bush, evensong in little Indian churches with Indian clergy as the oppressive heat of the day relaxed its grip, multilingual services in South Africa, the simplicity of nonconformist chapels, the grandeur of cathedral worship. The only question is whether what goes on nourishes one's relationship with and understanding of God. What suits one individual does not suit another. To me the happy-clappy services with tinkle-tinkle music and trite little songs provide no encouragement; to others they do. Nothing is right or wrong in this area. But to me mystery and awe and dignity are words of importance; and it is the beauty of holiness which provides me with spiritual stimulation.

So we established our retired lives in our new house, accompanied by our current cats Nimrod and Neptune though sadly the latter died quite soon after our move. In 1984 I was again on my travels, dispatched round the world (my third circumnavigation) to stir up support for the Kingsland Appeal – the raising of money for the school to celebrate the hundredth anniversary of the migration from the town. So I visited Salopians in Australia, in Hong Kong and on both Canadian coasts. On another expedition Joy and I took the coastal ship which went from Bergen on the Norwegian coast round the North Cape and back; this was a most successful holiday – marvellous scenery, much time for reading on the ship, constant calls at ports large and small, the midnight sun and, for me, a chance to see again those northern regions of Norway where I had spent the eventful summer of 1945.

On this our busy retired life a deep shadow fell. Joy had had some internal trouble which led to an operation on the bowel, which was carried out successfully. But it was revealed that the cancer was more widespread and was affecting the liver. Her days were numbered. Curiously the weight of this blow seemed to fall more heavily on me than on her because she, having participated in the healing ministry, a subject which she had studied, was sure that she would be healed. I had no such belief. I asked our doctor the obvious question as to how long we might expect; between six and eighteen months. For some time we were able to lead a fairly normal life, going to Bermuda again in the summer of 1986, seeing Joy's brother Jack and sister Jill – with the latter a healing of a relationship which had not always run smoothly. In the autumn life became more difficult. We were fortunate to have the constant attention of our GP, Tim Hill. At the outset, when I was in deep despair, Tim had said three things: that we should see that the quality of life was maintained to the highest level possible; that pain could in these days be largely controlled; and that we should see that she died at home. All these things were achieved. In addition to Tim we had the quite wonderful support of our Macmillan Nurse, Cathie Ingrouille, for whom no praise can be too high. She was with us constantly, anticipating what would happen and breathing confidence and comfort into all of us, for her brief was not only to look after Joy but the whole family.

Joy was able to play in her last concert in December 1986 at Ludlow under the baton of John Stainer, a friend whom she had always admired. That same month she was well enough to come with me to a dinner given to mark my retirement from the Governing Body of Moreton Hall – a fitting place to appear publicly for the last time – for it was from Moreton that I had abstracted her to marry me twenty-eight years previously. The whole family was together at Christmas time but in January she began to fail fast. It was only then, I think, that she gave up hope of healing and was able to talk about her death, emphasising that her passing should be a joyful occasion and asking to be buried rather than cremated so that her grandchildren should see something tangible to remember her by. She died very early in the morning of the 9th February 1987, firm in the Resurrection Hope; indeed this Christian doctrine was always before our eyes in those last days.

Joy was buried in Shrewsbury cemetery on a fine bright morning in the presence of the family: it was a time to mourn. In the afternoon we held a service at the Barnabas church: it was a time to rejoice – thanksgiving was the keynote. The service was taken by Frank Davies, who had been Joy's pastor for some time and had helped her greatly in the last weeks; there was a vibrant atmosphere of worship by a large congregation drawn from the different strands of Joy's life – the army, Shrewsbury School, musicians, Christians of various categories whose lives she had touched, fellow workers in the League of Hospital Friends at Shelton. Afterwards Eric Anderson wrote, ''Joy was a quite remarkable person, and one of the very few I have met whose faith was so strong that you cannot doubt that it was stronger than death''. Amen to that. I did not find it difficult to envisage her tuning up the heavenly double bass in the celestial orchestra.

CHAPTER XXVII

On the Touch Line

> ... who going through the vale of misery use it for a well:
> and the pools are filled with water.
>
> Psalm 84

In bereavement I lived through the phases which are, no doubt, common to many: the emotional high spirits of funeral and memorial service; the uplifting support of family and friends; the consolation of letters and messages which flood in and touch the heart; the stimulation of visitors and activity; and then the descent into the pit. Alan and Gillian were the last to depart. Having seen them off I went into the house and looked around – for the first time totally alone. It was only then that pent up emotions burst into tears. In my case those dark days were overshadowed further by having to have a prostate operation, an unpleasant experience at the best of times though excellent in the ultimate result. There is no disguising the depth of depression during those long weeks and months of 1987, and the strange feeling of the empty house.

Seeking the stimulation of change, I decided to go again to Pakistan; the Principal of Lawrence College said he would be pleased to see me. So, somewhat anxiously, I flew off to Islamabad; as I left the plane a limousine drew up and I was whisked off to the VIP lounge where the Principal, Brigadier Saeed, my old pupil (and Old Salopian) Changez Sultan and the head of the Prep School, Yusuf Qureshi, awaited me – this at 5 a.m.! Thereafter hospitality was lavished on me from every side. The Brigadier was kindness itself; on arriving at the Principal's residence he said, "Mr Charlesworth, this is still your home; the servants will get anything you wish; there will always be a car and driver when needed".

I came to admire very much what Brigadier Saeed was doing. He had been placed as Principal to get the College going again after years of neglect in which standards had fallen in every sphere. The lowest point had come when the Head Boy had murdered another boy on the College campus, inflicting thirty-eight wounds with a small knife. On another occasion, mass cheating had taken place, the invigilator being bribed by the offer of a television set. So Saeed had a lot of ground to make up. His strength was that he had powerful friends in government and he had persuaded the President of Pakistan, General Zia, to be patron. Thus he had both money and influence, launching a big building programme and restoring standards both academic and administrative, reverting to the name Lawrence College at the insistence of Old Boys, replacing the banal Pine Hills College, which name had been adopted in accordance with nationalist sentiment. I was interested in meeting the boys and, at my suggestion, was allowed to teach a different form every day; the standard of English was a good deal worse than it had been in my time but the boys were of much the same calibre. Saeed's complaint was the same as mine had been – how to find staff good enough for the boys.

One day I was told two visitors awaited me, both one-time students of mine. They had flown from Karachi (a thousand miles) to see me and insist that I go to Karachi where they would arrange a dinner for Old Gallians. ('Gallians' from Ghora Gali, the local village.) I could not but agree so they gave me a ticket and put me up in the Sheraton Hotel. At the dinner were forty-five Old Gallians, mostly of my time. Again at Lahore were gathered Gallians in similar numbers and also at Peshawar where the Commissioners of both Peshawar and Kohat were boys I had taught. The kindness I received everywhere was overwhelming.

Since Zulfikar Ali Bhutto sold his soul to the Islamic fundamentalist party for votes, Pakistan had been (in theory) dry so far as Muslims were concerned. One evening the Brigadier asked me, rather mysteriously, if I would like to come to the 'unIslamic room', which turned out to be heavily shrouded at the rear of the bungalow; on the mantelpiece was a bottle of Teachers whisky! An ex-army officer, Saeed continued to enjoy his whisky as formerly in the Mess.

This was a memorable visit – but it was not to be my last. I was urged to come back the next year and to speak at the College Founders' Day, sharing the platform with General Zia. On my expressing hesitation, I was impelled to accept by the offer of Old Gallians to pay my air fare. So again in 1988 I found myself in the Himalayan foothills; but, alas, General Zia had by that time been mysteriously killed in an air crash.

The anniversary of Joy's death had its obvious poignancy but by now I was getting into the rhythm of single living and finding enough activity in various spheres to maintain forward motion. My domestic foundation was secure thanks to Margaret Evans, who should have been mentioned previously in this narrative, for she had come to work for us back in 1974. She and Joy had a close friendship based on shared Christian faith; when Joy became ill, Margaret came to us every day and was a great source of strength. Now she continued to look after me on three mornings a week so I had no domestic worries.

James Hill, constant friend from days in Oldham's, had always urged me to write the biography of Basil Oldham whose life was, to put it mildly, most extra-ordinary. Bachelor housemaster in the old style, living as he had been brought up to live in Edwardian days, bibliographer and mountaineer, a man of complex emotions which found – or failed to find – expression in *amitiés amoureuses*. As he wrote (according to his own reckoning) about three thousand letters a year, there was a good deal of material on which to base a book together with the recollections of his old boys with some of whom he had formed enduring friendships and in some of whom he had engendered outspoken dislike. I enjoyed writing the book (which soon sold out) but, alas, James Hill had died before it was published.

Another book which I had long determined to undertake was a revision of the Shrewsbury School Register – a modified Who's Who – of the five thousand five hundred Salopians who were at school between 1925 and 1975. The bulk of the donkey work was done by the diligent Dee Dakers, my secretary, but I worked hard to try and collect the necessary information. Filling in forms is not an activity that Salopians are keen on. However, I was very pleased to extract what I needed from no less than 85% of those approached and it gave me much pleasure to be in touch with so many friends and acquaintances.

Although I have given up my function as a Lay Reader, I am nonetheless still asked to preach from time to time, to lecture and to present the prizes at various schools. At one – Arnold House in London – I was somewhat startled to encounter the penetrating gaze of Robin Day from the front row just as I was about to speak. On eight occasions I have given the Address at memorial services. Heavy responsibilities as these have been, I have been glad to pay tribute to such close friends as Jim Harrison of Abinger who set the whole course of my life; to James Hill, my study monitor when I was a new boy and a friend ever since; to my colleagues David Bevan and Stacy Colman; and to others to whom I have been close.

I have continued to enjoy travel, going every year to Bermuda where my brother-in-law Jack and his wife Celia give me a standing invitation. After some hesitation I joined an Oxford Society coach tour to Switzerland in 1990; the hesitation came from my single status. Most people on such tours are husband and wife and when joining strangers one never knows quite how one will fare. I should not have worried. I met the most delightful people with whom I had much in common. I have been on two other enjoyable tours with the Oxford Society, to Egypt and on the Orient Express to Austria, Hungary and Italy. I have also been to the USA a couple of times, on both occasions warmly welcomed by a remarkable American Old Salopian, Jim Pfautz, who was only at Shrewsbury for an English Speaking Union sixth form year, but a year which he remembers with enthusiasm and affection. I was his form master; and since that time we have always been in touch. Jim has now retired after rising to the rank of Major-General in the Air Force and is the soul of generous hospitality in his newly-built retirement house in Virginia.

My brother Richard, having retired from his not very absorbing work with British Rail, lived with his wife Freda in the Lake District for ten years but, when his health began to fail, moved to Courtyard Housing near Reading. Sadly Altzheimers overtook him and for several years he lived a deteriorating life before his death in 1990. I am peculiarly relationless: Richard's son David lives in North Devon where he teaches apprentices the art of the craftsman in wood; we seldom meet. Dorette, my second cousin, lives near Malvern where I call upon her when in the area. Otherwise I have no blood relative living, apart from my own children. My Aunt May, the last of my parents' generation, died at the age of ninety-five, her mind unclouded and with clear recall of Gladstone and Disraeli. The decline in Aunt population – particularly of maiden aunts – has been a sad feature of the last fifty years. (As has the dwindling number of spinster school-mistresses – once the very backbone of so many schools.)

Another death had already removed one who had influenced my life: Adam Fox, Dean of Divinity in my Magdalen years. When he was ninety, Keith Joseph and I organised a dinner for him at the Carlton Club to which came a dozen of his Magdalen friends of different generations – two Heads of House at Oxford in Robert Blake at Queen's and Greig Barr at Exeter; two MPs, the outspoken Ronald Bell and Keith himself, a main architect of Thatcherism; Cheslyn Jones, then Principal of Pusey House; Tony Hugill of Tate and Lyle, planner of the famous 'Mr Cube' campaign against the nationalisation of sugar; Ingram Cleasby, Dean of Chester; and others in the public service or the Church. Adam spoke briefly, still viewing life with affectionate and amused detachment; he never grew old in heart. I saw him shortly before he died at the age of ninety-three. He was largely bedridden and had grown a bushy white beard but his blue eyes were as penetrating as ever; Jehovah incarnate. During my time at Magdalen (when he did not expect to go elsewhere), he wrote about his own funeral. I make no apology for quoting these charming verses, so typical of his puckish humour. (His suggestion for the inscription on his tombstone was 'A Fox Gone To Earth'.)

> Deans of Divinity must die, but most,
> Before they die, secure some other post.
> I only, as one born out of due time,
> Before I came was some years past my prime,
> And it may be that I shall have to die,
> Lulled by the constant murmur of the High,
> In these fine rooms which back in 'Ninety-Four
> Displayed the present Primate's name above the door.

And if I die, think only this of me,
That you may burn me, bury me at sea,
Dissect me, or lay plainly in the ground,
Wherever any handy plot be found;
But do not let my body, I implore,
Enter the inner Chapel any more,
Lest I, who used to be all ears, all fire,
Should lie there at the last unheedful of the choir.

Yet, if a kindly President agree,
Some short memorial service there might be,
Thing decent to my thought and not amiss
For travellers between THAT world and this;
So three days from the day on which I pass
First let the Founder's Chaplain say the Mass,
And at whatever later hour is meet
Let choristers and clerks unite in concert sweet.

Croft's sentences be sung, and then a Psalm,
Best be the Ninetieth, so intense yet calm;
Then that long Lesson (or some part) be read,
The Collects in the natural voice be said;
But listen, Chaplain, oh whate'er you do,
Keep to the mind of Sixteen-Sixty-Two;
Let no false note from Nineteen-Twenty-Eight
Intrude upon my obsequies, for such I hate.

If there's an anthem I think Five-Ought-Seven
Lifts up the heart most quickly into heaven;
Those gentle Alleluias of Purcell
The best last greeting give and say all's well;
Then comes the Grace, and no more to be done
But go into the world and see the sun;
And pray have no Dead March, but might the choir
Sing for me Bridges *Love of Love* ere they retire.

It is interesting that four of our five children have, in adult years, committed themselves fully to Christianity. Bruce and Barbara play an important part in their local church in Cornwall and Bruce is now reading for ordination in the Church of England Non-Stipendiary Ministry. Robin is a Franciscan of the third order; he and Diane are members of a local house group. Martin is engaged in full-time ministry with the Barnabas community in which Jane also plays a part. Alan and Gillian are very active in their local parish church in Blackheath. Philippa remains untouched by religion. She has recently moved to Bristol where she works in the

Watershed Arts Centre. It is fortunate that the relationship of all five children both with each other and with those they have married has been of the happiest – as have their relationships with me. To have four such daughters-in-law as I am lucky enough to have has been a real blessing and they willingly help me in the domestic tasks of single living. Gillian has deployed a little of her very considerable expertise in leading me through the first steps in cooking, though I am not an apt pupil. But the little tasks of domestic life, such as winding my several clocks on Sunday mornings, do not bore me. I like regularity and order. The author O. Douglas once wrote of "the significant trivia of people's lives": 'For who hath despised the day of small things?' (Zechariah 4.10)

I have come to the end of most of my involvements with Governing Bodies and committees but I am still Chairman of the Diocesan Advisory Committee though probably not for much longer; I do not think one should be in such positions when nearer eighty than seventy. Edward King, the saintly nineteenth century Bishop of Lincoln, divided his clergy into three groups, those who had gone out of their minds, those who were about to go out of their minds and those who had no minds to go out of. I must say that my experience of the Lichfield Diocese clergy does not support the view of that Victorian Bishop of the Fens. Many priests, often in difficult circumstances, are working positively for the Kingdom in their parishes, unheralded and unsung but by no means unappreciated by those to whom they minister. The Church does indeed suffer from internal strains which the media delight to exploit but my experience over these last ten years has led me to a great respect for the work of the parochial ministry. I have been for some time a peripatetic churchgoer, attending services in different churches of the county, sometimes going to the Cathedral in Lichfield, sometimes to small rural churches, occasionally to nonconformist worship; this has led me to appreciate more fully Paul's words about 'diversity of activities' but the same spirit and the same God.

In 1986 I gave up editing *The Salopian Newsletter* after twenty-five years, handing it over to the safe care of David Gee. I had enjoyed the task of trying to make interesting a publication which all too easily becomes a chronicle of record – necessary but dull. As it is the only communication between the school and Old Salopians it plays an important part, the more so when major functions are envisaged or when Appeals are to be launched. It has been rewarding to hear from Salopians far spread through the world that they enjoy the Newsletter and sometimes from widows of Salopians who have died that their husbands looked back on schooldays with affection and enjoyed the continuing link through the Newsletter – often men whose passage through life as through schooldays appeared to be relatively undistinguished.

Through my connection with the Council for the Care of Churches I came to know Henry Stapleton, now Dean of Carlisle, who introduced me to the Redundant Churches Fund, the body responsible for the maintenance of churches no longer needed for worship but which need to be preserved because of their architectural, aesthetic or historical merits. The Fund, whose activities I much admire, have asked me to write Church Guides to half a dozen or so of their churches and also edit their gazeteer of the 250 redundant churches which was entitled *Churches in Retirement*, a publication distinguished for its quite excellent photographs of many of the country's most remarkable buildings.

I continue to view the activities of Shrewsbury School with close interest, still doing a little Old Salopian work, now also giving some assistance to the recently-established Shrewsbury School Foundation. Simon Langdale retired after seven years. Speculating with him one day as to his successor, we both simultaneously exclaimed, "and of course there's Ted". And Ted it turned out to be – Edward Maidment, then Headmaster of Ellesmere; and what a good appointment this has been. In times of recession the school has flourished remarkably, numbering 700 boys for the first time in history, while in many similar schools numbers have diminished, often to the point where it has been necessary to turn to co-education – ostensibly on educational grounds but in fact for hard financial reasons. As a governor of one newly co-educational school rather unfortunately expressed it to me, "We needed the girls to fill the boys' beds". It is a remarkable fact that Shrewsbury now belongs to a small league of major boys' schools which are predominantly boarding whose only members are Eton, Harrow, Winchester, Sherborne, Tonbridge, Sedbergh and Radley. Shades of the 'sacred seven' of the Public Schools Act of 1868. As were his predecessors, Maidment was fortunate in his housemasters, combining experience with a new younger crop – Stewart and Anna Roberts in Rigg's; Robin and Alex Case, who took over Ingram's from the safe hands of Nick and Annabelle Bevan; Jeremy and Isobel Goulding in Oldham's, sadly lost to the Site when they went off headmastering; and Peter and Jane Fanning, who have so successfully built up a brand new House, The Grove. All these have added to the life of the community in many ways, Anna by her delightful performances on the piano, Robin and Peter in some outstanding theatrical productions, Jeremy and Isobel in masterminding a seventy-fifth birthday celebration of Oldham's Hall, a House whose background and atmosphere – different from others – they sensitively understood.

What is the reason for Shrewsbury's success? Academic achievement may be a part of the answer but then boys do well academically in most of the big independent schools. I would advance three reasons. Firstly the school site itself – with its hundred acres so well maintained by Ken Spiby, groundsman without peer, and its riverine ambience. Secondly the personality of the Headmaster (and his immediate predecessors) together with the high standard of housemasters. And thirdly the boys who show round prospective parents who communicate what I think are particular Salopian characteristics in their articulation, their naturalness and their general attitude, confident yet relaxed. It seems unlikely that Shrewsbury will change from being the boys' school which it has been for four and a half centuries unless some new factors emerge. As I have already written, it is fortunate to be adjacent to but not part of a town; and in the town are girls' schools; girls come and act, play in the orchestra, sing in the choirs, disco and socialise. The old monastic community has long since died. Recently several Houses have made twinning arrangements with Houses at Moreton Hall.

Independent education should surely provide for the parents a choice. (I use the word 'surely' with hesitation. A.J.P. Taylor used to say to us, "If you hear a sentence which begins with the word, 'surely', prepare yourself for an appeal to ignorance or to prejudice or both".) Some parents may prefer single sex schools, some not; what is suitable for one child may not be suitable for another. No system – as I see it – is intrinsically better than another. The question is how well does a school, of whatever type, actually succeed in providing all round standards of excellence for its pupils? And this in turn will mainly depend on its staff. However well equipped, situated, endowed, supplied, as Wolfenden often used to remind us, a school is as good as its staff.

In Langdale's time what might be said to be the last outward sign of the old Public School disappeared when he ruled that formal dress (coat and tie) need no longer be worn when going down town. This was sensible; but it removed the last evidence of public school boys being 'different' which Salopians had been since the days of top hat and tails or straw hats.

In one of his books, John Rae, former Headmaster of Westminster, writes of the qualities needed in a headmaster: "a thick skin, a quick wit, stamina, a steady nerve, political dexterity, a capacity for ruthlessness and a keen sense of the absurd". To me these characteristics suggest a headmaster who is constantly manoeuvering, plotting and planning as though playing an immense game of chess. My own list of desirable headmagisterial qualities is this:

> Academic distinction
> Administrative ability
> Flair for public relations, especially with parents
> Skill in communication with staff and pupils
> Judgement – particularly in the choice of staff
> Vision; and a touch of charisma: leaders must be seen to lead

It is tempting in these days of League Tables to consider the seven Shrewsbury headmasters I have known and the two I have served under elsewhere with a view to establishing a Headmasters' League. But I think this is a temptation to be resisted; most of them are living and all of them I account (so far!) my friends. But I would say that, overall, I would place at the head of my table Eric Anderson and Sir James Darling. Eric, as he has demonstrated at Eton, has all the six abilities which I have listed. And in addition he has Poppy – a priceless asset. Jim Darling had a particularly inventive flair and style which I have not seen in anyone else.

Were the twentieth century Shrewsbury Headmasters to be described in musical terms we could start with Alington's *maestoso* followed by Sawyer's *giocoso*; then came Hardy with *alla marcia, tempo giusto* and Wolfenden with *presto, stringendo* followed by the different mood of Peterson – *andante sostenuto*. With Wright life was *allegro vivace pesante* followed by Anderson's *martellando un poco scherzando* and the *grave adagio molto tranquillo* of Langdale. With Maidment we proceed *maestoso fortissimo* as befits *profundo basso*.

CHAPTER XXVIII

Fin de Siècle

And I sat by the shelf till I lost myself,
And roamed in a crowded mist,
And heard lost voices and saw lost looks
As I pored on an old school list.

C.A. Alington

'If you are idle be not melancholy. If you are melancholy be not idle'. So wrote Dr Johnson. In the single life which has been my lot for these last seven years I have endeavoured to follow the Doctor's advice and have enjoyed activity both at home and abroad, happy to live still in the ancient borough of Shrewsbury. With a group of friends I went to a bridge course three years ago and the game gives me much pleasure: defying the old Anglo-Saxon Protestant work ethic, we play in the mornings after, in my case, a relaxed breakfast – one of the joys of retirement: 'The perfect breakfast all must own/ Is that which man enjoys alone/ Peace perfect peace is found they say/ Only with loved ones far away.' Music is a major enjoyment: I go (as I have since the War) to the Three Choirs Festival every year, to the Proms regularly and rejoice as do many others in the splendid cultural development of Birmingham, with the CBSO, Simon Rattle, Symphony Hall, the Royal Birmingham Ballet and the Welsh National Opera. I look back in gratitude to those Robert Mayer concerts in prep school days which gave me my first insight into music. When Sir Robert was ninety, his wife gave him a wonderfully imaginative birthday present. She persuaded eminent soloists and the London Symphony Orchestra to give their services, bought up the entire Festival Hall and gave seats to any who had attended the original children's concerts and who wrote to ask. Joy and I went and had a memorable evening. Twice a week I have lunch at the Salop Club, of which I am President. I help in the care of Battlefield Church, now redundant. I keep in touch with Moreton Hall where a former pupil, Jonathan Forster, is now Principal, a position for which he was obviously marked out after a fine performance in the Joyce Grenfell part of the games mistress (Miss Gossage – 'call me Sausage') in the Moser's production of

The Happiest Days of Your Life. (I was the headmistress, the Margaret Rutherford part.)

But I suppose one of my major preoccupations and enjoyments at this stage of life is my involvement with the great Salopian family, spread over this country and around the world. I am in regular touch with quite a large number of Old Salopians, in occasional contact with many more. If asked on *Mastermind* what my special subject was, I could only reply 'Old Salopians 1932–92'. Every year two hundred or so come to the Old Salopian Weekend and my powers of recall and recognition are put to a stern test. I travel the country a good deal in my admirable Metro and am the fortunate recipient of much Salopian hospitality and I equally enjoy my forty or fifty visitors who stay here. With the young too – both boys and girls – I still keep in touch to some degree; their forthcoming friendship is to me a privilege. Many years ago Ian Hay perceptively dedicated one of his books to those who teach – 'The worst paid and best rewarded profession'.

From time to time the media storm at the door or on the phone wanting to know all about the school careers of Old Salopians who are in the public eye, having acquired fame or notoriety. Having the longest memory, enquiries often end up with me and the nicely-balanced views and recollections I advance are duly savaged and distorted by journalists. Interesting contacts, however, are occasionally made. I appeared as a guest of Russell Harty on television as an adjunct to Willie Rushton, others in the programme being the delectable Toyah Wilcox and the deplorable Janet Street Porter.

The reader of this book will be relieved to know that at its conclusion he will get from me no educational punditry; not for me the role of the telephone in educational research. School is an important part of anyone's life obviously, but it is always the home which is the real influence on the growing child. To some, school is merely a passing and necessary phase and I am not one to trumpet its importance in influencing the lives of pupils though it has its contribution to make. Nor am I one who would claim to foresee the lives of boys who are later distinguished in the affairs of the world, though one can recognise talents which may come to fruition. School is a transitory period; boys who at eighteen seem outstanding may have already reached a peak of development, others may have much to come. Schoolmastering as a profession has suited me and it is to me the personal relations of teacher and taught which lie at the heart of education, partly in the form room but also in all the many activities made possible by boarding school life. When Moser was asked what he taught he would always reply with a terse monosyllable, 'Boys'. It is the interest in the boys as individuals which generates the energy which carries one through the long boarding school day. It was Moser again who, when speaking to new masters, would remind them that they were paid for twenty-four hours' work a day.

I have been glad to belong to an institution which has shown and still shows every sign of stability in an age in which foundations seem to be shaking whether of the Monarchy, Parliament, the Church, the Law, the Police, or other aspects of our lives which we have believed had permanence. Ted Maidment's vision of Shrewsbury is of a continuing school whose outlines have not much changed over the last hundred years but within whose structure new currents of energy constantly change and flow. In 1982 a contemporary of mine, Martin Adie, produced in the form of a video a film which he had made as a boy in the 1930s. It is remarkable both for its content and its technical quality, featuring cold swills, form rooms (with consenting masters), study and bedroom, tails and top hats, athletic pursuits (including Sgt Major Joyce in the Alington Hall) and Speech Day. I asked a fifteen-year-old who had just seen it what he thought of it. ''Well, it's all much the same, isn't it?'' A surprising but perhaps perceptive comment.

Having now been associated with Shrewsbury School for sixty years, I am occasionally asked which period I have enjoyed most. I can truthfully say that I have enjoyed each succeeding decade but perhaps – and it is no doubt only nostalgia – I look back on the Fifties with particular affection, partly because I was then between the ages of thirty and forty, maybe one's most physically energetic period. Of course those days would now be criticised as being narrow, restrictive, philistine and hierarchical. But such things as were done were done extremely well; there was a high sense of both endeavour and achievement allied to a strong commitment to the school by all but the few who found the going too difficult. Boys – and I think staff (numbering only fifty) – really did *belong* in a way which has partly disappeared. Every housemaster had made Shrewsbury his total career – a body of experienced though very diverse men. The younger element contained men of equal diversity but much vigour – and wit. A look in the Brown Book shows the younger versions of Alan Laurie, Robin Moulsdale, Adrian Struvé, Michael Hoban, Tony Trench, Peter Gladstone, Arnold Ellis, Laurence Le Quesne and others. Happy the school which could call on this diversity of talent. Taking up a random Brown Book, that for 1956, the praepostors form an interesting group who have made their mark in different fields. They are: Canon Christopher Hewetson, at present Vicar of C.S. Lewis's old parish in Oxford; Richard Quibell, a housemaster at Eton; Paul Foot, Daily Mirror and socialist journalist; John Mackenzie-Grieve, solicitor and ornithologist; Humphrey Ward and Edward Anderton, respectively consultant surgeon and GP; Bill Graham and James Baker, both engineers; Bill Lowry, chartered surveyor and prominent in the affairs of Newcastle; Willie Rushton, joker and cartoonist extraordinary; Archdeacon Douglas Bartles-Smith; Christopher Booker, journalist and author, scourge of Eurocrat (and home-produced) bureaucracy; Patrick Duncan, Chaplain at Christ's Hospital; and businessmen Peter Ward and Tony Duerr – the latter Shrewsbury's outstanding athlete in these last fifty years, now running his family firm.

It has been my good fortune to serve with and for people of the calibre mentioned in this last paragraph – not of course only in the 1950s decade but throughout my time. My lot has been cast in a fair field and I am very conscious of it, particularly in working with colleagues who have always been prepared to go the extra mile and with whom my relations, with only one exception, have been universally happy. When Eric Anderson left we presented him with a set of glasses each engraved with a suitable Salopian figure or scene. In his letter of thanks he wrote, "The delightfully un-expected is one of Shrewsbury School's hallmarks but on reflection we feel that we might almost have guessed at this present, since surely nothing else could so cleverly symbolise the excellence, individuality, elegance and wit of the Common Room. It has been a privilege and a pleasure beyond what I can express to enjoy these qualities for all too short a time."

What one actually achieves as a schoolmaster is a matter for conjecture. In retirement I recollect Stacy Colman saying that washing up gave him satisfaction – at the end one could see a material achievement whereas in teaching the results were incapable of assessment. Einstein expressed the same thought. "People like chopping wood because they can see immedi-ate results." A young Old Salopian did once make that remark to me which every schoolmaster hopes to hear, "I always remember what you said to us". Had I made a major contribution to his career or philosophy? But what he actually went on to say was, "I always remember you told us that if one had a honeymoon, have it in Kashmir. And I did!"

Were this book to have a title other than the one I have chosen, I should call it *On the Fringe*. Although I have played a central part at Shrewsbury, my talents lie on the fringe of real achievement. I have read much and dabbled in the academic world but am not a scholar; I shall never read Proust. I have read some theology but am not a theologian. I enjoy music but am not a musician. I look at pictures but my appreciation is untutored. I have some knowledge of architecture but it is superficial. I have spent much time on the stage without being an actor. I have written quite of lot of both verse and prose but am not an author. I have played cricket, football, fives, squash and tennis and achieved modest athletic success but have never moved out of the 2nd XI. Always on the fringe I think I can neverthe-less truly say that I "have warmed both hands before the fire of life". If I had my time again I would seek to know something of horticulture, ornithology and biology; I would seriously learn a musical instrument; I would try and master at least one foreign language. (Sadly I am in the class of those returned India hands who, leaving the ship at Marseilles to take the train, used to harangue the porters in Urdu.) And if I had my way I would be a left arm slow bowler.

Recently a friend asked me if I would do a Desert Island Disc programme for a discussion group which he ran. Surprised that anyone could possibly be interested in my life enough to want to listen to my choices, I nevertheless enjoyed the task, hoping that my audience would endure it. What music does one associate with what periods in one's life?

I started with *Anything Goes* which so well sums up the twenties and early thirties; (I nearly chose Coward's *Twentieth Century Blues*). The march *Colonel Bogey* is always to me inextricably connected with the Shrewsbury School Band which was so important to me. My pre-War university years, romantic days in recollection and in fact, were represented by the exciting last movement of Tchaikowsky's fifth symphony; the War and the East by *Mad Dogs and Englishmen*; and my Scandinavian involvement by Grieg. Marriage to Joy brings to mind the violin, so important a part of her life, and I chose a portion of the Bruch violin concerto. My interest in the Church and particularly in church music is summed up in Parry's great anthem, *I was Glad*. My last piece was devoted to Elgar, a composer who means a great deal to me, representing much that I have loved, the Border country, the Three Choirs, cathedrals and that Edwardian age of stability before 1914. Elgar's string tunes and tones have always pulled at my heart. I chose *Nimrod* from the Enigma Variations.

For a luxury I chose a permanently available hot bath, always to me one of the minor pleasures of life particularly missed in those long years living in the jungle. For a book I decided to take Wavell's anthology of poetry, *Other Men's Flowers*. Though I am reasonably conversant with Kek's 'Spells', which contain a lot of Auden, Eliot and twentieth century poets, my rather childish taste is still for narrative verse and poetry one can easily comprehend. Salopians should all be familiar with Housman and I am no exception, the fascination of form and word patterns overcoming the morbidity of his philosophy. I forget now the author of the brilliant parody of which the opening couplet was:

> What still alive at twenty two
> A fine upstanding lad like you?

It is natural for nostalgia to creep in as this autobiography nears its end. Distant days have a charm which is perhaps illusory but the structure of life in those distant pre-War days did seem to have a comforting permanence, when policemen were friendly Bobbies, when I, as a boy, could bicycle over half England by myself, when our harmless crazes were for pogo sticks, stilts and mah-jong. Films were not dominated by sex and violence, the theatre provided entertainment rather than challenge and shock, we awaited with anticipation the latest P. G. Wodehouse and Evelyn Waugh, soon available for sixpence in the first Penguin editions and I could watch the Cobblers for 1/6d, standing amongst unsegregated supporters of both sides without a policeman in sight. The words vandalism, graffiti, pollution, pornography and media were unknown. Now I have even abandoned my daily routine of reading *The Times* polluted, like so much else, by Rupert Murdoch.

The Nineties thus far has seemed a bleak decade, though I personally have few worries – as yet, – and from my vantage point on the touch-line it is good to see that Shrewsbury School flourishes abundantly. During the centenary celebrations of the move of the school to Kingsland I was rung up by a girl from the local newspaper who asked what the celebration was about. On being told we were celebrating 1882–1982, she simpered "Have there been any changes?". Apart from the thin thread of autobiography which runs through this volume, it has been my intention to comment on these changes as seen from the inside.

As an Old Salopian myself and the product of a traditionalist system the question may well be asked whether I have ever been out of sympathy with the developments which have led to a radically different school from the one I originally knew. I can say with confidence that I have been entirely in agreement with the broad sweep of policy which has been developed by succeeding headmasters and have always sought to aid the process rather than delay it. I have small reservations on minor matters: I mourn the disappearance of the *Salopian* magazine for instance, a journal which was extremely good in its day. We must be the only school in England without a school magazine, apart from a wretched sheet which boys write which is generally beneath contempt. I am sorry too that Central (the main tree-lined avenue leading to the School Building) has been taken over as a car park. The eighteenth century building has presence and the approach to it had dignity. Given my background I have never been able to reconcile myself to the presence of ladies in the Masters' stalls at the back of the Chapel, delighted as I am that the ladies take an increasing part in the school. When I used to sit in the Second Master's stall, the memorials to Moser and Chance, one behind each shoulder, were a stern reminder of the Salopian past. And I still see sitting there Sopwith and Street, Hope-Simpson and Bevan, Oldham and Brooke together with many others; an imaginative, subjective and out-dated view of course. But these are, as I said, minor matters.

On the school to-day I would make three unconnected observations. First, the school has to some extent changed in character because the boys now largely come from a geographically circumscribed area, though there are many exceptions. The homes of most are within fifty miles of the town of Shrewsbury. This tendency is echoed in all other similar schools except Eton. Whereas previous parents kept their distance, their active interest and participation has increasingly been sought which has naturally resulted in modern parents not wishing to be far away. Donald Wright used to stress to new boys' parents the importance of keeping the three concerned parties together – boys, parents and school. We used to call new boys' Sunday the Feast of the Holy and Undivided Triangle.

Secondly, the last thirty years or so have seen a development which puzzles me. In days gone by ninety per cent of the new boys joining at the age of thirteen-and-a-half had not reached the age of puberty; the exact opposite is now the case, ninety per cent having already reached puberty. There are few little boys in the physical sense – and a consequent shortage of trebles for the Choir. Recently two thirteen-and-a-half year old new boys were at once put in the Chapel Choir – as basses. Add to this that the media and advertisers do all in their power to make boys feel they are young adults with all the needs and 'rights' thereby implied and there is not much time to enjoy, as former generations did, the pleasures of boyhood. No longer adolescents, they are launched into the teenage world as fast as they can be propelled by the wiles of the adman, equipped with the right clothes, shoes, cosmetics, musical apparatus and attitudes.

Thirdly, never before has the staff been burdened with so much paper. Constantly changing educational policy works it way down slowly to the schools. The National Curriculum, the Children Act and the Health and Safety legislation – all so well intended – lay enormous administrative burdens on all; energy required for teaching is wasted on arcane procedures decreed from on high. The photocopier has, perhaps, turned out to be the teachers' worst enemy. When I first started at Shrewsbury there was no way of reproducing paper save on the typewriter of Sgt Major Blud who hammered away when he was not busy on Corps matters. The notice board in the Masters' Common Room was about three feet square; now there are one hundred and forty-four square feet of notice board and the photocopier is never silent. I salute those who presently labour in the vineyard where conditions have changed markedly even since I retired ten years ago. And yet the *genius loci* is still about; fancifully I trace it back to the lost world of Alington's Shrewsbury. Alington used to say that you could only understand the Public School world if you could appreciate that he might play fives with a boy in the afternoon, beat him after tea for a misdemeanour and have him to breakfast the next morning. The atmosphere in which these run-of-the-mill happenings could take place without comment is, *mutatis mutandis*, the atmosphere still.

All Ages Are Ages of Transition. Discuss. An old chestnut essay title for historians. The Nineties are presumably no exception and maybe there is a parallel with the last decade of Queen Victoria when people had that *fin de siècle* feeling. With luck I shall not see the twenty-first century. Walter Hamilton in his latter days was given to saying in his lugubrious way, "I shall never live to be 80". With perfect timing he died the day before his eightieth birthday. I should be happy to do the same. Although decaying only slowly thus far, around me friends and contemporaries develop the diseases and conditions of old age and for some has already come 'the blind Fury with the abhorréd shears'. Perhaps I should seek to imitate Housman whose rooms in his Cambridge college were at the top of a tower and who, in later life, used to run up the stairs two at a time in the hope that at the top he would collapse with a terminal heart attack.

In filling up his form for the Shrewsbury School Register, one Old Salopian noted, "What a dull life when laid out like this. Fortunately I never noticed at the time" – a sentiment which finds an echo with me. He or she who has read as far as this final paragraph has shown admirable powers of endurance. For me the compilation of this narrative over most of three years – written in spasms when there were no other more engaging things to do – has been a pleasant task. Though it is to compare the trivial to the tremendous I have something akin to the feeling of the author of the greatest of autobiographies in his summer house on that June evening of 1787 when, his History at last finished, Gibbon wrote that "a sober melancholy was spread over my mind by the idea that I had taken an everlasting leave of an old and agreeable companion...".